America and the World

America and the World

Culture, Commerce, Conflict

❧

LAWRENCE A. PESKIN

and

EDMUND F. WEHRLE

The Johns Hopkins University Press

Baltimore

© 2012 The Johns Hopkins University Press
All rights reserved. Published 2012
Printed in the United States of America on acid-free paper
2   4   6   8   9   7   5   3   1

The Johns Hopkins University Press
2715 North Charles Street
Baltimore, Maryland 21218-4363
www.press.jhu.edu

Library of Congress Cataloging-in-Publication Data

Peskin, Lawrence A., 1966–
America and the world : culture, commerce, conflict / Lawrence A. Peskin
and Edmund F. Wehrle.
p. cm.
Includes bibliographical references and index.
ISBN-13: 978-1-4214-0295-6 (hardcover : alk. paper)
ISBN-10: 1-4214-0295-5 (hardcover : alk. paper)
ISBN-13: 978-1-4214-0296-3 (pbk. : alk. paper)
ISBN-10: 1-4214-0296-3 (pbk. : alk. paper)
1. United States—Foreign relations.   2. United States—Foreign
economic relations.   3. United States—Civilization.   4. National
characteristics, American.   5. Civilization—American influences.
6. Globalization—Political aspects.   7. Globalization—Social
aspects.   8. Globalization—Economic aspects.   I. Wehrle,
Edmund F., 1964–   II. Title.
E183.3.P47 2011
973—dc22   2011009235

A catalog record for this book is available from the British Library.

*Special discounts are available for bulk purchases of this book.
For more information, please contact Special Sales at 410-516-6936 or
specialsales@press.jhu.edu.*

The Johns Hopkins University Press uses environmentally friendly book
materials, including recycled text paper that is composed of at least
30 percent post-consumer waste, whenever possible.

To our teachers at the University of Maryland:
James A. Henretta and the late Stuart B. Kaufman (1942–1997)

Contents

Preface

We live in the age of globalization, as pundits endlessly remind us. Integrated markets, blurring of national borders, and miraculous new technology—we hear constantly—have shrunk our world as never before. And it is true that we have entered a new epoch, both thrilling and ominous. Yet from a broader historical perspective, these trends are hardly novel. This book seeks to contextualize and historicize the phenomenon of globalization and America's connections to the world beyond its borders. Our aim is to provide a short, lively introduction for the general reader and the university student.

We view globalization as the process whereby the entire world has become linked through numerous and enduring networks, be they markets, transportation systems, diplomatic circles, cultural networks, or others. Unlike many historians, who see globalization as a recent phenomenon, we argue that globalization as a process has been going on for centuries. Through conquest and economic and cultural exchange, peoples have been forming connections throughout recorded history. Before the discovery of America, Europe, Asia, and Africa had been coming together in fits and starts for centuries, if not millennia. However, it was only with Columbus's voyage to America and the beginning of continual contact between America and the rest of the world that international networks could begin to become truly global. Connecting America to the larger world made full globalization possible for the first time.

Driven by this broad view of globalization, we chose to examine America's interaction with the world over a longer, more expansive period than most historians of globalization, who focus primarily on the twentieth century, when the United States became a global hegemon. Anyone trying to understand the pace of recent globalization and its varying effects on humanity, we believe, needs to be aware of this long history and to understand the ways people, ideas, and products from distant regions have been coming together (and occasionally drifting apart) over centuries.

To fit such copious subject matter into the narrow confines of a relatively short book, we provide chapters corresponding to the factors most crucial to globalization: commerce, culture, and conflict. In doing so we have sought to merge two approaches to America's relationship with the world. The older, more traditional approach is to focus on diplomatic and military history. We discuss these topics extensively under the category of *conflict*, which takes a wide view of warfare and diplomacy. Unlike standard military and diplomatic histories, ours is most concerned with how conflict and negotiation created connections between various parts of the world. From the great empires of the classical age on down, conquest, military alliances, and diplomatic networks have, for better or worse, served to link disparate portions of the world.

More recently, historians of America's relationship with the world have tended to focus on cultural and commercial ties, an approach particularly popular with historians of twentieth-century America. We deal with these topics as well, although our selection of subject matter may be a bit more capacious than the topic headings indicate. Under *culture*, we include all manner of cultural and intellectual trends, ranging from academic philosophy to popular music. We also focus on the international transit of ideas aimed at dramatically reshaping social and political relations—for example, seventeenth-century Christianity, eighteenth-century republicanism, and twentieth-century Progressivism. Under *commerce*, we incorporate all sorts of economic interactions, ranging from manufacturing to high finance. Wherever possible we incorporated the experiences of a wide range of peoples to suggest that globalization is first and foremost a human phenomenon, shaped by a remarkably diverse group of men and women.

Additionally, this book is divided into four chronologically defined sections. We have attempted to choose turning points that mark significant breaks in all of our three categories—culture, commerce, and conflict. The first section, from 1492 until 1763, covers the nearly three centuries between the beginning of sustained Euro-American interaction to the end of the Seven Years' War. It was the period in which Europeans gained control of all America, and then Britain gained control of North America. The end of the Seven Years' War prompted the revolutionary crisis that would mark the end of the former 13 colonies' participation in British mercantilism, as well as the beginning of the American idealism encapsulated in the Declaration of Independence and the Constitution. The second period, from 1763 to 1898, spans from the American Revolution through the Spanish-American war, thereby stretching from the end of America's colonial dependence on Britain to the point at which the United

States became an important imperial power in its own right. Additionally, 1898 marks roughly the time when the United States became the world's leading industrial producer and when Jim Crow racial segregation became the law of the land. The third period, 1898–1945, saw the United States emerge the world's leading military power, as well as its most formidable economy, and American culture, from movies to inexpensive consumer goods, began to make itself felt across the world. Finally, the period 1945–2010 marked the rise and fall of the Cold War and the dawn of modern globalization in which America reigned as the dominant military power and in which the so-called soft imperialism of American culture and economics seemed to predominate throughout most of the world.

From the first encounters between Europeans and Native Americans to the present, the very nature of commerce, conflict, and culture changed substantially, as did their relative significance in the story of America's interaction with the world. Commerce in the 1492–1763 period refers primarily to shipping and the mercantilist economy associated with it. Later, new transportation technologies, such as inland railroad trade, as well as factory production completely transformed what it meant to engage in commerce. By the second half of the twentieth century, new financial and communication technologies as well as previously unheard of issues such as intellectual property rights once again redefined the nature of commerce. In the colonial period, religion was perhaps the most important transatlantic component of culture, but during the nineteenth century and the era of Atlantic revolutions, America's political culture played a crucial role in world events. During the twentieth century, its political culture continued to be influential, along with popular culture and multiculturalism.

Likewise, during different periods, the relative importance of the different categories of globalization waxed and waned. For example, during the 1763–1898 period, the new nation was most influential on the world stage in the field of political culture. Conversely, by the 1898–1945 period, American military might became a far more important factor in the nation's relationship with the world. These shifts are also an important part of our story. The order in which we discuss these various issues within each part of this book reflects the changing relative importance of these categories. For example, we believe that during the colonial era commercial issues were crucial to America's integration into the world, but during the nineteenth century issues of political culture loomed larger. We elaborate our position on these issues within the introductions to each of the book's four parts. These introductions also provide background on the evolving transportation and communication technologies and immigration waves that facilitated global exchange during each period.

Examining such a wide expanse of time while trying to avoid the chauvinism of the old nationalistic history has also forced us to consider how to define America. One solution would be simply to limit our subject matter to the thirteen colonies that would eventually become the United States. We have rejected this approach because it would anachronistically limit our treatment of the early relations between America and the world to the area bounded by a nation that had not yet been formed. Rather, while making every effort to discuss relevant events and trends occurring north of the Rio Grande and south of modern Canada, in the early sections of this book we also consider modern-day Mexico, the West Indies, and Canada as part of America. We do so because the West Indies and Mexico were the most dynamic part of North America before the eighteenth century and because many of the events and interactions that occurred there shaped events and interactions that would later occur in the present-day United States. For the period after the American Revolution, however, we follow most historians of America and the world in focusing our attention on the United States of America and its interactions with the rest of the world—Europe, Asia, Africa, Australia, and the rest of the American hemisphere.

We hope that this book will contribute to an ongoing conversation, now nearly two decades under way, about how to reconceptualize United States history in a global context. No longer can America's history be told in a vacuum; no longer does the notion of American exceptionalism hold much water. Indeed, a new field frequently labeled "America and the world" has evolved, spurred by the emergence of world history and diaspora studies. Naturally, debates and differences have surfaced over just how to approach this new field of study. Some historians have focused primarily on U.S. history, situating it in the greater context of global trends, thus debunking notions of American exceptionalism. Others attempt truly transnational histories that jump back and forth across the Atlantic rather than rooting themselves in American, or any other national history. This book steers a middle course, organizing its narrative around American history but trying to show how that history was influenced by people, events, and trends that originated outside of America and how, in turn, it influenced non-American histories.

Throughout, we seek to portray America's history as a part of the larger history of globalization. The integration and interdependence that characterize globalization has not developed in a linear fashion. Far from smooth or inexorable, the pace of globalization often has been fitful and hesitant. Indeed, resistance to globalization, both among Americans and people everywhere, is central to this complex story (and is reflected over and over in the pages that follow).

Beginning the story, as many historians do, sometime in the late nineteenth century makes globalization seem far more inevitable and direct, suggesting to casual observers that the western world (at least), moved remarkably quickly from fragmentation to globalization over the last century. However, expanding the story backward to 1492 rightly complicates the picture. The 1492–1763 period was one of extremely rapid globalization from the perspective of America's relation to the rest of the world, while the next period (1763–1898) was one in which connections between America and the rest of the world grew at a slower pace, perhaps at times becoming less important. Examining 1492 to the present as a whole manifests the ebbs and flows of America's integration into the world—an unevenness caused by many factors, including economic downturns, disruptions from warfare, and popular opposition to global connections.

Nevertheless, despite the complex, varying rhythm of globalization, overall America's connections to the world were undeniably more important and more numerous than is usually apparent in standard histories, and they have certainly become even more important in recent years. To some extent, common wisdom about the nature of our increasingly globalized world does, in fact, reflect reality. Today we see this complexity in operation all around us. While this short book can only suggest some of the more important ways these connections have developed over the last five centuries, we hope it will provide readers with a broad historical understanding of this globalizing world and perhaps even inspire them to learn more.

Acknowledgments

As reflected in this book's dedication, we owe an enormous debt to our teachers at the University of Maryland, James Henretta and the late Stuart Kauffman, who taught us much about America, the world, and the world of historical research and writing. We also are grateful to Bob Brugger of the Johns Hopkins University Press for his unstinting support of this project, even when America and the publishing world plunged into the financial abyss.

Lawrence Peskin owes a debt of gratitude to Annette Palmer for piquing his interest in world history and the field of America and the world long before it attained its present popularity. He would also like to thank a number of individuals for their advice and assistance: Emeka Anaedozie, Brett Berliner, Stephen Feeley, James Fichter, Elizabeth Kelly Gray, Matthew Hale, John Hosler, Christian Koot, Matt Mulcahy, Allan Peskin, Glenn Phillips, Tricia Pyne, Shane Walsh, Mike Williams, and Natalie Zaceck. They are, of course, not responsible for any errors that remain in this text, but there would be many more without them.

Edmund Wehrle acknowledges Eastern Illinois University's Council on Faculty Research for generously supporting this project with a summer research grant. Thanks also to my colleagues at Eastern—in particular Lynne Curry, Newton Key, Sace Elder, Martin Hardeman, and Debra Reid—who unfailingly lent their particular expertise, read drafts, and provided encouragement. My gratitude also to Edmund S. Wehrle, David Sicilia, Alonzo Hamby, and the librarians and archivists at the Library of Congress and Newberry Library in Chicago. My wife, Jacqueline Wehrle, deserves particular recognition for cheerfully and patiently reading drafts, reviewing footnotes, and providing trenchant commentary.

Part I
1492–1763

INTRODUCTION

Columbus's arrival in America prompted an incredible transformation. Before 1492, Europeans and Americans essentially knew nothing of each other. Within fifty years, Europeans had conquered the two greatest empires in America and gained effective control of the wealthiest, most developed portion of the continent. They destroyed the largest city on the continent, replacing it with one built on a European model. They cajoled or forced millions of Americans into converting to Christianity and learning European languages. By 1763, Europeans had firmly integrated most of North America's Atlantic basin into their economies and brought it under their governmental control. Even Americans living far from the Atlantic had access to European trade goods, agricultural products, and livestock and exposure to diseases never present before 1492. Furthermore, most residents in European-controlled areas were now of European or African descent, with the Native American population in rapid decline. In eastern North America, Europeans and Africans transformed the landscape from forests and scattered agricultural towns to vast plantations, large areas of intensive family agriculture, and growing coastal urban centers. Before 1492, Europe, Asia, and Africa had been slowly coming together in fits and starts for centuries. The transformations that occurred after Columbus really marked the beginning of America's integration into the rest of the world and, therefore, the beginning of full globalization.

Historians have long debated why and how these transformations were able to occur so rapidly, but European geographical knowledge and maritime technology certainly were crucial. Mastery of the technology of sailing gave Europeans a crucial advantage over Native Americans. Still, European knowledge of American geography developed slowly. While European maps fairly quickly provided good detail of the eastern coast of South America and the Caribbean, understanding of the Pacific coast could not begin before Ferdinand Magellan's circumnavigation of 1519–1522, and Europeans remained ignorant of the contours of coastal regions of North America such as Chesapeake Bay and California into the seventeenth and eighteenth century, respectively. Exploration and mapping of the continental interior, begun by Hernán Cortés in 1519, largely depended on the knowledge and assistance of Native Americans, who were known to scratch detailed temporary maps on the ground to assist (and occasionally mislead) bewildered Europeans.

Columbus's landing in America led to a crucial new technological development: discovery and mastery of the wind systems that allowed Europeans to sail across the Atlantic easily and, more importantly, to be confident in their ability to return home. Native Americans could not retaliate against European advances by attacking their enemies' homelands, nor were they able to find sources of European goods or information about European technology and politics other than what came to America's shores. At the same time, maritime transport allowed a seemingly unending stream of European armies and settlers easy access to the so-called New World. Among other things, these travelers brought with them European diseases to which Americans had no immunity and new weapons and animals, such as horses and mastiff dogs, that could be used for military advantage. As a result of warfare and disease, the continent's native population dropped precipitously, creating more space for further European immigration.

Globalization was not, however, a one-way street. Even as America was being forcibly connected to the old world, Europe, Asia, and Africa were becoming Americanized. Most noticeable was the old world's rapid conversion to American crops such as Indian maize (corn on the cob), potatoes, tomatoes, cassava, and sweet potatoes, to name only a few. Contact with America accelerated European interest in geography, politics, and anthropology. Trading and warfare between Native Americans and Europeans ensured that the two cultures quickly learned about and adapted aspects of each others' military and manufacturing technologies. American wealth, particularly gold and silver, had a major impact on Europe's economy, and the effort to govern American territory helped to spur European imperialism and mercantilism. Finally, massive European immigration into America, as well as the forcible removal of millions of Africans to the new world, created connections that spanned continents and forged millions of personal links between the old and new worlds.

American interaction with the world changed dramatically by the second half of this period. During the first century or so of European-American contact, both sides were learning about each other and attempting to understand the future of the continent. Native Americans had to find ways to cope with new diseases, European military advances, and new economic challenges posed by the spread of European manufactures, crops, and livestock. Europeans, for their part, struggled first to gain control of the continent and then to determine how to profit from it. At first, Europeans treated Americans much as they had Africans and Asians in earlier decades, first as potential trading partners and then as potentially dangerous enemies. But, over time, as native Americans died off and Europeans gained control of much of the continent, they came to see America as an agricultural extension of Europe. Indians increasingly became peripheral to their vision of America as Europeans created a plantation system that integrated America into the European economy as a producer of valuable semitropical crops cultivated by the labor of African slaves. Increasingly, groups of Europeans fought wars to control these plantations and the wealth they produced. This warfare culminated in 1763 with the global Seven Years' War, which began in America and determined that Great Britain would become the world's leading colonizer. Paradoxically, it also accelerated the end of the colonial system in North America by catalyzing the American Revolution, the first step in wrenching the American colonies away from their European founders.

Commerce drove this early globalization. Columbus and other early European explorers hoped that by traveling west they would find a route to Asia's riches. After it became clear that would not be the case, they hoped to trade with the natives. When that failed, they searched for precious metals and other sources of wealth to extract from the New World. Had they not found anything, it is quite possible the invaders would have lost interest. However, Europeans found valuable products throughout North America, from southern silver to northern beaver pelts and cod. In some cases they relied on native expertise, and in others they relied on native labor. But, as the Indian population died out and as supplies of many of the commodities that the Europeans treasured dwindled, the conquerors looked for profits from new sorts of trade. Eventually they created the plantation system to produce staple crops such as rice, tobacco, and sugar using enslaved African laborers. The plantation system arose at different times in different regions, but it was primarily a product of the seventeenth and eighteenth centuries.

Bloody conflict also defined America's interactions with the world. First, Europeans and Americans fought for control of the continent. From the start, some Native Americans allied with Europeans against native enemies, continuing longstanding intercontinental hostilities reaching back well before Columbus. Europeans like Hernán Cortés made brilliant use of these alliances. For the most part, too, the earliest European colonizers, Spain and Portugal, each agreed to leave the other's settlements alone. Thus, Europeans in America were not beset by the divisions that plagued Native Americans. Over time, however, Europeans within the Americas began to spar with each other, both on the high seas (where they often engaged in piracy and privateering) and on land. Initially, Europeans informally agreed to keep these conflicts separate from wars in Europe. The great powers regarded conflict in America as "beyond the line," meaning it would not necessarily cause broader European conflicts. By the turn of the eighteenth century, Europe had largely won the battle for control of America over the natives, but inter-European conflict intensified, and it started to become more fully integrated into warfare in Europe and on other continents. The enormous Seven Years' War (1756–63)—described in these pages as the first world war—actually originated in America and saw, for the first time, large numbers of British troops fighting on this continent. By war's end, America was no longer "beyond the line." The new world had been fully integrated into European warfare.

Cultural exchange between old and new worlds also changed dramatically during this period. Initially, Europeans worked hard to indoctrinate Americans into the Catholic church. They succeeded at baptizing millions, although baptized Americans frequently secretly continued worshiping the old gods or fashioned a sort of syncretic American Christianity that incorporated Jesus into their existing religious structures. For their part, Europeans were surprisingly slow to develop interest in the details of the new world across the ocean, perhaps because it took them some time to figure out that it actually was new, rather than just an outcropping of Asia. Eventually, however Europeans became fascinated by the geography and, especially, the natives of America. This interest, spurred by many Indians who visited Europe, usually as captives, heavily influenced European thinking about what today would be termed anthropology, and it served as the crucible for modern conceptions of race and racism. Fascination with Native Americans also influenced European political philosophy, particularly the Enlightenment concept of the social contract. By the turn of the eighteenth century, however, as the Native American population dropped precipitously, European fascination with Native Americans correspondingly declined. Increasingly European colonists began to see themselves as true Americans (although occasionally, as in the Boston Tea Party of 1773 when they dressed as Indians to protest the British Tea Act, they continued to portray Indians as symbols of the New World). Transatlantic cultural connections now occurred primarily between Europeans in Europe and those in America and, to a lesser extent, between Africans in America and Europeans, while Native Americans increasingly seemed peripheral to the progress of globalization.

CHAPTER ONE

Commerce and Conquest

FROM PATUXET TO PLYMOUTH

Tisquantum, usually known as Squanto, lived a remarkable life that bridged two worlds. Born in the Wampanoag town of Patuxet sometime in the 1580s, he grew up to be a warrior and bodyguard to the tribal leader. From his seaside village, young Squanto frequently saw great European sailing ships fishing the rich North Atlantic waters. In the summer of 1614 he came face to face with a party of European explorers led by Captain John Smith, who had recently helped to found the Jamestown colony on Chesapeake Bay. When he later wrote about Patuxet, Smith called it Plymouth, the name by which it is still known today. Not long after Smith departed, his lieutenant, Thomas Hunt visited Plymouth, where he kidnapped approximately twenty Wampanoags, including Squanto, and carried them across the Atlantic to Spain. In Spain, Hunt attempted to sell Squanto and his compatriots as slaves, but Catholic priests who hoped to convert Indians to Christianity prevented the sale and rescued Squanto, eventually allowing him to go to London. There, Squanto lived for a time with a shipbuilder named John Slany, who exhibited Squanto to curious Londoners. There, too, Squanto learned to speak English fluently. Eventually the future proprietor of Maine, Ferdinando Gorges employed Squanto to assist his company's efforts to plant a colony in northern New England. Squanto crossed back to America, returning to England when a sailors' mutiny ended the mission. Finally, Squanto came home to America and to Patuxet/Plymouth in 1619 as part of another colonization expedition directed by Gorges.

When Squanto arrived in Patuxet/Plymouth he was shocked to find the village abandoned and the skeletons of many of its former residents lying unburied on the ground. The village, and many others along the coast, had been destroyed by disease in 1616. Historians presume Europeans fishing or exploring in the area carried microbes that proved deadly to Indians never before exposed to such lethal germs. This was the site where the ship Mayflower and the so-called Pilgrims landed in December 1620 and constructed what is today considered the first British colony in New England. Squanto impressed the Pilgrims with his English language skills, and he became their interpreter, helping them to negotiate with the natives. He also instructed them on how to plant Indian corn using fish as fertilizer. Perhaps more importantly, if less famously, he helped them to inaugurate a trade in fur in which the Pilgrims would serve as intermediaries between inland natives who captured beaver and otter and merchants in London who sold them to European consumers. Squanto died in 1622 while serving as an interpreter to Captain Miles Standish on a trip to trade with Indians to the south of Plymouth. The trade in furs, however, flourished without him. At its peak, in 1633 and 1634, Plymouth sent over 3,000 pounds of beaver pelts to London annually. From 1631 through 1636 they shipped 12,530 pounds of beaver fur and 1,156 otter skins.[1] Profits from these sales were the colony's major source of funding.

While Squanto's life was certainly remarkable, it also typified the changing nature of American-European commerce during the early years of conquest and colonization. This chapter chronicles the evolving economic role of America in the world from the period before Columbus to the rise of the eighteenth-century plantation economy. At first there was little in the way of formal trade networks between natives and Europeans. Nevertheless, they engaged in a great deal of exchange. Some of it was involuntary, such as the transfer of European diseases into America that devastated Squanto's village. Other exchanges involved the transfer of information, for example Squanto's instructions to Europeans on corn growing and fur trading. Both Europeans and Indians also engaged in much gift giving early on—for example, Europeans giving alcohol to natives or natives providing corn to Europeans. Historians often call this early phase the Columbian exchange, and this initial transfer of knowledge, technologies, disease, and products did much to Americanize Europe and Europeanize America. Soon European colonizers began to extract commodities from America, such as fur and silver, in a more systematic way, often creating large transatlantic markets in which Indians played a vital role. Eventually, however, as many of these commodities became depleted, Europeans in America began to forge a new economy based on massive plantations using enslaved African laborers to produce goods such as sugar and tobacco. This new form of commerce would tie together the three Atlantic-facing continents of Europe, Africa, and America, but Native Americans would play a far more marginal role than they had earlier.

COMMERCE BEFORE COLUMBUS

The world was much smaller and still overwhelmingly agricultural in the years before Columbus. For most people, on the Eurasian land mass as well as in America, commerce remained local and informal. Longer-distance trading was rare. Occasionally Europeans might buy and sell produce or manufactured goods at local markets or, less commonly, at large regional fairs that attracted people from many miles around. Nevertheless, in the centuries before Columbus, long-distance trade networks grew in importance and size, and European traders were becoming particularly proficient at linking together existing trading networks to create even larger ones.

By 1492 Europe's most influential traders resided in Italian port cities such as Venice and Genoa, Columbus's birthplace. Merchants in this part of the Mediterranean were well positioned to forge connections to the large and wealthy trade networks of Asia to the east, particularly the great Silk Roads over which silk and spices from more easterly portions of Asia flowed west toward Byzantium (now Turkey). The most famous Italian to walk these roads was Marco Polo, who claimed to have traveled to China, although some historians now dispute his claims. Rather than explorers, most Venetian and Genoese merchants served as middlemen directing the river of Asian goods flowing into Byzantium toward a series of large fairs in France. In this way, Mediterranean merchants traded with northern European merchants who, in turn, resold Asian goods to Scandinavian and eastern European markets. The Italians who dominated the European markets mostly excluded traders from the Iberian Peninsula (modern-day Spain and Portugal), which had recently been dominated by Islamic powers . Instead, Portuguese and Spanish traders began to look to the southern and western reaches of the Atlantic Ocean.

This focus brought them first toward Africa. While northern portions of Africa had long been integrated into Mediterranean trade networks, the Atlantic coastal people had not experienced much contact with Europeans or other outsiders. Beginning in the mid-fifteenth century, during the reign of Dom Henrique (Henry the Navigator), Portuguese explorers cooperating with Genoese and Venetian navigators probed southward along the Atlantic coastline of sub-Saharan Africa. They were particularly interested in tapping into what they believed were extensive gold-trading networks in Mali and Ethiopia. By the time of Columbus's voyage, they had penetrated far into the African interior, setting up a number of trading forts along the coast, most notably Sao Jorge da Mina in modern-day Ghana. Here the Portuguese traded textiles and other manufactured goods for gold, ivory, pepper, and other luxury items. They also participated in an initially small, but ultimately lethal, trade in African slaves.

By the late fifteenth century, Iberian explorers made inroads to the east and west. Portuguese were advancing by land and sea routes into eastern Africa. From there they hoped to connect to the rich Indian trade. According to a contemporary, Portugal's king expected the explorer Vasco da Gama to seize "those eastern riches so celebrated by ancient writers, part of which, by way of commerce, has made Venice, Genoa, and other Italian cities into great powers."[2] In 1497, Gama managed to round the Cape of Good Hope, Africa's southern tip, and sail into the Indian Ocean where he forced local navigators to help him cross in 23 days to Calcutta, India. Iberian and Italian interest in the Atlantic caused other explorers and traders to look to the west. As early as 1291 the Vivaldi brothers of Genoa disappeared at sea attempting to find a route across the Atlantic to Asia. Other Genoese, Spaniards, and Portuguese soon began to explore the Canary, Azores, Madeira, and Cape Verde islands located in the Atlantic to the west of Africa. Before Portugal gained a foothold on the African continent, Portugal's king, Henrique particularly valued the Canaries as a possible Portuguese-controlled gateway to the sub-Saharan gold trade. By the mid-fifteenth century, Portuguese colonists and enslaved Africans were raising substantial sugar crops in Madeira for sale in Europe. Spanish exploration of the Canaries revealed the Atlantic wind systems, which Columbus deduced would allow him to sail farther west to Asia.

Columbus's voyage can be seen as a continuation of Genoese and Iberian exploration of the Atlantic. A Genoese-born adventurer, Columbus began his voyage from the Canary Islands, and all of his financial backers had been involved in earlier ventures in the Canaries. Both he and Spain's monarchs, Ferdinand and Isabella, hoped that his westward voyage would create Spanish-controlled trade routes to Asia, much as Portugal hoped Vasco da Gama's southeastern route would give Portugal unfettered access to India. In fact, Columbus had earlier tried to sell the Portuguese on his western route but had moved to Spain after Henrique decided to back Vasco da Gama instead. Columbus's demand to be allowed to keep a tenth of all "gold, silver, pearls, gems, spices and other merchandise produced or obtained by barter or mining" in any land he would discover or acquire shows his expectations that his voyage would connect to Asian markets. Once he arrived in America, Columbus continued to focus on trade, noting that the natives brought him "parrots, cotton threads in skeins, darts and many other things" that they traded for "glass beads to put around their necks."[3] After the successful completion of his voyage, which Columbus always believed had brought him to Asia, the Spanish monarchs initially contemplated setting up a coastal trading fort as part of an operation they assumed would be similar to the Portuguese gold trade in Africa.

Historians know less about commerce in America before Columbus, but, like the people Europeans encountered in Asia and Africa, Native Americans had extensive trading routes of their own. More than 700 years before Columbus's arrival, the people of modern day Mexico traded far to the south and north. The Inca people of South America also commanded extensive trading networks, although they never seem to have connected to the Mexican-centered network. In what is now the United States, trade routes flourished in the Mississippi valley, which may even have been connected to the Mexican trade at some point. By the time of Columbus's arrival, however, these networks were diminishing.

Finding no apparent large-scale trade network in America and perceiving Indians as primitive and physically weak, Europeans opted for conquest. They would remake the American economy as an appendage of Europe rather than tie into existing trade routes as they had in Asia and, to a lesser extent, Africa. As a result, contact with Europe would more often than not lead to deadly consequences for native Americans. But it also enmeshed them, for better or worse, into a new European-dominated web of trade and transformed the economic structure of their continent. For Europeans, this economic transformation allowed for the creation of profitable new modes of commerce, as well as new trade routes.

THE COLUMBIAN EXCHANGE

Even before they established new markets in America, Europeans began to transform the continent's economy by introducing new items, ranging from germs to guns. They also brought American products back to Europe. This informal exchange, often known as the Columbian exchange, could be involuntary and unintentional, as with the transfer of diseases and weeds. Frequently, however, it was intentional on the part of Europeans, who hoped to make America into a more familiar, recognizable, and profitable place. These informal exchanges occurred wherever and whenever Europeans began to colonize the Americas. They nearly always had a devastating effect on America and Americans, quickly spreading deadly disease and dangerous invasive species ahead of Europeans wherever they went. In the more intermediate term, they began to transform the American economy and landscape as natives became accustomed, for better or worse, to new products and technologies. In the long run, they contributed to the process of worldwide homogenization and integration, as America began to look more similar to Europe and other old world continents and as people in both continents began eating the same foods and suffering from the same diseases.

The first exchanges between Europe and America were deadly and involuntary. As soon as Europeans arrived, and sometimes sooner, they spread unfamiliar and frequently lethal microbes to which most Europeans had gained some immunity over centuries of exposure. Unfortunately, American Indians had developed no such immunity. Once exposed, they died in extraordinary numbers from what are known as "virgin soil" epidemics of European diseases. On Hispaniola just two years after Columbus's arrival, a Spaniard reported that more than 50,000 natives of a population of around 300,000 had already died "and they are falling each day, with every step, like cattle in an infected herd."[4] Fifty years later, only 500 natives remained there. In early 1519 a devastating smallpox epidemic swept through the new world. Spaniards, who were largely immune to the disease, reported that it killed as many as half the natives of the island of St. Domingo before traveling to mainland Mexico. There, an observer traveling with Hernán Cortés's army noted that "when the Christians were exhausted from war [against the Aztecs], God saw fit to send the Indians smallpox, and there was a great pestilence in the city."[5] This pestilence—probably a combination of smallpox and other infections—allowed the Spaniards to triumph in what had earlier seemed a losing battle.

Similar devastation occurred in the present-day United States as soon as the English arrived. Thomas Harriot, one of the first Englishmen in Virginia noted in 1587 that soon after his party visited an Indian town "the people began to die very fast, and many in short space."[6] Although well versed in natural sciences, Harriot, like other Europeans, had no concept of microbiology and believed that the epidemic resulted from divine anger at the Indians' hostility to the English. Natives in New England and eastern Canada suffered from a disastrous epidemic in 1616–17. Three years later, when the English began to settle in Massachusetts, there were virtually no remaining Indians to oppose them. Massachusetts governor John Winthrop saw the epidemic as a sign of divine approval of his New England settlement.

Early conquest also proved environmentally challenging. Europeans inadvertently introduced new invasive plant and animal species into America. Perhaps the most enduring have been the rats, which no doubt were passengers on the first America-bound ships. Somewhat later, English ships brought them to the Bermuda islands where they quickly multiplied and became, according to one colonist, "a grievous scourge and punishment, threatening the utter ruin and desolation" of the island.[7] They ate so much that the colonists began to starve. European weeds also arrived with or ahead of the colonists. Kentucky bluegrass, which was well established across the Appalachians by the time colonists arrived, was actually a European plant brought to America as fodder and carried across the mountains by animals who deposited it in their dung. Other European transplants that flourished in North America included daisies, dandelions, white clover, thistle, and stinging nettles.

As soon as they began to settle in any portion of the new world, Europeans invariably introduced crops and animals from the old country into American soil. Spaniards, who disdained Indian corn bread, spread European wheat wherever it would grow, usually within a few years of settlement. Later, English colonists would introduce the crop into what is today the United States. Spaniards also brought European grapes for wine—a religious as well as a dietary necessity—into places such as Chile, which today remains an important wine-producing region.

European livestock proved more disruptive. Pigs, cows, sheep, horses, and other domesticated livestock did not exist in America before European arrival. Pigs, in particular, caused problems. Hernando de Soto brought thirteen with him to Florida in 1539. In three years' time they had multiplied to become 700. This porcine population explosion could be disastrous for natives. Because Indians did not use fences, pigs roamed at will, often eating the food that Indians relied on for their own diets, be it cassava and sweet potatoes in the Caribbean or shellfish in New England. European cattle also destroyed Indian hunting grounds by driving out deer and other animals. An early English colonist noted that "of all English cattle, the swine . . . are most hateful to all Natives, and they call them filthy cut throats, etc."[8] Consequently, conflicts between European colonists and Indians frequently were sparked by complaints over pigs and cattle. Europeans initially used horses to conquer native people. But over time, as Indians began to breed them, horses transformed native cultures and economies. While most Americans today picture the traditional Indian of the Great Plains riding a horse while hunting buffalo, the Indians in what is now the western part of the United States had no horses until the late seventeenth century. It was only in the eighteenth century that Comanche, Sioux, and Lakota arrived there and established the buffalo-hunting culture portrayed in the classic western movies of the twentieth century.

From the start, Indians admired European manufactured goods. European-made wampum beads became valuable prestige items in Indian society. Distilled alcohol, a novelty in America, proved to be attractive to Indians, albeit extremely detrimental. But most important was the European introduction of metal goods to Indians who had previously relied on stone and wood. Guns eventually would transform Indian society, but initially natives most desired European-made hatchets and brass tips for their arrows rather than clumsy, inaccurate muskets. They often cut up European-made metal goods such as kettles in order to re-use the metal for weaponry or ritual items. Metal hatchets and European flints made the laborious chores associated with building fires much simpler, and metal kettles and other utensils made cooking far easier. Nevertheless, the declining number of Indians and the slow development of Euro-Indian trading networks after initial contact limited the spread of manufactured goods in the first years of settlement.

American products also transformed the old world. It has long been thought that the venereal disease, syphilis, originated in America and spread to Europe with the earliest Spanish explorers; however, some historians now debate that claim. What is undeniable is that Indian agriculture, which was often highly sophisticated, had an enormous impact on European life. The most important and perhaps most technologically impressive of these crops was maize or Indian corn. Maize does not, and cannot, grow in the wild. Around 1500 BCE Indian cultivators in Mexico successfully bred wild grasses to produce the cobs associated with maize, a feat described by a modern day geneticist as "arguably man's first and perhaps his greatest, feat of genetic engineering."[9] Over the centuries, maize cultivation spread throughout most of the Americas, and native botanists developed countless varieties of it. Once discovered by Columbus, maize spread relatively quickly throughout Europe. Columbus himself noted in 1498, "There is now a lot of [corn] in Castille."[10] Maize spread from Spain into southern Europe, where it was more frequently used to feed cattle than humans. By the early eighteenth century, however, it had become a staple of peasant diets in southern France and Italy, where it was often consumed as polenta. It soon moved further east, becoming an important crop in eighteenth-century Hungary and in Balkan states such as Romania.

What maize did for southern Europe, the potato did for the north. Potatoes originated in pre-Columbian South America. Their tolerance of cold weather allowed potatoes to flourish in mountain highlands where other Indian crops struggled. Initially seen as an aphrodisiac by Europeans, it was only in the eighteenth century that the potato became an important crop in Ireland and other portions of Europe. In the nineteenth century it became a major food source in Russia, and by the mid-twentieth century the majority of the world's potatoes came from Europe. Because of the potato's resistance to cold and its unusually high caloric yield—a pound of potatoes provides about 80 percent more calories than a pound of wheat—the potato became the backbone of much of northern Europe's agricultural economy, not to mention its cuisine. Potatoes and other newly introduced American crops helped support rapid European population increases in places like Ireland, which grew from 3 million people in 1750 to 5.25 million in 1800. The mass starvation during the potato famine of the 1840s demonstrates how dependent the Irish had become on the American potato in only a century and a half.

Other American products also helped to transform European cuisine and culture. The tomato originated in South America and central Mexico but does not seem to have been cultivated much before Columbus's arrival. The plant began to spread into the Mediterranean during the seventeenth century. The earliest known Italian recipes using tomatoes date from 1692, making Italy's association with red pasta sauces surprisingly recent. Other American agricultural products initially entered Europe as luxury goods. Both chocolate and tobacco originated as native American plants that demanded heavy processing and novel rituals before they could be consumed. Chocolate is derived from the flower of the cacao tree. Indians prepared it by drying and fermenting cacao seeds, grinding and heating them, and mixing the processed seeds with water, maize, and spices. Europeans assimilated this process in America and began to drink chocolate on the home continent by the sixteenth century, but it was only in the seventeenth century that they began importing it in bulk. The story of tobacco was similar. Europeans learned to process and smoke tobacco from natives shortly after arriving in America and brought the habit with them to Europe. In 1574 a Spanish writer noted that Spaniards "bring from New Spain . . . canes covered within and without by a sort of gum and it seems that it is mixed with juice of tobacco."[11] Like chocolate, tobacco did not enter European markets on a large scale until the seventeenth century.

American products also transformed the diets of Africa and, to a lesser extent, Asia. Cassava (also known as manioc), the most important American plant in Africa, originated in pre-Columbian Brazil and was brought to Africa by the Portuguese in the sixteenth century. It only became a major product in Africa in the nineteenth century, but by the twentieth century it was the dominant crop in parts of West Africa and the third largest source of carbohydrates in the world. Other important African crops originating in America include sweet potatoes, peanuts, and maize. The sweet potato arrived in China by 1560, and by the twentieth century China had become the world's largest sweet potato producer. Maize, peanuts, cassava, and chili peppers, among other American products, also spread relatively quickly into East Asia and the Indian subcontinent where, as in Europe, they helped provide nutrition to a rapidly growing population. By the late twentieth century, two of the world's five largest crops had originated in America.

THE EXTRACTIVE ECONOMY

As it became clear that America was not part of Asia and natives would not be easily linked into a trading network for precious metals or spices, Europeans focused on extracting valuable commodities from American soil. Because, unlike in Asia and Africa, they claimed legal possession of the lands they had discovered, and because Indians were unable to resist their claims, Europeans had few qualms about seizing the riches of the New World. Much as they had in Africa, European explorers in America hoped to acquire large quantities of precious metals, which served as money in Europe. The earliest Spanish explorers thrilled at discovering gold in Hispaniola and Puerto Rico; however, they quickly exhausted these island deposits. Cortés and others soon discovered that mainland Indians owned significant quantities of precious metals. Where Indian populations remained relatively large and wealthy, the conquering Spaniards at first were content to take gold from the natives as tribute. But soon Spaniards began to establish their own mines using forced Indian labor. Spanish colonists sent more than 100 million grams of gold back to Spain by 1560. With the discovery of enormous silver deposits in Mexico and the Andes, silver exports to Spain over the decade of the 1540s rose to more than 170 million grams. Harnessing forced and voluntary Indian labor and making use of a new extractive technology that used mercury to draw silver out from the ore, production skyrocketed to well over 900 million grams by the 1560s. Precious metals would reign as the dominant export from Latin America into the seventeenth century.

These silver operations had an enormous impact on America. They demanded tremendous amounts of labor, much of it from Native Americans. While some Indians were experienced miners, Europeans recruited, often forcibly, many others to labor under miserable conditions in large mines. The concentration of laborers created intensive urbanization in the mining regions. The new silver mining city of Potosi, located high in the Andes Mountains of modern-day

Bolivia, had a population of more than 100,000 by about 1600, making it one of the largest cities in the western world. Because of its dual nature as commodity and money, silver pulled natives quickly into the market economy. Where it was available, silver soon replaced cocoa beans as the standard currency for Native Americans and allowed them to play a part in the money economy of the Spanish-American world.

American silver also had a tremendous influence in Europe and Asia. By the time of Columbus, Europe was experiencing rapid population growth, which caused the price of food and other goods to rise. One reason why Spain and Portugal were so interested in finding more gold and silver was to combat the effects of this price inflation. But instead of solving the problem of inflation, the vast quantities of American silver that began to flow into Seville by the mid-sixteenth century caused prices to rise still higher, thereby exacerbating the problems of inflation and scarcity for much of the population. While many in Spain became very wealthy, by the early seventeenth century much of Europe was in economic crisis, which was one of the factors pushing England to expand its program of colonization in America. American silver also found its way to Asia. In 1570, merchants started to link Asian, European, and American markets as Spanish ships began carrying American silver from Acapulco in western Mexico to Manila in the Philippines. From there, Spaniards traded large quantities of silver to China, which provided Asian luxuries such as silk and porcelain to Spanish-Americans in return.

To the north, in the area that would become the eastern United States and Canada, the earliest Europeans also developed an extractive economy. But the goods they extracted were not nearly as valuable as the silver and gold in Latin America. Even before the first settlements, enterprising European fishermen cast their nets into the rich waters south and east of Newfoundland, Canada. In 1578 an observer counted 350 European ships there, most French and Spanish. By 1618, two years before the Pilgrims arrived in Massachusetts, the 250 English ships working off Newfoundland earned the impressive sum of £135,000. The earliest European settlers in the region also felled trees and shipped them back to England, often to be used as masts for ships in the Royal Navy. By the mid-seventeenth century, shipyards and sawmills lined New Hampshire's Piscataqua River. In the early years of the Carolina settlements, colonists also cut down pine trees for masts or to be distilled into naval stores such as tar and pitch (used in ship construction and maintenance) to be exported to Europe. In 1718, for example, "tar heels" exported fifty thousand barrels of the black, sticky substance.

Shortly after settlement, English colonists began exporting animal pelts. In New England, they dealt in beaver and otter pelts, while Carolinians traded deerskins. Unlike easily extracted coastal items, these pelts proved difficult to capture, and Europeans were unable to gather large quantities on their own. Indians, however, already carried on some trade in these goods among themselves and were skilled hunters. European traders soon slipped into their customary role as middlemen, connecting Indian hunters and trade networks to European markets by channeling beaver pelts and deerskins to the Atlantic ports and then on to Europe. The burgeoning fur trade connected America more closely to Europe. Massachusetts colonists traded their products with a tight-knit group of London merchants centered on the Cheapside district of East London. These merchants, as well as their counterparts in Holland and France who traded with merchants in New France and New Netherlands, profited greatly from the colonists' trade. With furs flooding into Europe from North America, European consumers who could never have afforded fur clothing gained status and warmth by purchasing relatively inexpensive beaver hats, fur coats and hand and foot muffs, as well as fur ruffs, borders, and collars that could add a touch of class to their ordinary clothing, allowing them to imitate the fashions of the nobility.

Initially, much of this trade was conducted with Indian goods. Europeans first traded Indian corn for beaver pelts, much as Indians themselves had done for many years. But corn was awkward and bulky. Increasingly Europeans traded instead with white and purple beads made from shellfish and known by the natives as wampum. These shells, found primarily on Long Island, were rare and highly valued by New England Indians. Europeans expanded both the production of wampum and the size of the local networks trading it, making wampum into a common Euro-Indian currency, much as Spaniards had with silver in Latin America, and transforming old exchange networks into monetized markets. The trade in pelts also pulled Indians as far inland as the Mississippi River valley into the transatlantic market, creating new opportunities for consumption even among Native Americans who had little contact with Europeans. Initially, at least, natives leveraged their knowledge and hunting skills to good account with their European trading partners. One colonist wrote that the inland tribes "are rather shrewd and let no one outwit them easily." Soon natives could purchase large quantities of European-made goods, ranging from guns and metal tools to alcohol, cloth, mirrors, earrings, and even imported face paint. One historian has described this gravitation toward European goods as an Indian "consumer revolution."[12] An Iroquois joked to a

French missionary in the 1630s that the beaver "makes kettles, hatchets, swords, knives, bread; and, in short, makes everything."[13] It also, increasingly, translated into European guns. Archaeologists working at mid-seventeenth-century Iroquois sites have found that fewer than half of the surviving artifacts were made by Indians. While natives were doubtless happy with their new acquisitions, Europeans saw hidden benefits to this trade. Across the Atlantic, the Proprietors of Carolina, who managed the colony's affairs from England, observed with approval that furnishing the "bold and warlike" Indians with arms and ammunition made them so dependent on the English that whenever Native Americans "shall misbehave themselves towards us, we shall be able whenever we please by abstaining from supplying them with ammunition . . . to ruin them."[14]

Early Carolina colonists and Indians also collaborated in a massive trade in Indian slaves. Much as the Portuguese purchased African slaves from African intermediaries, British Indian slave traders purchased Indians who had been captured in war from the victorious tribes, most notably the aggressive Westo tribe, which had recently settled in the Carolina backcountry. From 1670 to 1715, the British sold from 30,000 to 50,000 Native Americans into slavery. Most were traded far from their homelands, as it was generally understood that Indians would escape into the backcountry if enslaved in familiar territory. While few records of this trade survive, historians believe a large percentage was sent to work in the West Indian plantations as a low-cost alternative to African slaves. A significant percentage also was traded to the New England colonies of Massachusetts, New Hampshire, and Connecticut, where they usually served as household servants rather than as field workers.

The importance of the extractive economy was declining in all colonies by the eighteenth century. The trade in pelts was necessarily short lived. As Indians began to hunt beaver and otter for European markets rather than for their own use, the animal populations began to drop. By the 1650s, only thirty years after European settlement, most of New England's fur trade was already in decline, and the paucity of beaver was transforming the region's former beaver ponds into pasture land used by Europeans for their livestock. In the Carolinas, deer remained fairly abundant, but the deerskin trade shrank in relative importance as a new plantation economy arose in the 1720s and 1730s. The Indian slave trade fell apart after the vicious Yamasee Indian War of 1715–17 in South Carolina, which caused the New England colonies to worry that southern slave traders were sending them the more rebellious Indians as a way of pacifying their own region.

THE PLANTATION COMPLEX

By the latter part of the sixteenth century in South America and the latter part of the seventeenth century in the north, a new plantation-based economy was replacing the extractive economy. This so-called plantation complex centered on the cultivation of products, known as staple crops, which were marketed far beyond America. In North America, the most important staple crops were sugar, tobacco, and rice. Cotton, which many people today associate with American plantations, did not become a significant staple until the eighteenth century (as discussed in chapter 5). In essence, American plantations amounted to agricultural factories designed to maximize production of staple crops for the benefit of European empires. Because plantation regions focused on producing a single crop, they usually depended on other regions for their supplies of basic foodstuffs and manufactured products. They also relied on distant regions, either Africa or Europe, for their supply of labor. Plantation owners usually (although not always) coerced workers to labor as servants or slaves, usually in harsh conditions. As with the extractive economy, the plantation complex tied America to the rest of the world. But, unlike the extractive economy, Indians played only a peripheral role in it.

The Spread of Staple Crops

Of the three major North American staple crops, sugar had the longest association with the plantation complex. Sugar cane first appeared in the Pacific island of New Guinea around 8000 BCE. Over the centuries it crept westward to the Philippine Islands and then to mainland India. Islamic conquest of the Mediterranean basin brought it into North Africa and southern Europe by at least the tenth century. As the Spaniards and Portuguese conquered Atlantic islands off the coast of Africa such as the Canaries and Madeira, they began planting large quantities of sugar there. By the time of Columbus, these islands had become plantation colonies, heavily oriented toward a single staple crop. As in subsequent plantation colonies, laborers in the Atlantic islands were overwhelmingly nonnative since most native Canary Islanders were wiped out due to disease and warfare in a process very similar to what would occur slightly later in the West Indies. The Portuguese Islands, which were mostly uninhabited before European conquest, also required imported laborers. Unlike the American plantation complex, however, these early sugar plantations relied on a mix of free and enslaved laborers.

Sugar crossed the Atlantic with Columbus, but it was the Portuguese who first cultivated it in large quantities in America. Portugal's Brazil colony began sending substantial shipments of sugar to Europe in the 1520s; within two decades, Brazil produced more sugar than all of Portugal's non-American colonies combined. By 1570 Brazil was sending well over 5 million pounds of sugar back to Portugal annually, accounting for more than 90 percent of the total value of Brazil's exports. Nevertheless, sugar remained a relatively expensive and rare product in Europe.

The greatest expansion of sugar production came in the seventeenth century when settlers in Caribbean colonies set about creating sugar plantations. The British island colony of Barbados played a leading role. Englishmen had unsuccessfully attempted to grow sugar in Virginia and Bermuda. Barbados in the 1640s became "the most flourishing island in all those American parts, and I verily believe in all the world for the production of sugar," according to a contemporary observer.[15] By the 1680s small farmers were unable to compete with the large sugar plantations that now dominated the island. By the end of the century Barbados alone annually produced more than 40 million pounds of sugar, and other British and French islands were also producing large quantities. As a result, sugar became commonplace in the typical English household over the course of the eighteenth century as a sweetener in the ubiquitous cup of tea (itself a product of Asia) as well as in pastries, puddings, and other sweets.

Unlike sugar, tobacco originated in America, as we have already seen. However, like sugar, it was not grown as a staple crop in America until the late sixteenth century, when Spanish and Portuguese colonists began cultivating it on the Caribbean island of Trinidad. In the next decades settlers started tobacco plantations on other islands and on the mainland in Mexico, Venezuela, and Brazil. In 1611 alone, more than a million pounds of tobacco arrived in London from Spain's American colonies. This boom made the English desirous of growing their own tobacco, despite King James's condemnation of smoking as "a custom loathsome to the eye, hateful to the nose, harmful to the brain, [and] dangerous to the lungs."[16]

The English soon established their own tobacco plantation complex along the shores of Chesapeake Bay in the colonies of Virginia and Maryland. Early experiments with tobacco in Virginia failed, as did almost everything else in the first years of that colony. But, by 1617, a decade after Virginia's first settlement, colonist John Rolfe began experimenting with new tobacco varieties from the West Indies, which flourished on the American mainland. Rolfe's successes led to a massive tobacco boom in the Chesapeake region, where production rose from 200,000 pounds in 1624 to 3 million in 1638 and 10 million by 1660. These colonies produced tobacco for exportation to Europe to the exclusion of just about everything else. Despite the Virginia government's efforts to force settlers to produce corn and engage in other useful projects, as early as 1623 one observer reported that "nothing is done in any one of them but all is vanished into smoke (that is to say into tobacco)."[17] In Maryland, where tobacco served as a currency for a time, the colonial assembly observed, "The trade of this province ebbs and flows according to the rise or fall of tobacco in the market of England."[18]

Rice was the least extensively grown and the last of British North America's great plantation crops to be introduced. Like sugar, rice originated in Asia and moved slowly west over the centuries. Also like sugar, it appears to have been introduced into southern Europe as a result of Islamic conquest around the tenth century. By the seventeenth century it played a small role in English cuisine, and some British writers hoped to introduce it into the American colonies to reduce dependence on imports from the Mediterranean. By this time, rice was also a fairly widespread crop in sub-Saharan Africa, where it had been introduced by Arabs as early as the twelfth century.

South Carolinians began to build rice plantations by the 1690s. The transformation to rice was a product both of English desire for a profitable staple crop and of their slaves' desire to grow a foodstuff that they had commonly eaten in Africa. Consequently, African practices shaped rice production in South Carolina, where farmers adopted methods and tools that originated on that continent. In turn, disruptions caused by the growing slave trade in some coastal portions of West Africa encouraged increased rice cultivation in Africa, too. Rice production in South Carolina grew impressively from approximately 268,000 pounds annually at the turn of the eighteenth century to 30 million by the late 1730s and 66 million by the late 1760s. Rice easily displaced buckskins and Indian slaves as South Carolina's largest export, causing one commentator in the early 1760s to observe that rice had become South Carolina's "staple commodity, as sugar is to Barbados and Jamaica, or tobacco to Virginia and Maryland."[19]

The Rise of Plantation Slavery

The growth of the plantation complex fueled an enormous demand for labor. All three North American staple crops demanded intensive amounts of work in deadly tropical or semitropical conditions. Initially, North American planters hoped to continue the practice of the extractive economy and use native laborers. Because of the low density of the native population north of the Rio Grande and Indians' aversion to agricultural labor, British plantation owners could never fill their labor needs entirely with Indian slaves. Consequently, they scrambled to find other sources.

Initially they looked to their fellow Englishmen. Early-seventeenth-century England was undergoing an economic crisis, and many poor people were without the means to support themselves. The American colonies, with their inexpensive land and developing economies, seemed to offer opportunity, but the cost of emigration was prohibitive. To tap into this potential labor force, Virginia's proprietors encouraged English people to come to America as indentured servants. In exchange for the cost of emigration, these servants were bound to work for whoever bought their time for a set period, usually four to seven years. As with Indian slaves, there developed a lively trade in servants who, once indentured, could have their remaining time sold and resold. Because of very high mortality in the American colonies, a great many of these servants died before their time expired. Servants made up three-quarters of the emigrants to Maryland and Virginia over the course of the seventeenth century, perhaps amounting to as many as 90,000 people. However, by midcentury, as English people became aware of the difficult conditions in America and economic conditions in England improved, servant emigration began to tail off. Nevertheless, European servants continued to play an important role in the colonial American workforce, with Irish and German servants becoming increasingly prominent in the eighteenth century.

Eventually, American planters adopted African slavery as their primary labor source, creating new and lasting connections between Africa and America. While African slavery was new to the British, it was relatively well established among the Spaniards and especially the Portuguese. The growth of the African slave trade can be closely correlated to the development of the plantation complex. Until 1550 or so, most African slaves were imported to Old World destinations, especially plantation island colonies off the coast of Africa such as the Canaries, Madeira, and São Tomé. It was only with the spread of the plantation complex to America that the New World began to dominate the slave trade. In sugar-growing Brazil, where the transition to a slave-based sugar plantation economy occurred in the final decades of the sixteenth century, importation of African slaves grew drastically from virtually none before 1550 to a total of 10,000 in the 1551–1575 period and 40,000 for 1576–1600. By the last quarter of the sixteenth century, Brazil had become the largest single destination for African slaves in the Atlantic world.

African slavery would not become an important institution in British America for another hundred years. As in Latin America, it grew with the emerging sugar plantation colonies. Barbados, the first British sugar colony, was also the first British colony to purchase many African slaves, beginning in the 1640s. By 1650 African slaves made up 30 percent of Barbados's population. Fifty years later, in 1700, approximately 50,000 black slaves lived on Barbados, constituting 76 percent of the island's population. However, throughout the seventeenth century, slaves remained rare in the British mainland colonies that would become the United States.

The eighteenth century would be the great age of slave acquisition for the plantation complex, with more than 5.5 million slaves exported from Africa. Rising prices made the slave trade more desirable to Africa's coastal elites, who were now frequently selling people who had been enslaved 50 or 100 miles inland. It was only during the eighteenth century that the mainland British colonies became heavily involved in the slave trade. As late as 1680 the population of only two colonies in the area that would become the United States—New York and South Carolina—was more than 10 percent black, and in New York slavery had been introduced by the colony's original Dutch settlers rather than by the British. All told, fewer than 7,000 black slaves lived in the mainland colonies at this time. Virginia's slave population jumped from 3,000 in 1680 to 16,000 in 1700 to 107,000 in 1750. South Carolina, which had 200 slaves in 1680, had 3,000 in 1700 and 39,000 by 1750. In both colonies, large numbers of early slaves came from British Barbados rather than directly from Africa. Despite the growth of slavery in eighteenth-century mainland rice and tobacco colonies, the wealthier West Indian sugar planters imported four times as many slaves as did the mainland colonists over the course of the century. In 1750 Barbados's population was 76 percent black, compared to 46 percent in Virginia and 61 percent in South Carolina.

Plantation slavery was devastating to the millions of Africans uprooted from their homelands and forced to work in sugar, tobacco, and rice fields in North America. However, the first generation of Africans, imported to the colonies before the plantation complex was in full swing, had a bit more flexibility than their descendants. A lucky few even managed to obtain freedom and purchase land. Once the British authorities began to formulate the codes that would equate race with lifelong servitude, subsequent generations lived very circumscribed lives with few opportunities for advancement and the certainty that their descendants would remain in lifetime bondage, subject to the whims of their owners in all things.

The African slave trade affected white Americans too. Many plantation owners and merchants became wealthy from the unsavory business of buying and selling people. Additionally, the influx of millions of Africans into the continent Africanized the New World to some extent. African languages, music, religious traditions, and cuisines would all have an impact on North American culture from the eighteenth century onward, causing it to diverge significantly from English and European culture.

Finally, the growth of the American slave trade had a significant impact on West Africa. From the first Portuguese arrivals onward, Europeans relied on African cooperation in the slave trade. Coastal Africans procured slaves for European traders, usually people from farther inland captured and enslaved during warfare. European traders invested heavily in efforts to engage in this trade with African merchants along the Atlantic coast of central Africa, which came to be known as the Slave Coast. British officials hoped by 1680 to "dispatch a ship from [Africa] every five weeks with upward of 500 negroes," but in actuality they likely shipped closer to 3,500 per year than the 5,000 predicted by their calculation.[20] With the eighteenth-century rise of the American plantation complex, however, exports expanded rapidly. As a result, a few West Africans grew quite wealthy while, on the whole, the area's population dropped due to slave exportations. European items such as metal goods, weaponry, and textiles flowed into the region, but the major trade good was cowrie shells, which West Africans used as currency. This influx of wealth and weaponry to slave merchants shifted political and economic power to the coastal leaders who controlled the slave trade with the Europeans.

The Mercantile System

Just as this vast plantation complex exploited millions of people, it also produced incredible wealth for others. European governments began to view the American plantation colonies as crucial components in their emerging trans-Oceanic empires. As a rule, these governments attempted to keep as much colonial wealth in Europe as possible and to make sure that it did not fall into the hands of rival empires or of colonists. Like most European colonial powers, Britain attempted to achieve this goal through a series of economic regulations. These efforts began with the Navigation Acts of 1651, 1660, 1663, and 1673, which regulated and set duties on shipments of goods between England and its colonies and between the colonies themselves. The acts aimed to ensure that profits from the American colonies accrued to the British merchants and the

British crown rather than to imperial rivals such as France or the Netherlands. New acts passed in 1696 created an administrative apparatus to enforce these rules, including the Board of Trade, which was to coordinate and control the components of the growing empire; an enlarged customs service; and a special court system to punish those who broke the rules. Like other European powers, the English crown also set up state-sponsored trading companies, most notably the Royal African Company (1672), which was granted exclusive rights to export slaves out of Africa to be sold within the British empire. Over the course of the eighteenth century, the British government would continue to refine this trading system, for example, by passing new laws forbidding large-scale manufacturing in the colonies, which primarily were supposed to be producers of raw materials and agricultural products.

These laws and administrative boards were the practical manifestation of the economic theory known as mercantilism. The rise of mercantilism, which would come to dominate European economic theory, was closely connected to the colonization of America. As early as 1585, Richard Hakluyt urged British colonization of America in order to gain access to goods such as wine, oranges, and rice that would normally have to be purchased from rivals such as Spain. While Hakluyt misunderstood the details of the Virginia climate, he pinpointed a central goal of mercantilism: creation of colonies that would allow the mother country to avoid purchasing goods from its imperial rivals. An impressive number of seventeenth- and eighteenth-century mercantilist economists, such as Josiah Child, Josia Gee, Malachy Postlethwayt, and Adam Anderson built on these ideas. In 1764, Anderson summarized the advantages of mercantilism when he wrote, "Probably about or near a million of our people are employed at home, many hundreds of stout ships, and many thousands of marines constantly employed; much wealth and considerable quantities of bullion of both gold and silver continually brought home to us."[21]

Although this mercantilistic focus on England's wealth might have been expected to annoy the colonists, throughout much of the eighteenth century most accepted the mercantilist system. Colonists understood it to be advantageous to them. It protected them from competition with the Dutch, French, Spanish, Portuguese, and their respective colonies. It gave them a privileged place within the world's richest empire. An American writing in 1766 observed that British encouragement of colonial raw materials enabled colonists to purchase British manufactures, allowing Americans and British to "become reciprocally necessary to each other."[22] In this way, mercantilism promoted the sort of economic integration and interdependence that is the hallmark of modern globalization. Unlike modern globalization, however, it did so through force of law and arms rather than through the less overtly coercive modern method of expanding free markets.

—૭ ૭—

The plantation complex and European mercantilism gave rise to economic activity that knitted together three continents. Far from acting as a barrier, the Atlantic Ocean became a conduit to trade, linking African, European, and American merchants into an enormous market. The staple crops grown in America with European investments drove this market. Without the forced labor of African slaves, profits would have been much lower. British colonies to the north, from Pennsylvania to New Hampshire, also played a role in this economy. Unable to grow the valuable staple crops in their cooler climate, Pennsylvania and New York farmers were able to provide flour and other food-stuffs to southern plantations whose owners sought to use as much land as pos-sible for rice, tobacco, or sugar rather than for growing foodstuffs. New En-gland merchants provided the capital and ships to move these products back and forth across the ocean. This Atlantic world was far removed from earlier European dreams of connecting Europe to Asia through America. Neverthe-less, the Atlantic economy linking three great continents marked a significant step in the long process of globalization.

CHAPTER TWO

The Many Wars for America

THE RAID ON DEERFIELD

On the wintry night of February 28, 1704, the 270 or so residents of the frontier village of Deerfield, Massachusetts, rested uneasily. A fear of Indian attacks had been hanging over the town for months. Not trusting the frozen roads and rivers to deter an assault, many townspeople now slept inside the local fort for protection. When the attackers did sneak into town that night, the first place they struck was the fort, where they "immediately set upon breaking open doors and windows," according to a contemporary account.[1] They fanned out, killing men, women, children, infants, and slaves, as well as livestock and dogs, and burned most of the town's houses (sometimes inadvertently incinerating people hiding in the cellars). The fires lit Deerfield with an ominous orange glow visible throughout the thinly settled region beyond the edge of town. Soon Englishmen from nearby villages rushed in to assist Deerfield, killing many of the attackers and forcing the rest to flee, but not before 48 villagers lay dead, with another 112 taken captive. Together, the dead and captured outnumbered the survivors.

On its face, this may have seemed like a simple, if deadly Indian raid. But in actuality it was more complicated. French men, in fact, led and organized the attack, although the townspeople did not immediately recognize it. Some of the Indians were local Abenakis who, no doubt, viewed the attack as an opportunity to avenge themselves against the English who had stolen their land. But others, notably the Kahnawake, came from much farther away and had no grudges against the settlers in western Massachusetts. French missionaries had recently converted them to Catholicism, and they fought as allies of the French. For their part, the French fought because their kingdom and England were at war and had been on and off since 1689. For them, the attack on Deerfield was a small part of a larger, worldwide struggle.

The raid on Deerfield occurred at a crucial time, with Americans involved in simultaneous wars, one winding down and one just beginning. The first, pitting the English and some Indian allies against local Indians such as the Abenaki, was part of a larger Euro-Indian struggle for control of the eastern seaboard of North America that had begun more than a century earlier. By 1704 England had essentially won this struggle. Deerfield was a late rearguard action by the natives. The second war, the Anglo-French War of the Spanish Succession (known in America as Queen Anne's War), was itself an early stage of an epic struggle sometimes known as the Second Hundred Years' War fought between France and Britain and their respective Indian and European allies. It began in 1689 and would continue for the rest of the century and beyond.

This chapter discusses both wars and argues that at about the time of the Deerfield raid, warfare in America underwent an important shift. Before, it was primarily a Euro-Indian struggle for control of the continent that was largely divorced from events in the rest of the world and was more often waged by colonists and privately sponsored raiders than by formal European armies. But sometime around the turn of the eighteenth century American warfare started to be integrated into European and global conflicts and to be characterized by formal battles conducted by European armies. By the time of the Seven Years' War (1756–63), warfare in America triggered what was the first world war in fact, if not in name.

THE FIRST SPANISH-AMERICAN WAR

Columbus's landing in America inaugurated a war of conquest. The war was, of course, fought between Americans and Europeans, but it was also fought among them. From the start, Europeans employed Indian allies in their struggle to control the continent. The Spaniards did not gain control of Latin America by themselves. The struggle was largely a fight between different groups of Native Americans, with technology and leadership provided by Spaniards. Later, as at Deerfield, warring Europeans would also fight each other, along with their various Indian allies. In this two-century-long struggle, intense periods of bloody, devastating warfare punctuated long, relatively peaceful periods in which Natives and Europeans often cooperated and lived in relative harmony.

The initial struggle for Mexico, the Caribbean, and South America pitted Spaniards and Portuguese against some of America's richest and most powerful cultures, most notably the Inca and Aztecs. A second phase, beginning roughly 100 years later, saw British, French, and Dutch soldiers take on the less centralized Native Americans of modern-day Canada and the United States. Although the conflict in Mexico and points south was never smooth or orderly, the early conquest was made easier by the fact that only two European powers were involved and that they did not usually interfere with each other. The Catholic church had issued several decrees in 1493 seeking to divide newly discovered portions of the world between Spain and Portugal. The papal bulls were supplemented by the 1494 Treaty of Tordesillas, which created a line dividing Portuguese New World territories (primarily Brazil) and Spanish territories to the north and west. This initial coordination freed the European powers, for a time, to concentrate on subduing Native Americans rather than jockeying with each other. It also ensured that New World conflicts would not develop into European warfare.

The Spanish conquest of Mexico and other portions of North America would prove to be a dramatic and hard-fought struggle permanently altering life for millions of Americans and destroying what was probably the richest culture ever created by Native Americans. It would also alter the very nature of warfare in America by introducing European tactics and technologies. The Spaniards quickly conquered the militarily weak and geographically isolated West Indian islands they first encountered. Through a combination of Spanish violence and widespread epidemics, the natives of the Caribbean basin rapidly disappeared, with estimates of millions of deaths in the first quarter of the sixteenth century. The Spanish friar Bartolome de Las Casas, who saw much of the killing firsthand, estimated that in only 40 years the Spaniards killed 12 to 15 million natives in the Caribbean.

After the Spaniards gained a beachhead in Cuba, and some understanding of New World culture and warfare, they encountered the far richer and more powerful natives of mainland Mexico. Their first sustained contact with the Mayan people of the Yucatán Peninsula began in 1517 with the ill-fated voyage of Hernandez de Cordoba. The size of the Mayan towns and their impressive architecture made an immediate impression on the Spaniards, who salivated at the prospect of great riches. Unfortunately for Cordoba, the Mayans were also militarily more sophisticated than their island neighbors and more hostile to the Spaniards, perhaps due to reports of early Spanish atrocities in the islands. Near what is today the town of Champaton, Mayan warriors led by their chief, Mochcouoh, surrounded the Spaniards overnight and attacked them with stone and copper axes, obsidian-edged swords, and bows and arrows in the morning. Their weapons and battle tactics proved far superior to those of the Caribbean islanders. They forced the would-be conquistadors from their boats, killing perhaps half of the 100 or so Spaniards, including Cordoba, who managed to reach Cuba before succumbing. The vanquished invaders managed to kill only approximately 20 Indians. It was the first time Americans had ever defeated Spaniards in battle, and it did not appear to augur well for the Spanish conquest of Mexico. The next year, Spanish Cuba's governor sent out another expedition to Mexico to try to mend relations with the natives and further explore the coast. Late in 1518 he made the fateful choice of Hernán Cortés to lead a third, ostensibly similar mission.

The relatively well-educated son of a prominent Medellin family, Cortés proved far more aggressive than his predecessors. He ignored his instructions and audaciously attempted to conquer all of Mexico with his band of, initially, only 500 Spaniards. Through a combination of superior military technology, keen diplomacy, and luck, he succeeded. Unlike Cordoba, Cortés used cannon, horses, and vicious mastiff dogs to terrify the Mayans, who had never seen any of these before. Cortés also benefited from his adversaries' understanding of war as a means to take captives rather than to kill enemies. Mexicans used stone weapons to knock enemies unconscious, while Cortés and his men used steel swords to kill them. Standard Mexican tactics of forming tight battle formations in which only the front column encountered the enemy also left them particularly vulnerable to Spanish artillery and horsemen.

Eventually, Cortés's demonstrations of military prowess and many Mexicans' unhappiness with their powerful Aztec overlords allowed the Spanish to make crucial alliances. Cortés was fortunate in locating two interpreters to assist him in negotiating with the Americans. The first, Geronimo de Aguilar, had been captured by Mayans in 1511 after he survived a shipwreck. He met up with Cortés's men in the early stages of their mission. The second, an Indian woman known as Malinali, or Marina, grew up speaking a dialect of the Aztec language, Nuhatl, before she was sold to the Mayans. She would later become Cortés's mistress. Using Aguilar to translate from Spanish to Mayan and Marina to translate Mayan to Nuhatl, Cortés would be able to communicate with the Aztecs.

Communication and miscommunication continued to shape the initial Spanish-Aztec encounter. The Aztec emperor, Moctezuma II, did all he could to dissuade the Spaniards, now reinforced with new arrivals from Spanish Cuba and thousands of Indian allies, from traveling into the Mexican valley. However, when Cortés's army arrived at the edge of his capital city of Tenochtitlán, Moctezuma personally welcomed them and invited them into the city. With a population of perhaps 200,000 and built on an island in the middle of Lake Texcoco connected to the mainland by a series of causeways, Tenochtitlán was the largest and grandest city that most of Cortés's men had ever seen, and its conquest presented them with the prospect of enormous wealth. Moctezuma most likely did not understand that Cortés's demands that he become a Spanish vassal implied he was to be subservient, nor did Cortés appear to understand that Moctezuma meant the lavish gifts he offered as demonstrations of the Aztecs' power rather than as tribute to the Spaniards. To this day it is impossible to say why Moctezuma allowed himself to become Cortés's prisoner in his own city. Perhaps he believed the Spaniards were gods whose return had been prophesied to occur in the Aztec year One Reed, which, coincidentally was the year of Cortés's arrival. Perhaps Moctezuma had some strategy that eluded Cortés and modern historians. At any rate, Moctezuma's submission gave the Spaniards and their allies control of the entire city for a time, until Moctezuma's own people began to turn against him. Eventually they forced Cortés and his men out, killing perhaps 600 Spaniards and thousands of Cortés's Indian allies.

Cortés and his allies regrouped. The Spaniards built small ships to launch a naval blockade and siege against Tenochtitlán, cutting the island city off from its food and water supplies. Although the Aztecs were familiar with land-based siege tactics, this was the first known amphibious siege in America. The Spanish ships with their guns generated terror and destruction, but the Aztecs quickly adapted to and sometimes anticipated Spanish tactics. Nevertheless, they were overwhelmed by the lack of food and water, the continual destruction, and a smallpox epidemic that reached Tenochtitlán by 1520, killing Moctezuma's successor. After three months of siege warfare, the Aztecs surrendered their devastated city to Cortés.

The battle had largely been an American one, with the great majority of combatants Native Americans. Some well-armed Cuban reinforcements brought the number of Spaniards in Cortés's army up to about 1,000 by the time of the battle. Although impossible to verify, contemporary estimates of the number of their Indian allies range from 150,000 to 500,000. But, even if the estimates were exaggerated by a factor of ten, Spaniards made up a tiny minority of the soldiers. The vast majority of the casualties also were not Spanish. Contemporaries estimated 100,000 to 240,000 Aztecs killed, along with 30,000 of Cortés's Indian allies and fewer than 100 Spaniards.

The fall of Tenochtitlán opened the door for Spaniards to conquer all of mainland North America. But the Spanish invasion proved slow and often unsuccessful as both Indians and Spaniards modified their approach to warfare. For example, no fewer than six Spanish expeditions failed to conquer the Florida Peninsula from the time of Ponce de Leon's 1513 expedition to Tristan de Luna y Arellano's 1559 effort. In Florida, the Spaniards found ineffective many of the techniques that had been successful in Mexico. For example, horses, which had so intimidated Mexican armies, proved useless in the Florida swamps, where Spaniards in Panfilo Narvaez's ill-fated 1527 expedition used them for food while building boats to escape to Mexico. Narvaez's men also discovered that their crossbows and armor were ineffective against Florida Indians' large and accurate longbows. Hernando de Soto's 1539–43 expedition had more success. Assisted by their horses and protected by the cotton armor they adapted from the Aztecs, the Spaniards defeated the Choctaw Indians in the Battle of Mabila. But even de Soto could not gain control of Florida. As his men fled the Indians by sailing into the Gulf of Mexico, their pursuers supposedly taunted, "If we possessed such large canoes as yours, we would follow you to your land and conquer it."[2] As late as 1680, 160 years after the fall of Tenochtitlán, Pueblo warriors expelled the Spaniards from New Mexico. In their carefully coordinated attack they vastly outnumbered the Spanish settlers and were able to use the Spaniards' own guns, swords, and armor to oust their enemy. They killed roughly one in six of the 2,500 Spaniards in New Mexico, destroyed every Spanish building, and kept the Spaniards away for another 13 years.

PIRATES AND PRIVATEERS OF THE ATLANTIC, 1523–1689

Spain's conquest of Mexico and its acquisition of vast new riches quickly aroused the interest of its European competitors. While no rival initially could threaten Spain's colonies, beginning in 1523 pirates, privateers, and other adventurers, most only loosely connected to European governments, began to attack Spanish ships in the Atlantic and Spanish colonial coastal fortifications as a way to tap into the wealth of the Americas. While there were nearly constant sea battles in the American Atlantic between 1523 and 1689, this was not a traditional war conducted by state-sponsored navies. Contemporaries viewed warfare in this region as "beyond the line," disconnected from the formal battles European monarchs and their allies pursued in Eurasia and Africa. European kingdoms that were at peace in the old world might occasionally come to blows in the New World without triggering warfare back in Europe. Furthermore, sailors and soldiers often only minimally connected to the European powers did most of the fighting beyond the line. Today they would be considered private military actors. European monarchs easily disassociated themselves from these military activities when necessary. Thus, while technically beyond the line of European warfare and peripheral to most nations' strategic considerations, the informal struggle in the Atlantic was a way for empires to jockey for power and wealth without initiating full-fledged warfare. Only after 1689 would American warfare become more formally connected to warfare in the rest of the world.

The major target for pirates and privateers in the sixteenth century was the Spanish treasure fleet carrying silver and other valuables from Peru and Mexico into Seville, Spain. Spain and France were at war during most of this period, and initially most of the attacks came from French pirates. France's tense relations with Spain, no doubt, encouraged some pirates; others were Protestants with a religious animus toward Catholic Spain. The enormous riches carried by the Spanish fleet motivated all. The earliest activities did not occur in America but rather in the eastern Atlantic. The first known attack, in 1523, occurred near the Portuguese coast when French pirate Jean Florin captured several ships loaded with Aztec gold, pearls, and sugar. As France struggled to build bases in South America, pirate attacks on Spaniards in America increased. French ships captured roughly 66 Spanish vessels, more than 20 of them in America, and raided Spanish West Indian islands 22 times between 1535 and 1547 despite an official truce during much of this period. During a slightly later truce, a Spanish court in America observed, "Although there is peace [the French] do not stop such robberies as long as such rich prizes are on offer at such small risk."[3] When war resumed in the 1550s, France sent naval squadrons into America for the first time. Like the pirates who continued to operate, they chased the Spanish treasure fleet and pillaged the Spanish West Indies. Even after peace resumed in 1559, French pirates continued to target Spanish ships and settlements. Six years later, in 1565, Spanish colonists attacked and destroyed a small French colony in Florida.

After Queen Elizabeth I ascended the English throne in 1558, that island nation also became a significant source of Atlantic pirates. Despite official peace between England and Spain, religious conflict and commercial rivalries made the new queen hesitant to crack down on English pirates such as John Hawkins who, in the early years of her reign, had some successes smuggling slaves and other goods into and out of Spain's Atlantic possessions. The most famous and successful of the Elizabethan pirates was Francis Drake. In the early 1570s he allied with French pirates and Maroon communities of runaway

Africans to raid the Spaniards, most notably capturing the mule train conveying Peruvian silver across the isthmus between Panama's Pacific and Atlantic
ports. In 1577 Drake and a number of wealthy Englishmen began to plan another voyage that would combine piracy and exploration. As relations with
Spain's King Phillip declined, they hoped to convince the Queen to invest as a
way to "annoy him by his Indies."[4] While the Queen gave Drake permission to
sail and probably provided some financial support, the voyage remained mostly
a private corporate affair.

Spaniards betrayed more than a little annoyance at Drake's bravado—
particularly when they spotted his ship, the *Golden Hind* off the Pacific coast of
South America after it successfully navigated the continent's southern tip.
Along the coast, Drake captured rich prizes, including one ship carrying silver
and gold valued at over 400,000 pesos. Although Drake had planned to return
the way he came, across the Atlantic, he now found it more expedient to attempt to cross the Pacific to Asia, a feat he accomplished relatively easily. He
returned home to a hero's welcome, becoming the first Englishman to circum-
navigate the globe and gaining much wealth in the process. However, he did
not become quite as rich as he might have hoped. In order to maintain good relations with King Phillip, Queen Elizabeth allowed some of the booty to be
restored to Spain. While the Queen did not mind irritating Spain and gaining
knowledge of the New World, she wished to avoid a formal war.

When war between Spain and England came, in 1585, the Americas played an
important but secondary role. There can be no doubt that the belligerents' main
focus remained on Europe, where the conflict culminated with England's victory in the famous sea battle of the Armada in 1588. England's willingness to
abandon Sir Walter Raleigh's American base in Roanoke to preserve military
resources in Europe demonstrates the secondary nature of the sea battles in
America. Nevertheless, as the source of much of Spain's wealth, America remained strategically important. Referring to Spain's king, Raleigh observed, "It
is his Indian golde that [endangers] and [disturbs] all the nations of Europe."[5]
Capturing that treasure would seriously weaken Spain's power and influence.
Consequently, Elizabeth now officially encouraged privately owned British
ships in the western Atlantic to attack Spanish vessels, providing them with
the documents that differentiated state-supported privateers from freelance
pirates. The queen sent Drake on another expedition against Spain's American
interests. More than 180 English ships followed him into American waters to
harass the Spaniards before peace returned in 1603. In addition to weakening
and impoverishing the Spaniards, these privateers brought much-needed

funds back to England. Estimates have British privateers in America and throughout the world netting at least £100,000 annually.

Similarly, Dutch pirates and privateers harassed Spanish ships in peace and war from the late sixteenth century into the seventeenth. The Dutch empire expanded rapidly across the globe, particularly in the Indian subcontinent, where the Dutch East India Company provided great wealth for the homeland. In 1621, imperial officials chartered the Dutch West India Company to fund attacks on Spanish ships in America and to oversee naval bases and colonies on land, including portions of Brazil, several islands, and New Netherlands, which hugged the Hudson River in modern-day New York. Like other European colonizers in seventeenth-century North America, the Dutch had to negotiate and fight with European and Indian adversaries. For example, in 1655 they attacked a small Swedish colony in the region of what is today Philadelphia. The Swedes surrendered before the Dutch could fire a shot, but in the meantime an alliance of Indian tribes attacked the Dutch settlement in the so-called Peach War, killing 50 Europeans and capturing more than 100 others.

In the latter part of the seventeenth century, the Dutch and English fought three major wars. Even when the two powers were technically at peace, English companies, such as the Company of Royal Adventurers Trading to Africa, continued to attack their Dutch rivals. America occupied a significant place for English planners in the early 1660s, when the heir to the throne, the Duke of York, hoped to gain control of New Netherlands for himself. The most important conflict on mainland North America occurred while England and the Dutch were still at peace. In the late summer of 1664 four English frigates and 2,000 soldiers and sailors landed in Gravesend Bay, Brooklyn. The Dutch, realizing they were hopelessly outgunned, surrendered the colony, which now became New York. The Second Anglo-Dutch war began soon after, in March 1665. One cause was the increasing conflict between English and Dutch traders on the high seas, but incidents in Europe, Africa, and Asia remained far more important than anything occurring in America.

THE NORTHERN FRONT

The European invasion of modern-day Canada and most of the present United States began nearly a century after Cortés's conquest of Mexico. Unlike native Mexicans, Indians in the north generally organized themselves into smaller, less centralized tribes, rather than a large empire on the Aztec model. Their military organization and technology appeared in many ways less sophisticated than that in the south. As a result, they generally presented a less formidable military threat to the invaders. However, this disadvantage was offset in part by the difficulty the Europeans encountered in defeating multiple groups of natives rather than having to defeat a single monarch, as Cortés was able to do. Additionally, because of the late arrival of Europeans in the north and the presence of competing European traders, these Indian tribes, unlike the Aztecs, acquired many European weapons and military technologies from the start of the European invasion. However, this early contact with Europeans also exposed northern Americans to disease epidemics so that, by the time Europeans began to plant colonies in the region, some Indian populations had drastically declined, along with the natives' ability to defend themselves.

Also unlike the Spanish experience in Mexico, during the seventeenth century, no European country held a monopoly on North America. Ongoing conflict in the Atlantic brought Spanish, English, French, and Dutch ships into contact with each other along the North American coast even before colonization began. After Europeans began planting colonies on the mainland, the colonies themselves threatened each other in a way that did not occur in Spanish Mexico. Thus, conflict on the northern front was frequently between different groups of Europeans, as well as between Europeans and Americans. The situation necessitated complicated diplomacy on all sides.

The first British colony in the modern-day United States emerged from European rivalries. Sir Walter Raleigh, a leader in privateering efforts against Spain, hoped that the island of Roanoke (in present-day North Carolina) would serve as a base for English ships. In 1585, about 100 Englishmen landed on Roanoke to set up the base. In less than a year they had become dependent on local Indians for food. Fearing attack, they lashed out at the natives, killed their chief, cut off his head, and attached it to a pole. When the privateering fleet returned, officials found the colony in such disarray that they shut it down and took the remaining settlers back to England. A second effort to colonize Roanoke in 1587, now known as the "Lost Colony," also failed due to British inattention during the Battle of the Armada with Spain in 1588. When British officials finally returned to Roanoke in 1590, all 110 settlers had disappeared, most likely killed or adopted by local Indians.

When England next attempted to colonize the area 20 years later at Jamestown, local Indians knew what to expect and may possibly have developed some immunity to European disease. They were initially quite successful at resisting the newcomers. They nearly destroyed the entire colony by starving the settlers in a siege. Reinforcements saved the English settlers just as they were preparing to evacuate. The local Indian leader Powhatan negotiated with the revitalized Jamestown settlement to establish relatively peaceful relations. Meanwhile, natives acquired many English goods through trade, including some weapons. As the Jamestown colony expanded, Powhatan's successor, Opechancanough, organized simultaneous attacks on a number of English settlements in 1622, slaughtering 347 of the 1,240 English colonists, employing methods resembling those used by the English in earlier raids on Indian villages. The English, who just barely escaped complete defeat, retaliated, in part by murdering Pamukey Indians with poisoned wine and scalping some of them in Indian fashion afterward.

To the north, the situation in New England proved far more complicated due to the proximity of French and Dutch colonies in Quebec and New York respectively. Both colonies built alliances with a broad web of powerful and lesser Indian tribes, including the Huron and Iroquois Five Nations, sold them weapons and other goods, and attempted to engage them in warfare against their European rivals. For their part, the Indians hoped to enlist their European allies against their own native and European rivals. For example, Abenaki Indians welcomed a short-lived British settlement at Sagadahoc, Maine, in the hope that the English might provide them with guns to use against their French-supported enemies, the Micmac.

At first the British invasion of New England went smoothly. The massive epidemic of 1616 that killed large numbers of coastal New England's natives removed much resistance to early English colonization. The rapid influx of Puritan settlers between 1620 and 1640 provided the colonies with an overwhelming numerical superiority over the local natives. They were able to forge an alliance with the Mohegan Indians and their tributaries against their mutual enemies, the Pequots. In 1637 the Puritans and Mohegans destroyed the Pequots in a war so horrifying that many of the Mohegans deserted the Puritans. The climax came when Puritan soldiers surrounded and burned a Pequot village on the Mystic River, killing nearly all of the roughly 500 inhabitants. The destruction of the Pequots and a temporary halt in Puritan migration to America reduced tensions for the next few decades. Rather than eying Indian lands to the west, Puritans instead moved more toward nominally Dutch territory to the south during the years of Anglo-Dutch warfare.

New England and Virginia colonists both fought their climactic battles against Native Americans in 1675–76, a time when colonial population expansion in both regions severely threatened Indian lands. In New England, the event known as King Philip's War pitted colonists against local Wampanoag and Narragansett Indians led by King Philip (also known as Metacom). Natives had great success waging guerrilla warfare against the English, burning and terrorizing frontier towns and effectively driving British settlers out of the western portion of New England. At times it appeared as though King Philip might just push the Puritans off the continent entirely. As one colonist recalled, had the Indians not become divided, "They might have forced us to some islands; and there to have planted a little corn and fished for our livings."[6] At the same time, Anglo-Virginians were busy fighting not only Indians but each other in the complicated war known as Bacon's Rebellion. Angered by a Doeg Indian attack on Virginia's frontier, Nathaniel Bacon and his followers began indiscriminately attacking frontier Indians, including the powerful Susquehannocks, despite opposition from the colony's governor, William Berkeley, who hoped to maintain peace with the Indians. The actions of Bacon and his followers initiated a war against the Susquehannock and other local tribes that produced great bloodshed on both sides. Finally Bacon destroyed the Susquehannock and the lesser tribes, ending the war.

Despite hard-fought battles and near disasters, both the Virginia and New England colonists won decisive victories, not only destroying the military prospects of the coastal Indians but also creating closer bonds between the English colonies and the powerful Iroquois Five Nations. The Iroquois inhabited the vast "middle ground" between British and French settlements ranging from the eastern Great Lakes down to the Ohio valley and west to the Mississippi. Both Bacon's Rebellion and King Philip's War initially strengthened their position by weakening or destroying their eastern rivals. In Virginia, the Iroquois' enemies, the Susquehannocks, had been English allies. By destroying the Susquehannock, Bacon unwittingly benefited the Iroquois. In New England, where King Philip and his followers, armed with European guns, won numerous victories and demoralized the British with guerrilla tactics, shortages of gunpowder and food finally doomed the natives' efforts. But, just as important, the English were greatly assisted, perhaps saved from defeat, when they allied with the Mohawks, one of the Iroquois nations, who then attacked and defeated King Philip's followers at their winter camp in present-day Albany, New York.

If Indians by themselves no longer posed an existential threat to the English colonies, they could still pose a serious threat when allied with other Europeans such as the French. Thus, for most of the following century, the three major powers in North America—Britain, France, and Iroquoia—would maintain a balance of power, depending on diplomacy and alliances to protect themselves and threaten their rivals.

THE FIRST WORLD WAR

Despite the English colonists' victory, they still faced threats from their French rivals, as well as from hostile Indians. The situation necessitated careful diplomacy, and for much of the following century the three great powers in the region—England, France, and Iroquoia—would maintain an uneasy balance of power through negotiations and alliances. These realities also brought about an important turning point in the Iroquois approach to warfare. In the sixteenth and seventeenth centuries, they fought what historians describe as mourning wars, aimed at capturing members of opposing tribes to honor and replace dead Iroquois and to provide glory for young warriors. As the Iroquois increasingly became involved in European diplomacy in the eighteenth century, however, their understanding of warfare became Europeanized, and they became integrated into the growing Anglo-French conflict known to historians as the Second Hundred Years' War.

England's Glorious Revolution of 1688 ended the rule of the Stuart dynasty, brought William and Mary to the crown, and (as discussed in chapter 3) prompted conflict in Britain's American colonies. King William's ascension to the throne also inaugurated a new series of wars with France that would ultimately pull the American colonies into the center of what was arguably the first global war. This series of Anglo-French wars, stretching from 1689 to Napoleon's defeat in 1815, has been labeled the Second Hundred Years' War to differentiate it from the earlier Anglo-French Hundred Years' War (1337–1453). At first, America played a peripheral role, as England and France focused on European issues. Over time, however, America became more central to the fighting. Anglo-French and Anglo-Spanish colonial conflicts in North America and the ongoing battle of the Atlantic all became absorbed into the Second Hundred Years' War, as would the continuing Indian-European warfare. This trend culminated in the Seven Years' War (1756–1763). The Seven Years' War originated in America, involved all the major European powers, and sparked battles in America, Europe, Africa, and Asia.

Most of the early activity in the Second Hundred Years' War occurred away from America, but significant skirmishing occurred in the New World. In North America it took the form of border skirmishes between English, French, and Indians (in the north) and English, France's Spanish allies, and Indians in the south. Brutal, terroristic attacks conducted primarily by Indian allies of European powers characterized much of the fighting. These attacks were often motivated as much by longstanding Indian or colonial objectives as by commands from Europe, and from the perspective of most Americans they must have looked like a continuation of the familiar century-long Euro-Indian struggle to control the continent rather than a new development.

As soon as word of King William's War (1689–97) reached New England in 1689 and shortly before it reached New France, English-backed Iroquois Indians used it as a pretext to attack their French enemies. In late summer 1689, 1,500 Iroquois launched a surprise attack on the village of Lachine, just south of Montreal. They burned 56 of the 77 houses in the village, killed more than 60 people and took another 90 prisoner. New France's governor, Count Louis de Frontenac, organized a three-pronged retaliatory attack on New England and New York consisting of terroristic raids by joint forces of Frenchmen and French-allied Indians. The first and deadliest attack occurred at Schenectady, New York, on February 8, 1690. The French and Indians completely surprised Schenectady's inhabitants, killing about 60, taking 27 prisoner, and burning nearly every house in town. Raids on Salmon Falls (modern-day Somersworth), New Hampshire, and Falmouth, Maine, followed with similar results. This pattern of Indian raids on European outposts continued into the War of Spanish Succession (called Queen Anne's War in America, 1702–13). Most notable was the 1704 Deerfield raid described above, but smaller groups of Indians also attacked English towns across Massachusetts and modern-day Maine.

Colonists also attempted to put together more traditional armies using European military tactics to capture enemy strongholds. Because of their larger population, the English colonies made more frequent use of these tactics than the French. During King William's War, New York and the New England colonies worked together to raise army and naval forces for a two-pronged invasion of Canada. Formulated without the knowledge or assistance of the British government, this plan called for an army consisting of colonists and Iroquois Indians to march up the Hudson River valley into Quebec, where they were to meet a naval force led by Sir William Phips of Massachusetts. Fierce resistance forced the army to retreat. Phips's ships arrived at Quebec in October 1690 but still proved unable to conquer the heavily fortified city; they too returned to New England. Later, during Queen Anne's War, New Englanders would again attack Canadian outposts with homegrown naval forces, and in 1711 a large British fleet would attempt to capture Quebec with no more success than Phips and his New Englanders had achieved two decades earlier. Similarly, along British North America's southern frontier, colonists organized attacks against colonial outposts belonging to France's ally, Spain. In 1702, Governor James Moore of South Carolina assembled a naval force manned by 500 colonists and 300

Native Americans. The expedition laid siege to the Spanish fortress guarding St. Augustine, Florida, but was forced to return home when Spanish ships from Cuba arrived to reinforce the Floridians. Anglo-Americans also encouraged Native Americans to attack French settlements along the Gulf Coast from western Florida to Louisiana.

When the Anglo-French conflict resumed after 26 years of peace, America became a greater focal point of the war. Known in America as the War of Jenkins' Ear, the next episode began as a British attempt to retaliate against purported Spanish brutality toward English ships and sailors (Jenkins alleged that Spanish sailors had cut off his ear), but it was really an effort to pick apart the dying Spanish empire. Despite a Franco-Spanish alliance, it would take some time before British efforts would provoke France into all out war. In America, Georgia's governor, James Oglethorpe, put together an army of 1,620 Americans to attempt another attack on the Spanish fortress at Saint Augustine. Despite support from the Royal Navy and the Cherokee Indians, this effort reaped no more success than its predecessor. Thousands of American sailors also volunteered their ships and service to assist extensive British naval operations in the Caribbean. Many died in a disastrous attempt to capture the Spanish base at modern-day Cartagena, Colombia, in 1741.

As the war dragged on, shading into the War of Austrian Succession, and especially after France officially joined with Spain in 1744, American issues became increasingly disconnected from the larger contest. New Englanders decided to organize an expedition to capture the French stronghold of Louisbourg at the mouth of the St. Lawrence River in modern-day Nova Scotia. Despite the British navy's refusal to assist them, more than 3,000 colonials set out for Canada in March 1745. Just after they sailed, British officials sent word that they would send a squadron of warships after all. Together, the American land forces and British navy succeeded in taking the town, despite one Louisbourg resident's comment that, "So striking was the mutual independence of the [American] land army and the [British] fleet that they were always represented to us as different nations."[7] When the victorious Americans returned to Boston, the evangelist George Whitefield wrote, "Numbers flocked with great joy from all quarters, and I immediately preached to them a thanksgiving sermon from these words, 'By this I know that thou has favored me, since Thou hast not permitted mine enemies to triumph over me.'"[8] The English public also cheered the victory with public celebrations, but at war's end, in 1748, Britain returned Louisbourg to France in exchange for French concessions on the European continent and in India, much to the dismay of many New Englanders.

The resulting peace did not last long, particularly in America. Tensions arose in what was then a remote portion of the Ohio River valley and is today the Pittsburgh area. Surrounded by New France to the west and north and British America to the east, Iroquois in this region had successfully played off French and British military and trade rivalries to create a relatively safe haven for themselves. After the War of Austrian Succession, the French began moving more aggressively into this country, building forts along the Ohio River valley. In the east, the British planned settlements of their own and became concerned that the French were trying to encircle their colonies with their new forts. Indians in the valley also began to jostle with each other for power as the Iroquois nation started to decline relative to more recently formed groups known as Indian republics.

These tensions came to a head in 1754. On May 27, Lieutenant Colonel George Washington and his small force of Virginians and Indians encountered a group of French soldiers in southwestern Pennsylvania. Young Washington's orders were to act defensively unless he should find the French attempting to hinder British settlements. The French leader, Ensign Joseph Coulon de Villiers de Jumonville had instructions to find Washington's party and deliver a letter to them insisting that they withdraw from French territory. But before Jumonville could do so, Washington's forces fell on the French. The inexperienced Virginian proved unable to control his men, and somehow Jumonville was shot in the fray. Next, Washington's Iroquois allies, led by the Half King Tanaghrisson, killed some of the Frenchmen, and according to one contemporary account, Tanaghrisson himself bludgeoned the injured Jumonville to death and "took out his brains and washed his hands with them and then scalped him."[9] This shocking act demonstrated Tanaghrisson's and other Iroquois's dissatisfaction with France and, probably, Tanaghrisson's personal desire to regain some of his waning influence.

Tanaghrisson's violence and Washington's ineptitude sparked the greatest war of the eighteenth century and the most important episode in the Second Hundred Years' War. Initially, the British government hoped to avoid provoking a wider war with France. Yet leaders also feared that if France gained control of the Ohio valley, all Britain's colonies would be threatened. Shortly after learning that Washington's forces had lost another engagement at Fort Necessity, Pennsylvania, the Duke of Newcastle, one of the government officials responsible for formulating military strategy, wrote, "All North America will be lost if these practices are tolerated; And no war can be worse to this country than the suffering of such insults as these."[10] Newcastle and others hoped that a quick demonstration of British might would force France to back down and make war less likely. To that end they sent two regiments under the command of General Edward Braddock to America with instructions to join with colonists, friendly Indians, and a British fleet to drive the French from four of their American forts. When these operations succeeded at alarming the French but failed in most of their military objectives, the war in America deepened, and a broader conflict with France became more likely. When Britain's ally, Prussia, invaded France's ally, Austria, on August 30, 1756, the alliance system triggered war in Europe. (A century and a half later, a similar system would launch World War I.)

After the war's inauspicious early stage, Britain appeared to triumph around the world. The American theater continued to be crucial, as Britain began the invasion of Canada with approximately 50,000 British and American troops, the largest British force deployed in North America up to that time. With the fall of Quebec in 1759, the end of French control of Canada was near. In that same year, at the battle of Quiberon Bay off France's Brittany coast, Britain completed its destruction of the French navy. In the meantime, an up-and-coming official of Britain's East India Company named Robert Clive was making his reputation by defeating French and native troops throughout the northern portion of India, ultimately gaining control of Bengal at the Battle of Plassey in 1757. In southern India, British forces repelled French attacks on their posts, and in 1760 they decisively defeated the French at the Battle of Wandiwash, ending for the time any French designs on India. In the latter stages of the war, Britain took the Spanish ports of Havana, Cuba, and Manila in the Philippines, where they would also capture more than $4 million in Spanish treasure.

The peace treaty, signed in Paris in 1763, revealed the extent of Britain's victory. France surrendered all of its North American territory east of the Mississippi River, all of its possessions in India, and many of its valuable West Indian islands. Great Britain returned some West Indian islands to France and Spain. But with its acquisition of Canada and Florida (from Spain), it now controlled nearly all of the European-settled portions of North America above Mexico— emerging the clear victor in the struggle for North America. Britain also appeared to have won the war against Native Americans for control of the eastern portion of the continent. Many Indians who had relied on France to be their ally had lost their military and commercial partner, and all Indians had lost a strong counterweight against British ambitions. While Tanaghrisson and the Iroquois briefly stood at the center of world events in the 1750s, by war's end Native Americans were increasingly peripheral to European concerns. With the

French ousted from most of North America, the delicate three-sided English-French-Iroquoian diplomacy ended. England no longer needed Iroquoia as a counterweight against the French, and without European allies the Iroquois faced the prospect of losing their land along with their power.

Recognizing the danger inherent in this post–Seven Years' War situation and inspired by a revival of Indian religion, an alliance of Native Americans attacked Detroit and seven British forts in the 1763 war known as Pontiac's Rebellion. As a concession, and an attempt to preserve peace, the British government figuratively drew the Proclamation Line of 1763 across the top of the Appalachian Mountains, banning white settlement west of the line in what was to become an Indian reserve and allowing Indians to retain control over their land for a time. This respite would not last long. In little more than a decade, the American Revolution would bring still greater difficulties to the Indians of the Ohio valley and would renew the Anglo-French wars as well.

_᷍ ᷍_

By 1763, America was at the center of European warfare, and European methods of battle, now integrated with Indian tactics, dominated American warfare. This marked a notable change from earlier centuries when America had been "beyond the line" of European warfare, and when state-sponsored military forces rarely fought there. The peace following the Seven Years' War would prove short-lived. In little more than a decade, the American Revolution would bring still greater difficulties to the Indians of the Ohio Valley and would renew the Anglo-French wars. Once again, European armies would fight on American soil, and conflict in America would spark a war fought around the world.

CHAPTER THREE

De-Indianizing
American Culture

POCAHONTAS GOES TO COURT

The annual Twelfth Night masque held in the court of King James was a high point of London's social calendar. In 1617 the lavish production, entitled *The Vision of Delight*, was written by famed playwright Ben Jonson, and noted architect Inigo Jones created the sets. Conspicuous in the audience, seated very near the king himself, was an American woman known variously as Lady Rebecca, Matoaka, or Pocahontas, the daughter of Virginia's most powerful Indian leader and wife of a leading English colonist. As a real live Indian princess and a representative of both Virginia's Indian and English leadership, Pocahontas aroused great curiosity among Londoners who had never before viewed a Native American. Moreover, the princess was an important diplomatic figure whose marriage to an Englishman would protect Virginia from Indian attacks, or so the colony's directors hoped.

Just a decade after England founded its first permanent settlement in Virginia, Pocahontas and her people knew much more about English culture than most English people knew of Indian life. Her father and other leading Indians in Virginia had learned about English ways through their continual negotiations with colonists, beginning with the first, abortive efforts to create an English Virginia in the 1580s. All of Virginia's Indians lived with the products of European technology every day and must have devoted much energy to understanding and countering the British technological advantage, most notably their control of guns and ships. Pocahontas, who had been kidnapped by the colonists and converted to Christianity before marrying her English husband, John Rolfe, lived her life more as an English woman than as an Indian princess. But there were also many aspects of British culture that she and Virginia's Indians still did not fully understand. What was life like across the ocean? What was the source of England's power? Why did so many English people come to America, and what plans did they have for their colonies?

Pocahontas and her father hoped to use her visit as an opportunity to answer such questions about the people who were colonizing their homeland. Accompanying her and her new husband was one of her father's advisers, Uttamatomakin. In London, Uttamatomakin met well-educated English people with whom he spoke about religion and other matters. He told them that he had been instructed by Pocahontas's father, Powhatan, to determine the size of England's population, and he also expressed interest in English agriculture. Quite likely, Powhatan and other Virginia Indians speculated that the English wished to colonize America because of their lack of agricultural resources. If so, Uttamatomakin must have realized that the existence of extensive farms in England meant that British people did not depend on their American colonies for sustenance. The enormous population that he found in London and other cities he passed through would also have troubled him deeply. Clearly the British had great resources in population, agriculture, and technology. Inigo Jones's sumptuous sets and the rich costumes worn by the spectators at the Twelfth Night masque, which Uttamatomakin also attended, no doubt reinforced his sense of awe. If the king who presided over this spectacle and over the rich, populous lands and large cities the Virginians had passed through wished to conquer all Virginia, Uttamatomakin now realized it would be extremely difficult, perhaps impossible, to resist.

The Virginians' visit to England was an outgrowth of the mutual curiosity of two races of people who had only recently discovered each other. English men and women marveled at Pocahontas's exotic dignity and supposed savageness, while she and Uttamatomakin struggled to understand the strange people who had become so important to their survival. In this way, the Virginians' experience mirrored important aspects of early European-American cultural interaction, which tended to focus on religious, racial, and technological differences.

Powhatan and Uttamatomakin's trepidation about the English reflects the reality that Native Americans had much to fear from European culture. From Columbus's first day in the New World, Europeans sought to conquer and remake America in their own image. They imported Christianity and developed new notions of racial superiority and inferiority even as they brought along the trade goods and military aggression discussed in the previous two chapters. Once Europeans realized they had found a new continent (and this took a surprisingly long time) they became fascinated by the natives. In time, the

European discovery of Native Americans would influence European science and philosophy in important ways. But even during this period of European fascination with America and Americans, actual Native American culture had very little influence on Europeans or their lives. By contrast, European culture threatened the very existence of the Native American way of life as Christian missionaries, backed by powerful European armies and the invisible weapon of communicable disease, attempted to Christianize and Europeanize people they viewed as newfound "savages."

By the eighteenth century, as natives succumbed to disease, warfare, and westernization and were, more often than not, physically removed from Euro-America, Europeans began to lose interest in them. Rather than a strange and exotic land peopled by a novel, savage race in need of Christianization and civilization, America increasingly seemed to be a cultural extension of Europe, albeit one with some unusual customs. Meanwhile, eighteenth-century Native Americans and African newcomers seemed, to Europeans, to be merely inferior, subjugated races. Uttamatomakin's worst fears had been realized.

FIRST ENCOUNTERS

Sixteenth- and seventeenth-century Europeans mostly defined America as a new world with new people. Revelations of this New World, unknown to the ancients, spurred Europeans to better understand their own world in the Renaissance and early Enlightenment. As the example of Pocahontas suggests, the arrival of Europeans also prompted native Americans to learn more about the world beyond the Atlantic. Cultural exchange took place. Each side tried to understand and conceptualize the other. Yet power relations inevitably shaped these exchanges. As Europeans gained the overwhelming share of power, they were increasingly able to impose their vision on the New World.

Christianity in Latin America

Christianity was the first, and arguably the most important, big idea Europeans attempted to impart to the New World. Columbus himself described his voyage as, in part, an effort to convert the people of Asia to Christianity. When he first landed in America, he professed pleasure in finding peaceful natives who might be "more easily freed and converted to our holy faith by love than by force."[1] On Columbus's second voyage, undertaken in 1493, he carried a former envoy to the Holy See and five friars belonging to the Benedictine, Jeronymite, and Franciscan orders, assigned to oversee construction and outfitting of the first Christian church in America. The first Catholic dioceses in America were soon established in Hispaniola (1508) and Puerto Rico (1511), initiating a relentless campaign that would transform America.

Columbus's landing did not mark the start of Catholic missionary work. The church had sought to spread its word throughout the Islamic world for centuries, most notably with the Crusades. The reconquest of Spain from the Muslims who had ruled portions of it for nearly eight centuries and the ensuing Inquisition, begun the year of Columbus's first journey, were the culmination of a long effort to bring Christianity to Iberian Muslims and Jews, frequently through force of arms. Columbus's expectation of converting Asians reflected the Church's hopes for conversions in the Far East. Six years before Columbus sailed, Pope Innocent VII proclaimed the Church's mission as promoting "the propagation of the orthodox faith, the increase of the Christian religion, the salvation of barbarian nations, and the repression of the infidels and their conversion to the faith."[2]

The Catholic Church's interest in conversions accelerated with the onset of the Protestant Reformation just a little more than two decades after Columbus's first voyage. The growing influence of German theologian Martin Luther and others who rejected the authority of a Catholic Church they labeled as corrupt and theologically incorrect caused a religious schism in Europe. Within a few short decades much of western and central Europe joined Luther's Protestant camp, rejecting the pope and the rites of Catholicism. As a result of these mass defections and increasing success in converting Native Americans and Asians to Catholicism, the sixteenth-century Catholic Church became less European and far more global than it had been for centuries.

At the same time, the rise of the Catholic religious orders played a leading part in missionary work. Some orders, such as the Franciscans and Dominicans, predated Columbus and the Reformation and had long been active in missionary work both in Asia and within Europe, where pagan beliefs commingled with Christianity into the sixteenth century. During the Reformation, Catholics formed new orders, sometimes described as part of a Catholic counter-reformation aimed at checking Protestantism. The most consequential of these orders were the Capuchins, Ursulines, and Jesuits. All three would play a role in spreading Christianity beyond Europe, but of the three, the Jesuits were perhaps the most influential. Founded in 1534 by a former Spanish soldier, Ignatius of Loyola, the Jesuit order from its beginning focused on education and missionary work. As early as 1540, Francis Xavier, one of the most important early

Jesuit leaders, became the new order's first missionary in Asia when he sailed to India aboard a Portuguese ship. He would later continue to work throughout South and East Asia.

The Jesuits and the other religious orders played a crucial role in the massive effort to convert Native Americans. In New Spain (modern-day Mexico), which contained the continent's most populous and sophisticated native population, the first twelve Franciscan missionaries arrived in 1524, just three years after Cortés's conquest of the Aztecs. Thirty-five years later, New Spain boasted 160 church buildings overseen by more than 800 Franciscans, Dominicans, and Augustinians. To convert natives, missionaries had to become fluent in languages no Europeans had ever heard before the sixteenth century, such as Mayan. They constructed schools and created curricula to educate natives in European culture and theology. They also sought to deter Indians from practicing native religions. One cleric went so far as to destroy 500 temples and 20,000 idols. By 1550, missionaries had baptized as many as 10 million natives in America.

These impressive efforts were part of an international drive to expand Christianity. Portuguese missionaries initially had some limited success in Africa, converting the king of Congo to Catholicism in 1491. However, they gained far more converts in Asia. Francis Xavier himself baptized 10,000 people in southern India in 1544, and the Portuguese Inquisition opened an office in Goa, India, in 1561. By the late sixteenth century, Spaniards began missionary efforts in the recently conquered Philippines. Roughly 100 years later, they could boast of more than 600,000 Catholic Filipinos. In Japan, where Francis Xavier arrived in 1549, there were already an estimated 150,000 Christians by 1582 and well over 200,000 by 1614, when the Japanese government expelled all foreign missionaries and began to execute Christians who refused to renounce their faith. Missionary activity by the Jesuits, Dominicans, and others in China resulted in between 200,000 and 500,000 converts by the end of the seventeenth century.

Alongside this enormous missionary effort, the church also invested impressive capital and labor into a spiritual infrastructure that transformed the physical and intellectual landscape of America. Throughout the sixteenth and seventeenth centuries, church officials directed the construction of imposing churches and cathedrals, frequently located symbolically atop the sites of the Indian temples missionaries had destroyed. The resulting structures, built with forced Indian labor and often relying on skilled Indian craftsmen, rivaled their European counterparts in size and grandeur. An Englishman visiting

Mexico City in the 1620s described the city's 50 "gold daubed" churches as "the fairest that ever my eyes beheld." Inside, "[m]any altars have sundry marble pillars, and others are decorated with brazilwood stays standing one above another with tabernacles for several saints richly wrought with golden colors."[3] Church members also funded educational structures to spread the word of God to converts and ecclesiastics alike. In Mexico, Franciscans funded the first school in America in 1523, while Dominicans sponsored the first American university in 1538. Other universities aimed primarily at training clergy followed in Mexico and Peru. The Mexican church established the first printing press in America in 1539 as a means of further spreading the gospel to Indians and colonists. Together, these institutions began a massive transfer of European religious culture and literacy to America.

Nevertheless, Native Americans, even those who accepted baptism, rarely accepted Christianity entirely or in the prescribed European manner. Mexico's Mayan Indians initially seemed very receptive to Christianity, introduced to them by Franciscan missionaries. However, the Franciscans soon accused the Mayans of hiding idols in caves and secretly practicing human sacrifice. Franciscan leaders tortured thousands of Indians in an effort to prove these allegations. Church authorities in southern Mexico charged that even the leaders of supposedly Christian Indian groups continued to worship idols and practice human sacrifice. Other Indians created a syncretic Christianity that blended European and American culture. Among the earliest and most important examples is the Mexican worship of the Virgin of Guadalupe, who was supposed to have appeared above a hill near Mexico City in 1531. Indians painted her image to resemble their own features, and they associated her with the Indian deity Tonantzin, whose pre-Christian shrine had been located on the hillside where the virgin was said to have appeared. Despite church authorities' unease with the Indian origins of the Virgin of Guadalupe, they ultimately came to accept her cult, which became a central feature of Mexican Catholicism. Some three centuries later, in 1810, she would be adopted as a symbol of Mexican independence from Spain by the rebel leader Miguel Hidalgo y Costilla. Few could deny that Catholicism had conquered Latin America.

Christianity North of Mexico

A more complicated process unfolded to the north. Missionaries soon began to spread Christianity into the remote, thinly populated areas that are today the southern United States. By 1566, Jesuits arrived in the area known as La

Florida only to be superseded by Franciscans a few years later. In 1597, natives living near St. Augustine revolted when a missionary attempted to prevent one of their leaders from having multiple wives. Despite this setback, Franciscans renewed their activity in the next century, and by the 1650s they claimed to have baptized 21,000 natives in the area. In New Mexico, where Franciscans arrived in 1629, they soon boasted of baptizing 86,000 Pueblo, Navajo, and Apache Indians. One Franciscan wrote of the New Mexico natives, "If we go passing along the roads, and they see us from their pueblos or fields, they all come forth to meet us with very great joy, saying: Praised be our Lord Jesus Christ! Praise be the most holy sacrament!"[4] As in Florida and Mexico, natives practiced a syncretic Christianity, viewing the Franciscans, and probably Jesus, as one of their many katsinas or minor deities. By the late seventeenth century, however, Pueblo Indians had tired of the Franciscans and the Spanish culture they brought with them. In the Pueblo Rebellion of the 1680s, Indians desecrated missions and tortured and humiliated Franciscans. After expelling the Spaniards, Pueblo leaders attempted to obliterate Catholicism and Spanish culture entirely from their lands. They prohibited Indians from speaking Spanish, annulled marriages performed by the Spaniards, and ordered their people to burn any Spanish seeds and return to planting only Indian corn and beans.

When the British began to settle North America a century after their Catholic rivals, they initially professed an interest in following the Spanish missionary model. Referring to Spain's efforts, William Strachey, one of the leaders of the Jamestown colony, asked, "Have we either less means, fainter spirits, or a charity more cold, or a religion more shameful?"[5] Virginia's early leaders made big plans for converting Indians. Colonists were to bring native children into their homes to begin their Christian education at an early age. Later these youths were to be educated at a special college and, eventually, a planned Indian university. Virginia's promoters raised substantial sums for these projects, but they were never executed. No doubt renewed Indian-English warfare in 1622 played a large part in scuttling them.

Massachusetts, the second British mainland colony, had as its official seal a picture of an Indian pleading, "Come over and help us." But the pious Pilgrims and Puritans who began settling the Bay Colony in the 1620s did not get around to converting Indians in a serious way until the 1640s. John Eliot, the "apostle to the Indians," led these efforts as he worked tirelessly to master the natives' language, publishing the *Indian Primer* (1654) and the *Indian Bible* (1663). These works, both printed on the Cambridge press, the first in British North America, were the first book and first Bible ever printed in the Algonquian language. At about the same time, Massachusetts began setting up "praying Indian towns" to separate Eliot's converts from their supposedly savage brethren. In England, the Massachusetts colony's agent helped organize the Society for the Promoting and Propagating the Gospel of Jesus Christ in New England (1640), which raised money for more missionary work and founded the Indian College at Harvard to educate Christian Indian leaders. These efforts, which may have converted about 2,500 New England Indians, were pretty much abandoned as a result of the vicious Indian-English warfare in the mid-1670s.

The contrast between the millions of baptisms in New Spain and the thousands in British North America is striking. It cannot be explained by any single factor. Rather, colonial British and Spanish religious cultures diverged in a number of respects. While Britain's established Protestant Anglican church professed interest in competing with Catholicism for American converts, it had neither the financial resources of the Catholic church nor the assistance of the Catholic orders such as the Dominicans, Franciscans, Ursulines, and Jesuits. Unlike the Catholic church, the Anglican church never installed a bishop in North America before the American Revolution. More importantly, dissension wracked British Protestantism. While the Anglican church remained the majority church in some colonies (most notably Virginia), dissenters, who strongly disagreed with the leadership and theology of Anglicanism, dominated other colonies. Puritans held sway in Massachusetts, and Quakers dominated in Pennsylvania. Meanwhile, Catholics founded Maryland as a refuge from the persecution they faced in England. Within colonies, too, there were frequent disagreements over religious practice. As a result, internal doctrinal conflicts superseded any mandate to convert Native Americans.

These conflicts stemmed from the British reformation of the sixteenth century, when England broke from the Catholic church and established the new Church of England, or Anglican church. Many Protestant dissenters found the Anglican church too similar to Catholicism and wished to institute new, unorthodox practices and theologies. At the same time, those who remained Catholic also resented Anglicanism. British authorities who sought to deter dissenters and Catholics wielded the power of the state, frequently heavy handedly, but their efforts failed to destroy the dissenters. This conflict and increasing multiplicity of churches spread into North America with the earliest British settlements.

The opening of North America spurred a diaspora of British dissenters who sensed that lack of established religious authority and distance from Britain would provide them with the freedom to practice (or not practice) as they wished. The most famous of these dissenters were the Puritans, who are best known for creating the Massachusetts Bay colony as a Puritan commonwealth in which religious authorities largely governed the entire colony. Massachusetts, with its population of perhaps 20,000 Puritans by 1640, was just one node in the greater Puritan diaspora. Puritans also launched colonies in the Caribbean islands of Providence and Bermuda, and significant numbers settled in non-Puritan colonies such as Virginia, where Puritans requested a "supply of faithful ministers" from Massachusetts in 1642.[6] Despite their arrival in the Americas, these Puritans maintained close connections with their homeland, and when a Civil War broke out in England in the 1640s that led to the temporary disestablishment of the Anglican church and a new Puritan-friendly regime, many returned to England from New England.

The large number of dissenters immigrating to America inevitably caused conflict. Even in relatively homogeneous New England, different Puritan factions exerted great energy disputing among themselves. Farther south, where no single group dominated, a remarkable level of religious diversity was apparent to seventeenth-century observers. In New York, one wrote, "Here bee not many of the Church of England, few Roman Catholics; abundance of Quaker preachers . . . Sabbatarians, anti-Sabbatarians; Some Anabaptists; some Independents; some Jews; in short, of all sorts of opinions there are some, and the most part [are] of none at all." Another wrote that in nominally Catholic Maryland "many [Protestants] daily fall away either to Popery, Quakerism, or Phanaticisme . . . it is become a Sodom of uncleanness and a Pest house of iniquity."[7] While Maryland Catholics initially made some efforts to convert Indians, over the course of the seventeenth century they focused more on fighting off hostile Protestants in the miniature religious wars of 1645, 1654, 1676–77, 1681, and 1689. Maryland's famous Toleration Act of 1649 amounted to a failed attempt to create peace between religious factions.

As a result of this diversity and conflict, British North America diverged sharply from the Spanish model. Rather than a new, Euro-American syncretic Christianity, British colonists created an uneasy mixture of Anglicans, Catholics, and dissenting Protestants. Tensions in the New World mirrored those in England, and British dissenters retained close ties with the homeland. America became an important site in the ongoing British religious conflict rather than a site for missionary work among the natives.

Savagery and Race

Ambivalence about converting Indians reflected European uncertainties about the fundamental nature of Native Americans. Just as European geographers did not immediately recognize the true dimensions of the American land mass, philosophers did not recognize the extent to which Native Americans differed from people Europeans had already encountered. The term *Indian*, widely used to describe Native Americans from the start, reflects the European propensity to see Native Americans as essentially similar to the Asian Indian peoples with whom they had recently become familiar. The conquistadors who planned to subject the natives and the church officials who hoped to convert them were the first Europeans to think in a systematic way about the origins of Americans. They learned Indian languages, investigated the sources of native wealth (if only to take it), examined native religion (if only to eradicate it), and gauged natives' intelligence (if only to judge their suitability for conversion). Perhaps the most perceptive and sympathetic early observer of the natives was the Spanish friar, Bartolomé de las Casas, whose *Apologetica Historia* concluded that Indians were fully rational and, therefore, capable of truly converting.

Las Casas never published his work in his lifetime, and most sixteenth-century publications about the Indians were either produced by Europeans who had not traveled to the New World or were modified by European publishers. As a result, sixteenth-century Europeans tended to view America as a sort of primitive Europe. Frequently, they understood the Native Americans to be similar to the ancient European civilizations that predated Christianity. For example, the Englishman John White, who first visited Virginia in 1585, produced a series of watercolors on the spot depicting Native Americans and their activities; his illustrations are still the standard source for colonial historians trying to understand early Virginians. However, back in Europe publishers significantly modified White's watercolors to produce engravings in which the native Virginians came to resemble familiar images of classical Greeks and Romans. Significantly, White and his collaborators also used Virginians as models for images of the Picts, whom they described as savage people who had inhabited Britain long before Christianity. The analogy was clear: Americans represented an early stage of human society, much as so-called savage Picts and classical Greeks predated modern Christian Europeans. Additionally, this analogy implied that so-called savage Americans were not inherently savage and might in time become civilized Christians like the sixteenth-century English.

Many Europeans learned about the newly discovered Americans firsthand without crossing the Atlantic. Perhaps as many as 2,000 captured Indians traveled against their wills to Europe during the first century of contact. Columbus started this practice on his first voyage when he brought ten Americans to Spain to prove to his king and queen that he had reached the Indies. Subsequent American captives came to work as slaves, but others were brought specifically to demonstrate to Europeans the nature of the New World's inhabitants. An Eskimo man captured by the English explorer Martin Frobisher in 1577 demonstrated his kayaking methods as part of the entertainment at a dinner party given by the mayor of Bristol in the 1570s, more than a decade before the first English effort to settle North America. Captives also taught explorers and conquistadors native languages and customs in advance of journeying to the New World. Some captives learned European languages in order to become guides for Europeans. One such American, captured by the Spanish in 1559 and renamed Don Luis, met Spain's King Philip II before returning to America, where the Spaniards hoped he would help them win influence among the native population. Instead, he led his people in a revolt against the Spanish colonists. As noted above, Pocahontas's 1616–1617 tour created a sensation in London society when she met the king and queen and other notables.

Written accounts of the New World and physical demonstrations of native Americans influenced a number of important sixteenth-century European humanists. The influential English politician and writer, Thomas More, chose America as the setting for his *Utopia* (1516). Describing a fictional island in the Atlantic, More used his American setting to portray a perfect society free of the problems that he perceived in European society. Supposedly prompted by his acquaintance with a Brazilian native in France, Michel de Montaigne wrote an influential essay, "Of Cannibals" (1580), suggesting that Europeans, rather than Native Americans, were the true savages. "I think there is more barbarity in eating a man alive than in eating him dead, in tearing by tortures and the rack a body still full of feeling," he wrote. Montaigne's countrymen may have called Americans barbarians, but he concluded that Europeans "surpass them in every kind of barbarity."[8] Montaigne's essay helped establish the myth of the "noble savage," which incorporated the commonplace notion that Americans represented an early pre-Christian stage in human development. Unlike the views of many missionaries who deplored Indians' ignorance of European culture, the noble savage myth valorized Americans precisely because of their innocence of corrupt European ways. By setting *The Tempest* (1611) on a West Indian island, William Shakespeare brought some of these ideas to the British stage, including a Native American character named Caliban, whose name is an anagram of *cannibal* and who decidedly was not a noble savage.

THE EIGHTEENTH CENTURY

By the turn of the eighteenth century, America's position in the global imagination began to change. With a shrinking native population and a growing European settler population, America, and particularly British North America, appeared more of a province of the old world than a dramatically different New World. An important difference was the growing population of enslaved Africans, whose presence mixed aspects of African culture with Euro-American culture, thereby differentiating the developing American culture from that of Europe. Furthermore, a pernicious blend of emerging racism and evolving slavery would have tragic repercussions in the coming centuries. At the same time, English institutions, architectural forms, religion, and scientific approaches came to dominate eastern North America, and North Americans of European descent themselves now began to make some important contributions to European thought.

Eighteenth-Century Christianity

Before the eighteenth century, Europeans in America focused on the task of converting the "savage" natives to Christianity. Authorities in British North America continued to stress the importance of converting natives throughout most of the seventeenth century. However, by the dawn of the eighteenth century, that emphasis was shifting toward the need to convert other Europeans to "proper" forms of Christianity and, to a much lesser extent, to convert Africans. In addition to the diversity of British faiths, a large number of non-British colonists supported other Protestant faiths such as the German Moravians, French Huguenots, and the Dutch Reformed Church, which had been the established denomination in the New Netherlands colony before it became British New York in 1664. In an attempt to spread Anglicanism and bring some uniformity to these colonies, the Church of England created the Society for Promoting Christian Knowledge (SPCK) in 1698 and the Society for the Propagation of the Gospel in Foreign Parts (SPG) in 1701. The SPG sent more than 600 clergymen to the colonies before the American Revolution, establishing approximately 300 new churches outside the Anglican strongholds of Virginia and Maryland. It also attempted to convert African American slaves. The SPG made some inroads, even converting several influential leaders at Yale College. Between 1750 and 1770 the number of Anglican congregants in America increased by about a third.

However, beginning in the 1730s, the explosion of evangelical Protestant sects sometimes known as the Great Awakening greatly outpaced the growth of Anglicanism. Some view the expansion of these diverse groups as a uniquely American phenomenon and the foundation of remarkable religious diversity and toleration in the United States. The movement, however, had a strong transatlantic dimension. The leading ministers in America and Britain kept close contact throughout this period. Jonathan Edwards, an early and influential revival leader in New England, wrote to a correspondent in Scotland, "The Church of God, in all parts of the world, is but one; the distant members are closely united in one Glorious Head."[9] British and American evangelicals soon began circulating newspapers and magazines that allowed the faithful on either side of the Atlantic to read about revivals and conversions in Britain and America. In the early 1740s they instituted the United Concert for Prayer, which established a common day of prayer and Thanksgiving for evangelical churches on both sides of the Atlantic. The culmination of transatlantic revivalism came in the person of George Whitefield, nominally an Anglican priest but in practice the first nondenominational celebrity evangelist. He visited America seven times between 1738 and 1770, staying for three and a half years in one long stretch between 1744 and 1748. He preached to men and women of all ethnicities and races in every colony from Maine to Georgia. Describing Whitefield's 1739-40 visit to Philadelphia, the normally skeptical Benjamin Franklin wrote, "It seem'd as if all the world were growing religious; so that one could not walk through the Town in an evening without hearing psalms sung in different families of every street."[10] Philadelphia, with its diverse population was a microcosm of the British colonies, and as in Philadelphia, the Great Awakening brought colonists from Germany, France, the Netherlands, and many other lands besides England together into a new form of Protestant belief.

It also played an important role in the evolution of African American Christianity, which would fuse elements of African religious practices together with Euro-American evangelical Protestantism. It was during the Great Awakening that African Americans first became Christian in large numbers. Beginning in the mid-eighteenth century, and then accelerating in later years, African Americans would create a distinctive and ultimately influential form of Christianity, one that blended surviving African religious practices, such as death and marriage rituals, with European Christian practices to create an approach to Christianity that diverged from European models.

Race and Slavery

As Europeans' interest in converting Indians declined, they began to develop a more modern and insidious conception of race. Well into the seventeenth century, Europeans continued to see Indians as noble savages who might well become their equals if they would only become Christians. As the eighteenth century dawned, however, Europeans generally began to see Native Americans as racially distinct and inferior. Early European settlers in America believed European-American physiological differences were a product of America's unique environment, and they feared that their American-born children would emerge as Indians. When that did not occur, Europeans began to consider that physical differences between themselves and Indians might be biologically determined. European scientists initially suspected that color differences between Europeans and Africans related to the different amounts of exposure to the sun that they received in their homelands. If true, then the two races would logically become the same if both lived in America. The French scientist Georges Louis Leclerc, Comte Buffon, for example, expected them to become similar within eight to ten generations. Over time, however, Americans realized this theory was not borne out by reality. Furthermore, Indians' heavy susceptibility to disease led Europeans to conjecture that their constitutions were inherently inferior to their own. (These seemingly more robust Europeans still did not understand the true causes of their own immunity to European diseases). Together, these strands of thought pushed aside older notions that Indians might be transformed into Europeans (and vice versa) and laid the foundation for the emerging notion of fixed racial categories.

At the same time, Europeans and Anglo-Americans came to see Africans as another, inferior race. Late-seventeenth-century slave codes articulated and enforced this notion. English slave colonies in the West Indies and American mainland repeatedly outlawed interracial sex. By the last decade of the century, records in the British slave colonies of Barbados and Virginia both began to refer to blacks and whites rather than Christians or English, thereby emphasizing color over previous distinctions of ethnicity or religion. Furthermore, by equating blackness with servitude, colonial slave codes created a legal basis of racism. Such distinctions were useful to American planters, who now could justify slave labor on the basis of racial inferiority. In turn, the daily distinction between white landowners and black slaves, further reinforced American racism.

Across the Atlantic, Swedish botanist Carl Linnaeus created a hierarchical method to classify animals. This system, which essentially ranks animals from least to most developed, led some Europeans to believe that Africans, as allegedly less developed humans, were not far removed from apes. This association was reinforced by the geographical proximity of Africans and apes on their home continent. Religious figures, who stressed the great divide between men and beasts, denied this association, as did most scientists. Buffon, for one, saw a large gap in understanding between men and beasts, but his comment that Africans were "almost equally wild, and as ugly as these apes," did nothing to diminish the growing impression of Europeans that Africans were inherently different and inferior.[11]

Some Europeans applied these theories to all Americans, not just natives and African Americans. Certain scientists, including Buffon, subscribed to a theory of degeneracy that held that America's supposedly harsh climate made it difficult for large animals to thrive there and that European species would decline in stature when transferred to America. Others took the logic further, arguing that when transplanted to America's climate, even the Europeans themselves would begin to degenerate. This idea spread widely in the second half of the eighteenth century. Its most famous proponent, French scientist, Abbe Raynal, insisted that English people had visibly degenerated in America. The New World, he maintained had not yet produced a good poet, an able mathematician, or a man of genius in any art or science.

Enlightenment and America

Not surprisingly, such rhetoric angered Anglo-Americans, who saw themselves as racially superior to Native Americans and equal in faculties to other Europeans. Their participation in the European scientific and philosophical revolution known as the Enlightenment, they insisted, manifested their equality with Europeans. Benjamin Franklin was far and away the best-known American scientist. According to John Adams, Franklin's reputation in France "was more universal than that of Leibnitz or Newton, Frederick or Voltaire, and his character more beloved and esteemed than any of them." Even in faraway Bavaria, a doctor read Franklin's work and lay awake at night worrying about the electrical danger from a lightning strike.[12] Franklin and other Philadelphia thinkers, most notably astronomer David Rittenhouse, formed the American

Philosophical Society in 1769 to spread American scientific discoveries by publishing scholarly papers and to exchange information with similar European organizations. The growing transatlantic book trade and the international circulation of newspapers also linked Americans to Enlightenment thought, and popular publications such as Franklin's *Poor Richard's Almanack*, spread scientific information to the American masses.

While Native Americans did not contribute much to the Enlightenment directly, the notion of the American continent and the allegedly "noble savages" who had populated it influenced European thinkers whose ideas, in turn, would later influence America's founders. Enlightenment political philosophers emphasized humans' rights to liberty and property, the basis of the liberal democracy that continues to dominate much of the modern world. Probably the most important political philosopher of the era, and certainly the most important in England, was John Locke (1632–1704). His *Two Treatises of Government* (1690) ranks among the most popular and influential works of political philosophy ever published and is generally considered one of the foundational texts of liberal democracy. One of Locke's crucial contributions is the notion that human existence began in a primitive "state of nature" in which people had certain natural rights, most notably the possession of property. He argued that civil societies emerged when people in a state of nature voluntarily agreed to join together and bond themselves by certain rules to protect themselves from others who threatened their property and liberty.

Although Locke hardly invented such arguments, he was unusual in the extent to which he likened the state of nature and its inhabitants to early America and Native Americans. In the *Two Treatises* he famously observes, "Thus in the beginning all the world was *America*, and more so than that is now; for no such thing as *money* was any where known."[13] Locke was not unique in connecting the state of nature to pre-Columbian America. Some years earlier, the Dutch philosopher Hugo Grotius made a similar observation when he wrote, "The primitive state . . . exemplified in the community of property arising from extreme simplicity, may be seen among certain tribes in America which have lived for many generations in such a condition."[14]

Locke's *Two Treatises* was, in part, a justification for England's Glorious Revolution (1688), itself a transatlantic event, occurring two years before the publication of Locke's book. In this relatively peaceful revolution, Parliament and its allies, angry at King James II's alleged tyranny and Catholicism, forced him to flee to France and relinquish his throne to his daughter Mary and her husband, William of Orange. News that James had been overthrown triggered smaller uprisings in many of the British American colonies. In Maryland, which was ruled by the Catholic Calvert family, Protestants saw the Glorious Revolution as an excuse to depose their own Catholic leaders. They accused Maryland Catholics, the French, and nearby Indians of fomenting a conspiracy against them. They cheered the "happy change in England" and promised Marylanders a new government that would protect them from "tyranny and popery." Although governed by Protestants, rebel leaders in New York intimated that the officials appointed by King James might be part of a Catholic conspiracy. In overturning those officials they proclaimed that New Yorkers had long suffered under the "same oppression" as their counterparts in England, and they hoped that the new king would support them. Unfortunately, this uprising, known as Leisler's Rebellion, grew into a messy civil war that led to several years of sporadic disorder and violence.[15]

Recently, scholars have argued that *Two Treatises* was also written to justify Britain's colonization efforts in America. For most of his career, Locke was closely tied to colonization. He invested profitably in a Bahamas trading company in 1672. His employer, Anthony Ashley Cooper, Earl of Shaftesbury, was the proprietor of colonial South Carolina. Locke served as secretary to the Lords Proprietors of Carolina from 1668 to 1675 and helped draft the colony's first constitution. He also served as secretary to Britain's Colonial Council of Trade from 1673 to 1675 and as a commissioner for the Board of Trade and Plantations from 1696 to 1700. Because Locke wrote much of his *Two Treatises* before the Glorious Revolution, the colonial background may well have influenced him as much as the rebellion itself. In this context, Locke's emphasis on the transition from a state of nature to civil society and on the superiority of private property and a monetary economy to the Indians' communal, pre-monetary economy can also be seen as justification for English settlement of Indian lands. When he wrote, "As much land as a man tills, plants, improves, cultivates, and can use the product of, so much is his *property*," he seemed to create a justification for enclosing land that Indians had shared in common.[16]

From a modern perspective, it seems paradoxical that John Locke, the philosopher of liberty and property, lived at the center of British mercantilism. The Board of Trade, on which he served, was the body that oversaw imperial colonial administration. However (as noted in chapter 1), for most of American colonial history the majority of American colonists were not hostile to mercantilism. It was only just before the American Revolution that Anglo-Americans began to view mercantilism as a threat to their liberty, and even then they complained more about specific aspects of British regulation than about the theory of mercantilism itself. Coincidentally, in the very year the colonists declared their independence, a Scottish economist named Adam Smith published what would become the most influential critique of mercantilism, *The Wealth of Nations*. Smith built his critique of mercantilism around an analysis of the British administration of the American and East Indian colonies. Calling the discovery of America and the passage to India "the two greatest and most important events recorded in the history of mankind," Smith deplored the mercantile system they gave rise to.[17] This system, he concluded, misused resources that would be employed more efficiently if allowed to flow without regulation, thereby costing ordinary consumers money while benefiting the great merchants. Smith's book would serve as the foundation for modern-day economics, which replaced mercantilism with a theory of free trade. In time, this economic philosophy became a crucial component of western culture, and, still later, much of the ideological struggle of the twentieth century would be based on the conflict between free trade and Soviet-style managed economies.

_____

In culture, as in commerce, the eighteenth century marked a change in the nature of European notions of America's place in the world. In the earlier part of the colonial period, the European vision for America was arguably more global than it would later become. The earliest explorers, missionaries, and conquerors imagined America and Native Americans would become a node in a global trading network stretching from Europe to Asia and a portion of a Christian church that would cover every continent. By the eighteenth century that vision had only been partly realized. Well-established cultural and commercial ties linked the people on both sides of the Atlantic, but while western Europeans, western Africans, Euro-Americans, and African Americans were far more connected than ever before, they had yet to become fully integrated into truly global cultural and commercial networks.

Part II
1763–1898

INTRODUCTION

New technology sped globalization and transformed America and the world during the long nineteenth century, from 1763 to 1898. At the dawn of this period, the fastest way to travel was still by sailing ships, which typically would take four to six weeks to cross the Atlantic; by the turn of the twentieth century, steamers routinely crossed in six days. In the revolutionary era, news could travel only as fast as the fastest ship; by the late nineteenth century, information traveled across the Atlantic nearly instantaneously via transoceanic telegraph cables. These changes increased exponentially the flow of news and people across the oceans and throughout the world. New manufacturing technologies that made these developments possible also spurred widespread movement of peoples throughout the world as industrializing regions pulled in ever-growing numbers of laborers from less-industrialized or less-prosperous regions.

Few nations reaped greater benefits from these advances, or contributed more to them, than the United States. In 1800 it took six weeks to travel from New York to Chicago and many months to reach California. By 1900 transcontinental railroads whisked travelers and goods from New York to Chicago in hours and New York to San Francisco in days. Improved transportation and communications, as well as industrialization, spurred a massive global flow of immigrants into the United States. Before the Civil War, western Europeans, especially from the British Isles and Germany came to America to work in early manufacturing and agricultural areas. During the 1850s, the peak of this migration wave, 2.5 million immigrants arrived in the United States, making up 11 percent of the nation's total population. With expansion toward the Pacific, Asians began emigrating, too, especially Chinese and Japanese. By the end of the century, inexpensive steam ship transport, warfare, and religious persecution in Europe and massive American industrialization together pushed and pulled enormous numbers of emigrants, including growing numbers of Catholics and Jews from eastern and southern Europe. At the peak of this immigration, during the 1880s, more than 5.2 million new immigrants arrived in the United States, making up 10.5 percent of the nation's total population.

A burst of nationalism, which overspread most of the western world and parts of the east, also distinguished the nineteenth century. Nation building involved a mostly inwardly focused process of securing boundaries and the allegiance of the inhabitants within those boundaries. European nations experienced this process through a series of wars and nationalistic movements over the course of the nineteenth century. Places such as Italy and Germany, which had been little more than collections of states at the start of the century, became great nations by its end. The United States also followed this path, developing from 13 separate British colonies to a unified nation as a result of the American Revolution and the ratification of the Constitution. The Civil War, in which more than half a million Americans died, completed the process of nation building by forcing the secessionist, slaveholding southern states to remain in the Union against their will and guaranteeing the new nation would hold together for the foreseeable future.

In Europe the inward-looking process of nationalism was balanced by the late-nineteenth-century growth of imperialism, an outwardly directed effort to rule territories considered to be inhabited by less-civilized races. Imperialist European nations gained control of much of the Indian subcontinent, portions of East Asia, and, by the end of the century, most of Africa. While the United States was neither capable of nor particularly interested in taking part in Asian and African imperialism until the very end of the century, the new nation engaged in a sort of continental imperialism in which it wrested control of the Indian and Hispanic territories to its immediate west, subjected the native inhabitants, sent out waves of Euro-American settlers, and eventually incorporated the newly settled territories into the United States itself rather than ruling them as imperial possessions. As a result of this process, the United States began to orient itself away from the Atlantic, which traditionally had been the umbilical cord between the colonies and their mother country, and instead looked west toward the interior of the continent. In many ways this new, inward focus signified a turning away from the connections to Europe and Africa that had been so significant during the colonial period, prompting many Americans to imagine that their nation might become self-sufficient enough to remove itself from much of the turmoil of the Atlantic world.

However, it was never possible for the new nation to avoid the wider world entirely. Millions of immigrants from Ireland, Germany, China, and other lands poured into the United States to find work in its factories, farms, and mines, and along its developing canals and railways. But, beyond this massive influx of immigrants, the very effort to fix its boundaries and create a more independent economy brought the new nation into contact, and sometimes conflict, with the world.

_ᴄ⌒⌒⌒_

During this period, the United States made its biggest impact on the world through its political culture. The American Revolution and the U.S. Constitution created a sensation throughout the western world. George Washington and Benjamin Franklin gained international renown, and the republican ideals of "life, liberty, and the pursuit of happiness" that Thomas Jefferson wrote into the Declaration of Independence would become incorporated into subsequent revolutions, most notably in France in 1789. Thus, the United States was at the center of the great age of revolutions, which reordered the western world by ending the reign of kings, remaking colonies into independent nations and ripping apart the old Atlantic world economy. The Atlantic world was further rocked by the notion of freedom for slaves, which the new United States initially seemed to champion but which, by mid-century, prompted a Civil War that nearly destroyed the new nation.

The nineteenth-century United States was far less influential commercially and militarily. Americans focused mainly on the home continent in the world of commerce, with an emphasis on developing an independent national economy, in contrast to the earlier colonial dependence on British mercantilism. Conquests and acquisitions in the west, from the Allegheny Mountains to the Pacific, brought the new nation millions of acres of farmland, which ensured its agricultural independence. Similarly, massive industrialization in the East and Midwest helped to alleviate earlier dependence on European manufacturers. Nevertheless, both these developments ultimately tied the new nation to expanding world markets in new ways. The remarkable success of American farmers produced surplus agricultural goods frequently sold for profit in worldwide markets stretching to Europe and Asia. American agriculture became largely dependent on such markets so that, by the end of the century, falling prices for grain in distant places such as Poland could bankrupt farmers in Kansas and the Dakotas. Likewise, America's growing and productive manufacturing sector began to look for overseas markets. This development, in turn, would further push the United States to seek overseas influence in the coming twentieth century as a means of gaining secure outlets for surplus merchandise.

Despite its victory over Britain, the post-revolutionary United States was paradoxically more vulnerable militarily than it had been as a colony to a powerful empire. The very republican ideals of the American Revolution prompted unease at the notion of a large standing army, especially among those who remembered the trouble the British military had caused them. What little military muscle the new nation had was used not to jostle with the European powers on the Atlantic but to secure the western territories from Native Americans and potential European rivals. For the most part, the new nation avoided military conflict with the great European powers, seeking instead to become a neutral power that would not need to maintain a large military but could, instead, profit commercially by trading with warring European powers. After 1815 or so, the United States became more confident militarily and began to look overseas for possible conquests. Nevertheless, its greatest military struggle would be the Civil War. It would only be at the very end of the century that the United States could begin to think in earnest of establishing an overseas influence.

CHAPTER FOUR

The Idea of Freedom in an Age of Slavery

GETTYSBURG AND THE WORLD

On a clear November day in 1863, as the American Civil War neared the end of its third year, President Abraham Lincoln joined a procession of more than 12,000 veterans and war widows through the little town of Gettysburg, Pennsylvania. Less than five months before, one of the most brutal battles in military history raged through the surrounding countryside, resulting in more than 50,000 casualties. When the processional arrived at the new Soldiers' National Cemetery, where many of these soldiers recently had been buried, Lincoln, in his high, undistinguished voice, delivered one of the most memorable speeches in American history. "Four score and seven years ago," he began, "our fathers brought forth on this continent a new nation, conceived in liberty, and dedicated to the proposition that all men are created equal."

Generations of school children have memorized these words as a patriotic duty. They may not realize that this first sentence of the Gettysburg Address paraphrases the Declaration of Independence of 1776, but, like Lincoln, most people who write or think about American ideals have that document in mind. Even today, these words remain central to Americans' and the world's understanding of what is best and most appealing about American culture. Yet the ideas declared by the American Revolution were not native to America. They were, in large part, a product of European culture that crossed the Atlantic with America's colonists.

This chapter explores the international origins and global impact of the revolutionary notions of self-government and individual rights central to American political culture. The Declaration of Independence brought those ideas together in an unprecedented and alluring package, but as Lincoln well knew when he spoke at Gettysburg, the new nation that claimed them as its heritage did not always follow them in practice, nor was it always the world's leading exemplar of the ideas of liberty and equality in the century following independence.

THE AGE OF REPUBLICAN REVOLUTION

America's revolution was the first in a series around the Atlantic world that pitted republican revolutionaries and liberal ideals against monarchical rulers. The ideals of the Declaration of Independence and the reputation of George Washington would serve as inspirations for many of these revolutions. As a result, the United States appeared to be at the leading edge of western political culture for many years after the American Revolution.

Europe and the American Revolution

In the decade before the Declaration of Independence, the American colonies underwent a series of local disturbances, conflicts, and particularized rebellions. England's tax policies sparked riots and protests from Massachusetts to Georgia. By 1774, these various protest movements were beginning to coalesce under the guidance of a revolutionary committee calling itself the Continental Congress. This body, consisting of experienced political leaders from all 13 colonies, would declare independence in July 1776. By so doing, they transformed a series of local conflicts into what would prove to be the first successful colonial rebellion in modern history. A committee of the Continental Congress dominated by Thomas Jefferson of Virginia encapsulated the two central ideas of this rebellion within the Declaration of Independence. First, by asserting that it was necessary for the colonies "to dissolve the political bands" connecting them to England, they implied that, under certain conditions, colonized people had a right to break away from their colonizers to create their own nation. Second, by listing a series of "self evident" truths—"that all men are created equal, that they are endowed by their creator with certain inalienable rights, that among these are life, liberty, and the pursuit of happiness"—and by asserting that the governed had a right to overturn any government that violated these basic rights, they attempted to transform the rebellion from a particularized conflict between Americans and their English governors into a universal revolution for freedom.

Jefferson's effort to universalize the American Revolution reflected his commitment to Enlightenment liberalism, particularly his references to "inalienable rights," "self-evident" truths, and "Laws of Nature" (for more on Enlightenment thought, see chapter 3). One reason Jefferson invoked these ideals was to

gain European approval, and to attract enlightened Europeans to the American cause. Famously, the declaration attracted a young, dashing, fabulously
wealthy French nobleman, Marie-Joseph Paul Yves Roch Gilbert du Motier,
Marquis de Lafayette. One of many French officers seeking to enlist in the American army, Lafayette quickly rose to prominence and gained an appointment as
General George Washington's aide-de-camp, in part because of his sympathy
for the revolution's Enlightenment ideals. A self-described "soldier of freedom,"
Lafayette volunteered his services to make America "the respected and secure
haven of virtue, honesty, tolerance, equality, and a peaceful freedom."[1] A young
French-educated Polish nobleman named Tadeusz Kosciuzko joined Lafayette
in America, probably out of similar idealistic motivations. A student of Jean-
Jacques Rousseau and other Enlightenment thinkers, Kosciuzko viewed himself
as a friend to liberty throughout his eventful life. In America, he gained notice
for his engineering skills, attaining the rank of colonel in the rebel army and
serving as an aide to General Nathanael Greene.

In addition to Enlightenment ideals, American revolutionaries employed a
second strand of thought more particular to England. Described as Real Whig
ideology, or republicanism, it had roots in the opposition to the king that
emerged during the English Civil War (1640–49), when rebels executed King
Charles I, and the so-called Glorious Revolution of 1688, when they forced King
James II into exile. Codified by the writings of John Trenchard and Thomas
Gordon, Real Whig thought extolled republican government (i.e., one that was
representative but not fully democratic) and warned of corruption and incipi-
ent tyranny on the part of the king and his court. While Real Whig political culture lost influence in eighteenth century England, it continued to be important
in the American colonies, where fears of a corrupt and tyrannical king seemed
far more plausible after 1763 when colonists, who could not elect representatives to Parliament, became targets of new taxation schemes. This republican
philosophy emerged as the dominant political ideology among revolutionary
leaders, who frequently described themselves as "whigs."

Another English tradition known as "popular radicalism" influenced other
American patriots. Popular radicalism was most closely associated with arti-
san culture—that of the men who performed skilled labor in trades such as
blacksmithing, printing, and shoemaking, usually in cities or towns. These individuals sought to protect what they thought of as their customary rights, including fair prices, equitable taxes, and respectful treatment from their social
superiors. Any perceived violation of these rights might drive protesters into
the streets, where they performed elaborate "rough music" rituals aimed at

humiliating their oppressors, such as tarring and feathering (in which the offending party was stripped, dipped into hot tar, covered with feathers, and forced to run through the streets) and, occasionally, violent rioting. To popular radicals of the 1760s, no figure was more inspiring than John Wilkes, a member of Parliament and editor of a newspaper called *The North Briton*. When Wilkes implied in his newspaper that King George III was a liar, authorities quickly arrested him. He was eventually expelled from his seat in Parliament but not before his supporters staged massive popular demonstrations and riots. "Wilkes and Liberty" would be the battle cry of English radicals for many years to come. In the American colonies, middle- and lower-class radicals in places like Boston, Philadelphia, and New York employed similar tactics as their displeasure with British rule grew during the 1760s, sometimes even invoking the name of Wilkes. For example, Paul Revere, a Boston silversmith and whig leader, crafted an elegant silver bowl commemorating Massachusetts's defiance of the king, on part of which he engraved "Wilkes and Liberty" and "No. 45," a reference to the offending volume of Wilkes's newspaper.

The man who most exemplified both Real Whig republicanism and Anglo-American popular radicalism was an English-born corset maker turned journalist named Thomas Paine. In England, young Paine embraced radical politics and likely met Wilkes in 1770. In 1774, he met Benjamin Franklin, then colonial Pennsylvania's agent in London. The two shared a common background as artisans (Franklin was trained as a printer) and similar political sensibilities. In 1775, carrying a letter of reference from Franklin, Paine arrived in Philadelphia to begin a career in journalism, a profession for which he apparently had no training or experience. Nevertheless, by January 1776 he published his pamphlet *Common Sense*, which would prove to be the most influential piece of literature in the entire American Revolution, and one of the most important catalysts for independence. Although Paine's ideas were original and idiosyncratic, his pamphlet clearly drew both on Real Whig republicanism and on popular radicalism, particularly in its direct attack on the "monarchical tyranny" of the king—a charge most Americans were still hesitant to voice. Paine's writing was also rooted in Enlightenment thought, and like Jefferson he sought to universalize the Revolution when he wrote, "The cause of America is in very great measure the cause of all mankind," and accused England of "declaring War against the natural rights of all mankind." Perhaps it was Paine's ability to combine all these strands in easy-to-read language that made his pamphlet the best-selling publication printed in America to that time and undoubtedly the most influential in precipitating independence.

The Atlantic Revolutions

Nearly continual revolution throughout Europe and the Americas marked the half century following the Declaration of Independence. Revolutionary ideals bounced back and forth across the Atlantic and throughout Europe so frequently and from so many directions that it is impossible to trace how any one revolution influenced the others. Because it was the first, and because of the universal ideals expressed by its leaders, the American Revolution served as an important example to subsequent revolutionaries. After 1789, however, the French Revolution, which would depose a king and explode the entire social structure of one of the world's great powers, probably proved more influential. Nevertheless, subsequent rebellions, particularly those of colonies, would continue to draw from the rhetoric of the American Revolution and the new nation's constitution.

Even before the French Revolution, the American Revolution proved influential in places such as Holland and Ireland, where groups sought to overturn ruling monarchs or reform existing governments. Benjamin Franklin, who served as America's wartime representative in pre-revolutionary Paris, became a huge favorite of the French people and a friend to influential Enlightenment thinkers such as Voltaire, many of whom admired his scientific experiments on electricity. After the Revolution, Thomas Jefferson replaced Franklin, serving as the new nation's minister to France during the early years of the French Revolution. His old friend the Marquis de Lafayette, now an important revolutionary leader, frequently consulted with the author of the Declaration of Independence, and the two collaborated on an early draft of what would become the Declaration of the Rights of Man and Citizen (1789), which would seek to universalize the French Revolution much as Jefferson's declaration had done for the American Revolution. Parallels between the two documents are striking, including the French declaration's assertion that "men are born free and equal in rights" and that all governments must preserve the "natural rights" of "liberty, property, security, and resistance to oppression."

As the French Revolution commenced, the United States was implementing its new Constitution, written in 1787, and inaugurating George Washington as the first president. The Constitution, with its three-part division of government into legislative, executive, and judicial branches, owed much to British political practices, as well as to earlier state constitutions written in 1776 and after. However, the notion of a written constitution to be ratified by the population at large was uniquely American, and it would become one of the new nation's greatest and most influential contributions to the world. The French followed suit, enacting a written constitution in 1791 that delineated the executive and legislative branches and, like its American predecessor, incorporated a bill of rights. In 1799, when France's first emperor, Napoleon Bonaparte, overturned the 1791 constitution, he drafted a new American-style document delineating the government's executive, legislative, and judicial branches and had it ratified by popular vote.

By the 1790s France's republican revolution took a radical, violent turn. Early leaders, including Lafayette and Thomas Paine (who came to France in 1789 and soon published his *Rights of Man,* perhaps the most important defense of the French Revolution) soon lost favor, eventually landing in prison. Under the "Terror," thousands of former revolutionaries and members of the old regime lost their heads to the guillotine, a new and supposedly more humane form of execution. Radicals executed King Louis XVI and Queen Marie Antoinette in this fashion in 1793. France's radical new leaders sought to export antimonarchical revolutionary ideals throughout Europe by invading neighboring countries and overthrowing their kings and princes. The French army's successes buoyed revolutions in Belgium, Poland, Holland, Switzerland, and Italy. Some were relatively elite republican revolutions resembling the earlier stages of the French Revolution, while others were more broadly democratic and radical.

Although the ideals of "liberty, equality, and fraternity" associated with France were most influential, aspects of the American Revolution also proved inspirational, particularly in Poland, which experienced two revolutions, in 1791 and 1794, to gain independence from Russia and to implement a more republican government. There, King Stanislas, who initially supported the revolution, placed a bust of George Washington in his study and assented to a new, written national constitution, the second such document in history after the U.S. Constitution (and just before the French). Tadeusz Kosciuzko, who had returned home from America after a short stay in France, became commander-in-chief of Poland's 1794 revolution, for which he also wrote the Act of Insurrections, the equivalent of America's Declaration of Independence. In it he called for "freedom, integrity, and independence" as well as "life, security, and property," a clear echo of the Declaration of Independence and the Declaration of the Rights of Man.[2] Unlike Jefferson, who sidestepped the slavery issue, he went so far as to attempt to free the Polish serfs, who served in a state very similar to American slavery. Sadly, Kosciuzko was crippled by a war injury and captured by the Russians as the revolution fell apart. After his release from prison he returned to the United States, where he resumed his friendship with Jefferson, trying unsuccessfully to convince the author of the Declaration of Independence to free his slaves.

An important, unintended consequence of the French Revolution was a series of revolts by slaves and "free men of color" in France's West Indian colonies. Even before the French Revolution began, antislavery ideas then popular in France and a rumor that King Louis XVI planned to abolish slavery prompted a slave uprising on the island of Martinique in 1789. French revolutionary idealism as embodied in the Declaration of the Rights of Man proved particularly influential among free blacks on the sugar-producing island of Saint Domingue. One of their representatives, Vincent Ogé, pressured France's revolutionary Constituent Assembly to grant full citizenship to free black men. The assembly eventually did so in 1791, but by then it was too late to stop rebellion in Saint Domingue, where enslaved and free blacks had initiated the only successful slave revolt in the Atlantic world, eventually creating the new nation of Haiti, the second independent nation in America and the first to be ruled by people of African descent. The Haitian Revolution also prompted an uprising on the nearby island of Guadeloupe and may have influenced other Atlantic-world slave revolts and conspiracies, including Gabriel's Rebellion in Virginia (1800).

The leaders of the Haitian Revolution were well aware of the ideals of the American Revolution. A regiment of free colored men from Saint Domingue fought against the British in America where they, no doubt, learned of efforts to abolish slavery in Massachusetts and other northern states. Many of these men subsequently became active in the Haitian Revolution. An early draft of Haiti's Declaration of Independence had been modeled on the American Declaration of Independence, but the revolutionary leader Jean-Jacques Dessalines thought it too moderate, prompting a new, more radical version calling for "independence or death" and pledging to "forever ensure liberty's reign in the country of our birth."[3]

In Latin America, where revolution came in two waves, the example of the American Revolution and George Washington also proved influential. Although presaged by a 1780 Indian revolt led by Tupac Amaru II in Peru, the first widespread round of Latin American rebellions was triggered by Napoleon's 1807 invasion of Spain and the subsequent collapse of the Spanish monarchy. The leaders of these and subsequent Latin American revolutions were primarily elite native-born men of European descent. The most significant early leader, Francisco de Miranda, was a close student of the history and government of the United States who fought against England as a Spanish captain off the coast of

Florida during the American Revolution. Afterward, he lived briefly in the United States, where he met Alexander Hamilton, and possibly George Washington and Thomas Paine. Later, he would also meet Thomas Jefferson before leaving the United States to fight in the French Revolution and live in Paris. After a long period of planning failed revolutionary attempts, he helped push Venezuela to declare independence from Spain July 5, 1811, making it the second mainland American colony to declare independence.

Spain soon crushed these Latin American revolutions, but a second round, beginning in 1816, enjoyed greater success. A series of southern revolts in modern-day Chile and Argentina led by José Francisco de San Martín and Bernardo O'Higgins followed the French and American precedents of declarations of independence and written constitutions securing liberty, equality and property. To the north, Simon Bolívar had fought with Miranda earlier and, like his compatriot, drew on the ideas of the French and American revolutions. Like Miranda, too, he lived for a time in France and visited the major cities of the United States. After the first round of revolutions failed, he escaped to Haiti, where President Alexandre Pétion pledged to support him, provided he free Venezuela's slaves. Bolívar admired the U.S. Constitution, although he doubted whether it would be appropriate for the united states he dreamed of forming in South America. When, in 1826, Lafayette awarded him a medallion symbolizing the connection between Bolívar and George Washington, Bolívar acknowledged Washington as "the outstanding citizen-hero, the champion of freedom, who on the one hand has served America and on the other the Old World of Europe." [4]

PURSUING HAPPINESS AND FREEDOM

After the American Revolution a flood of European visitors washed ashore in the United States to view the new republic. Perhaps the most famous was a French nobleman named Alexis-Charles-Henri Clérel de Tocqueville who grew up in the years following the French Revolution, when his nation reverted to monarchy. In 1830 Tocqueville left France, as he wrote, "with the intention of examining, in detail and as scientifically as possible, all the mechanics of that vast American society which everyone talks of and no one knows." After completing his tour he wrote, "I saw in America more than America; it was the shape of democracy itself which I sought . . . I wanted to understand it so as at least to know what we have to fear or hope therefrom." [5] For another famous visitor, Englishwoman Frances Trollope, American culture represented a disturbing example of social democracy in which there was little respect for high birth or high rank. What she found most worrisome in Americans' way of life was its "leveling effects on the manners of the people."[6] Yet, whether admiring or critical, Tocqueville, Trollope, and many other European visitors shared a sense that the United States provided a window onto their own future.

Democracy and Liberalism

At the time of the American Revolution, the United States was neither a political democracy, a government of the people by the people, nor a social democracy in which social rank was nonexistent. Nearly all of the new state constitutions, written shortly after the Declaration of Independence, established property requirements for voting, barring poor people from the ballot box. And nearly all women and African Americans were unable to vote. However, by the time of Tocqueville's visit, America was in the process of becoming more democratic; nearly every state allowed all white men to vote, regardless of wealth. England was moving in a similar direction, particularly with the Reform Acts of 1832, which made Parliament far more representative of the population at large, even though voters faced property requirements.

More than political democracy, foreign visitors to the United States like Mrs. Trollope feared the social and cultural leveling associated with social democracy. Tocqueville noted that "the social state of Americans is eminently democratic" and worried that Americans' love of equality might exceed their love of liberty.[7] Elite Americans, too, chafed at the social equality celebrated (if not always practiced) by the supporters of President Andrew Jackson. A wealthy Washingtonian named Margaret Bayard Smith wrote approvingly of the majesty of President Jackson's 1829 swearing in, but she scorned the "rabble" who attended his inaugural ball. The celebration at the White House resulted in "scrambling, fighting, [and] romping" and the celebrants destroyed "cut glass and bone china to the amount of several thousand dollars" in their rush to secure alcoholic refreshment. Tellingly, Mrs. Smith compared Jackson's supporters to the "mobs in the Tuilleries and at Versailles" during the height of the French Revolution.[8]

The age of Jackson was also one of economic liberalism. Succinctly described by the Scottish economist Adam Smith as a policy of "let us alone" (*laissez-nous faire*), economic liberalism rested on the proposition that individuals ought to be able to make their own economic calculations free of government interference. As discussed in chapter 3, economic liberalism was a reaction to the oppressive policies of European mercantilism, which restricted trade both at home (through price fixing, licensing fees, state-supported monopolies, and the like) and abroad (through tariffs, duties, and prohibitions on imported and exported goods). President Jackson announced a policy of "equal rights" whereby government would not interfere in the domestic economy, creating, at least in theory, a level playing field for all, in contrast to Europe, where government was expected to confer benefits on the well born. Nevertheless, the administration continued to impose tariffs, sometimes quite heavy, on foreign goods under the logic that there could be no level playing field until other nations also dropped their tariffs. Smith's ideal of "free trade"—that is, duty-free international commerce—remained unattainable.

At the same time, under Prime Minister Robert Peel, England also moved toward economic liberalism. There, the controversy was over the so-called Corn Laws, which set tariffs on imported wheat and other grains. Liberals and others concerned about the price of wheat held enormous mass meetings in the 1840s to protest these laws. After the Corn Laws apparently made it impossible for starving Irish people to buy wheat during the potato famine of 1845, Parliament repealed them, much to the joy of English liberals and to the disappointment of the old elites whose profits came from their large agricultural holdings.

Transatlantic Reformers and Radicals

In Europe and America, this period of democratization and liberalization was also one of social reform and radical experimentation. For example, prison reform had long been an issue in England, where cruel conditions and the high incidence of capital punishment began to seem inhumane. Ideas of English reformers such as Jeremy Bentham and Samuel Romilly influenced construction of state-of-the-art American penitentiaries in New York state (1819) and Philadelphia (1829). In turn, these American prisons attracted European reformers interested in duplicating them in their own countries. In fact, examining these prisons had been the original motivation for Tocqueville's journey to America. Officials from England and Prussia also visited on similar missions.

While the impetus for prison reform came largely out of Enlightenment philosophy, religious enthusiasm inspired many other reform movements in the United States. At the dawn of the nineteenth century a great religious revival known as the Second Great Awakening swept through the new nation. Longstanding Protestant denominations drove much of the excitement, but the highly democratic denomination of Methodism, founded in England by John

Wesley in the 1730s and only recently transplanted to America, was also very influential. In turn, Methodists and members of newly formed American denominations such as Mormonism sought to spread the revival throughout the Atlantic world as they proselytized in Africa and Europe. In America, reformers and radicals were also influenced in countless ways by the idealism unleashed by the American Revolution and encapsulated in the Declaration of Independence's insistence on the rights to life, liberty and the pursuit of happiness.

The women's movement is a good example of how these strands wound together. Although Americans and Europeans generally expected women to stay at home and avoid public affairs, they made an exception for participation in church activities, understood to be appropriate for women because of their importance to the moral well being of families. Consequently, during the Second Great Awakening, when American churches became more and more involved in moral reforms, ranging from the temperance movement (anti-drunkenness) to Sabbatarianism (prohibiting work on Sundays), women became active participants and even leaders. Many of these activists developed strong ties to a transatlantic network of reform-minded women. Some American women, including Elizabeth Cady Stanton, attended an international antislavery convention held in London in 1840. When the men who dominated this event refused to allow women to be seated as delegates, Stanton and others began to consider the inferior position of women. She later wrote, "As the convention adjourned, the remark was heard on all sides, 'It's about time some demand was made for new liberties for women.'"[9] In London, Stanton met a fellow American, Lucretia Mott, and the two determined to form a society to advocate for women's liberty in America and to hold a women's rights convention.

It took eight years, but they eventually held that convention at Seneca Falls, New York, in 1848. In her opening speech, Stanton linked the progress of women to the advance of civilization and to the movement toward a religious millennium. The famous Declaration of Sentiments produced by the convention connected women's liberty to the ideals of the American Revolution by employing the language of the Declaration of Independence. It proclaimed, "We hold these truths to be self-evident: that all men and women are created equal; that they are endowed by their Creator with certain rights; that among these are life, liberty, and the pursuit of happiness." The Seneca Falls Convention and subsequent women's rights conferences caught the attention of many European women, including another British visitor to America, Harriet Martineau, who wrote a long letter supporting the cause. From a Paris prison, two French women also wrote, urging all women to support the cause and blaming the failure of European reform efforts on the exclusion of women and the refusal to acknowledge their "right to liberty, equality, and fraternity."[10]

While female reformers worked to improve American society, some radicals sought to create entirely new worlds, perfect communities that followed reformers' ideas to their logical extremes. These utopian communities derived from influences ranging from Christian millenarianism to secular socialism. Many were founded by non-Americans, such as the famous Shaker communities, which followed the teachings of the English religious figure, Mother Ann Lee. European ideas influenced others, such as the various "phalanxes" that followed the philosophy of French socialist Charles Fourier. The United States offered an attractive location for such experiments partly because of the ready availability of land but, more importantly, because of the lack of repressive government authorities and the widespread commitment to the "pursuit of happiness."

The little frontier town of New Harmony in southern Indiana offers a particularly useful example. It was founded as a religious community by a German religious sect that followed the teaching of George Rapp. Rappites were millenerianists (they believed the second coming was imminent) and communists (they did not own private property) who did not believe in hell and, like the Shakers, eschewed marriage and practiced celibacy. Persecution by the established Lutheran church in Germany prompted Rapp and hundreds of his followers to cross the Atlantic and settle in western Pennsylvania beginning in 1803. In 1815 the entire community, now 800 people strong, moved west to New Harmony. The experiment was prosperous enough and well-enough known for the famous English poet, Lord Byron, to refer to it in his comic epic *Don Juan* when he wrote that Rapp, "either meant to sneer at Harmony / Or marriage, by divorcing them thus oddly. / But whether reverend Rapp learn'd this in Germany / Or not, 'tis said his sect is rich and godly, / Pious and Pure, beyond what I can term any / Of ours."[11]

By the early 1820s, Rapp had decided to sell the New Harmony property and move his prospering community back to Pennsylvania. He found a buyer in Robert Owen, who rose from poverty to become, paradoxically, both a wealthy British industrialist and a socialist. Owen was already famous for his model factory town, New Lanark, Scotland, but by the 1820s he was hoping to found a more purely socialist settlement. After purchasing New Harmony, he appealed to Americans to join his ideal city. "By a hard struggle you have attained political liberty," he told them, "but you have yet to acquire real mental liberty, and if you can not possess yourselves of it, your political liberty will be precarious and of much less value."[12] By 1825 about 900 people had followed him into Indiana, including some Europeans, many of them advocates of the radical methods of the Swiss educator, Johann Heinrich Pestalozzi. Despite early successes, like most utopian experiments, New Harmony soon succumbed to infighting. Owen intensified the problems with his July 4, 1826, Declaration of Mental Independence, which angered many Americans with its denunciations of private property, organized religion, and marriage.

Another European radical to find fertile ground for utopian experiments in the American West was the pioneer feminist, Frances Wright. Born in Scotland to a father who was a follower of Thomas Paine, she was exposed early to radical ideas. She first learned of America through the writings of Carlo Botta, an Italian, and soon set off to the United States to explore "a new country inhabited by free men."[13] After coming back to Europe, she became a close companion of the Marquis de Lafayette, with whom she returned to America in his triumphal, nostalgic 1824 tour. While there, she met Robert Owen and became intrigued with New Harmony. The dismal plight of American slaves prompted her to create her Nashoba colony in Tennessee as a place where slaves might work to buy their freedom. The experiment lasted four years but finally failed, in part due to controversy over Wright's support for universal desegregated education, opposition to marriage, and implied approval of sexual relations between the races. In the end, Wright freed the 30 slaves still living at Nashoba and arranged for them to emigrate to Haiti.

Meanwhile, in Europe, radicals staged a spectacular but short-lived series of revolutions in 1848. Combining elements of nationalism, liberalism, democracy, and radicalism, they overturned the French monarchy for a time (it would be restored in 1852). Tocqueville now reissued his book so that the new French republic might learn from America's example. In Germany, Italy, and Hungary, revolutionaries attempted to institute democracy and national unification. Like many of their American counterparts, these European radicals often subscribed to various types of socialism and admired the *Communist Manifesto* published in 1848 by two young German radicals named Karl Marx and Friedrich Engels, both of whom had moved to England. Americans initially embraced European revolutionaries as kindred republican spirits. They held enormous mass meetings celebrating the revolutions in most major cities and, according to one observer, "with one universal burst of enthusiasm [they] hailed the late glorious revolution in France in favor of liberty and republican government." [14] In her keynote speech at the Seneca Falls Convention, Elizabeth Cady Stanton specifically linked the American women's movement to the European revolutions that had occurred just months earlier. Another prominent

American feminist, Margaret Fuller, was an acquaintance of the Italian revolutionary leader Giuseppe Mazzini and participated in his "Risorgimento" while working in an Italian hospital.

These revolutions failed quickly, sending many of their leaders and participants into exile in the United States. Most famously, Lajos Kossuth, leader of the Hungarian revolution, stayed in America for several months in 1851 and 1852. He charmed Americans with his glamor and his insistence that Hungary wished to become "a republic like that of the United States."[15] Perhaps more importantly, many immigrants arriving in the United States shortly before and after 1848 brought radical European ideas with them. German artisans, in particular, had imbibed these ideas in their homeland and in France, where many of them learned their crafts. One of their leaders, a tailor named Wilhelm Weitling, had been an important socialist thinker in France and Germany during the 1848 revolutions and was an acquaintance and rival of Marx. Thanks to him and others, Germans played a major role, along with Irish workers, in the New York City labor uprising of 1850, in which thousands struck for better working conditions and higher wages and, in many cases, called for socialist-inspired innovations such as workers' cooperatives.

SLAVERY AND THE LIMITS OF FREEDOM

After an initial burst of enthusiasm for the 1848 revolutions, many Americans grew uncomfortable with events in Europe. While some radicals appreciated the turn toward socialism in France and Germany, many Americans, including the growing class of northern industrialists, believed in private property and mistrusted labor radicalism. In the South, the slaveholders who controlled the region were very uncomfortable with the idea of worker revolutions. By 1848, American slavery increasingly seemed abhorrent, if not anachronistic, in many parts of the world. European travelers noted it with distaste. Harriet Martineau called it a "tremendous anomaly" and "a deadly sin" against American principles.[16] For her and other European observers ranging from Tocqueville to British novelist Charles Dickens, the United States, once in the vanguard of revolution, now appeared out of step with the worldwide progress of liberty.

Abolitionism in the Atlantic World

Fifty years earlier, the United States had been a leader in the first wave of antislavery sentiment, aimed primarily at ending the Atlantic slave trade. This movement was, in part, rooted in religious sentiment. Quakers and Methodists in England and America were vocal opponents of slavery even before the republican revolutions of the late eighteenth century. The ideology of liberty that emerged from these revolutions served as a second spur to abolitionism. Opponents of slavery banded together to form abolitionist societies in Philadelphia and New York City in 1784, followed by the British Society for Effecting the Abolition of the Slave Trade in 1787 and the Société des Amis des Noirs in France in 1788. During and after the American Revolution, black and white Americans petitioned their legislatures to abide by the logic of republican ideals and abolish slavery and the slave trade. British abolitionists presented 102 such petitions to Parliament in 1788 and 519 in 1792. As many as half a million people signed these documents.

As a result of these groups' efforts, and economic and political factors, the international slave trade rapidly diminished. In 1788, the founding fathers of the United States gave Congress power to end American participation in the slave trade in twenty years, and Congress complied, outlawing slave importation as of January 1, 1808. The British Parliament followed suit, withdrawing from the slave trade on that same day. Denmark had preceded them in 1803. Other European empires now felt pressure to do the same. The Netherlands did so in 1814, and in 1815 France, which had resumed its participation in the slave trade under Napoleon, finally withdrew. In 1815, all the major European powers signed on to a declaration against the international slave trade at the Congress of Vienna. In the meantime, all of the U.S. states north of the Mason-Dixon Line had enacted legislation freeing their slaves. In most cases they passed gradual abolition or "free womb" acts, which allowed slave owners to keep their chattel but mandated that children of the slaves be freed when they reached a certain age, usually in their twenties. The only nations to free large numbers of slaves without conditions at this time were in the French Caribbean, where the revolt in Haiti, rather than abolitionist societies, prompted action.

After the abolition of the international slave trade, public interest in slavery declined for a time. In England, the success of the anti-slave-trade movement and the small number of slaves within the British Isles contributed to complacency, while the Napoleonic Wars distracted the public. France, under the government of Napoleon Bonaparte and his successors, suffered economically from the loss of Haiti to slave rebellion and was not inclined to initiate further antislavery measures. In the United States, attempted slave rebellions in Virginia and South Carolina and a large revolt in Louisiana made slave owners reluctant to free more people, lest they instigate further unrest. Additionally, the increasing popularity and profitability of the cotton crop in the South made slavery more economically viable. Consequently, many southern states passed laws forbidding the freeing of slaves. Perhaps the only option remaining to planters wishing to divest themselves of their slaves was to send them elsewhere. The American Colonization Society, founded in 1816 to facilitate the emancipation and relocation of slaves, created the colony of Liberia in West Africa, to which it shipped approximately 6,000 former slaves. This project followed the example set by England's Sierra Leone colony, located near Liberia. The only significant attack on slavery during this period came in Latin America, where Bolívar and other rebels freed numerous slaves partly due to ideology and partly to strategic needs.

By the late 1820s, abolitionism began to regain popularity in England and the United States as part of the movement toward democratic and liberal reform. Prompted in large part by a pamphlet written by an Englishwoman named Elizabeth Heyrick entitled *Immediate, Not Gradual Emancipation* (1824), the new wave of "immediatist" British activists called for a complete end to slavery in the British empire without delay. The Anti-Slavery Society, reestablished in 1830, garnered widespread support for abolition and other democratic reforms, as did dozens of female anti-slavery societies. In 1833 large public meetings in the major cities and petitions containing roughly 1.5 million signatures, including one signed by 350,000 women, put additional pressure on Parliament. An influential Anti-Slavery Society convention held that year insisted on immediate abolition. As a result of this public pressure and other political and economic concerns, Parliament passed the Abolition of Slavery Bill, which promised to free roughly 800,000 colonial slaves once they completed a transitional "apprenticeship" period. Parliament also provided substantial financial compensation to the former masters.

Similarly, American abolitionists moved toward immediatism by 1830. Far more than in Britain, part of the impetus came from slaves and free blacks. David Walker, a free black man living in Boston, wrote an important immediatist pamphlet, *An Appeal to the Colored Citizens of the World*, in 1829. Later, many former slaves toured the country as abolitionist lecturers demonstrating the evils of slavery with examples from their own lives. Perhaps the best known were Frederick Douglass and Sojourner Truth. William Lloyd Garrison, the most famous and arguably most radical of the white abolitionists, was inspired in part by Elizabeth Heyrick's pamphlet and, quite possibly, by David Walker, who was a fellow Boston journalist. He began printing his influential immediatist newspaper, *The Liberator*, in 1831. He incorporated a women's section into this publication and made heavy use of the image of a kneeling female slave with the motto "Am I not a woman and a sister," which had earlier been pioneered by British female abolitionists.

Black and white women in the United States played an important role in the abolitionist crusade. They were tireless antislavery speakers, often causing controversy when they addressed mixed audiences of men and women. Heyrick's influence on the American movement prompted Lydia Maria Child, an American, to ask, "Has not the one idea that rose silently in Elizabeth Heyrick's mind spread until it has become a world's idea?" [17] Maria Weston Chapman, educated in England, became a leader in Boston's abolitionist movement and wrote a book that later influenced Harriet Martineau. As already noted, Elizabeth Cady Stanton, Lucretia Mott, and many other American women traveled to London to attend the 1840 World Anti-Slavery Convention.

African Americans, too, forged connections with British abolitionism. For many years they held large celebrations in American cities on August 1 to commemorate the implementation of the British Abolition of Slavery Bill and to show support for similar measures in the United States. Many leading African American abolitionists, including Frederick Douglass, journeyed to England in the 1840s to lecture on American conditions and meet English and European allies. Charles Lenox Remond, a free black from Massachusetts, served as a delegate to the London World Anti-Slavery Convention where he and Garrison staged a dramatic walkout when the convention refused to seat women. Remond stayed in Britain for nineteen months, busily lecturing on abolition and other reforms. There he met Daniel O'Connell, one of Ireland's most influential reformers and an abolitionist who called for the British antislavery movement to turn its attention to the United States after 1833. At O'Connell's request, Remond returned home carrying a petition signed by 60,000 Irishmen urging Irish-Americans to join the fight against slavery.

Despite Revolutionary-war era antislavery efforts and the end of the slave trade in 1808, the number of slaves in the United States jumped from roughly 1.2 million in 1810 to nearly 4 million by 1860. Without a doubt slavery was more entrenched than ever before in the American South.

Emancipations and Reconstructions

Outside the United States, the revolutions of 1848 led to a dramatic increase in the pace of emancipation. Alexis de Tocqueville and other French abolitionists attempted for more than a decade to convince their government to follow Britain's lead and free the quarter million people enslaved in the French colonies. Finally, after the 1848 revolution, the new French republic agreed, despite much opposition from West Indian planters. In central and eastern Europe, the events of 1848 helped to topple the ancient institution of serfdom. Although the same race as their masters, serfs occupied a position similar to that of slaves on American plantations. By law they were bound to the land they worked and, therefore, they were essentially bound to the lords who owned that land. During the early nineteenth century, serfdom in Russia was already beginning to collapse in the face of economic problems and serf rebellions. The 1848 revolutions, with their promise of widespread liberty, prompted further serf uprisings—161 in Russia in 1848 alone. As a result of these developments, Austria freed 12 million serfs in 1848, Hungary freed 7 million in 1853, and Russia freed over 20 million in 1861. In sum, nearly 40 million people had been freed during this 13-year period.

By 1860, the American South was one of only four remaining slave societies in the Americas, along with Puerto Rico, Cuba, and Brazil (although slavery still existed in some countries undergoing gradual abolition under "free womb" laws). Southern slave owners, feeling threatened by the election of President Abraham Lincoln, attempted to secede from the United States in 1861 to create a plantation society that would be safe from antislavery measures contemplated by Lincoln and his Republican party. This effort prompted the U.S. Civil War (1861–65), which, to the rebels' dismay, ended slavery in the United States, much as other wars such as the Haitian Revolution, the Latin American revolutions, and the 1848 revolutions ended bondage in Haiti, Latin America, and Central and Eastern Europe. As in these places, enslaved people in the United States played a part in ending their bondage, in some cases by escaping from plantations and joining with Lincoln's army. By the end of the war African Americans made up roughly 10 percent of the Union Army.

Ultimately, however, American emancipation was a legal process. During the war, Lincoln used his war powers to issue an Emancipation Proclamation. It was a measure aimed at undermining the rebels' morale and eroding their ability to procure slave labor. However, as the war progressed, northerners increasingly saw emancipation of the slaves as a crucial end in and of itself. In the Gettysburg Address, Lincoln attached this goal to the revolutionary ideals of the Declaration of Independence when he described the United States as a nation conceived in liberty and equality. Looked at this way, there could be no place for slavery in the union. Abolitionists such as Frederick Douglass had long made the same point, but with the success of the Union Army, this interpretation of national ideals now triumphed. As a result of this wartime victory and the disenfranchisement of most white southerners, Congress and the states ratified the Thirteenth Amendment to the Constitution, which made slavery illegal and immediately emancipated nearly four million American slaves in 1865.

Like all emancipations, this one forced the former slave society to reorganize itself. Because the southern states were under federal control following the Civil War, this task fell largely to the U.S. Congress, controlled by northern Republicans, most of whom remained hostile to the former slave owners. As they attempted to reconstruct their society, Americans sought to learn from British West Indian emancipation. Some found inspiration in the rise of a landowning black peasantry in Jamaica, while others, particularly in the South, were appalled by the former slave owners' loss of control of Haiti and other West Indian islands. After recounting the history of these places, a writer in a Kentucky newspaper concluded that the emancipated slave must be taught that "he is *free*, but free only to labor." Even Russia's example entered the discussion when Congressman Thaddeus Stevens praised "that wise man, the Emperor of Russia," on the grounds that after setting free the serfs, "he compelled their masters to give them homesteads upon the very soil which they had tilled."[18]

Despite the expectations of some former slaves that they were to receive "forty acres and a mule," Congress ultimately did not grant them land. However, unlike virtually all other former slave societies, the United States did agree to provide the freed men with full citizenship and the right to vote with the Fourteenth and Fifteenth Amendments respectively (1868 and 1870). These amendments, coupled with disenfranchisement of white southerners led to a brief period during which former slaves gained significant political power. During this period of Reconstruction (1865–77) more than 600 African Americans were elected to state legislatures, and throughout Reconstruction they served as a majority in the lower house of the legislature of South Carolina, formerly the most virulently pro-slavery state. At the national level, voters elected 16 African Americans to the House of Representatives.

Racism and American Exceptionalism

As the United States fell out of step with much of the Atlantic world over slavery, American racism and pro-slavery sentiment also became increasingly virulent. During the revolutionary era many southern planters, like Thomas Jefferson, viewed slavery as a necessary evil. The acquisition of new states and territories due to the Louisiana Purchase and the Mexican War of 1846–48 vastly expanded the amount of land open to slavery, forcing Americans to assess whether they wished to continue that institution. Slaveholders, frightened by the Nat Turner rebellion (1831), were reluctant to free slaves or loosen restrictions. In the decades before the Civil War most southerners convinced themselves slavery was a positive good for slaves, whom they assumed to be racially inferior and incapable of self-government. George Fitzhugh, an important apologist for southern slavery wrote of the slave, "He is but a grown up child, and must be governed as a child, not as a lunatic or criminal."[19] Additionally, the radicalism of America's abolitionist leaders created a backlash in the South and many parts of the North. Even in Massachusetts, a center of abolitionist activity, William Lloyd Garrison was attacked by a mob and nearly lynched. In 1857 the Supreme Court's decision in *Dred Scott v. Sandford* opened up all United States territories to slavery and suggested that the courts might eventually allow slavery in the northern states where it had long been abolished

At the same time, Euro-Americans increasingly viewed Native Americans as racially inferior people. By the 1830s, rather than signing treaties with Native Americans as Europeans had for centuries, American officials determined that Indians were not separate nations but were subject to the laws of the United States and could therefore be removed from their territory by law rather than by negotiation. This approach famously led to the Cherokee Trail of Tears in which the army forced the remnants of the Cherokee Nation to march 1,200 miles from their homes in the southeastern United States to reservations in what would become the state of Oklahoma. Anti-Indian racism was also clearly expressed in the new ideology of continental expansion: manifest destiny. A New York newspaper editor named John O'Sullivan coined the term in 1845. But the concept that it was the God-given right of white Americans (frequently described as "Anglo-Saxons") "to overspread and to possess the whole continent which providence has given us for the development of the great experiment of liberty and self government" reached deep into American history while clearly excluding Indians and Hispanics from the experiment of liberty and self-government.[20]

Pre–Civil War inequalities had been justified on the basis of servitude—i.e., that slaves could not own property or participate in politics— but Americans after the war justified inequality upon the idea of racial inferiority. They drew in part from anthropological notions of racial inferiority known as "scientific racism" that were on the rise in Europe, prompted in part by the debate over abolition. In 1847 the scholars who made up the French Societé Ethnologique held a conference to discuss "the distinctive natures of the white race and the black race" at which most participants agreed the white race represented intel-lectual superiority, scientific creativity, and progress. American Indians, they decided, were somewhat closer to whites than to blacks. In the United States, an Alabama physician named Josiah Nott, who argued that blacks and whites were two entirely separate species, borrowed heavily from scientific racists such as Frenchman Arthur De Gobineau, whose major work, *The Inequality of Human Races*, Nott translated into English.

After 1877, white southerners used these ideas of white superiority and black inferiority to justify their efforts to subvert the Fourteenth and Fifteenth Amendments by disenfranchising African Americans, frequently through the terroristic activities of the Ku Klux Klan and other vigilante groups. As a result, African Americans lost the political gains of the Reconstruction era. In the state of Louisiana, for example, there had been 130,334 black voters as late as 1896, but by 1904 there were only 1,342. This loss of political power allowed southern legislatures to pass a series of "Jim Crow" laws in the 1880s and 1890s mandating segregation of the races. Economically, most southern African Americans became tenant farmers who were often so heavily indebted to white storekeepers and landowners that they were unable to attain financial indepen-dence. As a result of these developments, by the 1890s American society, par-ticularly in the South, was now reorganized along racial lines. This situation gained the imprimatur of the Supreme Court through the *Plessy v. Ferguson* de-cision of 1896, which approved of Jim Crow legislation, provided that blacks be allowed "separate but equal" facilities, a proviso that was generally ignored by local and state governments, which relegated blacks to crowded, inferior schools, hospitals, and other public facilities.

_⌒ ⌒_

American political culture brought the new nation to the world's attention during the Revolutionary era. The combination of Enlightenment values, evan-gelical religion, and inexpensive real estate made the early republic a mecca for utopian experimenters from throughout the western world. Nevertheless, de-spite Jefferson's and Lincoln's egalitarian rhetoric, crucial inequalities re-mained. Most glaring was the contradiction of racism. The "color line" would, as W. E. B. Du Bois famously predicted, become the crucial problem of the next century, along with new forms of inequality produced by the dawning indus-trial age.

CHAPTER FIVE

Developing a Continental Market

EXPLORERS AND TRADERS

November 1805 brought steady, chilly rains and low-hanging fog to the Oregon coast. Through the mist, the Lewis and Clark party paddled down the Columbia River. This small group of Euro-Americans and their Native American guides had begun their epic journey more than two years earlier and nearly 4,000 miles to the east. Now, as they approached the mouth of the Columbia, Lewis and Clark were on the verge of becoming the first white men to cross the North American continent. As they neared the Pacific, they were surprised to see native Americans carrying muskets, pistols, and tin powder horns and wearing European-made sailors' jackets, overalls, shirts, and hats. Some cursed at the Americans in English. One native who was particularly fluent told Lewis and Clark that he and his people received many of their goods from an American named Mr. Haley. Others indicated that there were more white men on the nearby coast.

The man the Indians called Haley was most likely Captain Hill of the Boston, Massachusetts, brig *Lydia*. Massachusetts merchant ships had begun trading with Native Americans in Oregon nearly twenty years earlier. In the single year of 1801, 14 Boston ships had traded here, and this activity was one reason why Lewis and Clark came to Oregon. Even before the United States purchased the vast inland territory known as Louisiana, President Thomas Jefferson had planned to send them across it to seek a quicker route to the Pacific than the torturous four-to-six-month journey around South America that Captain Hill and other American traders endured to reach the Northwest. This was nothing less than the old dream of a Northwest Passage to connect the Atlantic world to the riches of Asia. Once the United States purchased Louisiana, President Jefferson added a new dimension to Lewis and Clark's mission, requesting that they report on the nature of this new territory and its native inhabitants.

Today, Lewis and Clark are remembered primarily for successfully completing this aspect of their mission. But, in fact, they failed at the primary objective: identifying an easier passage to the Pacific. However difficult Captain Hill's voyage had been, it was far preferable to Lewis and Clark's two-year trek, which included a grueling portage over the Rocky Mountains.

Nevertheless, this chapter demonstrates that Lewis and Clark's expedition and the Louisiana Purchase helped to spur the development of a vast new continental empire that transformed American commerce. Proponents of this westward expansion sometimes praised it as a way to free the United States from its dependence on Europe by enabling the new nation to create its own inland markets and produce all that its inhabitants needed on its rich new farmlands. But Lewis and Clark's voyage also demonstrated that the development of internal American markets was never entirely independent of foreign trade. However much some Americans might hope to retreat from their global connections, in the end, domestic economic developments would always result in new commercial connections to the wider world, just as Lewis and Clark's journey down the Columbia River had linked them to the markets of the Pacific rim.

ESCAPING MERCANTILISM

In declaring the colonies independent of England, the American Revolution separated the United States from British mercantilism just as surely as it severed the Anglo-American political connection. It was only after the successful, but enormously expensive, Seven Years' War that many North American colonists became profoundly dissatisfied with British mercantilism. In the decade between 1764 and 1774, Britain enacted a series of new laws designed to raise revenue from the colonies in order to pay the war debt. These acts, which included the Sugar Act (1764), Stamp Act (1765), Townshend Duties (1767), and Tea Act (1773), employed various strategies, but they all met with heated, often violent colonial protest. Colonists saw them as marking a fundamental shift in British mercantilism. They believed the acts saddled them with a new role: creating tax revenues. To their minds, this shift meant that they were now expected to contribute to the empire twice: first as producers of raw materials exclusively for Britain, and second as taxpayers. Additionally, many of these new acts sought to close old loopholes that had facilitated colonial smuggling and to create new legal authorities to crack down on the smugglers themselves.

Consequently, the colonists began to see their struggle as one against British mercantilism, as well as British political authority. The first Continental

Congress attempted to combat both with its Association of 1774. The Association called on the colonies to begin a program of domestic manufacturing and to curtail most trade with Britain. In so doing, the Continental Congress hoped that it could use economic pressure to force repeal of the new taxes. But, as events proceeded and the king and Parliament refused to back down, the Association also marked a first strike against British mercantilism by essentially pulling North American raw materials out of Britain's economic empire and by introducing the possibility that the colonies might build up their own domestic manufacturing sector rather than relying on British goods.

After declaring independence, Congress was free to take stronger measures to break the United States away from British mercantilism. Some members of Congress, including future president John Adams, hoped to open up free trade with the world. In 1776, Adam Smith had just published *The Wealth of Nations,* which would become the most important attack on mercantilism and exposition of free trade ever written. Most Americans were still unaware of this book and its arguments, but their dissatisfaction with the strictures of the British empire pushed some of them toward similar conclusions. Adams and his supporters in Congress proposed a "new model treaty" that would allow "a free trade . . . with all nations." The measure did not pass, and even if it had it would have been unenforceable so long as the British navy could deter other nations from American ports and capture American ships on the high seas. However, the model treaty set a precedent for the new nation's Treaty of Amity and Commerce with France. Signed in 1778, this treaty created a system of free trade between the United States and the French empire and protected neutral countries from having their ships seized during times of war.

After the Revolution, American merchants worked hard to expand trade into European markets that had been closed to them under British mercantilism. Between 1790 and 1807, American exports more than quintupled, from $20 million to $108 million. The majority of exports were actually "re-exports," goods such as coffee, sugar, cocoa, and pepper, which American merchants bought in one part of the world and sold in another. Before the Revolution, mercantilism dictated that most such goods flow between colonies and mother country before they could be sold outside of the empire. Now freed of the British empire, American merchants could trade these items between colonies and between empires, provided more powerful nations did not force them to stop. American ships also were now able to carry domestic products such as tobacco, rice, and indigo to parts of Europe and the European-controlled West Indies that had been off limits before the Revolution. In 1780 they began trading tobacco directly to Sweden, and throughout the 1780s and 1790s, they shipped large quantities of tobacco and rice directly to the Netherlands. None of this activity would have been allowed under the Navigation Acts. Most notably, exports to France soared, so that by 1791 France and her colonies took nearly one quarter of all American exports. At the same time, American merchants began to trade frequently with Spain and Portugal, which together accounted for about 16 percent of American exports in 1791.

Despite these developments, America's post-Revolutionary trade hardly operated in a free, open atmosphere. Because it was no longer part of the British empire, the new nation could no longer trade freely with Britain or its colonies, and the British government was disinclined to allow their former colonies access to the British West Indies, which had once been crucial and lucrative trade destinations for American merchants. For a time during the French Revolution and the ensuing Anglo-French Wars, America's neutrality led to its ships being welcomed into European and West Indian ports where ships flying the flags of belligerent countries were forbidden. However, by the early 1800s both France and Britain increasingly confiscated ships belonging to America and other neutral nations in order to prevent the cargoes from reaching their enemies. As a result of these confiscations and the onset of the War of 1812 between Britain and America (which was itself, in part, a reaction to these confiscations), American exports plunged from a high of $108 million in 1807 to a low of $6 million in 1814. After 1815 they began to recover, but they would not match the 1807 level for nearly two decades. Furthermore, despite opening new markets to neutral traders, America's merchants continued to depend on trade with the British empire, which remained the nation's most important trading partner throughout the nineteenth century, despite British restrictions on American shipping. Even Thomas Jefferson, a great advocate of trade with France, regularly purchased British goods. "It is not from a love of the English but a love of myself that I sometimes find myself obliged to buy their manufactures," he confessed to Lafayette after purchasing an expensive riding harness from England.[1]

American ships seeking to enter new markets in and around Africa also ran into restrictions. After the Revolution, American merchants, particularly those from Rhode Island, rushed into the African slave trade. During parts of the 1790s American ships annually carried as many as 10,000 Africans to be sold as slaves. Rhode Island ships alone made at least 200 slaving voyages to Africa between 1794 and 1804 despite new limitations on the slave trade. Estimates suggest that in the 20 or so years after the Revolution, America's share of this trade increased eight-fold to reach roughly 16 percent of all slaves exported from Africa. Reformers cheered, but slave merchants were hit hard when the federal government outlawed American participation in the slave trade in 1808. The U.S. government usually enforced this ban, with the notable exception of the Brazilian slave trade of the 1840s, when American traders may have played a part in as many as half of the 350,000 slave importations.

American traders hoping to take advantage of new markets in Spain, Portugal, and other parts of southern Europe found themselves restricted by North African pirates or corsairs who captured hundreds of American sailors and numerous ships sailing in and near the Mediterranean between 1785 and 1815. North African states such as Algeria, Tripoli, and Morocco had long sponsored piracy as a means of raising revenue, by ransoming captives back to their homelands or by signing treaties with the captives' government guaranteeing tribute to the North Africans as a sort of protection payment. No longer protected by British payments and the British navy, the new nation found itself particularly vulnerable to these pirates and, consequently, the promising Mediterranean trade was severely limited.

Perhaps the most spectacular result of American neutrality in the Anglo-French wars was the development of new commercial connections throughout Asia. The first American merchant ships reached the Indian Ocean in 1784, where they had particular success in the Mascarene Islands, especially on the island of Mauritius, located approximately 600 miles to the east of Madagascar. During the Napoleonic Wars, more American ships arrived in Mauritius than from any other nation. Trade with the French-controlled Mascarenes allowed Americans access to spices, coffee, sugar, and other products that they had obtained primarily from British merchants previous to the Revolution. American traders also created important links to the Dutch East Indies, the Spanish Philippines, and Hawaii during this period, creating trading networks that would have been impossible under the rule of British mercantilism.

The most important new Asian market during this period, however, was the supposedly insular empire of China. The first American ship, the *Empress of China*, arrived there in 1784. The ship's New York owners turned an impressive profit when it returned with a cargo of tea, the very product on which British taxes had helped spur the American Revolution just a decade earlier. America's trade with China rapidly increased over the next three decades, particularly when British shipping to Asia decreased during the Napoleonic Wars. More than 600 American ships arrived in Canton between 1784 and 1814, with 40 or more arriving annually during the peak years of the Napoleonic Wars.

The growing China trade helps to explain the English-speaking Native Americans that Lewis and Clark encountered when they reached the mouth of the Columbia River. American merchants, who had discovered that the Chinese were willing to pay a good price for otter fur, had already begun to trade with Native Americans in Oregon and Alaska for pelts on their journey to China, thereby pulling Indians into the expanding trade between the Atlantic and Pacific worlds. The most famous American merchant to facilitate this trade was John Jacob Astor, a New York millionaire who established the short-lived town of Astoria near the mouth of the Columbia in 1811 as a port where furs purchased from Native Americans could be loaded onto ships bound for China. Similarly, American merchants also traded with natives on the Pacific island of Hawaii for sandalwood, which sold well in China where it was used for wood carving and various medicinal purposes. Sadly, this China trade nearly led to the extinction of the sea otter in the Northwest and the depletion of Hawaiian sandalwood stores. Despite this environmental destructiveness, furs and sandalwood made up a relatively small portion of the new nation's China trade. Far more important, and even more international, was the trade in silver, which the Chinese valued more as a precious metal than as currency. Initially mined by enslaved Indians, Spanish-American silver had begun to flow into China by the sixteenth century. Silver, acquired primarily from Latin America by American merchants, probably accounted for about three-quarters of U.S. exports to China.

This newly developed trade to Asia dramatically demonstrated the new nation's growing contact with world markets after having freed itself from the strictures of British mercantilism. By the mid-nineteenth century, the value of American exports to Asia neared $3 million per year, at times exceeding the value of U.S. trade to Africa. Nevertheless, the value of this trade remained quite small in comparison to the more than $60 million in goods annually sent to Europe, and, despite the new republic's efforts to develop new markets worldwide, Great Britain remained its most important trading partner. Furthermore, once the Napoleonic Wars ended in 1815, the United States would lose its advantage as a neutral carrier, and trade with Asia would decline.

LOOKING INWARD, 1815–1860

As the U.S. population began to move away from the Atlantic coast and into the interior beyond the Appalachian mountains, the new nation's trade also began to move into the interior of the American continent. Settlers created an enormous continental empire that, by the 1840s, stretched from the Atlantic to the Pacific. Within this expansive territory they developed new transportation and communication networks that facilitated active and profitable new markets. Additionally, Americans constructed large new manufacturing projects that eased their dependence on imported goods and further contributed to the growth of inland markets serving eastern industrialists as well as western farmers. As a result of these developments, the U.S. economy became far less dependent on overseas imports and exports than it had been during previous years, allowing some Americans to dream of a nearly autonomous domestic economy that would not be affected by the volatility of the larger world.

The Continental Empire

The Democratic-Republican presidents Thomas Jefferson and James Madison, his successor, envisioned a nation that would be large enough to enable all its citizens to gain sufficient land to become independent farmers. Jefferson lauded yeoman farmers as "the most vigorous, the most independent, [and] the most virtuous of citizens."[2] For Jefferson, the Louisiana Purchase and westward expansion would serve to provide yeoman farmers with land for the foreseeable future, thereby ensuring that the new nation would become a self-supporting agrarian republic that would not depend on overseas trade for its survival. As a result of this vision and, later, the ideology of the new nation's "manifest destiny" to advance across the continent, the United States grew extremely rapidly. In 1763, British Americans occupied a narrow strip of land along the Atlantic coastal plain. By 1848, the United States occupied its current territory, with the exception of Alaska, Hawaii, and a small strip of land in the Southwest. This remarkable expansion embroiled the new nation in negotiations, threats, and warfare with Spain, France, Great Britain, Russia, Mexico, and numerous Native American tribes, a process described in the next chapter. The combination of land purchases and the removal of resident Native Americans and Mexicans prompted millions of yeoman farmers, land speculators, and others to pour into the West. However, in contrast to the vision of the independent yeoman farmer, they and the new territories quickly became entangled with world markets.

Even Jefferson and his followers understood that the virtuous independence of the yeoman farmer was partly mythical. Most farmers, even in the early nineteenth century, grew crops in order to sell at least a portion for profit. That was certainly the case with most migrants to the West. Consequently, the expansion in territory created new markets, both domestic and overseas. This market expansion was intimately connected to the nineteenth-century revolution in transportation, which began with the construction of new roads and new canals. The 363-mile long Erie Canal, completed in 1825, linked the Hudson River to the Great Lakes, opening up the western portions of New York and the upper Midwest to settlement by farmers who could use it to transport their grain across the mountains to New York City and sell it to merchants throughout the world. This trade also helped transform New York into the nation's most important Atlantic port and largest city. While Americans did not invent the steam engine, they immediately recognized its potential. Steam-powered railroads and steamboats could transport goods cheaply and quickly across the vast continent. By 1840, the United States had 3,000 miles of railroads, compared to only 1,818 in all Europe.

This transportation revolution linked even the most remote western households to world markets. On the rude southern Indiana frontier in the spring of 1828, twenty-year-old Abraham Lincoln agreed to take a load of farm produce to market. He and his partner saw the crop loaded aboard a nonmotorized vessel known as a flatboat at the Ohio River town of Rockport. They guided the boat 200 miles down the Ohio River until they reached the Mississippi at Cairo, Illinois. From there they floated nearly 700 miles down the great river to New Orleans, where they sold their cargo and Lincoln pocketed $25 for his trouble. From New Orleans, the Indiana grain and other farm products from the Mississippi and Ohio valleys floated over the ocean to ports around the world. Lincoln and his partner returned home, spending part of the journey upstream aboard one of the new steamboats that helped to make the Mississippi into America's most important trade route. Lincoln and his frontier neighbors might have been yeoman farmers, but they were hardly independent of each other or the larger world.

The wave of westward movement became a tsunami when the United States acquired California in 1848 just after James W. Marshall discovered gold at Sutter's Mill, near present-day Sacramento. Fortune hunters from Asia, Chile, Hawaii, Britain, continental Europe, and Mexico, as well as the eastern United States rushed in, boosting California's non-Native American population nearly 20 times, from 14,000 in 1848 to 250,000 by 1852. Most notable was the arrival of America's first substantial Chinese immigration. More than 65,000 Chinese made their way to antebellum California, where they worked primarily as merchants or miners. In 1852 alone, 20,026 Chinese arrived in the new state, making them California's largest ethnic minority. The gold rush turned San Francisco into an important Pacific port nearly overnight, as its population rose from 800 in 1848 to 35,000 by 1850. Such spectacular growth prompted easterners and Californians to dream of a new transcontinental railroad connecting San Francisco to the Atlantic. Jobs in the new mines and construction of the railroad pulled even more immigrants, many of them Asian, into California, further connecting North America to Asian economies. By the 1860s roughly half of all Chinese Americans worked at railway construction.

The westward wave could hardly stop at San Francisco. Fusing manifest destiny with a quest for profits, many Americans now saw the Pacific islands and Asia as the new western frontier. A Washington, D.C., publicist called for Americans to continue across the Pacific in order to "arouse the sluggish and dormant nations of the East into activity," and another writer described "'a far west' on the isles of the Japanese Empire and on the shores of China." Senator Daniel Webster lauded expanded commerce in the Far East as a means "to enable our enterprising merchants to supply the last link in that great chain which unites all nations of the world."[3]

Manifest destiny, the push for profits, and new transportation technologies all played a role in America's dramatic encounter with Japan in the 1850s. Japan's Tokugawa shogunate had essentially closed their island nation to western trade by 1640. The United States, Britain, and other European nations made unsuccessful efforts to end this policy of seclusion in the early nineteenth century. Japan allowed only a few Dutch ships to dock in the port of Nagasaki, far from the center of population. Throughout the 1840s an American merchant and promoter named Aaron H. Palmer made efforts to convince the American and Japanese governments to establish trading relations. But it was not until the conquest of California and the gold rush that relations with Japan became an important priority for Washington. The growth of the port of San Francisco and various plans for transcontinental railroads and canals, as well as for an American trans-Pacific steamship line, forced American business interests to think seriously about Pacific markets. While the new steamships could reach East Asia relatively quickly, they depended on coal, which was scarce in most of Asia but was believed to be abundant in Japan. Americans now hoped that Japan could supply them with fuel as well as valuable markets for trade.

As a result, President Millard Fillmore ordered Commodore Matthew C. Perry to take an armed squadron of four ships to Japan in order to initiate relations with the Tokugawa regime. In July 1853, Perry's ships became the first western squadron to reach Japan in more than 200 years. Perry arrived with a letter from the president stressing America's new proximity to Japan. The

United States, Fillmore wrote, "now extend from sea to sea . . . [and] our steamers can reach the shores of your happy land in less than twenty days." [4] Well aware of the realities of western transportation technology, which had already been revealed to them by the Dutch, and intimidated by Perry's heavily armed squadron and the likelihood of even more fearsome British squadrons in the future, the Tokugawa leaders agreed to initiate diplomatic relations with the United States. Soon after, they made similar arrangements with Britain and Russia.

Five years later, in 1858, the United States became the first western nation to negotiate a trade agreement with Japan. Japanese agreements with France and Britain soon followed. The United States took great pride in its role opening the Japanese market. When the first Japanese delegation arrived in New York in 1860, the poet Walt Whitman exulted, "I chant the world on my western sea . . . I chant the new empire, grander than any before." [5] In Japan, however, stresses created by the end of seclusion soon led to the violent overthrow of the ancient shogunate in 1868. World markets transformed Japan as well as America.

Manufacturing and Self-Sufficiency

Many Americans thought it was important to develop domestic manufacturing to escape dependence on Britain. The colonies had supported very little manufacturing, in part because of mercantilist strictures against it. During the Revolution some Americans, particularly artisans, viewed the boycott against British goods as an entering wedge for developing America's manufacturing capacity. Revolutionaries initiated some early manufacturing projects, most notably the American Manufactory in Philadelphia (1775), which hired several hundred employees and purchased some of the earliest industrial textile machinery in America. In lauding this project, the patriot leader Dr. Benjamin Rush noted, "A people who are entirely dependent upon foreigners for food or clothing must always be subject to them." [6] Not all agreed. In the 1780s Thomas Jefferson hoped Americans would "let our workshops remain in Europe." He feared that manufacturing would lead to factory towns on the order of Manchester, England, which would undermine his vision of a nation of independent farmers. But by 1816, like many members of his party, Jefferson had modified his position, writing, "Experience has taught me that manufactures are now necessary to our independence." [7] Nevertheless, much like westward expansion, the growth of manufacturing soon created greater national and global interdependence than self-sufficiency and independence.

The early industrial revolution, in which American manufacturing played a small part, was an international phenomenon. It originated in late-eighteenth-century England, where large coal deposits provided the energy for newly developed steam engines. English innovators found these engines useful in extracting more coal and in powering early railroads to transport the coal, which in turn powered more steam engines. The need for this machinery also led to the development of new iron and steel manufacturing techniques. But the hallmark of the early industrial revolution was the textile industry. From the seventeenth-century onward, Britain had admired cotton textiles produced at low cost in India. With the development of steam power, innovators soon realized that mechanization could allow England to produce textiles that could compete with Indian products. Soon English merchants were able to sell inexpensive mass-produced textiles throughout the world, particularly to colonies such as those in North America, where mercantilist regulations gave British textiles a monopoly. These profits further enriched Britain, providing more capital and more profit as incentives for further industrialization.

Freed from British mercantilist restrictions and seeking to strengthen their shaky economy after the Revolution, many Americans sought to bring their new nation into the industrial revolution. To do so, they needed to understand the new technology being developed in Britain. But this valuable technology was zealously guarded by its owners, who did not welcome competitors. As a result, American manufacturing enterprises resorted to stealing. As early as 1783 an Englishman named Benjamin Phillips smuggled textile manufacturing equipment into Philadelphia. A second Englishman, purportedly seeking to "check the advancement of the cotton manufactory in America," disassembled it and returned it to England.[8] To escape infuriated American manufacturing proponents, the Englishman went into hiding, eventually escaping the United States only with the assistance of the British consul. The most famous early American manufacturer, Samuel Slater, emigrated from England in 1789 after reading that a group of New Yorkers was offering a large reward to anyone able to build British-style machinery in America. Having memorized the details of such machinery, he disguised himself as a farmhand to fool British officials who were trying to prevent technology smuggling. After arriving in the United States, Slater went on to found one of the most important and well-known eighteenth-century American textile mills in Pawtucket, Rhode Island. His factory may have been the model for nearly all other New England factories of the 1790s and early 1800s. Somewhat later, a Boston merchant named Francis Cabot Lowell managed to memorize the details of British textile machinery while visiting Glasgow and Manchester. On his return, he used the information to set up the famous Lowell, Massachusetts, textile mills, which would become the world's first integrated cotton mills and among the largest American industrial enterprises established before the Civil War.

America's new manufacturing sector depended on British expertise as well as British technology. Despite British restrictions prohibiting the emigration of skilled artisans, a large proportion of the men who operated, repaired, and modified the new nation's industrial machinery were recent immigrants trained in Britain. Great Britain's first American consul, Phineas Bond, frequently urged his government to clamp down on skilled artisans leaving Britain and Ireland for America and bringing valuable equipment with them. However, as Bond himself admitted, it was extremely difficult to restrict this emigration, and by the 1790s skilled British and European workers had become the backbone of American manufacturing.

Perhaps the biggest challenge to American manufacturers was the new nation's relative shortage of labor compared to densely populated European nations. Early industrialists hoped to solve the labor problem by using the new "labor saving machinery" smuggled in from Britain and by employing women and children in their factories. The Lowell mills were particularly noteworthy for their early reliance on farm girls as factory operatives. The mills' managers defended this decision as a way to avoid creating a poverty-stricken working class like the one that had emerged in industrial England. The farm girls could be expected to work only a few years before marrying and moving into the world of middle-class respectability. Initially these temporary female workers did dominate Lowell's workforce. They expressed pride that as "daughters of freemen," they did not depend on the factories in the same way that England's impoverished working men did. However, this very sense of independence, when it translated into resistance to wage and benefit cuts, ultimately caused American manufacturers to reject the use of native-born women laborers and seek, instead, to employ immigrants.

By the 1840s the increasing need for immigrant industrial labor coupled with economic and political turmoil in Ireland and Germany contributed to massive emigration to the United States. In the latter part of the decade, more than 100,000 Irish immigrants were arriving in America annually, with 221,000 arriving in the peak year of 1851. Similarly, 215,000 Germans arrived in the peak year of 1854. A majority of Germans arriving in the 1850s already had manufacturing experience, making them valuable industrial employees in their new home. Irish immigrants, too, often were familiar with the craft of weaving, making them particularly well suited to work in the textile industry. As a result, foreign-born workers soon dominated the American industrial workforce. In Lowell, foreign-born workers made up a majority of the workforce by 1860, with nearly half of all workers born in Ireland. These developments prompted a backlash in the form of the Know-Nothing or American Party, which won a great deal of support for its anti-Catholic, anti-immigrant platform in the 1850s.

While American industry came to welcome foreign laborers, it sought to exclude foreign products that might compete with American goods. Hoping for a more integrated, interdependent national market, industrialists and others called for an "American System" in which southern cotton and northern wool would be sold to the new industrialists to produce American textiles. The role of the government would be to keep out foreign competition, to fund a modern transportation network to allow for exchanges between the regions, and to spur the creation of a more efficient banking system to make capital available for these improvements. Hezekiah Niles, one of the chief promoters of this system envisioned "an internal commerce . . . compared with which the foreign trade is of no great importance, except in cotton only."[9] Pre–Civil War protectionism reached its apex in 1828 when the so-called Tariff of Abominations imposed duties as high as 50 percent on some imported textiles.

Unfortunately for American System proponents, the South never quite conformed to their vision of an integrated national economy. While Hezekiah Niles and other proponents understood that the South would continue to export cotton, they underestimated the extent to which cotton exports would dominate the southern and, indeed, the national economy. Southern cotton production had been minimal in the eighteenth century, but with the introduction of Eli Whitney's cotton gin, which cut production costs by drastically reducing the amount of labor needed to produce the crop, annual cotton production grew nearly 100-fold from about 18 million pounds in 1800 to 1.7 billion in 1860. This enormous increase resulted, in part, from the rapid westward expansion of the cotton growing zone, which had been limited to a narrow sliver of the coastal Southeast in 1800 but, by 1860, included a vast conglomeration of plantations centered on Alabama and Mississippi and stretching from coastal South Carolina all the way into Texas. By 1840 nearly two-thirds of the world's cotton originated in this belt. Indeed, the growth of southern cotton production far outstripped the growth of American textile manufacturing. As a result, growers exported the majority of their cotton to Britain, where the industrial revolution had advanced much farther. From 1820 to 1860 the United States consistently exported 70 to 80 percent of its cotton crop, and by 1860 the value of exported cotton was greater than the value of all other exported goods combined.

Thus, rather than relying on trade with northern industrialists, southern cotton producers depended primarily on British and New York merchants who brokered exchanges of southern cotton for a variety of imports. Rather than contribute to an interdependent American system, cotton primarily expanded the foreign trade sector, tying southern planters as closely to England as to the northern United States. Southern planters' dependence on this overseas trade combined with their reliance on slave labor differentiated their economy from that of the North and West. This divergence caused serious tensions between the regions when, in the early 1830s, southerners vehemently protested the so-called Tariff of Abominations. Because they depended on trade with Britain, southerners feared that this tariff on imported textiles, most of which came from Britain, would eat into their profits, which were already declining due to the declining price of cotton. These fears very nearly led to civil war when, in 1832, South Carolina adopted an "ordinance of nullification" declaring both the Tariff of Abominations and the slightly more moderate 1832 tariff null and void. President Andrew Jackson threatened to subdue the rebels with force, but ultimately he negotiated a peaceful settlement through delicate diplomacy.

By the dawn of the Civil War, despite calls for economic independence, westward expansion and the development of manufacturing by no means severed the new nation's economic dependence on Britain and the wider world. Nor was the United States transformed into a predominately industrial society. The majority of Americans continued to work on farms, although nearly 20 percent now worked in manufacturing. America's exports continued to rise rapidly, with their value jumping six-fold from $52.5 million in 1815 to $333.5 million in 1860. The enormous size of cotton exports meant that, despite the anti-British, anti-mercantilist rhetoric of the Revolution, Britain continued as post-Revolutionary America's most important economic partner.

GLOBALISM AND ITS DISCONTENTS, 1860–98

After the Civil War, the United States grew still more connected to the worldwide economy due to technological developments and the rapid growth of the domestic economy. New manufacturing techniques and agricultural equipment improved American productivity. The ever-widening transcontinental railroad network insured that products from every corner of the continental United States could find their way to market. Improved shipping and the inauguration of the transatlantic telegraph cable in 1866 allowed American merchants to learn of international price fluctuations as they occurred and to use that information to sell American products for the best price, whether it be to Britain or Brussels. For some, particularly manufacturers and bankers, this expansion of global trade provided great wealth. But for others, particularly American farmers, late-nineteenth-century globalization proved more troubling.

Agriculture

The Civil War dramatically transformed American and world agriculture. Because of the ravages of war and the Union blockade of southern ports, the cotton crop was virtually destroyed during the five-year conflict. At the start of the war, England depended on the enormous southern cotton crop for raw materials for what was by far the world's largest textile industry. Southerners hoped that the "cotton famine" created by these wartime disruptions would bring Great Britain into the war as their ally. But, instead of supporting a slave regime in America, Britain decided to encourage cotton production in other portions of the British empire and around the world. Consequently, new cotton kingdoms sprung up from South America across Africa and into Asia. During the Civil War the value of cotton exports nearly quadrupled in Egypt and Brazil and nearly tripled in India, transforming these local economies and tying together America, Africa, and Asia into a global agricultural market. After the Civil War, American cotton production quickly rebounded, but falling prices, due in large part to increased global production, severely curtailed southern prosperity. A combination of increased competition and increased demand from American textile manufacturers also contributed to a decrease in the percentage of American cotton exported. While American cotton farmers regularly exported 75 percent or more of their crop before the war, afterward they rarely exported more than 65 percent.

During much of this period, wheat farming made more dramatic gains than cotton. After the Civil War, the amount of wheat grown in the United States shot up dramatically from roughly 151 million bushels in 1866 to more than 675 million in 1898. This rise was due to a variety of factors, including rapid settlement of the wheat-producing plains states, better rail and steam ship transport, and increases in efficiency due to the introduction of factory-made labor-saving equipment such as steel plows, mechanical reapers, binders, and mowers. Exports of wheat to the world market also grew dramatically, from 4 percent of the total crop in 1866 to, briefly, more than 30 percent in the early 1880s. However, as with cotton, closer connections to world markets also created increased price volatility, leading to a boom-and-bust cycle for American farmers, who now competed with grain producers in Europe, Asia, and throughout the world.

By the late nineteenth century these developments contributed to what is sometimes described as an "agrarian revolt." Small farmers in the South and West found it increasingly difficult to turn a profit. The high cost of farm machinery, the need for ever-larger plots of land, volatile crop prices, tight credit, competition from larger mechanized farms, and an inordinate number of natural disasters created frustration. To combat these problems, farmers joined together into self-help associations and ultimately formed a political party known as the People's or Populist Party. Populists sought to solve the agrarian problem through increased regulation of railroads, grain elevators, banks, and other organizations they believed were profiting from the farmers' distress. They also hoped to move the dollar from the gold standard, which limited the amount of currency issued to the amount of gold held in reserves, to a silver or bimetallic standard, which would allow the government to print a great deal more money, thereby making credit more readily available to farmers and other businessmen.

In its rhetoric at least, the agrarian revolt was also a revolt against globalization. Farmers frequently expressed hostility against foreigners—usually British or Jewish—who they believed controlled the world financial system. Farmers and others often talked of a plot by the "Anglo-American Gold Trust" to limit credit and control world markets. An agrarian politician warned his listeners to beware "Wall Street, and the Jews of Europe."[10] In his famous 1896 Cross of Gold Speech, Populist presidential candidate William Jennings Bryan equated support of the gold standard with "surrender[ing] the right of self-government and plac[ing] the control of our affairs in the hands of foreign potentates and powers."[11] Bryan and his agrarian supporters saw global markets and, particularly, the emerging international financial system as a threat to national sovereignty and prosperity rather than as an engine of economic development. In this regard they shared much in common with late-twentieth- and early-twenty-first-century residents of the developing world who expressed similar fears at the rise of the World Bank and other international agencies.

Industrial Revolution: the Second Phase

In the latter half of the nineteenth century, the Industrial Revolution entered a new phase. Earlier, it had been centered in the textile industries of western Europe and England. Despite the marked increase in manufacturing in pre–Civil War America, from a global perspective the United States had remained a secondary player. Now, the Industrial Revolution began to fan out through North America, central and southern Europe, Russia, and parts of Asia. Heavy industry replaced textiles as the most important product, and large corporations replaced or swallowed up smaller firms. It was during this new phase that the United States replaced Britain as the world's leading industrial economy.

After the Civil War, America's industrialization continued to be fueled by the needs of the continental empire. The Homestead Act of 1862, which provided cheap land for those willing to settle it, prompted farmers to begin breaking ground in formerly remote portions of the Great Plains and far West. Railroads soon followed, with more than 150,000 miles of new track constructed between 1865 and 1898. This construction created an enormous demand for metal rails and heavy equipment, which, in turn stimulated the nation's nascent iron and steel industries. Iron production more than doubled in the seven years following the Civil War from 856,000 tons in 1865 to 1.8 million in 1872, while steel production grew more than fiftyfold, from 3,400 tons in 1867 to 174,000 in 1873. The enormous extent of America's new railway system also spurred creation of the nation's first large corporations and its first corporate bureaucracies as railroad companies hired new managers and created new, complex corporate structures to integrate their far-flung enterprises. Like the railroad and steel industries, makers of farm implements also benefited from America's continental expansion. Perhaps most notable of these was Chicago's McCormick Reaper works, which produced the harvesters, mowers, and binders that were becoming necessities for American farmers. As early as 1851, McCormick's machinery impressed Europeans when it was displayed at the famous London Crystal Palace exhibition, often considered the first world's fair. By the 1880s McCormick's 1,500 employees were producing roughly 1,000 machines per week.

Despite the importance of the continental empire, America's industrialization also owed a debt to the nations of the world. Roughly 14 million immigrants, many of them skilled laborers, poured into the United States in the last four decades of the nineteenth century. As in previous decades, they were disproportionately represented in the industrial workforce, particularly in factory districts springing up in burgeoning inland cities such as Chicago, Cleveland, and Detroit. Some immigrants rose very high in the ranks, perhaps none more so than Andrew Carnegie, the son of a Scottish weaver whose way of life was destroyed by industrialization. His impoverished family migrated to industrializing Pittsburgh in 1848, where the father found work as a weaver and young Andrew found work as a "bobbin boy" in a textile factory. Carnegie would later work for the Pennsylvania Railroad before becoming a capitalist in his own right and, by the end of the century, America's most powerful industrialist and one of its richest men.

During this period, American industry also continued to acquire some of its technological processes from abroad. Carnegie learned of Henry Bessemer's new process for blasting steel during a visit to England. He eventually acquired the patent rights to the Bessemer process in America and used the new technology in his first major industrial venture, the Edgar Thompson Steel Works in Pittsburgh. The plant, which initially focused on producing steel rails, became the nucleus of Carnegie Steel. By the end of the century, Carnegie's company employed 20,000 people and was probably the world's largest industrial unit. Carnegie sold it for an astounding $480 million in 1900.

Besides foreign laborers and technologies, American industry also benefited from foreign investment. Despite the turmoil of the Civil War years, the United States, with its vast continental empire, growing population, and relatively stable government, looked like a very attractive investment to Europeans. American railroad securities became so popular that the London Stock Exchange opened a special section for them, and by 1875 more than half of all railroad securities quoted on Amsterdam's stock exchange were American. By the end of the century, 52 percent of the Pennsylvania Railroad, 65 percent of the Illinois Central, and 75 percent of the Louisville and Nashville were held by foreign investors. Public utilities, steel makers, and even large retailers also profited from foreign investment. Occasionally, foreign companies purchased entire firms, such as flour maker Pillsbury Washburn. Between 1870 and 1895 foreigners invested roughly $1.5 billion into the American economy, a sum that, while a significant source of capital, was still only a fraction of that provided by domestic investors.

By the end of the nineteenth century, the United States was, without a doubt, the world's greatest industrial powerhouse. In the 1880s, for the first time, the value of American manufactured goods surpassed that of agricultural products. In 1899 the value of American manufactures ($11.4 billion) was nearly 2.5 times that of agricultural products and more than a quarter of the nation's labor force was now directly engaged in manufacturing. By 1900 America's manufacturing output surpassed that of Great Britain, Germany, and France combined—quite a feat for a nation that had produced less than each of these competitors 40 years earlier. As a result of increased production, American firms also grew much larger, and by the end of the nineteenth century they entered into a "merger mania," in which they became enormous. A total of 319 mergers occurred between 1894 and 1904, and, in the peak merger year of 1899 alone, 106 firms were combined. By the end of the merger mania, 318 huge firms controlled an estimated 40 percent of American industry, and the size of these corporations would have important ramifications in the new century.

—◦ ◦—

Despite this remarkable industrial expansion, the United States continued to export a much smaller share of its manufactured goods than other leading industrial nations. As late as 1900, manufactured products made up only 32 percent of American exports, compared to 61 percent for agricultural products. This statistic illustrates the continuing importance of the growing home market, which, presumably, was able to consume those manufactured goods that were not exported—probably more than $10 billion worth by the end of the century. This massive domestic consumption and the heavy tariffs that promoted it by keeping out foreign competition did, to some extent, fulfill the earlier vision of American System promoters who had hoped to create a relatively independent home market. However, with a shrinking quantity of undeveloped land available in the continental empire and the continual rapid growth of American industry, this unusual reliance on the growth of domestic consumption could not last forever.

CHAPTER SIX

From Colonies to the Threshold of Empire

ON THE SHORES OF TRIPOLI AND ALGERIA

Commodore Stephen Decatur was America's greatest military hero in the six decades between the Revolution and the Mexican War. He led the United States to spectacular victories in two North African wars. The first, in Tripoli, would be immortalized in the opening of the Marines' hymn ("From the Halls of Montezuma to the Shores of Tripoli"). The second, against Algiers in 1815, was still more triumphant. For 30 years, corsairs from that North African capital had bedeviled American ships trading in the Mediterranean, capturing more than a dozen and holding their crews for ransom. With few options at its disposal, the United States had long paid an annual tribute for protection to the leader of Algiers, the Dey. But, by 1815, a strengthened American navy held the upper hand. In just a week of fighting, Decatur's squadron captured two of the Dey's warships, took nearly 500 prisoners, and killed their admiral. Decatur now successfully demanded that the Dey cease all hostilities against American shipping and release the United States from paying tribute. Next, Decatur sailed on to Tunis, another North African city-state that frequently harassed American and European shipping, to force their leader to sign a treaty similar to the one with Algiers. Finally, he led his squadron to Tripoli (now Libya) where he intimidated the ruling Bashaw into signing a similar treaty and then forced him to release ten European captives.

When he returned home, Decatur was treated to ceremonial dinners and parades in towns up and down the East Coast. In Washington, admirers wrote songs about him to the tune of "Yankee Doodle" and "The Star Spangled Banner." Newspapers across America praised him. One lauded him the "champion of Christendom," noting he attained "a glory which never encircled the brow of a Roman pontiff; nor blazed from an imperial diadem." Another, referring to the rescue of the ten captive Europeans in Tripoli wrote, "How delightful it was to see the stars and stripes holding forth the hand of retributive justice to the barbarians, and rescuing the unfortunate, even of distant but friendly European nations, from slavery."[1] Americans were jubilant, not only because of Decatur's victory itself but because, combined with America's perceived success against the powerful British military in the War of 1812, it seemed to mark a turning point.

After decades in which the United States was little more than a pawn in the larger global game played by France and Britain, Americans sensed Decatur's victory marked a sea change in their relations with Europe and the world. An American officer in Gibraltar wrote home, "You have no idea of the respect which the American character has gained by our late wars." Algiers's prime minister supposedly told Britain's consul, "You told us that the American navy would be destroyed in *six months by you* . . . and *now* they make war upon *us* with *three* of *your own vessels* they have taken from you."[2] Nevertheless, Decatur and the wars he fought are nearly forgotten today, despite the many towns and counties named for the hero throughout the United States. What was once perceived as a crucial turning point now seems almost a footnote to history.

This chapter argues that 1815 did mark a turning point when the United States emerged out of the shadows of European warfare to begin to become an empire itself. But the shift was only partly due to Decatur's exploits or any American actions. What was most important was the vicissitudes of the Second Hundred Years' War. While the war was under way, the United States was merely a pawn in the wider global conflict, but the nation's remote location and position of neutrality allowed its merchants to profit from the war and its farmers and speculators to gain from France's misfortunes when Napoleon sold it the massive Louisiana Territory in 1803. After the Second Hundred Years' War ended with Napoleon's defeat at Waterloo in 1815, the United States, invigorated by Decatur's display of naval power in North Africa and its survival in the War of 1812, moved toward assuming a greater role in global geopolitics. For most of the pre–Civil War period these ambitions were focused on North America, as the new nation built a continental empire by conquering Native American and Hispanic peoples. After the Civil War clearly established the new nation's continental boundaries, some Americans tentatively began considering the possibility of creating an overseas empire to rival that of the great European powers.

IN EUROPE'S THRALL

The American Revolution marked a critical turning point in the Second Hundred Years' War. While the Seven Years' War saw Britain at the height of its power (see chapter 2), the Revolution brought a bit more balance to Anglo-French relations by humbling Britain to some extent and depriving it of much of its American empire. After the Revolution, France would have its own revolution, which would result in the rise of Napoleon Bonaparte and a new, more aggressive Anglo-French struggle for control of the European continent and beyond. Any overseas activity on the part of the United States and its citizens before 1815 had to take into consideration this ongoing global struggle, whether it be Americans' fight to win independence from Britain during the American Revolution (discussed below), or the efforts of its overseas merchants to trade profitably during the Napoleonic Wars (discussed in chapter 5).

The Global American Revolution

The American Revolution began as a colonial revolt in a remote portion of the world and ended as a global struggle between France and Britain and their allies in which the new United States played the role of interested spectator. From the beginning, the colonies realized that their best chance for success against Britain was to tie themselves to France. However, they also feared that an alliance with France could ultimately become a matter of replacing one master with another. Therefore, they initially hoped to receive only financial assistance from the French rather than cementing a formal military alliance. In 1776, John Adams wrote, "I wish for nothing but commerce, a mere marine treaty with [France]."[3] This arrangement also suited the French government, which had suffered a financial crisis as a result of the Seven Years' War and had to balance its desire for revenge against the potential for further devastation from an all-out war against Britain. Thus, shortly before the colonies declared independence, France's King Louis XVI appropriated the modern equivalent of several million dollars in aid to the colonies. To maintain secrecy, the French government funneled the money into a dummy company headed by the celebrity playwright Pierre-Augustin Caron de Beaumarchais, best known today as the author of *The Marriage of Figaro* and *The Barber of Seville*. Beaumarchais's company then used the money to purchase shiploads of military supplies, including guns and ammunition, and send them to the rebellious colonies.

The Americans cleverly played France off Britain as they fought desperately against superior British forces. By late 1776, as the war slowed for the winter, it was clear that more assistance was needed. But France remained wary of becoming entangled in a new war, and the Americans remained wary of France. What broke the logjam was the Americans' massive and unexpected victory at the battle of Saratoga in September 1777. There, the Americans utterly destroyed a large portion of the British army and drove the enemy out of most of the strategically vital Hudson River valley. The victory was so unexpected and impressive that the French began to fear that Britain might negotiate a peace with the colonies, a prospect that would allow Britannia to turn all its forces against its traditional Gallic enemy. France wanted very much to prevent any such Anglo-American entente, and American diplomats stoked those French concerns by appearing to consider British overtures. These negotiations prompted the French foreign minister to wonder, "If we dissuade [the Americans] from listening [to Britain], what shall we give them as an equivalent?" The answer, he suggested, was "to enter the breach and make an engagement [with the Americans]."[4] In the end, the rebels signed two treaties with France on February 6, 1778: a commercial treaty and a Treaty of Alliance to maintain "the liberty, sovereignty and independence absolute and unlimited of the said United States." As a direct result of the latter, France would soon enter the war against Britain.

The importance of the French alliance to American victory can hardly be overstated. Not only did France provide money, supplies, troops, and artillery, but the French navy was able to offset the overwhelming superiority of Britain's navy, which, before French entry, was able to go pretty much wherever it wanted in North America. Perhaps even more significantly, France's entry into the war forced Britain to turn its attention and resources away from the American war in order to defend its navy and possessions around the world.

French support was crucial at the climactic Battle of Yorktown, Virginia, in October 1781. While it is largely known today as the battle that secured American independence, Yorktown more resembled a battle between France and Britain than one between colonists and colonizers. Despite the genius of George Washington's leadership, the battle could never have been won without French assistance. French pressure on British West Indian colonies (and the greed of British naval officers who plundered the West Indian island of St. Eustasia) kept a significant portion of the British navy away from the American mainland, allowing the French navy, under the command of Admiral le Comte de Grasse, to gain control of Chesapeake Bay. The combined American and French forces marching toward Virginia from the north numbered nearly 17,000 men, nearly half of them French. At the same time, the French admiral the Comte de Barras sailed out of Newport to carry French artillery toward Yorktown where Britain's General Cornwallis, unaware of these events, had set up camp after months of sparring with American troops under the command of the Marquis de Lafayette. All of these forces converged on the lower Chesapeake in late September. Once de Grasse's fleet blocked the British from entering the bay, Cornwallis's 6,000-man army was essentially trapped on Yorktown peninsula, surrounded by 7,800 French troops and 8,800 Americans, all supported by Barras's artillery. Cornwallis soon realized the hopelessness of his position, and the British commander surrendered to Washington, effectively ending the fighting in the United States.

However, the war continued for nearly two years without the United States. Instead, it became a far more global conflict, fought on four continents between four major world powers—France, Britain, Holland, and Spain. Britain had some successes, partially redeeming its American losses and pleasing the British public more than in the earlier stages of the war. In North America, fighting continued in the West Indies. After some setbacks, the British finally defeated the French navy at the Battle of Saints in April 1782. There they captured several French ships, including the one carrying Admiral de Grasse, who was forced to surrender to his British counterpart. This victory allowed Britain to retain its West Indian holdings, including Jamaica. When this news arrived in Britain, it filled the newspapers and caused widespread public elation. Britons also cheered successes in Europe and Africa. Ever since the French joined the war, Britain had feared an invasion across the narrow channel separating the two enemy nations. In 1778 France had gotten the best of a battle with a British fleet off the small island of Ushant but proved unable to follow up on its victory. In December 1782, when French and British ships again met near Ushant, the British gained a measure of revenge by capturing more French ships, further weakening France's navy. Farther south, along the western coast of Africa, British forces captured rich trading posts from the Dutch, who had entered the conflict when Britain declared war against them in December 1780. Most importantly, Britain managed to defeat the Spanish when they attempted to lay siege to the British-controlled Rock of Gibraltar, which guarded the entrance to the Mediterranean at Spain's southern tip.

These victories thrilled the British public, erasing the stain of defeat in America enough to allow the king to move toward an honorable end to the war. As it had during the war, the United States continued to play Britain off France in the peace negotiations, which resulted in the Treaty of Paris (1783). Concerned by French moves to preserve territory east of the Mississippi for Spain, American diplomats began to negotiate a separate treaty directly with Great

Britain rather than work with France as the terms of the Franco-American alliance dictated. By doing so, they were able to wrest favorable terms from England, including cession of all the territory below Canada and east of the Mississippi. France reluctantly went along with these negotiations rather than lose its American ally.

But before the war could end, one last set of battles had to be fought halfway around the world. India, which was being colonized by both Britain and France, presented a situation somewhat reminiscent of that in North America before the Seven Years' War. The two great rivals each sought influence over a vast region populated by natives and colonists—although India contained far fewer European colonists than America. As in North America, local people sought to play the two rivals off each other. In particular, a rebel leader named Hyder Ali enlisted French support in his struggle against Britain. After Yorktown, a large French fleet arrived in India, bringing with it soldiers to assist Hyder Ali's war against the British. As a result, France and Britain fought several battles off the Indian coast. By June 1783, British forces were near defeat, but, luckily for them, word arrived that the war had ended five months earlier. Britain had just managed to save southern India, which it would make into the nucleus of its nineteenth-century empire.

These eight years of warfare affected the lives of people on every continent. They also prompted a remarkable amount of movement of people between countries and between continents. The early stages of the war, of course, brought many British soldiers to North America for the first time. About 12,000 of the 32,000 British soldiers sent to America in 1776 were actually Germans recruited from central European states allied with the King of England such as Hesse-Cassel (hence the common description of these men as "Hessians"). By war's end, nearly 30,000 Germans fought in King George's army. One described his comrades as "a bankrupt tradesman from Vienna, a fringemaker from Hanover, a discharged secretary of the post office from Gotha, a monk from Wurnzburg, an upper steward from Meinungen, a Prussian sergeant of hussars . . . and others of like stamp."[5] Thousands of these soldiers remained in the new nation after the war, joining their fellow Germans who had arrived in the colonies earlier.

The war vastly accelerated the forced westward movement of Native American peoples, many of whom had supported the British against their expansion-minded patriot neighbors. The patriots' war against the natives continued after Yorktown, often using the same troops that fought the British, who were no longer present to protect their Indian allies. By 1783 an Indian delegation observed that the Americans were "extending themselves like a plague of locusts in the territories of the Ohio River which we inhabit."[6]

Other Native Americans who had allied with the British moved northward, crossing into the British colonies of Canada. They were followed by tens of thousands of white loyalists, who also supported the British during the Revolution. Many had their land and property confiscated by the victorious Americans. All told, as many as 100,000 loyalists fled the United States. While the majority settled in Canada from the maritime provinces west to Ontario, many others settled in the British West Indies in places like Jamaica and the Bahamas, and still others fled to British-controlled portions of Florida or back to England. Finally, thousands of African Americans followed the same pathways, either as slaves of departing loyalists or as freed people who managed to escape slavery by fighting with the British army.

Betwixt and Between

The great war powerfully affected all who fought it. The enormous expenses of fighting a war overseas and of maintaining a large army at home bankrupted King Louis XVI's government, eventually contributing to the French Revolution of 1789 and his execution. As France's republican revolution transformed itself into the prolonged violence known as the Terror, its new leaders began to conquer other European lands, purportedly to spread revolution and end monarchy. Great Britain also struggled under heavy debts after the war, not to mention the loss of much of its American empire. But, unlike King Louis, England's monarchy retained power and even flourished. The successes in the latter part of the war, the retention of India, the West Indies, and Canada as the centers of a new empire, and a new sense of pro-imperial patriotism on the part of the public made post-1783 Britain arguably more stable than ever. This spirit of nationalism and patriotism combined with the strength of the monarchy put England on a collision course with its traditional enemy, a newly revolutionized, anti-monarchical France.

The United States wanted nothing more than to remain neutral, avoiding alliances or warfare with either of the great European powers. President George Washington famously warned his countrymen to "steer clear of permanent alliances with any portion of the foreign world." Avoiding military entanglement with the great powers was also good for business. Under the theory that ships belonging to neutral countries should be allowed to trade with whomever they pleased—a principle held dear throughout American history—U.S.

commerce thrived after 1793 when France declared war on Britain. However, the resumption of Anglo-French warfare also posed new problems for the United States. Inconveniently, the new nation was still technically allied with France under the 1778 Treaty of Alliance which, it seemed, would inevitably pull it into war against Britain. Washington's declaration of neutrality essentially renounced U.S. obligations to France, causing new fears that France would try to force the new nation into the war. Those concerns seemed to become reality when the French minister to the United States, Edmund Genet, allowed French privateering vessels to use America's supposedly neutral ports in 1793, against the wishes of George Washington's administration. Additionally, France sought to force American ships to stop sending grain to England.

Ultimately, however, the greater danger came from England, which began stopping American ships in the West Indies in late 1793 as a means of preventing supplies from reaching the French Caribbean. In addition to seizing more than 250 American ships, Britain also provoked Indian attacks against American settlers in the upper Great Lakes and supposedly played a role in the seizure of American ships by Algerian pirates in the Atlantic. In response, many Americans now pushed for a second war against Britain, particularly those who were beginning to form the new Democratic-Republican party. Angry Americans threatened British officials in Baltimore, Philadelphia, and Norfolk, Virginia.

American anger waned after Britain rescinded its policy of seizing American ships and signed Jay's Treaty with the United States in 1795, resolving some of the two nations' disagreements. Conflict with Britain was soon replaced by a new war threat from France. The problems stemmed initially from the Anglo-American rapprochement. Tensions were greatly exacerbated when it became public that France had demanded a bribe from American diplomats seeking to repair the Franco-American relationship in what came to be known as the XYZ Affair of 1798. The public cried "millions for defense but not one cent for tribute" in response to this insult. The government took heed, spending millions to expand the army and navy. The latter had been disbanded after the Revolution but reinitiated in 1794 in response to the Algerian attacks on American shipping. Congress also poured money into a network of coastal forts to prevent French invasion of American cities. To do otherwise, according to a War Department memo, "would be to offer up the United States a certain prey to France."[7] While France never invaded, the two nations did fight an undeclared "quasi-war" at sea for more than two years, much to the delight of Great Britain and the pro-British Federalist Party in the United States.

The quasi-war ended after the United States and France signed the Convention of 1800, in which the United States paid an indemnity to terminate the alliance of 1778. This treaty ushered in a period in which U.S. ships were once again able to sail relatively unmolested by the warring powers. However, after a short Anglo-French truce, warfare between the powers escalated after 1803. British ships, and to a lesser degree French vessels, now resumed their practice of intercepting American merchant ships and impressing (or seizing) their crews to solve their naval manpower shortages. It has been estimated that nearly 3,000 American sailors were impressed during the 1803–6 period. American resentment came to a head in 1807 when a British ship sought to retrieve four alleged deserters aboard the USS *Chesapeake*. When the *Chesapeake*'s commander refused to return the men, the British opened fire, killing three Americans and wounding eighteen others. President Jefferson resisted the ensuing public clamor for war against England, instead proclaiming an embargo, signaling America's withdrawal from the world of trade. The president hoped this measure would reveal the great powers' dependence on American agriculture, forcing them to agree to treat American ships with more respect in return for a resumption of trade. Instead, the experiment was an economic disaster, proving that the United States depended more on its overseas trade than the great powers did on American products.

Eventually, tensions with England boiled over into outright conflict with the inconclusive War of 1812. The United States won some impressive naval battles on the Great Lakes and Lake Champlain and a land victory in the Battle of New Orleans, which actually occurred after the peace treaty was signed (but before the news reached remote Louisiana). However, the war nearly bankrupted the United States, which failed in its efforts to conquer Canada and was badly embarrassed when British troops burned down Washington, DC, in 1814.

Ultimately, the fate of this war depended more on the final stages of the Second Hundred Years' War in Europe than on developments within America. With the French, now led by Napoleon Bonaparte, in retreat, it made little sense for indebted, war-weary Britain to prolong the stalemated war in America. Ending the war enabled Britain to redirect valuable troops destined for America to fight the Battle of Waterloo, at which Napoleon was finally and decisively defeated. Additionally, as Anglo-French fighting ended, the issue at the center of the War of 1812, American rights as a neutral trader, no longer was a concern. Consequently, there would no longer be much need for Britain to seize American ships or impress their crews. Neutral rights were not even mentioned in the Treaty of Ghent, which finally ended the War of 1812.

Despite all evidence to the contrary, many Americans viewed the War of 1812 as a great victory. One Massachusetts newspaper crowed, "*We have triumphed*—let snarling discontents say what they will—*we have gloriously triumphed.*"[8] Americans began to see the war as a second war for independence—not only in the military sense but also due to the emergence of a more viable domestic economy and the related growth of American territory in the West. Decatur's glorious victories in the Mediterranean, which served as much clearer evidence of growing American power than the complicated War of 1812, further fed that sense of new found maturity and independence. By 1815, Americans hoped that their nation was finally emerging from the conflict and bloodshed of European warfare into a new era in which it could, perhaps, become an empire in its own right.

THE CONTINENTAL EMPIRE

During the early nineteenth century the United States began to turn away from Europe and to concentrate on building an American empire. The bedrock of the continental empire was the 828,000 square miles of land known as Louisiana, reaching from the Gulf of Mexico to Canada and purchased by the United States for $15 million in 1803. The Louisiana Purchase roughly doubled the size of the United States, which now stretched from the Atlantic Ocean to the Rocky Mountains. Just as importantly, the purchase secured U.S. control of the Mississippi River, which provided mid-western farmers with a safe, reliable route to send goods to Atlantic markets. Later in the century, the United States would further expand through a series of land purchases and wars. While, this expansion potentially enabled the United States to look away from Europe and foster its own, more independent empire, it also further entangled the United States in diplomacy with the European powers that controlled or claimed various portions of the American continent. Acquiring the continental empire also further exacerbated existing American divisions over slavery and, in turn, the growing commitment to slavery in the American South complicated America's relations with the rest of the world.

From Louisiana to Oregon

The Louisiana Purchase was the product of several military and diplomatic decisions, many of which were beyond the control of the United States. Most important was France's trouble in the expensive Napoleonic wars, the final

stage of the Second Hundred Years' War. The violent revolution led by Tous-
saint L'Overture in France's St. Domingue colony (renamed Haiti by the rebels)
exacerbated France's war woes. Napoleon expected to regain control of Haiti,
in which case basic agricultural supplies for the sugar colony would be obtained
from Louisiana. When efforts to retake Haiti failed, Louisiana became much less
valuable to France, and with money needed to pursue the war with England, it
became even more expendable.

For its part, the United States worried about being deprived access to the
Mississippi River, which served as an important, if circuitous, conduit between
mid-western farms and Atlantic markets via the port of New Orleans (a path
young Abraham Lincoln followed, as detailed in chapter 5). After the Spanish officials who still controlled that port in 1802 suspended Americans' right to de-
posit goods in New Orleans warehouses, Congress considered sending 50,000
troops into Louisiana to take New Orleans. When President Jefferson learned
that France had regained control of Louisiana, he famously wrote, "The day that
France takes possession of New Orleans . . . we must marry ourselves to the
British fleet."[9] No doubt the United States' fierce determination to maintain its
rights to ship goods freely down the Mississippi was another factor convincing
Napoleon to sell the territory rather than to try to maintain control of it.

While the Louisiana Purchase provided the territorial foundation of the
continental empire, the Monroe Doctrine, issued in 1823, provided its diplomatic underpinning. Reflecting both the post-1815 self-assurance of the United
States and its lingering fear of European powers, President Monroe declared
North and South America off limits to further European colonization and insisted that European interference in America's hemisphere would be seen as a
threat to U.S. "peace and safety," implying the United States might respond to
such action militarily. In essence, Monroe proclaimed the United States the
primary power in the Americas. In addition, he asserted that the United States
had not and would continue not to "interfere in the internal concerns" of the
European powers. On its surface, this proclamation reflected the United States'
new sense of its own strength—or, perhaps, its preposterous overconfidence.
But beneath the surface lay the Monroe administration's fears of once again being sucked into European rivalries and warfare. To the Northwest, Russia's czar
issued an edict claiming much of the Pacific coast and forbidding all non-
Russian ships from sailing within 100 miles of Russia's claims, on paper banning Americans from trading in the Pacific Northwest. To the south, Spanish
weakness and the republican revolutions in Latin America had caught Europe's
interest, specifically the monarchical Holy Alliance of Russia, France, Prussia,

Austria, and England. Americans feared these countries might take advantage of the chaos in Latin America to restore Spanish rule in that quarter, and in 1823 a persistent rumor had it that France would soon take control of Cuba.

In the decades after the Monroe Doctrine, Americans began moving west in ever-larger numbers and over ever-greater distances. By the 1840s, settlement had reached the Pacific coast. Popular histories often portray this migration as a grassroots movement, in which hundreds of thousands of rugged individuals, motivated by the quest for farmland, gold, or just more space, trekked across the Great Plains and the Rocky Mountains in search of their American dream. While aspects of this interpretation are certainly true, westward migration also relied on government action. Government negotiators worked out treaties with Native Americans, while the military pushed them from place to place to make room for white settlers. The federal government sold cheap land to settlers and speculators. And, from a more international perspective, global diplomacy and warfare made all of this activity possible.

Texas and Oregon, the two most important early settlements west of the Mississippi, exemplify the interaction between individual migration and international diplomacy. Both became diplomatic issues because of the rapid influx of American settlers, and in both cases the settlers' presence ultimately strengthened the diplomatic hand of the United States. Americans in the southern states had long eyed Texas, which, although a province of Mexico, was underpopulated and ideally suited to cotton farming. For its part, Mexico's government encouraged a limited number of Americans to settle in Texas in the hope that the grateful settlers would remain loyal to Mexico and would serve as a barrier to further incursions by the United States. Initially, Stephen F. Austin, whose American father had become a Spanish citizen, headed the settlement. Austin earned the right to begin settling Americans in Texas under the stipulation that settlers become Mexican citizens, and, therefore, Catholics. He began bringing families into Texas in 1821, and by 1834 Americans outnumbered Mexicans in Texas, by about 20,000 to 4,000. What is more, the vast majority of American settlers were not Catholic, and many of them owned slaves, a practice that had been outlawed by Mexico's government. Mexico realized its policy of using the American settlers as a buffer was on the verge of backfiring. When the Americans declared independence and threatened armed rebellion in 1835, the Mexican general Antonio López de Santa Anna marched an army of 600 men north to "subdue the rebels and . . . establish the boundary between Mexico and the United States."[10] Despite early success at the old mission known as El Alamo, Santa Anna eventually suffered defeat at the hands of the Texans at the Battle of San Jacinto, where General Sam Houston's army captured him and ensured Texas's independence.

Oregon presented a still more tangled web. The Pacific Northwest had been claimed by three European powers: Spain, Russia, and Britain, in addition to the United States. Spain's claims dated to the late fifteenth century, but by the nineteenth century it had abandoned them. Russia's claims stemmed from its possession of Russian America (modern Alaska). By 1824 the United States had pushed the Russians to withdraw all of their claims south of latitude 54° 40′, the southern tip of modern day Alaska. That left Great Britain (which controlled Canada) and the United States contending for Oregon (which included the modern states of Washington, Oregon, and Idaho, as well as Canadian British Columbia). When Americans began to make their way along the Oregon Trail into the Pacific Northwest in the 1840s, the issue of ownership became more pressing. By 1845 roughly 5,000 Americans resided in Oregon, most in the rich farmlands of the Willamette Valley. This influx of American settlers not only threatened British control of the region, but their presence and their farms also threatened the fur trade Britain's Hudson's Bay Company had conducted with the Native Americans in the region. At this point, the United States government under President James K. Polk took a hard line with Great Britain, demanding all of the Oregon Territory under the slogan "54° 40′ or fight." When Britain began to prepare its navy for war, Polk strategically retreated, agreeing to a compromise boundary at the 49th parallel. After further negotiations, the two sides finally fixed the northern boundary of the United States at its present location, opening the door for another 60,000 or so migrants to find their way into Oregon before the Civil War.

Slavery and Manifest Destiny

All of this migration further exacerbated the great American debate over slavery. Most of Oregon's settlers originated from northern states and were antislavery. They also initially banned African Americans from owning land. As a result, only 207 of the 13,294 Oregonians listed in the 1850 census were black. On the other hand, Texas, with its plantation agriculture, had allowed slavery since Austin's arrival, despite Mexican laws prohibiting it. By 1840, Texas's 60,000 whites owned approximately 15,000 slaves. Along with fear of war with Mexico, this slave population was one of the most important factors discouraging the United States from accepting the Texas Republic's overtures to join the union. Politicians from both parties worried that admitting a large new slave state would cause internal conflict by disrupting the balance of power between pro- and antislavery forces in Congress.

Slavery impinged on American diplomacy in other ways during this period. Despite the 1808 ban, some overseas slave trading continued, prompting the U.S. Navy to create an African Squadron in 1843 to enforce the ban. Matthew Perry, who later gained fame for opening Japan to western trade, served as the squadron's first commodore. Slavery also lay at the root of what was arguably the first U.S. overseas colony. The American Colonization Society (ACS), founded in 1817, argued vigorously that American slaves should be freed and repatriated in Africa, under the assumption that former slaves could not live as equals with white Americans. Reactions of most African Americans ranged from discomfort to outright hostility, but by 1822 the ACS founded the African settlement of Liberia, which was ruled from the society's headquarters in Washington, DC, until it gained independence in 1847.

Slavery also played a central role in America's largest 19th-century foreign conflict, the Mexican War. The closest thing to a pure war for conquest ever waged by the United States, the Mexican War brought together most of the remaining pieces of the Continental empire. The war might well have been avoided had the United States not finally decided to annex Texas in 1845. Still technically at war with Mexico, the Texas Republic had instituted diplomatic relations with France and Britain. In the early 1840s, British abolitionists began scheming to end slavery in Texas by using British influence to create a Texas-Mexican rapprochement and settling Texas's vast underpopulated lands with non-slaveholding free people from Britain or the northern United States. British officials saw this as a way to expand their influence in America and burnish their worldwide antislavery image. Instead, fear of a renewed British presence in America pushed the John Tyler administration to negotiate for annexation with Texas president Sam Houston, who, quite possibly, had been working toward that outcome all along.

Britain was not particularly unhappy about annexation, but Mexico, which still claimed Texas as its province, was incensed. To add insult to injury, newly elected president James K. Polk sent American troops under General Zachary Taylor to the Rio Grande River in 1846. Mexico and the Republic of Texas had generally agreed that the Neuces River, roughly 150 miles north of the Rio Grande, was Texas's southern boundary. By sending Taylor into territory that nearly everyone agreed belonged to Mexico, Polk was almost certainly trying to provoke war rather than just protect Texas from Mexican invasion. That was the conclusion of an American colonel in Taylor's army who wrote, "We do not have a particle of right to be here. It looks as if the government sent a small force on purpose to bring on a war, as to have a pretext to take California."[11] Whatever Polk's motivation, the Mexicans did attack, and Congress declared war. Polk's war message accused the Mexicans of "invad[ing] our territory and shed[ding] American blood upon the American soil."

Mexico's attack helped to galvanize the American public. But the war and ensuing expansion were not entirely popular, in part because of fears that it would bring more slave states into the union. Conflict over expansion and empire would become a recurring theme in American politics over the rest of the nineteenth century. However, for the time being, such concerns were largely overcome by the new ideology of the continental empire: manifest destiny (discussed in chapter 4). Because volunteers performed the majority of the fighting (there was no standing army to speak of), the grandeur of manifest destiny helped in recruiting and motivating soldiers, particularly in the antislavery North. For example, one Pennsylvania volunteer predicted the American flag would soon "be the banner under whose folds the inhabitants of all Mexico will find shelter and protection." He added, "The Anglo-Saxon race, that land loving people, are on the move."[12]

Militarily, the war was a spectacular victory. American forces easily captured California, a prize that Polk long desired. General Winfield Scott and 14,000 troops landed at the Mexican port of Veracruz, performed a tortuous six-month-long march through the mountains, and, once across, captured the capital of Mexico City, thus adding the "halls of Montezuma" to the "Shores of Tripoli" in the Marines' hymn. In the end, Mexico surrendered claims to modern-day California, Nevada, New Mexico, Arizona, Utah, and most of Colorado in exchange for an indemnity of $15 million in the 1848 Treaty of Guadelupe-Hidalgo, which ended the war. The war was a disaster for Mexico, which not only suffered the humiliation of losing its northern provinces and having its capital occupied but also had to contend with revolts by native people touched off by the war. The government even resorted to hiring American soldiers to combat Mayan Indians involved in one such uprising. The aftereffects of the war so severely destabilized the government that by the 1850s the country descended into bankruptcy and civil war. Despite the Monroe Doctrine, European powers threatened to intervene, and in 1864 France appointed Ferdinand Maximilian, a member of the Hapsburg dynasty, as Emperor of Mexico. He served until 1867, when he was executed by Mexican revolutionaries.

The war's impact on the United States was no less dramatic or destructive. Conflict over whether to allow slavery into the new territories was nearly continuous from the start of the war to 1860 and was one of the primary causes of the Civil War, in which more than 600,000 Americans died. But, the Mexican War also had its positive results for the United States. The continental empire was nearly complete. The boundaries of the lower 48 states as they exist today were essentially settled by 1848. The 1853 Gadsden Purchase added the last small piece of the puzzle, when the United States purchased what is today southern New Mexico and Arizona from Mexico for $10 million.

TOWARD A NEW EMPIRE

From the Civil War nearly to the end of the nineteenth century, the United States further consolidated its territory and began some tentative, controversial steps toward overseas expansion. The Civil War proved perhaps the most important factor in strengthening the continental empire, although the war initially threatened to destroy or fragment it. At the war's beginning, in 1861, President Lincoln cast it as a struggle for the United States to "maintain its territorial integrity against its own domestic foes." But Lincoln and his cabinet also understood that the war presented a threat to American territory from abroad.

Much as the American Revolution had sparked a worldwide war of imperial conquest, the Civil War, by destabilizing the United States, threatened to spark a new European scramble to control America. Certainly Great Britain would not be disappointed were the Union to break apart. The Russian minister to Britain observed, "The English government, at the bottom of its heart, desires the separation of North America into two republics, which will watch each other jealously and counterbalance each other."[13] And, he might have added, such a separation would have lessened the danger of American expansion northward into British Canada. France, for its part, took advantage of the Civil War to set up Maximilian as emperor of Mexico. For France, Confederate victory and a weakened union would not only lessen the prospect of American interference under the Monroe Doctrine but would also create a Confederate buffer to protect French Mexico from the United States. Finally, even the declining Spanish empire took advantage of the Civil War to reclaim its former territory in St. Domingo and a small portion of Peru. American victory and renewed ability to enforce the Monroe Doctrine would threaten their gains.

For their part, the leaders of the Confederacy hoped to exploit European hostility toward the United States and European textile manufacturers' reliance on "King Cotton"—the South's major export—to gain recognition and support for their rebellion. Their efforts failed, partly because England was able to do without southern cotton but also because the prospect of supporting a pro-slavery regime was distasteful to much of the British public. African Americans living in Britain, who relentlessly attacked slavery at public forums discussing the Civil War, helped feed this distaste.

Just as important as slavery in determining European policy was the growing international respect for American military power following the Mexican War. One of President Lincoln's first acts as commander in chief was to declare a blockade, meaning that foreign ships would be prevented from trading with the rebellious southern states for cotton or any other product. This policy soon provoked conflict as the United States seized British ships for violating the blockade. It nearly resulted in war, when in 1861 an errant American captain took it on himself to stop the *Trent*, a British ship, and forcibly seize the Confederate diplomats who were on board, thereby violating accepted international guidelines for blockades. Ultimately, however, Britain backed down from war, largely because it feared American power and calculated that it could do better to emulate America's course during the Napoleonic Wars and profit from neutral trade. As the American military grew during the course of the war, it created growing concern for Britain that any interference on behalf of the Confederacy would lead to the United States seizing Canada. Similar calculations concerning Maximilian's vulnerability in Mexico helped to prevent France from entering the war. Confederate failure to convince these great powers to assist them ultimately sealed the rebellion's defeat.

At war's end, Lincoln had achieved his goal of securing American territory from the threat of domestic rebellion and foreign interference. However, in the western territories one obstacle remained: the much-weakened but still coherent Native American tribes. Before the Civil War the United States government generally treated negotiations with Native Americans as a matter of foreign policy insofar as it regarded such agreements as formal treaties, even if those negotiations were very unequal and usually conducted under the threat of military action against the Indians. After the Mexican War, the federal government increasingly considered Indians to be a domestic concern, moving the federal Indian Bureau from the War Department to the newly created Department of the Interior. But even in the 1850s the federal government continued to negotiate treaties with the Indian tribes that it moved onto reservations. The U.S. Senate, however, refused to ratify such treaties, arguing that Indians had no title to their lands. While such legalistic distinctions probably made little difference to Native Americans, they signified the increasing confidence of a continental empire, which, unlike the new republic of 50 years earlier, now had clearly defined western borders within which the federal government could ignore Indian claims entirely.

Despite the new found posture and power of the United States, Native Americans and settlers continued to spar during and after the Civil War. Armed conflict usually proved disastrous for Indians, with the exception of their victory against General Custer at Little Bighorn in 1876. This defeat soon led the U.S. Army into an all-out effort to eradicate Indian resistance, culminating in the Battle of Wounded Knee (1890), really a massacre in which U.S. soldiers surrounded and slaughtered a group of unarmed Sioux. Official tallies showed 146 Indians killed, but the actual total may have been much higher. At the same time, the federal government sought to break up tribal rule by integrating Indians into the continental empire as individuals. Most notable was the General Allotment Act of 1887, also known as the Dawes Act, which broke tribal possessions into individual allotments.

When combined with the land purchases, warfare, and diplomacy with European powers and Mexico, these policies marked the final stage of the domestication of the American West. In 1800 this region had been an ill-defined borderland, portions of which were claimed by various European powers, American states, and native tribes, all of which engaged in nearly constant negotiation and frequent armed conflict to preserve their claims against the others'. By 1890 all that had ended. The entire region was under the sole sovereignty of the United States, with its borders clearly defined and well defended. The U.S. Census Bureau declared that the West had become so densely settled that the frontier was officially closed.

American expansion did not end, however. Before the Civil War, when the United States acquired new territory for the continental empire, it was generally adjacent to and west of the nation's existing boundaries. Usually, too, it had already begun to be settled by intrepid Americans who had moved west on their own initiative, as in Texas and Oregon. After the Civil War, the pattern began to change. New U.S. possessions would not be contiguous to existing territory; frequently, they would be quite distant. As a result, this new expansion often proved far more controversial than the earlier march across the continent. It aroused opposition from many Americans who did not want their nation to emulate the imperialistic European powers with their massive non-European holdings and their talk of civilizing the allegedly inferior races who inhabited those lands. American imperialism, beyond the confines of the present-day lower 48 states, remained hesitant and often very controversial.

Alaska, purchased from Russia in 1867 for $7.2 million, marked an early effort by the United States to control a large, distant territory. Separated from the United States by more than 700 miles of Canadian wilderness, its 586,000 square miles contained approximately 30,000 natives and only 900 non-natives, many of them Russians. Criticism of the Alaska purchase resulted less from anti-imperialism than from the widespread belief that the new territory—nicknamed "Seward's Folly" after the secretary of state who approved its purchase—would be useless. Supporters justified the Alaska purchase as a way to forestall Russian expansion into North America. Alaska also provided a useful Pacific outpost for the U.S. Navy as well as the promise of natural resources such as furs and salmon. Nevertheless, American settlers would not become a significant presence until the gold rushes of the 1890s.

After their successes in the Mexican War, Americans also increasingly turned their attention to Latin America and, especially, the Caribbean basin. Cuba, in particular, with its vast sugar plantations located less than 100 miles from the Florida Keys, seemed a natural next step for the expansion of the southern plantation system. In 1848 John O'Sullivan, the formulator of Manifest Destiny, wrote Secretary of State James Buchanan, "Surely the hour to strike for Cuba has come . . . Fresh from our Mexican triumphs, glories and acquisition, the inevitable necessity for which the United States must sooner or later have Cuba, will force itself on the minds of the Spanish ministry."[14] However, despite the efforts of American diplomats and private adventurers known as filibusterers, Cuba remained a Spanish colony. After the Civil War, the Cuban question reemerged when Cuban rebels launched their Ten Years' War (1868–78) against Spanish control. Despite some American interest in intervening in and perhaps annexing Cuba, the idea failed to gain traction due to fears of war with Spain and the problem of dealing with Cuba's large slave population should the island be annexed. President Ulysses S. Grant showed more interest in acquiring the island republic of Santo Domingo, even drawing up an annexation treaty in 1869. The idea proved unpopular, however, in part because of the prospect of acquiring Santo Domingo's large slave population, and the Senate rejected Grant's treaty the next year.

The United States also threatened to intervene in other Latin American affairs in the early 1890s, primarily as a way to counter growing British influence in the region. The most serious of these incidents was the Venezuela crisis of 1895–96, prompted by a boundary dispute between British Guiana and

Venezuela. When Venezuela appealed to the United States for assistance, Secretary of State Richard Olney composed what came to be known as the Olney
Corollary to the Monroe Doctrine, declaring, "Today the United States is prac-
tically sovereign on this continent, and its fiat is law upon the subjects to which
it confines its interposition." British refusal to accept this American declaration of control over North and South America nearly prompted war, but in the
end Britain was not willing to risk armed conflict over a relatively small slice
of territory, and it agreed instead to have the dispute mediated by an international arbitration board.

Looking to the west, the United States also became interested in a number
of Pacific islands following the Civil War. After unsuccessfully chasing a Confederate ship through the south Pacific during the war, the United States realized it needed a coaling station for its steamships in that region. In 1878 it signed
a treaty with the ruler of the Samoan Islands giving the United States rights to a
coaling station in Pago Pago in return for protecting Samoa from foreign powers. This agreement nearly sucked the United States into war with Germany,
which sought to colonize Samoa, but the conflict was settled for the moment
when Germany, Britain, and the United States agreed to establish a joint protectorate over the islands in 1889.

Further north, Americans had long been interested in the Hawaiian islands. American- owned sugar plantations flourished there beginning in the
1840s to serve the growing California market. By the 1880s tens of thousands of
Chinese, Japanese, and Portuguese laborers worked Hawaiian plantations.
Seeking to gain more control over Hawaii's independent government, Ameri-
can citizens led a successful revolt against Queen Liliuokalani in 1893. The new
provisional government pushed the United States to annex Hawaii, and the U.S.
Senate Foreign Relations Committee drew up a treaty, but the new president,
Grover Cleveland, opposed it and urged the rebels to restore the queen to power.
They refused, and the situation remained unsettled for most of the decade.

Along with these multiple engagements in the Atlantic and Pacific, the United
States began a major expansion of its navy, culminating in Congress authorizing
construction of seven new battleships between 1890 and 1895. At the same
time, Alfred Thayer Mahan articulated a new theory of American naval power
in his famous book, *The Influence of Sea Power upon History, 1660–1783* (1890),
and a popular article, "Hawaii and Our Future Sea Power." He argued that
America would soon need to trade with more markets around the world and
that in order to do so it needed to establish a powerful navy and to acquire strategic colonies to be used as naval bases. The growing U.S. Navy and Mahan's

strategies would soon be put to the test as America began to build a new empire in earnest.

—⟐ ⟐—

The acquisition of the continental empire had prompted Americans to direct much of their commercial and military energy toward North America rather than the old dream of overseas connections. They developed new trading and communication networks to connect the far-flung western frontier to the established eastern states while dedicating substantial military and diplomatic resources to acquire and keep control of the new western acquisitions. By the 1890s, the closing of the frontier, the rapid growth of American naval power, and the incredible rise of American industry would once again cause many Americans to look outward, across the Pacific as well as the Atlantic, as they sought new markets, new territories, and new influence.

Part III
1898–1945

INTRODUCTION

Momentous, often crippling, challenges faced the world in the first half of the twentieth century. Rapid industrialization, urbanization, economic turmoil, and social upheaval shook a world that seemingly careened toward total breakdown. Socialism, communism, anarchism, imperialism, fascism, and a host of other "isms" prompted two global wars, despite the efforts of reformers who hoped to reorder the increasingly chaotic world.

All these forces, especially the cataclysms of the world wars, remade America—forcing it into a leadership role for which it was often unprepared. Some activist-minded Americans eagerly embraced this new calling. For them, the United States was an exceptional nation with a moral duty to spread—by force if necessary—the benefits of democracy and free market capitalism. These Americans pushed for greater military, diplomatic, and economic influence throughout the world. Despite the obvious dangers and hardships awaiting them, many of these Americans pressed for U.S. entry into the world wars, believing their involvement literally necessary to save the world.

At the same time, many other Americans resisted the role of world leader with an equally determined vehemence. Citing George Washington's warning against entangling alliances, they hoped that geography—the security of two oceans—would safeguard their country as the world grew more dangerous. Ironically, like their interventionist opponents, isolationists often evoked American exceptionalism, insisting their uniquely endowed nation must chart its own separate destiny apart from the corruption of other nations.

Such reveries, however, ignored America's already deep involvement in global affairs. U.S. progressives closely followed social and economic reforms overseas, often modeling their own reforms on what they witnessed and studied in other countries. American artists flocked to Europe for training, inspiration, and to escape their supposedly provincial homeland. Meanwhile, though an avowedly anti-imperialist country, the United States took colonies in the Pacific and Caribbean. U.S. troops went to China to subdue an anti-foreigner rebellion, and the U.S. Navy became an increasingly potent presence worldwide. Backed by American military power, U.S. business interests forged an "informal empire" in their own hemisphere. Likewise, American products and cultural influence increasingly permeated the world.

Between 1900 and 1910, 8.8 million immigrants, mostly from southern and eastern Europe (although nearly 300,000 arrived from Mexico), poured into America. The "new immigrants," so known to differentiate them from earlier migrants from western and northern Europe, settled largely in American cities, spurring unprecedented urban growth. "Within 19 miles of New York's City Hall," noted the *New York Times* of July 31, 1912, "there are today more foreign born than were in the whole United States in 1850." Drawn by the wealth of available industrial jobs in America, the immigrant work force in turn fueled surging U.S. industry. These immigrants, among them Marcus Garvey, Samuel Gompers, Emma Goldman, Nicola Sacco, and Bartolomeo Vanzetti, also provided powerful connections to the rest of the world.

Nor could America's natural borders, as the isolationists hoped, assure a separate destiny. Advances in travel and communication shrank the world in previously unfathomable ways. Transoceanic travel grew faster and cheaper. Wireless technology promised to link peoples together at ever greater speeds. From the first experiments of the Wright Brothers, the airplane quickly advanced—by the 1930s providing transatlantic passenger travel. By the early twentieth century, transoceanic cables had accelerated dramatically the speed at which financial information spread. Only three minutes separated the New York and London stock exchanges. The development of the wireless telegraph, invented by Italian Guglielmo Marconi in the 1890s, opened yet more vistas for improving the speed and quality of communications. In 1903 President Theodore Roosevelt and Britain's King Edward VII traded wireless messages to demonstrate the potential of radio waves.

Conversely, American technology, including the telephone, phonograph, and the incandescent bulb transformed life around the world. But perhaps more important than any single invention bequeathed by Americans, was a broad approach to manufacturing dubbed the "American System" and already well known around the world. Key to this system was interchangeable parts and standardization.

There was little hope that Americans could escape the hardships and horrors of the first half of the twentieth century. Like the rest of the world, America struggled to come to grips with the chaos bequeathed by industrialization and urbanization. As elsewhere in the world, strikes and labor unrest wracked the United States—causing many to fear for their nation's future. An increasingly globalized economy brought worldwide recessions and depressions. Americans experimented with a host of remedies for the afflictions they faced—many borrowed from Europe, where the crises of modernity weighed even heavier. Nationalism, imperialism, and socialism sparked European wars in 1914 and 1939. In both cases, Americans initially resisted the conflict—only to be drawn in later. In the end, hundreds of thousands of American lives were lost in Europe and Asia.

By the end of World War II (as was also the case briefly after World War I), many around the world turned to America to lead a path away from the destruction and privation that so characterized the first half of the twentieth century. Concurrently, an increasing number of Americans, shelving remaining isolationist sentiments, also came to think of themselves as world leaders—even as a people with a special mission to renew the world.

_⌒ ⌒_

Conflict in the form of global warfare, then, unquestionably proved the arena in which Americans most shaped the world—and the global force that most shaped America. Twice in the first half of the twentieth century, American intervention in world wars shifted the tide bringing victory to the Allies. These conflicts reshaped the way Americans conceived of the larger world. Two generations directly experienced warfare outside U.S. borders—and hundreds of thousands lost their lives doing so. By 1945, few Americans dared advocate isolationism or envision an American future without their country playing a central role in world affairs.

The world of commerce, also, drew Americans dramatically beyond their borders. An ever-expanding economy required raw materials and new markets for finished goods. Most prominently, Americans moved into Latin America creating a commercial or "informal" empire based on economic interests backed by the threat of American force. Elsewhere in the world, American commerce, particularly commodification of movies, music, and other aspects of popular culture, became impossible to ignore. Some on the receiving end resentfully complained of an "American invasion." Others admired the utility and modernity of U.S. products and celebrated the freedom and sophistication of American jazz records and movies.

Around the world, a culture of reform, marked by movements for social and political change arose during this period fed by ideas that bounced back and forth across the oceans. Americans often felt behind Europe and nations such as New Zealand, which advanced unique and imaginative social and economic reforms. Early in the century, America appeared to some a backwater, ruled by disorganized chaos. U.S. reformers flocked overseas for exposure to supposedly superior European methods for organizing modern, industrial society. By the 1930s, however, perspectives began to shift. The New Deal, with its pragmatic dedication to serving the "forgotten man," drew worldwide attention—even as some New Dealers looked to countries like Sweden for inspiration. By the advent of World War II, some Americans too began envisioning themselves as reshaping the world through inspired modernization projects such as the Tennessee Valley Authority—which reformers planned to export to the world.

Compared to most major nations, America emerged from the darkness of the first half of the twentieth century—an era marred by world wars, revolutions, depressions, and genocide—stronger and more prepared to offer a redemptive model to a crippled world. This represented a dramatic change in the course of five decades, from a country with few financial investments in the outside world and limited interest in the affairs of outside nations—to a country in many ways eager to assume world leadership.

CHAPTER SEVEN

Reluctant Global Warriors

"A LIVING HELL"

At first war seemed exciting to Lieutenant Clifton B. Cates from Tiptonville, Tennessee, a small town north of Memphis, nestled along the Kentucky border. After graduating from the University of Tennessee, he eagerly reported for active duty in June 1917. Assigned to the Sixth Marine Regiment, Cates sailed for France in early 1918. There, he joined millions of young American men reinforcing exhausted French and British forces fighting the Germans in what later became known as World War I. As he and his division (numbering 27,000) moved through France toward the front lines, the local population cheered them as saviors, throwing flowers and kisses at the Americans they hoped would turn the tide after four devastating years of war. Just behind the front, the marines enjoyed a dinner of chickens, rabbits, potatoes and French wine. Cates' first taste of battle over the next several days brought a rush of adrenaline and excitement. "[I]t is a wonderful thrill to be out there in front of a bunch of men that will follow you to death," he wrote his mother.

Days later, Cates's tone had changed. "It's been a living hell since I started this," he admitted in another letter. "We were shelled all night with shrapnel and gas shells. At times, I wished that one would knock me off." Worse than the shelling was the mustard gas. Cates watched gas soak the clothes of his men, burning their bodies and causing temporary blindness. Exposed himself, Cates stripped naked and washed "with a heavy lather of soap." His quick action, he concluded, "saved me, but I have bad blisters between my legs, around my neck and on my forehead." The "strain," he confessed, "has been terrible."

Still, Cates remained committed to the cause, refusing a doctor's pleas to leave the front to recover from his wounds. He recognized that the American presence "has put new energy in the allied troops," and he remained deeply committed to the cause of defeating the Germans. He wrote home of his pride fighting alongside "about a dozen different kind of troops," including Algerians, French, English, Moroccans, and Scottish Highlanders, who, Cates noted, the Germans called "the ladies from hell"—referring to their kilts.

When the armistice was declared on November 11, 1918, at the eleventh hour, of the eleventh day, of the eleventh month of the year, Cates heard no cheering nor celebration on the battlefield, "but there was not a man that did not thank God that rainy, muddy, cold morning that it was all over." That night the survivors worked on "thawing out and getting dry; there must have been a million bon fires along the front. It was a beautiful sight."[1]

Cates's encounter with bloody world war, however, was far from over. He remained a loyal marine for several decades. During World War II, he served in the Pacific theater, leading men into some of the most brutal engagements of the war—including Guadalcanal and Iwo Jima. He retired at the rank of general in 1954—in the middle of the Cold War. As his career suggests, intense warfare on a worldwide scale defined the American experience in the first half of the twentieth century. But beyond this, Cates, in his overriding sense of commitment and dedication, embodied the larger theme of American mission and sense of exceptionalism that drove its diplomatic and military interaction with the world in this violent era. Americans long had seen themselves as exceptional—in Lincoln's words, as "an almost chosen nation." Geography and devotion to the ideals of democracy, equality, and liberty, many Americans believed, had created a uniquely endowed and prosperous nation. Ironically, Americans were not exceptional in viewing themselves as exceptional: nationalism, which chauvinistically exulted the nation-state, had swept up much of Europe in the nineteenth century. Still, flexing new might as a new century opened, Americans sought new opportunities to pursue a unique mission. Bitter debates exploded, however, over the exact nature of that calling. Likewise, when they took up their charge, Americans often found, as did Cates in Europe, their ideals tested to the breaking point.

WAR AND EMPIRE

America in 1898 bustled with energy and an emerging sense of the special role it might play in the greater world. This consciousness materialized as European powers began aggressively expanding their empires. While imperialism dates to ancient history, a new, more virulent brand developed in the last quarter of the nineteenth century. No longer content with loose control of a few centers of commerce, imperialists moved forcibly into Africa and Asia, creating colonial bureaucracies, employing large parts of local populations, and imposing western culture and values on their new holdings. Soon, millions from West Africa to the Solomon Islands in the Pacific came under colonial control. Colonies furnished raw materials such as rubber, cotton, diamonds, and gold, while also providing markets for finished goods produced by "mother" countries. Colonizers, informed by scientific racism and nationalism, saw themselves as bearers of the "white man's burden," tasked with the mission of bringing development and civilization to "lesser" peoples.

As the "new imperialism" took hold in Europe, some Americans worried their nation was falling behind. "As one of the great nations of the world," admonished Senator Henry Cabot Lodge, "the United States must not fall out of the line of march."[2] Indeed, argued some U.S. imperialists, Americans bore a unique obligation to spread their democratic ideals. Meanwhile, an equally adamant group, quickly labeled the anti-imperialists, objected, arguing that despite the nation's expansion in the 1840s, imperialism represented a betrayal of American ideals (see chapter 9). Empire, worried anti-imperialist Harvard University professor Charles Eliot Norton, would mark the end "of the America exceptionally blessed among the nations."[3]

While Americans mostly avoided the early rush to empire, by the very last years of the nineteenth century, imperialists were gaining ascendancy. Both sides, however, framed arguments in terms of American exceptionalism. The 1890s, plagued by social tension and economic depression, proved to be an especially stressful decade for Americans. The anxiety and "psychic crisis" of the times without question rendered Americans more susceptible to the imperialist cause, which included calls to foster new markets, bolster U.S. security, and spread the glories of American democracy.

Spain's brutal suppression of a revolution against its colonial rule in Cuba provided an opening for the imperialists. Stories promoted in America's "yellow press" of disease-ridden "reconcentración" camps riled Americans. Imperialists pushed a reluctant President William McKinley to act. Theodore Roosevelt, then assistant secretary of the navy, recalled that he "preached, with all the fervor and zeal I possessed, our duty to intervene in Cuba."[4] In 1898, when the USS Maine, a naval battleship sent by McKinley to Havana Harbor, exploded without warning, killing 266, most Americans blamed Spain and demanded war. Unable to stop the momentum, congressional opponents of war focused on passing the Teller Amendment, renouncing any interest in annexing Cuba. Imperialists could have their war, but they would not get Cuba. Compensating for what they lacked in training with enthusiasm, American forces easily overwhelmed Spain both in Cuba and in the Philippines, Spain's Pacific island colony.

The Teller Amendment disappointed those seeking territorial gains from the war. Still, imperialists and those with a financial stake in Cuba refused to walk away from the newly liberated island. The Platt Amendment, granting the United States right of intervention in Cuba "to restore order," guaranteed future American dominion over the island. Cuba essentially became a U.S. protectorate. Meanwhile, during the war, America annexed Hawaii, and as part of the peace agreement with Spain, it gained Puerto Rico and the island of Guam in the Pacific.

The outstanding question, however, was the Philippines. Americans had given little thought to the matter beforehand. "Few of us had ever heard of the Philippines until that year [1898]. We had heard of Manila rope, but we did not know where Manila was," recalled George C. Marshall, then a cadet at Virginia Military Institute.[5] Initially indecisive, McKinley finally cast his lot with the imperialists. It was America's duty, the president told a gathering of fellow Methodists, to "uplift and civilize and Christianize them [the Filipinos], and by God's grace do the very best we could by them." The question then shifted to the Senate, which would have to approve annexation. Debate was acrimonious. Each side sought to harness the rhetoric of exceptionalism for its purposes. Annexation, imperialists insisted, would provide access to Asian markets, stymie the claims of other nations such as Germany to the archipelago, and—echoing McKinley—allow America to spread its values. God "had marked the American people as His chosen nation to finally lead the regeneration of the world," waxed Senator Albert Beveridge, leading the charge for annexation. In the midst of the debate, British poet Rudyard Kipling published "The White Man's Burden" in *McClure's Magazine*. Subtitling his poem, "The United States and the Philippine Islands," Kipling cast annexation in philanthropic terms but cautioned that serving "half devil, half child" peoples was a "thankless" burden. Meanwhile, anti-imperialists took both the high and low roads. A magazine editor recoiled at the specter of "ignorant Catholic Spanish negroes" joining the union,[6] while Senator George Frisbie Hoar warned that a democracy "cannot rule over vassal states without bringing in the elements of death into its own constitution."[7] In the end, the treaty passed by a one-vote margin, reflecting deep divisions over the matter.

As charges shot back and forth, tension mounted in the Philippines between U.S. soldiers and the local population, who expected their liberators to leave soon. A naval officer touring the country noted the "colder manner of the people."[8] Filipino rebels found themselves barred from Manila and subject to racial taunts of "nigger" and "goo goo" from U.S. troops. Rumors circulated among Filipinos that Americans, having freed their slaves, were seeking a new population to enslave in the Philippines. On the eve of the Senate vote, war broke out between Americans and Filipino "insurgents."

Maintaining a colony proved infinitely more trying than claiming one. Eventually the U.S. military dispatched some 125,000 troops to the islands to subdue the Filipino "insurrection." Both sides committed atrocities. While the earlier Spanish practice of herding Cubans into concentration camps provoked outrage in the United States, Americans essentially adopted the same practice—forcing Filipinos into "protected zones," where food shortages and disease quickly developed. Anti-imperialist newspapers devoted heavy coverage to stories of American malfeasance.

Discomfort over actions that seemed to belie American ideals swung the pendulum back away from the country's imperialist experiment. Running for president in 1900, William Jennings Bryan proclaimed: "It is not necessary to own people to trade with them."[9] Bryan lost the election, but the continuing toll of the war convinced growing numbers he was right. As the Americans finally subdued the resistance—after four years of fighting at a cost of 5,000 U.S. and 200,000 Filipino lives—Americans lost their taste for overt empire. Still, as Bryan suggested, many remained interested in building "informal empire," allowing Americans simultaneously to reap the benefits of imperialism yet preserve a cherished sense of American uniqueness.

ALTERNATIVE TO EMPIRE?

Costly warfare in the Philippines and mounting anti-imperialism at home forced U.S. officials to shift course away from direct imperialism imposed by force. Instead, American leaders explored a softer form of power. Secretary of State John Hay's "Open Door Notes," issued in 1899 and 1900, set the tone for what many Americans viewed as an alternative to empire. Economic penetration, rather than formal military conquest, would be the goal. Wherever necessary, however, Americans would wield force to maintain this informal empire—yet always under the guise of preserving democracy and legitimate leadership, ideas consistent with American exceptionalism.

The immediate issue for Hay was China. Following defeat in the Sino-Japanese war of 1894–95, China faced an uncertain future. Sensing opportunity, foreign imperial powers moved to seize the moment. Weak and divided, the Chinese acquiesced to the creation of "spheres of influence" throughout coastal China. Native governments maintained nominal authority over these zones, but foreign powers, not subject to local laws, controlled affairs and profited from commerce, often from behind walled-in compounds.

Lacking its own sphere, Hay worried America would lose influence and market shares in strategically important Asia. In 1899, he circulated the first of his "Open Door Notes," urging that powerful nations not practice trade discrimination in China. Instead he proposed an "open door" for trade in which all nations had equal access to China's markets. A year later Hay issued a second note, demanding respect for China as a "territorial and administrative entity." Beyond promoting U.S. commerce, Americans believed they were playing an altruistic role by curbing imperial designs on China—all the while keeping a door open to U.S. influence and trade.

Still, Americans never consulted the Chinese about the "Open Door Notes," and anger brewed throughout China over foreign incursions. In 1900, between the circulation of Hay's first and second notes, Chinese rebels calling themselves the Boxers led a bloody rebellion against imperialistic influence in China, culminating in a siege of the foreign compound at Beijing. The Boxers took primary aim at western missionaries but also targeted merchants and destroyed railroads and telegraph lines as an expression of indignation at western economic exploitation. Eventually an international force, including U.S. Marines sent from the Philippines, put an end to the rebellion. Rather than an act of imperialism, U.S. intervention, Americans insisted, aimed to protect China from both the Boxers and overzealous foreign powers. Americans even devoted the bulk of their share of reparations payments received from China for the Boxer uprising to the education of Chinese in America. Still, many Chinese saw little difference between the Open Door policies of the Americans and more blatant imperialism practiced by Europeans.

It was in Latin America where the full force of informal empire was felt— often backed by U.S. military power. Unlike in China, where America operated as one of many rival imperial powers, the United States possessed a freer hand in Latin America. During the early twentieth century, it moved to consolidate control over the Caribbean and Latin America. As in China, the publicly stated goal was to serve the region, not to create an empire. In Cuba, the Platt Amendment and frequent military interventions firmly established the island as an American protectorate. But, as in China, "preservation of Cuban independence" was the official goal. In 1904, President Theodore Roosevelt extended this policy to all of Latin America with his Roosevelt Corollary to the Monroe

Doctrine. Again, selflessness not imperialism, Roosevelt insisted, guided his actions. "It is not true that the United States feels any land hunger or entertains any projects as regards the other nations of the Western Hemisphere," explained Roosevelt, "save such that are for their welfare."[10]

The construction of a canal between oceans through Central America was one such "project" occupying Roosevelt's mind. Such a route would cut the long transoceanic trip around Cape Horn by more than half—providing a great boon to trade and to America's expanding navy. From the start, acquiring land for the canal proved a sullied affair. Already a French company had failed miserably trying to dig such a canal across the isthmus of Panama. Eager to salvage something, the French moved to sell their interest in the Panama operation to the United States. The French went so far as to spread false rumors of an active volcano along an alternative route through Nicaragua previously of interest to Americans. Persuaded of the superiority of the isthmus route, Roosevelt secured French rights at a cost of $40 million. He then negotiated the Hay-Herran Treaty with Colombia in 1903, leasing land along the proposed canal for 100 years at a cost of $10 million upfront and $250,000 annually. The Colombian senate, however, rejected the treaty, sending Roosevelt into a rage. "I do not think the Bogota lot of Jackrabbits," he huffed, "should be allowed permanently to bar one of the future highways of civilization."[11]

Seeing its $40 million prize slipping away, agents of the French company fomented revolt among land-owning families in Panama, the region of Colombia where the canal was to be constructed. To secure his planned contribution to civilization, Roosevelt dispatched the USS *Nashville* to the region to block a Colombian response. His administration then negotiated a treaty with the new government of Panama—actually with an agent of the French owners of the Panama concession, who presented himself as a representative of Panama. The Panamanians, now caught between the United States and Colombia, had no real choice but to accept the treaty as handed them. Later, Roosevelt defended his actions in terms of mission and obligation: "[I]t was our duty to the world to provide this transit in the shape of a canal."[12] In 1904, construction began on the canal, which was formally opened in August 1914. Until 1979, Americans controlled the Canal Zone, a 553-square-mile territory that included the canal. The U.S. military maintained a strong presence in the zone as well as in Guantánamo Bay, Cuba, making it an intimidating force in the Caribbean.

America also attempted to extend its informal empire to resource-rich Mexico on its southern border. U.S. investment in Mexico grew tremendously in the early twentieth century—as did Mexican discomfort with their aggressive neighbor to the north. Even pro-American Mexican president Porfirio Díaz lamented that "poor Mexico" was "so far from God, so close to the United States." A revolution beginning in 1910 that ousted Díaz from office, however, strained America's designs on Mexico to the breaking point. U.S. president Woodrow Wilson watched with alarm as violence and factionalism overtook Mexico. Dismissing American economic claims, Wilson professed to be most concerned with establishing a stable democracy—resembling that of the United States— in Mexico. Victoriano Huerta, who took control of Mexico in 1913, was not Wilson's idea of a good leader. The high-minded U.S. president worried the new Mexican leader would set a bad example for the rest of Latin America. He told the British he "wanted to teach those countries a lesson by insisting on the removal of Huerta."[13] When soldiers loyal to Huerta arrested and briefly held U.S. sailors who came ashore in Mexico to collect supplies, Wilson retaliated by dispatching the U.S. Navy to the port city of Veracruz. A battle for the city cost the lives of 19 Americans and several hundred Mexicans. Argentina, Brazil, and Chile (the so-called ABC powers) provided mediation, allowing the Americans to exit and Huerta to flee to Europe.

Wilson sent his military to Mexico a second time in 1917 to hunt down legendary revolutionary Pancho Villa. Villa, who had raided the border town of Columbus, New Mexico, killing 17 Americans, was another Mexican who Wilson thought needed to be taught a lesson. The 7,000 men Wilson sent south under General John J. Pershing ploughed 350 miles into Mexico but never found Villa. Pershing and his men withdrew just as Germany announced unrestricted submarine warfare against the United States. To the end, Wilson remained steadfast that he acted in the best interests of Mexico. "What makes Mexico suspicious of us is that she does not believe as yet we want to serve her interests," Wilson told a gathering of Michigan businessmen. "But I will try to serve all America, so far as intercourse with Mexico is concerned, by trying to serve Mexico herself."[14]

AMERICA AND THE "GREAT WAR"

President Woodrow Wilson brought this same righteous sense of mission to the horrific war that besieged Europe in 1914. From start to finish, he approached the Great War from a perspective of American exceptionalism—an often distorting view that ultimately proved his undoing.

Son of a Presbyterian minister with an uncompromising moralistic streak, Wilson envisioned America as a singular force for global reform and renewal.

Rarely has an American leader spoken so emphatically of his country's special place and mission to the world. He told a July 4, 1914, crowd at Independence Hall in Philadelphia, "America has lifted high the light which will shine unto all generations and guide the feet of mankind to the goal of justice and liberty and peace."[15] Over and over, Wilson spoke of a mandate to put America's greatness to work for the benefit of the world. "[T]he idea of America," he insisted, "is to serve humanity."[16]

Mounting tension in Europe in 1914 put Wilson's ideals to a grueling test. Surging nationalism, bitter imperial rivalries, rapid economic development, and a series of military alliances made early-twentieth-century Europe a tinderbox awaiting a spark. The spark came when Germany vaulted to the defense of its Austro-Hungarian allies in a war against Serbia and Russia. Swiftly, most of Europe joined the fray, breaking into two warring camps: the Central Powers of Germany and Austria-Hungary, and the Allies, made up of Britain, France, and Russia. Fighting grew particularly fierce in northern France where trenches stretched for thousands of miles, and new technology—including machine guns, poison gas, and airplanes—generated the deadliest combat in human history.

Watching the man-made catastrophe from a distance, Wilson and many Americans became ever more committed to celebrating the virtues of their still peaceful land. "It is the genius of our people," wrote *Emporia (Kansas) Gazette* editor William Allen White, "to live in peace." An Indiana newspaper added that Americans owed their ancestors a debt of gratitude for having left Europe, now aflame in war.[17] Wilson echoed the sentiment, urging all Americans to maintain neutrality: "We are the only one of the great white nations that is free of war today, and it would be a crime against civilization for us to go in." Still Wilson felt compelled to use his country's "great character and her great strength in the interest of peace."[18] He dispatched his close confidant Colonel Edward House to Europe to seek negotiations between warring parties.

The growing peace movement, with roots in the older anti-imperialist tradition (see chapter 9), applauded the president's efforts to mediate while remaining neutral. William Jennings Bryan, a three-time Democratic presidential candidate and Wilson's secretary of state, emerged as the most vocally peace-minded cabinet member.

On the other side, former president Theodore Roosevelt blasted "ultra-pacificists" and Wilson, insisting America could never serve as "spiritual example to them [Europeans] by sitting idle, uttering cheap platitudes." While assailing his antiwar foes, Roosevelt actually shared their overriding sense of American exceptionalism and mission. "Our country should not shirk its duty to mankind," he admonished. War in Europe is "terrible and evil," he acknowledged, but also "grand and noble." The United States must involve itself, militarily if need be, to defend the world from "oppression and subjugation."[19]

While dismissing Roosevelt as "a clever and adroit demagogue . . . wedded to the belief that rhetoric is action," Wilson was hardly a model of neutrality.[20] The son of an English-born mother, Wilson viewed Great Britain and France as worthy, albeit flawed, democracies. He fretted about the dangers of German militarism and authoritarianism. Increasingly he allowed the United States to become an arsenal supplying the Allies. Germany in turn bitterly protested and dispatched U-boats to disrupt U.S. trade with the Allies. When a U-boat torpedoed and sank the British liner *Lusitania* in 1915 at the cost of 128 American lives, the Wilson administration framed the issue in decidedly moral terms. America was "contending for nothing less high and sacred than the rights of humanity" rather than defending "property or privilege of commerce" as might a lesser nation.[21] Upset by Wilson's insistence on maintaining trade with belligerents, Secretary of State Bryan resigned. Wilson replaced him with the decidedly pro-British Robert Lansing.

Meanwhile, Britain launched an aggressive propaganda campaign to persuade Americans to side with the Allies. J. P. Morgan's banking empire, which loaned millions to Britain and France, actively promoted the allied cause. "In America there are 50,000 who understand the necessity of the United States entering the war. But there are 100 million who have not thought of it. Our task is to see those figures are reversed," explained a Morgan associate.[22]

Interventionists established the National Security League in 1914 to encourage preparedness and support the Allies. The league helped spread word of supposed "Hun" atrocities, such as the "rape of Belgium" (later revealed to have been exaggerated by the Allied press). President Wilson personally received a Belgian delegation at the White House, which shared stories of mistreatment under the Germans. Concurrently German-Americans often supported their motherland, and Irish-Americans chaffed at any suggestion Britain was an archetype of democracy while holding Ireland as its colony.

For a time, Wilson managed to placate all parties. In 1916 he ran for reelection as the candidate of peace and preparedness under the slogan "he kept us out of war." After narrowly winning a second term, Wilson revived his peacemaking mission, asking both warring parties to state their war objectives with the goal of negotiating "peace without victory." Neither belligerent took up Wilson's good offices. From there things rapidly fell apart. Beginning February 1,

1917, Germany announced unrestricted submarine warfare on any ship sus-pected of trading with the Allies. An intercepted telegram from Arthur Zim-merman, the German foreign secretary to Mexico, proposing an alliance against the Americans and promising Mexico help in regaining land lost in the Mexican-American War further inflamed U.S. public opinion. As U-boats be-gan sinking American ships, Wilson decided he had no choice but to declare war against Germany.

Although the president pivoted from his earlier antiwar stance, he remained firm in his vision of America as a transcending force that would change the world. In his soaring war message to Congress on April 2, 1917, Wilson declared America would fight for the "ultimate peace of the world and for the liberation of its people—the world must be made safe for democracy." The United States, Wilson continued, "is privileged to spend her blood and her might for the principles that gave her birth."

As the president spoke, dissenters converged on the Capitol. One protester held a sign reading: "Is this the United States of Great Britain?" Earlier that day, a fistfight broke out between a protester and ardently pro-war senator Henry Cabot Lodge. Wilson responded to the protests with righteous determination to eliminate all obstacles to his sacred mission to "serve mankind." He autho-rized a campaign to silence opposition to his war aims. German-Americans be-came frequent targets for suspected disloyalty. "Any man who carries a hyphen about with him carries a dagger that he is ready to plunge into the vitals of this Republic," blurted Wilson at one point.[23] Just as America was taking up a grand crusade to remake the world, intolerance, stoked by the president, seemed to be sweeping the land. The black mood culminated with the lynching of a German-American in 1918 and the imprisonment of key opponents of the war, including Eugene Debs, the socialist leader who received nearly one million votes in the 1912 presidential election. "If you are really for America first . . . then you are classified as pro-German," lamented Congressman Charles A. Lindbergh (father and namesake of the famed aviator and notorious isolationist).[24]

Even as it prepared to join the Allies in Europe, its first alliance since the Revolutionary War, the American military also remained guided by a sense of exceptionalism. General John "Black Jack" Pershing, appointed by Wilson to lead U.S. forces in Europe, shared the president's conviction that Americans were an extraordinary people. He rejected allied proposals that his men be amalgamated into European units. Instead, he insisted, Americans would fight as a separate army in their own sector. (Eventually some U.S. forces—in particular African American soldiers—did fight under French command.) Like-wise, Pershing, a veteran of the Indian wars and the hunt for Pancho Villa in Mexico, dismissed calls that he train his recruits for trench warfare. Positive his men were superior to the tired Europeans, Pershing focused instead on open battle techniques. "If the Americans do not permit the French to teach them," French president Georges Clemenceau coolly retorted, "perhaps the Germans will do so."[25]

Despite the protests of at least one U.S. senator—"You're not actually going to send soldiers over there, are you?"—America raised a remarkable fighting force of over four million, two million of whom eventually went to Europe.[26] Dire circumstances for the Allies in the spring of 1918 forced Pershing to agree to limited temporary amalgamation of his forces, and he acceded to the creation of a Supreme War Council under French general Ferdinand Foch. While U.S. forces fought bravely in engagements such as Belleau Wood and St. Mihiel, they were ill-prepared for battle and suffered heavy casualties. By war's end, over 100,000 American lives were lost.

Undaunted, Wilson took his crusade into peacetime, determined to push the world toward his vision of democracy and international cooperation aimed at avoiding future costly conflicts. In January 1918, he issued his famous Fourteen Points, proposing a new world grounded in the principles of open diplomacy, self-determination, and free trade. In part, Wilson hoped to counter the growing attraction of Bolshevik communist revolutionaries who swept to power in Russia in 1917. Under Vladimir Lenin, the Bolsheviks fashioned a strong appeal to the dispossessed based on "self-determination," a magnetic term they actually seized on before Wilson. In late 1918, Wilson, the first president to leave U.S. borders while in office, journeyed to France to oversee peace negotiations. On the streets of Paris, millions cheered Wilson as a savior. Around the world, people taken with his vision of peace and self-determination embraced his cause. A Chinese journalist celebrated the president as a "champion of human rights generally and of the rights of China in particular." In India a prominent press published a series of the president's speeches under the title *President Wilson: The Modern Apostle of Freedom.*[27]

Wilson, however, would be negotiating not with his admirers but with his British and French counterparts, David Lloyd George and Georges Clemenceau. Together they faced an intractable set of problems: remaking the borders of Eastern Europe, disposing of colonies possessed by vanquished powers, addressing the sundry needs of various nationalistic and ethnic groups, and arranging reparations payments. Over and over, Wilson compromised on key provisions. Unwilling to challenge colonialism, he disillusioned many who saw themselves now excluded from the ideal of self-determination. Wilson, leader of a country where segregation reigned in the South, also crushed a Japanese proposal for a treaty amendment promoting racial equality.

In the end, the Treaty of Versailles, as Wilson put it, was "the best that could be made of a dirty past."[28] He placed all his faith on the inclusion of the League of Nations in the treaty. Wilson hoped the league, an international assembly of countries dedicated to settling conflict peacefully, would resolve all lingering and future diplomatic issues. But a provision in Article 10 of the league's covenant, which appeared to oblige member nations to protect each other "against external aggression," deeply disturbed key U.S. senators, who would have to approve of the treaty. Fears grew that an international body could force America into wars against its will. Wilson, now returned from France, was in no mood to compromise. Touring the nation to promote his treaty in the fall of 1919, Wilson charged, "The whole freedom of the world depends upon the choice of America. The world will be absolutely in despair if America deserts it."[29]

Toward the end of his speaking tour, Wilson suffered a massive stroke. As he lay incapacitated, the Senate, worried America would concede its sovereignty and moral power by joining the league, defeated the Versailles treaty. In a sense, one brand of exceptionalism, mandating that America remain above and separate from world affairs, defeated Wilson's vision of a singular nation actively perfecting the world.

As the treaty crashed in flames, the country seemed to veer toward chaos. Race riots, debilitating strikes, and a deadly flu virus brought back by returning soldiers all rattled postwar America. The 1917 Bolshevik Revolution in Russia aroused fears that a similar communist movement was brewing in America. In the repressive atmosphere that followed, government officials arrested and disrupted the activities of suspected radicals, many of whom were foreign born. By 1919 a dark and intolerant tide (to which the president greatly contributed with his campaign against radicalism and suspected foreign intrigue) overtook Wilson's sweeping vision of world democracy forged by a benevolent American mentor.

RETREAT FROM WILSONIANISM

The voting public in 1920 rebuffed entirely the Wilsonian program of intensive American involvement in world affairs. Republican Warren Harding, promising a "return to normalcy" and professing "not to know anything about this European stuff," handily defeated his opponents.[30] For the next two decades, America would avoid overt world commitments—essentially reverting to Washington's Farewell Address dictum that "permanent, inveterate antipathies against particular Nations, and passionate attachments for others, should be excluded." Talk of American exceptionalism and a crusade to remake the world dissipated.

Instead Americans balked at overt international commitments, endorsing only general measures aimed at preventing future wars. U.S. diplomacy after the world war generally followed the pacifistic mood of the country. In 1921 the Harding administration sponsored the Washington Naval Conference in which Japan, Britain, the United States, and six other nations committed themselves to disarmament in the Pacific. Secretary of State Charles Evans Hughes opened the conference with a dramatic pledge to destroy 30 American naval ships. In 1927, the French requested that Washington join in a Franco-American treaty renouncing war between the two nations. Seeking to avoid any impression of an alliance, the Americans invited all nations of the world to sign the treaty, abolishing war. Fourteen countries eventually signed the resulting Kellogg-Briand Pact, which exemplified the nation's determination to avoid a repeat of conditions that led to the recent world war.

Beyond disarmament and peace initiatives, the U.S. government did encourage international business contacts during the 1920s (explored in chapter 8). The country, however, shunned the League of Nations, avoided direct involvement in European affairs, and made only symbolic gestures of protest against international acts of aggression, such as when Japan brazenly violated the Washington Naval Treaty and the Kellogg-Briand Pact by invading Manchuria in 1931.

Taking the oath of office in 1933, Franklin D. Roosevelt remained well aware of the failings of his former boss Woodrow Wilson. While he hoped to influence world affairs, with the Great Depression ravaging the country, Roosevelt focused on pressing domestic concerns. When he moved modestly to join the League of Nation's World Court in 1935, he suffered a rare defeat in Congress.

As FDR's first tentative moves to expand America's diplomatic presence met with failure, the Great Depression and the rise of fascism in Germany only further cemented the isolationist currents flowing through the country. Isolationism traditionally was strongest in the Midwest and far West, but by the mid-1930s it was spreading. Books like Walter Millis's *America's Road to War* (1935), arguing that British propaganda and greedy arms manufacturers tragically drove America to war in 1917, found wide audiences. When members of

Oxford University's debating society voted in 1933 to "under no circumstances fight for King and country," they inspired American college students to adopt their own versions of the "Oxford pledge." In 1935 some 175,000 college students across the country walked out of classes to protest militarism and war. Brandishing signs with slogans like "Abolish the ROTC" and "Scholarship not Battleships," the strikers drew international attention. That same year, hearings conducted by North Dakota senator Gerald Nye resulted in the first of a series of Neutrality Acts, restricting American trade with countries at war.

Sensitive to the isolationist climate, President Roosevelt moved cautiously. When he addressed international issues, his early initiatives reflected the mood of national retrenchment. In Latin America, Roosevelt set out to repair damage committed by his aggressive predecessors with his "Good Neighbor Policy." At the 1933 Pan-American conference held in Montevideo, Uruguay, the United States supported a motion that "no state has the right to intervene in the internal or external affairs of another." The next year, Roosevelt repudiated the Platt Amendment that had so plagued U.S.-Cuban relations since the Spanish-American War. South Americans greeted Roosevelt with enthusiasm when the president journeyed to the region in 1936. When he visited Argentina, two million people flooded the streets of Buenos Aires to hail the American leader.

As Hitler further consolidated power in Germany and Japan invaded China, Roosevelt began speaking more forcefully about world affairs and the dangers of aggression. In 1937 he urged peace-loving nations to "quarantine" those promoting "anarchy and instability from which there is no escape through mere isolation or neutrality." But recognizing he had little public support, Roosevelt offered no program to enforce any such quarantine.

When France and Britain declared war on Germany, following Hitler's invasion of Poland in 1939, positions hardened in the United States. Roosevelt grew increasingly determined to find flexibility with which to help the French and British, while isolationists rallied to block American entry into the war. In 1939, Roosevelt did manage to persuade Congress to amend the Neutrality Act to allow the export of arms on a "cash-and-carry" basis. Desperate to aid Great Britain following the collapse of France, Roosevelt arranged to "swap" aging American destroyers for bases on British holdings in the Western Hemisphere. While the president remained frustrated he could not do more, the isolationist-leaning *St. Louis Post-Dispatch* greeted the "bases-for-destroyers" announcement with the headline "Dictator Roosevelt Commits Act of War." "I am fighting against a public psychology, which comes very close to saying, 'Peace at any price,'" Roosevelt privately lamented.[31]

Encouraged by Roosevelt, interventionists formed the Committee to Defend America by Aiding the Allies (CDAAA) in May 1940. Isolationists responded with the formation of the America First Committee (AFC) later that year. Both groups hoped to muster public opinion for their opposing views. Debate often grew heated. AFC members, one of Roosevelt's cabinet members charged, were little more than "anti-democrats, appeasers, labor baiters, and anti-Semites."[32] In return, the AFC compared Roosevelt's 1941 declaration of emergency to Hitler's seizure of power in 1933.

Despite the acrimony, much of the debate focused on concrete issues related to national security. Little in the way of a crusading spirit, so prevalent in earlier debates over U.S. foreign policy, could be found on either side. The perceived failure of the previous war and Wilson's high-minded ideals had discredited such talk. Still, American exceptionalism remained central to the context of the debate. One side believed America should forge a separate destiny apart from a corrupt, warring world. The war, insisted the AFC, was "another chapter in the series of conflicts between Europeans for hundreds of years"[33] U.S. involvement would bring only "another conquest motivated by hate and another peace containing the seeds of the next war."[34] Meanwhile, the interventionists implied that only U.S. activism could save the world from a despotic future. German victory, Roosevelt claimed, would mean "living at the point of a gun— a gun loaded with explosive bullets, economic as well as military."[35]

Convinced he alone could mobilize the country against the threat, Roosevelt ran for an unprecedented third term in 1940. His assurance to a Boston audience that "[y]our boys are not going to be sent into any foreign wars," ensured victory.[36] Roosevelt then moved to extend what he considered a necessary lifeline to Britain and China. In early 1941, proclaiming that America would become "the great arsenal of democracy," FDR proposed the Lend-Lease Bill, authorizing the president to supply weapons and necessary materials to "any country the President deems vital to the defense of the United States." Over bitter isolationist objections, the bill passed into law in March 1941. When Germany suddenly turned and invaded its former ally the Soviet Union in June 1941, Roosevelt wasted little time in tendering lend-lease to the Soviets. Americans, however, remained of two minds about the conflagration in Europe. A highly placed AFC member lamented a recent poll showing "people overwhelmingly want to stay out of war and at the same time want to save Britain. They don't understand that these two worthy objectives contradict each other."[37]

As debate heated up, both interventionists and anti-interventionists continued to draw on the language of American exceptionalism. Charles Lindbergh, the famed aviator and most prominent AFC spokesman, told a Madison Square Garden audience that America was "a civilization in many ways never previously approached," boasting a "racial tolerance such as the world has never seen." "Why must all of this be jeopardized," Lindbergh asked, "by injecting the wars and hatreds of Europe into our midst?"[38] Harnessing some of the same language, Roosevelt retorted that failure to act would be "to reject the destiny which Washington strove so valiantly and so triumphantly to establish. The preservation of the spirit and faith of the Nation does, and will, furnish the highest justification for every sacrifice that we may make in the cause of national defence."[39] In his 1941 State of the Union message, Roosevelt laid out "four freedoms" that he proclaimed would be the basis of a better world "attainable in our own time and generation. That kind of world is the very antithesis of the so-called 'new order' which the dictators seek to create."[40]

That summer Roosevelt secretly journeyed to the North Atlantic Sea to meet with British prime minister Winston Churchill. There the two issued a joint declaration outlining common values to shape the postwar world. Among the principles articulated in what became known as the Atlantic Charter was the right to self-determination, reduction of trade barriers, disarmament, and freedom of the seas. Isolationists quickly objected that Roosevelt was reviving Wilson's Fourteen Points, laying out the same utopian vision that drove the United States into an unnecessary war in 1917. But Roosevelt insisted his aim was to save the world, not remake it. "I dream dreams," he protested, "but am, at the same time, an intensely practical person."[41]

By the time of the Atlantic Charter, American ships regularly were tangling with the German navy in the north seas. The road to war, however, came through Asia not Europe. Japanese resentment and distrust of America had deep roots. Theodore Roosevelt's Gentlemen's Agreement in 1908, cutting Japanese immigration to the United States, angered many Japanese. Wilson's cavalier treatment of the Japanese amendment declaring "racial equality" at Versailles contributed to antipathy, as did Congress's formal ban on Japanese immigration as part of the 1924 National Origins Act. Offended by Western colonialism, Japan moved brutally to incorporate Asia into its own sphere of influence, which it christened the "Great East Asia Co-Prosperity Sphere." Japan's invasion of China in 1937 set it on a collision course with the United States. In 1940, Roosevelt slapped a series of trade restrictions on Japan. A year later, together with Britain and the Netherlands, Roosevelt embargoed oil shipments to Japan in response to Japanese movement of troops into southern Indochina. Japan's alliance with Germany, its threat to the Philippines, and American "open door" principles in Asia no doubt also moved Roosevelt. Most certainly Roosevelt did not expect his actions to result in war in Asia. The Japanese, unable to live with the oil embargo and unwilling to retreat from China as the Americans demanded, planned a secret attack on the U.S. naval base at Pearl Harbor for December 7, 1941. The day after the attack, amid a mood of public fury, Roosevelt declared war on Japan. On December 11, Germany and Italy declared war on the United States.

WORLD WAR II

The second World War drove America infinitely deeper into world affairs and utterly transformed the country in the process. Millions of U.S. military men and women served around the world. At home Americans intensely followed events in corners of the world few had heard of only years before—Guadalcanal, Saipan, the Ardennes Forest, Tunisia. Isolationism as a political force evaporated. Internationalism, the recognition that America's fate was profoundly intertwined with the rest of the world, reigned unchallenged.

In the wake of Pearl Harbor, Winston Churchill traveled to America. President Roosevelt initially worried the prime minister's presence might offend lingering isolationist sentiment in the country. To the contrary, Americans warmly greeted Churchill, who immediately struck up a close working friendship with Roosevelt. Together they issued the "Declaration of United Nations" on January 1, 1942, signed by Britain, the United States, China, the USSR, and 23 other countries—"four fifths of the human race," boasted Churchill—committing themselves to the principles of the Atlantic Charter and to defeat of the Axis powers. Britain and the United States also forged a Joint Anglo-American Combined Chiefs of Staff, headed by U.S. general George C. Marshall, to oversee this truly global war.

Despite America's full-scale entry into the war, diplomacy remained of paramount importance. Although fighting together, serious differences divided the Allies. Contentious issues included diplomatic relations with the Vichy (German-controlled) French regime, pressure from the Polish government in exile, and China's demand for increased aid. Divisions even strained the strong Anglo-American alliance. Tensions were such that a fistfight over military tactics almost broke out between an American admiral and the British chief of staff at the Cairo Conference in 1943.

These divides however paled in comparison to mounting stress between the Soviets and their British and American counterparts. Suffering devastating losses while barely holding off German invaders, Soviet leader Joseph Stalin pressed his allies to open a second front to lift pressure off his exhausted forces. Meanwhile, Soviet designs on the Baltic States and Eastern Europe unsettled its allies. Partly to placate Stalin, the Americans and British invaded North Africa in 1942, then pressed into Italy in 1943. In a further gesture to reassure Stalin, in 1943, the Allies pledged at the Casablanca Conference to accept nothing short of "unconditional surrender." Nevertheless, real relief for Stalin would not come until the June 1944 cross-channel D-day invasion. The delay contributed mightily to postwar tension that later spiraled into the Cold War.

As the Allies bargained and pressed ahead against Germany, the U.S. home front dramatically transformed. War mobilization put an end to the Great Depression and reshaped the nation's economy. Millions migrated to centers of wartime industry such as San Diego and Norfolk, Virginia. Women, many of them married, found work in "Rosie the Riveter" jobs in wartime industries. African American activists also mobilized, pushing Roosevelt to bar racial discrimination in defense jobs and promoting a "double victory" over Nazi racism abroad and Jim Crow at home.

Consumed as he was by military planning, mobilization at home, and maintaining his wartime alliances, Roosevelt also strove to focus on the postwar world. Like Wilson, Roosevelt sought to promote international cooperation with the United States playing the central, indispensable role. But Roosevelt's idealism was more muscular than Wilson's. The president frequently spoke of China, America, Britain, and the Soviet Union serving as the "Four Policemen," enforcing postwar order. He also moved, in Wilsonian tradition, to organize an international organization to replace the failed League of Nations. In 1943, the Soviets agreed to participate in what eventually became the United Nations. Preliminary planning took place at Dumbarton Oaks, a mansion in Washington, DC, in 1944. In April 1945, delegates from 50 countries gathered in San Francisco to dedicate the UN to saving "succeeding generations from the scourge of war which twice in our lifetimes has brought untold sorrow to mankind." In contrast to Wilson's League, designers injected a strain of power politics into the UN. At the core of the organization would be a fifteen-member security council, with five permanent members, charged with maintaining world peace through force if necessary and each possessing veto power over council decisions.

Also unlike Wilson's League of Nations, the United Nations immediately gained widespread support at home. On January 10, 1945, Senator Arthur Vandenberg, formerly an ardent isolationist and FDR foe, took the Senate floor. Urging "that the present fraternity of war becomes a new fraternity of peace," he strongly endorsed U.S. participation in the United Nations. One of the Senate's most ardent isolationists was now a committed internationalist.

—⌒◦ ◦⌒—

As a result of World War II, isolationism had lost all credibility. Triumphant internationalists believed they were providing to the world a clear-eyed program to promote stability and prevent war. Yet elements of the old crusading spirit, anchored in American exceptionalism, remained. In his widely read 1941 editorial "The American Century," *Life* magazine editor Henry Luce urged Americans "to accept wholeheartedly our duty and our opportunity as the most powerful and vital nation in the world to exert upon the world the full impact of our influence." [42] The next half of the twentieth century would see the full exertion of America's influence guided by a commanding sense of mission, but debates about the nature and propriety of that influence would continue.

CHAPTER EIGHT

Emerging Economic Hegemon

UNCLE SAM AND THE BANANA MAN

Samuel Zemurray, later popularly known as "Sam the Banana Man," left his family home in present-day Moldova (then a part of Russia) to journey to Selma, Alabama, at age 15. He arrived in 1892 virtually penniless, but bananas, the tropical fruit most Americans considered an expensive delicacy in the late nineteenth century, soon changed his fortunes. Sam understood bananas were perishable and had to be transported to market quickly. He began buying ripening bananas (as opposed to "greens," yet to ripen) off the docks of Mobile, Alabama. He then immediately shipped them by train to waiting grocers down the line, alerting his buyers by telegraph with the message "Sam the Banana Man is coming!" [1] Instead of rotting on the dock, Zemurray's bananas sped onto store shelves—and into the hands of hungry customers. Bananas soon became an abundant, low-cost staple of the American diet.

Tropical produce made Sam rich by his early twenties, but he yearned to compete with the big boys—United Fruit Company (UFCO), which dominated the fruit industry, owning thousands of cultivated acres in Latin America. In 1910, Zemurray purchased land along the Cuyamel River in Honduras, where he planned to grow his own bananas. The Honduran government, however, had other ideas. It refused Zemurray important concessions for railroads necessary to ship his fruit. Instead, government officials entered negotiations to obtain generous loans from American banking kingpin J. P. Morgan—an arrangement likely to shut out Zemurray's nascent operation. Refusing to concede, Sam took the low road. He hired Lee Christmas and Guy "Machine Gun" Molony, two nefarious soldiers of fortune. Flush with Zemurray's money, the mercenaries armed themselves and led a private army of 600 against the Honduran government, which they quickly toppled and replaced with leaders more sympathetic to Zemurray.

Now enjoying the full favor of local authorities—Zemurray liked to boast that "a mule costs more than a congressman" in Honduras—the Russian immigrant, still speaking with a thick accent, prospered.[2] His Cuyamel Fruit Company gained ever growing shares of the market, soon competing directly with UFCO. In 1930, "the Banana Man" sold his company to UFCO at a hefty profit. Three years later, with UFCO reeling from the Great Depression and mismanagement, Zemurray organized a stockholders' revolt and emerged as UFCO's new president. Sam quickly turned the company around and continued its aggressive expansion into Latin America.

Along the way, Zemurray and UFCO earned a reputation for ruthlessness, which Sam later regretted. "All we cared about were dividends. I feel guilty about some of the things we did," he confessed in the early 1950s.[3] Yet even as he made that admission, Sam joined in activities that would eventually lead the CIA to overthrow a leftist government in Guatemala, a government that appeared hostile to UFCO's interests.

As Sam the Banana Man's story demonstrates, America's informal empire (discussed in chapter 7) benefited American businessmen who, in turn, spread American influence around the world during the crucial first decades of the twentieth century. While force often backed American economic expansion, an ideology promoting free trade and the benefits of commercial progress propelled U.S. commercial interests in the Western Hemisphere—and beyond.

Expanding American commercialism was not without its critics abroad. Likewise, not all Americans acquiesced to this new form of imperialism; some strenuously objected. The majority, however, while viewing aspects of the informal empire as unsavory, appreciated the benefits of emerging globalization (including cheap bananas). Two world wars and a severe depression failed to arrest the march of American commerce. By the end of the first half of the "American Century," the United States was poised to expand its informal empire worldwide.

INDUSTRIAL LEADER WITH GLOBAL REACH

"That the United States of America have now arrived at such a pitch of power and prosperity as to have a right to claim the leading place among the nations cannot be denied," pronounced journalist William Thomas Stead in 1901.[4] Indeed, by the early twentieth century, America had risen to be the leading industrial nation in the world. Huge factories practicing economies of scale unthinkable only decades before dotted the landscape, especially in the Northeast and Midwest. A swelling population, which grew by 16 million between 1900 and 1910, furnished industry with markets and labor. Americans enjoyed the highest per capita income in the world, an abundance of natural resources, and rich reservoirs of capital backing the nation's mushrooming industries.

However, the American economy continued to rely on domestic rather than foreign markets. U.S. exports never amounted to more than 10 percent of its gross national product (GNP) until World War I. Of that small amount, the bulk until the 1930s remained primary products such as cotton, grain, tobacco, oil, and meat. High tariffs erected barriers to imports, strengthening the domestic market but impeding globalization. The United States, in fact, competed with Russia as the most protectionist of the great powers.

Still, the growing American economy proved quite attractive to investors worldwide. Foreign bankers and financiers invested not only in U.S. industry but also in mining, ranching, and lumber. Great Britain served as primary patron, contributing 60 percent of international investments, followed by Germany at 15 percent. Several financial developments, most notably movement toward an international gold standard, encouraged foreign investment in America. Still lacking a central bank and plagued by political divisions over currency, nineteenth-century America appeared a financial muddle compared to Europe.

By the late nineteenth century, however, order began to replace chaos. Following the defeat of the silver lobby in the 1896 presidential election, the Gold Standard Act of 1900 defined the dollar exclusively at a convertible fixed amount of gold, making clear to all parties the absolute value of a dollar, and allowing foreign investors to feel more secure expanding their American ventures. The Federal Reserve Act of 1913, which created a central banking system similar to ones in European countries, also stabilized the American economy and made it more attractive to investors. Improving communications and growing immigration (detailed in the introduction to part 3) further connected America's economy to Europe and the rest of the world.

In turn, Americans began to think more about cultivating international markets. The sharp recession of the 1890s fed this growing interest. Many blamed agricultural and industrial overproduction for the economic crisis. The development of foreign markets, trade proponents reasoned, offered a remedy to the "glut" crisis facing the U.S economy. "We must have new markets," urged influential senator Henry Cabot Lodge, "unless we would be visited by declines in wages and by great industrial disturbances of which signs have not been lacking."[5]

Informal Empire in Latin America

America's own hemisphere offered the most hospitable terrain for expanding U.S. business interests —as the tale of Sam "the Banana Man" Zemurray attests. While U.S. officials pushed for an "open door" to trade elsewhere (such as in China), Americans, operating in closer proximity and with increasing power, sought to establish a monopoly in their Latin American "backyard."

The lingering presence of Spain, which maintained possession of Cuba and other Caribbean holdings, however, remained an obstacle to U.S. ambitions. By the late nineteenth century, U.S. investment in Cuba had far outpaced that of Spain. The McKinley Tariff of 1890 exempted Cuban sugar, the island's primary crop, from levies, greatly enhancing Cuban-American trade. American holdings in Cuba—including ranches, mines, railroads, and large plantations—reached $50 million by the mid-1890s. Some 87 percent of Cuban exports during this period came to the United States. The 1895 rebellion against Spanish rule (discussed in chapter 7) worried U.S. investors in Cuba, many of whom feared that American military action would only further threaten their assets. Supporters of war were undeterred. "We will have this war—in spite of the timidity of the commercial interests," insisted Theodore Roosevelt, then assistant secretary of the navy.[6]

Roosevelt got his way; the Spanish-American War put a swift end to Spain's rule in Cuba—but not to continuing foreign domination. The short war and subsequent Platt Amendment, guaranteeing American control of the island, opened new opportunities for U.S. commerce. As the Spanish exited, Americans entered, buying up plantations and estates at bargain-basement prices. "Nowhere else in the world are there such chances for success for the man of moderate means as well as for the capitalist, as Cuba offers today," waxed one U.S. investor. Cubans, meanwhile, watched in anguish as, in the words of one government official, Americans "leap ashore from steamboats from the north—with wallets full of banknotes—ready to buy at low prices our immense land. We shall be left powerless."[7]

Thriving in what was essentially a U.S. colony, American investment in Cuba topped the $200 million mark by 1911. By 1921, U.S direct investment climbed further to $1.3 billion. Yet heavy outlays, especially in the sugar industry, discouraged diversification, leaving the Cuban economy vulnerable to market fluctuations. Exasperation at American exploitation frequently boiled over in Cuba. U.S. troops returned to the island several times over the three decades after 1898 to safeguard American investments. Americans "treat us as a people incapable of acting for ourselves, and have reduced us to obedience, to submission, and to tutelage imposed by force," bitterly lamented one Cuban. "It is America who is the enemy, in the mind of the average Cuban—between Americans and Cubans no love exists," reported an American traveler to Cuba in 1910.[8]

Cuba quickly became a model for informal American imperialism in the region. While the United States established no formal colonies, U.S. business interests expanded aggressively—backed, when necessary, by military force. The United States increasingly integrated Latin America into its economic system. The region provided cheap raw materials and agricultural products for the industrial colossus to the north.

Panama, where in 1904 Americans began digging a monumental canal to connect two oceans, also emerged as part of this economic system. U.S. support for Panamanians against their Colombian government in 1903 produced not only territory for the canal but also a country ripe for American economic investment. As was the case in Cuba, the new Panamanian constitution gave Americans the right to intervene "to reestablish public peace and constitutional order." The U.S. military established bases along the canal—from which it made frequent shows of power, often to protect growing American commercial interests.

U.S. commerce spread in Panama—both inside and outside the canal zone. Sailing down Panama's Bayano River in 1912, Chicago newspaperman William Dickson Boyce passed "several plantations, owned by American companies which were from six to over a hundred thousand acres in extent. At San Antonio, the Illinois Lumber Company of Peoria had a tract of 8,000 acres." Upriver, Boyce found "the United Fruit Company has a large tract and just beyond this concession is land owned by some California people." Panama, Boyce concluded, "is the southern boundary line of the United States."[9] As in Cuba, however, the omnipresence of American businesses and often racist wealthy Americans bred deep resentment, especially among Panama's poor. "[T]he lower classes of this republic hate us," admitted a U.S. minister to Panama.[10]

For many Latin Americans, the United Fruit Company, later run by Sam "the Banana Man" Zemurray, symbolized their increasing subservience to American economic imperialism. Founded in 1899, the Boston-based UFCO gobbled up hundreds of thousands of acres in Central America, the Caribbean, and South America, converting them into vast tracts of fruit-producing land. UFCO owned its own fleet of ships (sailing under foreign flags), railroads, banks, and even published a daily newspaper entitled *El Diario Commercial* for its nearly 100,000 workers.

Where native workers were unavailable, UFCO imported thousands of West Indians, some fresh from building the Panama Canal. The company sought strict control over its labor force—creating a system essentially modeled on the Jim Crow South. Theaters, dance halls, and eating facilities in company towns were strictly segregated. UFCO overseers viewed both their imported and native workers as commodities—much like the land on which they worked. "[T]he attitude of the average white employee," acknowledged a former manager, "is one of sneering contempt for the native of the country."[11]

UFCO, its critics charged, created "Banana Republics": Caribbean and Central American countries dependent on one crop, exploited by U.S. commercial interests, and dominated by a small wealthy elite while the general population remained mired in poverty. UFCO and other American fruit growers depended on the U.S. government and military to physically protect its interests. Over and over—following the dictate of the 1904 Roosevelt Corollary—the American military mobilized in defense of UFCO and similar U.S. operations. Beginning in 1918 for instance, U.S. soldiers occupied the Panamanian province of Chiriqui for three years to secure American holdings, including those of UFCO.

The threat of American military intervention and the aggressive practices of UCFO and other U.S. enterprises generated antipathy throughout Latin America. Locally, UFCO was known as *el pulp*, or "the octopus," suggesting the company's far-reaching, all-pervasive influence. At times workers did organize against the octopus, but they faced fierce resistance. In 1909, Guatemalan troops put down a strike by black UFCO employees. Later, many of UFCO's black workers became followers of Marcus Garvey (who had briefly worked for UFCO in Costa Rica) and his Universal Negro Improvement Association (discussed in chapter 9). UFCO officials, however, remained ready and willing to use force to control their workers. Most notoriously, Colombian troops fired into a crowd of striking UFCO workers in 1928, killing hundreds. Author Gabriel García Márquez later immortalized the episode in his novel *One Hundred Years of Solitude*.

A similar tale of exploitation and resentment took place in Mexico, which received more U.S. direct investment in the early twentieth century than any other country in the world. Americans aggressively drilled for oil, dug mines, built railroads, and constructed company towns where U.S. employers controlled everything down to the police force. Mexican resentment of such incursions contributed to the bitter revolution that began in 1910. As revolutionary fervor settled, Mexican officials looked to secure control of their natural resources. The 1917 Mexican Constitution placed severe restrictions on foreign ownership of oil.

In the 1930s, President Franklin Roosevelt attempted to right past wrongs and exploitation with his "Good Neighbor" initiatives. Roosevelt renounced the right to intervene in Latin America and attempted to set trade on a more equitable footing. While his initiative yielded some success, U.S. exploitation of the region continued—leaving a legacy of exploitation, poverty, and resentment.

Open Door Dreams in China

Although U.S. economic penetration of Latin America was well under way as the century opened, the distant lure of the "China market" rather than nearby spoils drew the attention of many twentieth-century Americans. This was nothing new. For decades, the fabled "romance of the orient"—a supposed exotic, erotic world of adventure and enchantment—had mesmerized certain romantically inclined Americans. The economic collapse in the 1890s lent new urgency to efforts to open Chinese markets, already heavily exploited by European powers. Sheer numbers alone—400 million potential Chinese customers (the U.S. population in 1900 was 77 million)—entranced American businessmen. "If the Chinese should spend only one cent per day per capita," computed American railroad magnate James Hill, "it would amount to 4,000,000 a day."[12]

American designs on the China market encouraged the Philippines annexation in 1899. Robert La Follette, later an outspoken anti-imperialist, threw his support behind annexation because it would allow the United States "to conquer [its] rightful share of that great market now opening [in China] for the world's commerce."[13] In 1899 and 1900, Secretary of State John Hay issued his "Open Door Notes" (discussed in chapter 7), which caused some Americans to trumpet a "special relationship" between the American and Chinese people. Yet the plight of Chinese immigrants in the United States belied such claims and emerged as an obstacle to American commercial ambitions in China. Numbering just under 100,000 at the turn of the century, Chinese immigrants made invaluable contributions to economic development in America, especially in railroad construction. But a series of restrictive immigration acts beginning in 1882 impeded Chinese wishing to come to the United States—more so than any other nationality. Once in the country, Chinese immigrants often faced hostility and outright violence from American workers, who acted out of racism and fear of economic competition.

Stories of restrictions and harsh treatment facing immigrants ricocheted back to China, triggering resentment. With American influence and commerce spreading in China, the Chinese decided to strike back. Demanding liberalization of immigration laws and better treatment for immigrants, in 1905 the Shanghai Chamber of Commerce declared a boycott of American businesses operating in China. From Shanghai, protests quickly spread up and down the coast of China. Songs, posters, and pamphlets stirred support. Chinese in America raised money to aid the cause, while Chinese in the Philippines joined the boycott. Eventually the U.S. government, concerned about access to the Chinese market, made slight adjustments to its immigration policies, and the boycott petered out. But the size and vehemence of the protests certainly called into question any notion of a "special relationship" between Americans and Chinese—and the wisdom of U.S. investment in the troubled country.

Undeterred, American businessmen pressed on—with limited results. Among those beguiled by China was railroad tycoon E. H. Harriman. Unlike most sharing his interest in Asia, Harriman actually traveled in 1905 to Japan, Korea, and China. Impressed by the potential of the region, he attempted to purchase a Manchurian railroad line that he planned to extend to the Russian border. The 1907 financial panic put an end to his immediate designs, but he continued planning a China venture to his death in 1909.

Under the administration of President William Howard Taft, who boasted he would expand U.S. trade through "dollar diplomacy," China took on renewed importance. Sharing Harriman's vision of a railroad through resource-rich Manchuria, the Taft administration began rallying businessmen to the cause. For their part, the Chinese were eager to counterbalance the growing influence of other foreigners in the area. In the end, however, Japanese and Russian resistance to threats to their own interests in Manchuria combined with Chinese impotency doomed the plan.

Dreams of 400 million Chinese consuming American products unraveled one after the other in the decade and a half before World War I. In the arena of railroad construction, where Americans had invested significantly, results proved particularly disappointing: Americans by 1911 had built a mere 29 of China's 5,771 total railroad miles. Exports to China in 1911 accounted for a measly 1 percent of total U.S. exports. Increasingly, U.S. businessmen recognized China was too poor and unstable to serve American interests. In 1911

anger in China at ineffective leadership and continuing foreign economic incursions spilled over into revolution and the overthrow of the Manchu dynasty.
By 1916, China collapsed into full-scale civil war and disarray. American commercial goals for the region would have to be put on hold.

Fordism and Mass Marketing

American manufacturers also moved to expand their worldwide market share
in the early twentieth century. U.S. companies like the Singer Manufacturing
Corporation, makers of sewing machines, already had made significant inroads overseas. The real international breakthrough, however, came in the
first years of the new century. The automobile—the product most associated
with twentieth-century American industry—led the way.

Ironically, the "horseless carriage" so associated with America, had its beginnings almost exclusively in Europe. Familiar French and German names
like Carl Benz and Louis Renault made major contributions to the early automobile. Americans, however, quickly seized on the car and made it their own.
The name Henry Ford stands out. In 1908, Detroit-automaker Ford introduced
his Model T, a simple stripped-down automobile sold at an unprecedented low
price. To reduce costs and increase output, Ford standardized and accelerated
production by introducing a moving assembly line driven by conveyor belts
that towed parts between workers. Soon, Ford plants were assembling 1,000
cars a day. In 1916, Ford sold 577,000 Model Ts. Partly to stabilize his workforce
and partly to empower workers so they could afford cars like the Model T, Ford
began paying his employees generous wages of five dollars a day in 1914. Ford's
revolutionary approach, which seemed to portend a bright democratic future
spurred by industrialization, brought the automaker worldwide fame.

Although a man of deep personal prejudices and intense isolationist leanings,
in business Ford was an internationalist. His Ford Motor Company emerged
a multinational corporation from its inception. In fact, the sixth car ever produced by Ford was sent to Canada. By 1914, Ford had dealers in France, Germany,
Belgium, Holland, Sweden, Denmark, Austria, and Russia. He also built factories across Europe—all directly owned and controlled by the Ford corporation.

Ford became a hero to many for placing car ownership within the reach
of the common man. Others, however, looked with annoyance at the upstart
American and his simple, unadorned cars. "It is to the credit of our English
makers that they choose rather to maintain their reputation for high grade

work," commented the British trade magazine *Autocar*, "than cheapen by the use of the inferior material and workmanship they would be obliged to employ to compete with American manufacturing of cheap cars."[14]

The same Fordist commitment to standardization and mass marketing also began to transform the retail industry—in America and abroad. In 1879, Frank W. Woolworth introduced a new variation on the department store: the discount "5 and 10 Cent Store." Woolworth dealt directly with manufacturers, allowing him to offer steep discounts on general merchandise. Everything in his stores sold for five or ten cents. Like Ford, Woolworth aimed to bring the wonders of industrialization to the masses. The concept quickly took off with the average American. Soon Frank Woolworth moved to take his concept worldwide. In 1909, a band concert and fireworks show, attracting thousands, inaugurated the opening of the first Woolworth store in Britain. The company chose the industrial town of Liverpool in northern England as the site of its new store—a four-story building (with three sales floors) that included a restaurant serving free afternoon tea. Within a year, several other Woolworths—known as "three and six stores" (to reflect English coinage)—opened throughout Britain. In less than two decades' time, Woolworth had hundreds of stores throughout Britain, and the company was moving into Germany.

Not all Europeans welcomed brash American entrepreneurs with their modern uniform products aimed at the common man. Social critics blasted the American "invasion" in books and articles with titles such as *America the Menace: Scenes from the Life of the Future*. Unapologetic, Americans continued to construct the base of what increasingly was becoming a commercial empire.

WAR AND THE AMBIVALENT TWENTIES

World War I, beginning in 1914, elevated America from a net debtor to the status of the world's major creditor. Initially, however, the outbreak of fighting in Europe portended disaster for the American economy. Facing war, Europeans moved to sell assets in America, and continental markets for American products and materials dried up. Hoping to head off collapse, the New York Stock Exchange closed for four months in 1914. The U.S. economy, already in recession since 1913, teetered on the brink of full collapse. By early 1915, however, circumstances reversed themselves again. Orders began piling up in American factories from Europeans desperate for resupplies as fighting entered a stalemate. American banker J. P. Morgan emerged as the unofficial representative of allied (French and British) interests in America, extending credit and arranging for $3 billion in shipments to France and Britain. American loans, allowing the Allies and (to a lesser extent) Germans access to U.S. markets, bolstered the American economy. Companies like Bethlehem Steel and DuPont, the chemical manufacturer, thrived—forging success from European distress. Flush, Americans in turn bought up European securities at bargain prices. Between 1915 and 1917, U.S. investors purchased $900 million in British and $700 million in French securities.

American trade with belligerents, however, roused controversy. Critics claimed such trade inevitably would lead to U.S. involvement in the war— especially as Americans increasingly traded more with Britain and France and less with Germany. While dealings with Germany dwindled, by 1916 U.S. banks were loaning Britain roughly $10 million a day. Seeking to snap America's lifeline to the Allies, Germany declared unrestricted submarine warfare in 1917, pushing America into the war on the side of the British and French. Once the nation entered the war, the U.S. government replaced private creditors as the primary lender to the Allies. Through bond sales and taxes, Wilson provided a staggering $10 billion for struggling France and Britain from a total of roughly $31 billion spent on the war.

While winning the war, of course, remained the priority, Americans also sought to advance their commercial and financial interests. Over objections from Britain, President Wilson insisted that "freedom of the seas" be a key allied war aim—a provision sure to enhance American commerce. Secretary of the Treasury William McAdoo also aggressively prodded Britain to sell remaining holdings and formally assume responsibility for wartime debts. In another example of wartime exigencies pushing commercial interests, the U.S. government moved to control the growing communications field. Government officials worked to break the British monopoly of cables carrying telegraph messages. The potential of wireless communication proved of even greater interest to Americans. During World War I, the U.S. government nationalized its radio system and enhanced radio technology. Although radio returned to the private sector after the war, President Wilson encouraged the creation of a new company, the Radio Corporation of America (RCA), from the mergers of several companies. RCA almost immediately became the international leader with the pronounced goal of making "America the center of the World."

At the dawn of World War I, foreign holdings in the United States eclipsed its investments in other countries. By war's end, the reverse was true; America emerged the world's greatest creditor nation. U.S. foreign liabilities dropped from $5 billion in 1914 to $2 billion in 1919. Meanwhile, America's international holdings grew by $7 billion. The United States appeared poised to assume the mantle of global economic leadership. But after an exhausting and costly war, in which over 100,000 young Americans died, few Americans felt excitement at the prospect. Many, in fact, hoped to reestablish some distance from the rest of the world.

While American relief efforts under future president Herbert Hoover provided some immediate needs in war-torn Europe, European pleas for debt cancellation were met with stony indignation. "They hired the money, didn't they," curtly retorted President Calvin Coolidge. As the burden of repayment, amounting to $10 billion, slowed reconstruction, Europeans began maligning the United States as "Uncle Shylock."

Meanwhile, in 1922, protectionists in Congress passed the Fordney-McCumber Tariff, raising duties from 15.2 percent to 36.2 percent. Europeans howled that the tariff would further impede their postwar recovery, while American exporters warned of European retaliation against U.S. goods. Still Congress stood its ground.

Europe's economic and political struggles, however, soon became impossible to ignore. Painful inflation ravaged Germany, which shortly defaulted on its reparations payments, totaling $33 billion. In 1923 France and Belgium responded by invading and occupying the Ruhr Valley area of Germany, home to significant coal resources and important factories. The ensuing crisis pushed Americans to act. Prompted by the State Department, American businessman Charles Dawes negotiated an end to the French occupation. Under the Dawes Plan, U.S. banks, especially the ubiquitous House of Morgan, loaned Germany money permitting it to make reparations payments. In turn this allowed former allied countries to repay debts owed to the United States.

While the Dawes Plan aimed primarily to ease the burden of debt and reparations, it also generated markets for American manufactures. This helped the U.S. economy recover quickly following a postwar recession. Between 1922 and 1929 industrial output almost doubled. Flourishing, U.S. businesses moved even more assertively beyond American borders. Direct investment abroad by U.S. firms nearly doubled in the 1920s to $7.55 billion. American corporations like General Electric, General Motors, U.S. Steel, and DuPont aggressively marketed products and established operations overseas. Automobiles again led the way. By the late 1920s, cars accounted for nearly 10 percent of all U.S. exports, and 10 percent of American-made cars became exports (up from 5.5 percent in 1913). Expansion failed only in Italy, where U.S. automakers ran up against a fascist government (foreshadowing future troubles).

Meanwhile, American businesses moved into new regions of the world. Tire magnate Harvey Firestone leased land in Liberia for a rubber plantation (land previously promised to Marcus Garvey's UNIA). Backing Firestone, the U.S. government floated loans to the west African nation with the stipulation that American advisers would take control of Liberian finances, an agreement that lasted until the 1950s. Not to be outdone, Henry Ford purchased 2.5 million acres in the Brazilian Amazon in 1928, hoping to produce rubber. But unlike Firestone's initiative, Fordlandia, as the automaker modestly named his undertaking, failed miserably. Despite ideological differences and the absence of formal diplomatic relations, American businessmen also established operations in the Soviet Union. Among other projects, General Electric constructed a damn along the Dnieper River, and Ford built a plant in Nijni-Novgorod.

As in the case of Firestone's Liberian enterprise, the U.S. government worked to facilitate U.S. foreign trade. The Webb-Pomerene Act (1918) exempted business combinations involved in international trade from antitrust laws, and the Edge Act (1919) permitted U.S. banks to establish foreign branches. Meanwhile, Secretary of Commerce Herbert Hoover expanded the Commerce Department and devoted it to promoting trade abroad.

American cultural products also penetrated the world in the 1920s. Jazz records, first introduced by U.S. soldiers to Europeans during the war, appealed especially to the young. American movies spread to the far reaches of the globe. Clara Bow, Douglas Fairbanks, Mary Pickford, and Charlie Chaplin became international phenomena. By the 1920s, Hollywood provided a quarter of the films shown in Japan, 70 percent of those in France, and 80 percent of those in South America. Hollywood not only introduced the world to U.S. products but also to a distinctly American universe of attitudes and expectations. British film audiences, complained one English critic, "talk American, think American, dream American; we have several million people, mostly women, who, to all intents, are temporary Americans."[15]

Many around the world began using the term "Americanization" in reference to the commercial and cultural tidal wave washing up on their shores. Americanization, however, engendered strikingly different reactions among different people. To some it suggested modernity and freedom. "American gasoline and American ideas have circulated throughout France, bringing a new vision of power and a new tempo," waxed French poet and diplomat Paul Claudel.[16] Others feared an "American invasion," with its "gray monotone, mechanistic uniformity," would destroy community and tradition.[17] Imperial America, warned Argentine critic Manuel Ugarte, had become "the new Rome,"

conquering the world with its culture rather than its armies.[18] Seeking to still
the American tide, corporations in several European countries changed their
bylaws to prevent foreigners—most likely Americans—from purchasing company stock. "Buy local" campaigns also sprang up. "My Country First—Protect
its Industries—Buy its Goods—Be Australian—Buy Australian-Made Goods,"
urged the Australian Industries Protection League.[19]

Despite ambivalence both at home and abroad, American commerce and
culture continued its worldwide march in the 1920s. Prosperity helped ease the
contradictions and tensions at the core of America's rapidly coalescing informal empire. Worldwide economic crisis, however, beginning in 1929, exposed festering nationalism and resistance to globalization. Everywhere,
the 1930s would be very different from the 1920s.

ECONOMIC NATIONALISM AND THE GLOBAL DEPRESSION

Good times never last. In October 1929, the New York Stock Exchange crashed.
Bank failures, deflation, unemployment, and industrial breakdown followed.
The gross national product in America fell from $98.4 billion in 1929 to half
that by 1932. During the same period, the value of manufactured goods fell
by one quarter, thousands of banks failed, and 15 million Americans lost their
jobs. The Great Depression had arrived.

America's collapse quickly infected the rest of the world. U.S. credit
dried up, and Americans scrambled to sell off foreign holdings before they
too became worthless. Between 1929 and 1932, industrial production worldwide declined by a staggering 38 percent. As in America, European banks
began failing. In 1931 the Viennese Credit-Anstalt, the leading bank in Eastern Europe, collapsed, sending shock waves through Europe and leading to
more bank failures. Agriculture-based economies, already struggling in the
1920s, faced calamity. By the early 1930s, a bushel of wheat sold at the lowest
price in 400 years. Cotton, cocoa, corn, and coffee prices all went into free
fall. In rapid succession, Americans halted loans to Europe, Germany defaulted on its reparations, and the Europeans stopped repaying wartime
debts. In 1931, President Herbert Hoover announced a one-year moratorium
on debt repayments, but Europeans proved unable to pick up their payments after the respite. Desperately trying to salvage the situation, Hoover
offered to cancel Britain's debts in exchange for its colonies in Trinidad and
British Honduras (present-day Belize). Great Britain, however, balked at the
offer.

For self-preservation, nations, including America, turned inward—reverting to economic nationalism. Import quotas, trade discrimination, and high tariffs replaced open trade and international outreach. In 1931 Great Britain abandoned the gold standard. More than 20 countries, including Japan, quickly followed its lead. Nations began devaluing their currencies to gain the upper hand in trade at the expense of other countries. Such "beggar-thy-neighbor" strategies only further undermined the international economy.

The nationalist mood rapidly turned ugly. In Hitler's Germany, officials assailed the American Gillette Company, makers of safety razors, as a Jewish-controlled "octopus" and mandated that only "pure" German companies operate in the Fatherland (still, several American firms maintained operations in Germany, including DuPont, Standard Oil, and Union Carbide). In 1934, the Japanese announced the Amau Doctrine, essentially a Monroe Doctrine for their region: henceforth Japan would reserve the right to intervene in the affairs of East Asian countries to "preserve peace and order." Meanwhile, Mexico nationalized its petroleum reserves, infuriating British and American oil companies. Everywhere the "open door" ideal of free trade receded. Correspondingly, worldwide trade fell by 40 percent in the early 1930s.

American actions mirrored the nationalistic retreat. With President Hoover's approval, Congress passed the Smoot-Hawley Tariff in 1930, sending rates to dramatic highs in hope of protecting American domestic production. On his last day in office, Hoover signed legislation requiring the federal government to buy only American-made products.

Although he pulled the United States off the gold standard, President Franklin Roosevelt initially indicated an openness to international action on behalf of the beleaguered economy. In June 1933, he dispatched representatives to an international conference in London aimed at forging a joint response to the crisis. Conference delegates began exploring a coordinated return to the gold standard, believing it would lend needed stability to the global economy. An early draft agreement, approved by American representatives, in fact, endorsed restoration of the gold standard.

Roosevelt, however, was coming to a very different conclusion. Sailing off the coast of New England, he read a *Saturday Evening Post* article that took a hard nationalist line on economics. Each nation, the piece argued, must "find how it shall balance its own budget, reemploy its own people, restore its own solvency." Roosevelt found himself agreeing that America must first look after itself. At earliest opportunity he sent his delegation in London a sharply worded telegram, dubbed "the bombshell message." Condemning "old fetishes of so-called international bankers," Roosevelt denounced cooperative moves toward currency stabilization. The United States, FDR made clear, was going it alone. The president's volley stunned his advisers in London—and infuriated Europeans. The Manchester *Guardian* decried the message as "A Manifesto of Anarchy." British prime minister Ramsay MacDonald lamented: "How could [Roosevelt] have sent such a message to me?"[20]

The nationalistic trend continued the next year. Congress passed the Johnson Act, banning private loans to countries that defaulted on their debts. Seeking to stem deflation and promote U.S. products overseas, in 1934 Roosevelt devalued the dollar by increasing the value of gold to $35 an ounce from $20.67 (thus rendering American exports cheaper in countries with tighter currency).

American direct investment abroad, which peaked in 1929 at $602 million, receded—not reaching 1929 levels again until 1956. "Americanization," so hotly debated only years before, also ebbed. Woolworth reorganized its British stores as a public company and sold 48 percent of its stock in Britain. In 1932, UFCO revalued its assets, acknowledging the loss of millions.

Public anxiety and anger fed economic nationalism in America. Many Americans blamed cheap imports for the depression. Newspaper publisher William Randolph Hearst mounted a "Buy American" campaign, vigorously promoted by his media empire. "My Mother and Dad say everyone should buy American so lots of people will get jobs," pleaded a young girl in a Hearst Metrotone newsreel.[21] Meanwhile, from his headquarters outside Detroit, Father Charles Coughlin broadcast populist attacks on bankers and European "money-changers" to his radio audience of millions. Hostility toward globalization reached a crescendo in the mid-1930s when Senator Gerald Nye sponsored hearings that ultimately blamed international trade and greedy U.S. corporations for America's intervention in the world war in 1917.

Yet some Americans remained committed to a vision of global economic integration. Cordell Hull, the U.S. secretary of state, had devoted his life to the Wilsonian principle that, as Hull put it, "trade between nations is the great peacemaker and civilizer within human experience."[22] Trade, Hull told a skeptical Roosevelt, could engender both economic recovery and world peace. By 1934, the secretary of state made some progress. That year the president threw his support behind the Reciprocal Trade Agreements Act, one of Hull's pet projects. The act empowered the president to cut tariff rates up to 50 percent with nations granting similar concessions. Roosevelt also created the Export-Import Bank in 1934, to provide loans to countries wishing to purchase U.S.

goods. Likewise, Roosevelt's decision in 1934 to peg the dollar to gold at $35 an ounce provided some stability to the world's currencies.

By the mid-1930s, then, America appeared to be backing away from overt economic nationalism. Still, despite Hull's best efforts, international trade remained anemic compared to its highs in the 1920s. While American exports rose from $1.61 billion in 1932 to $3.18 billion in 1939, trade remained well below the 1929 level of $5.24 billion. By this time, however, war in Europe and Asia increasingly defined discussions and debates about trade.

ISOLATIONISM, TRADE, AND WAR

By the late 1930s, trade increasingly became entangled with security concerns—sparking intense debate about its role in an ever more dangerous world. While commerce did not cause World War II, developments in Asia and Europe clearly threatened America's long-held "open door" ideals regarding trade. Japan's pronounced policy of forging a sphere of influence in Asia—its Greater East Asia Co-Prosperity Sphere—challenged the century-old notion of a Sino-American "special relationship" and persistent dreams of harnessing the "China market" for America. Japanese control of Asia more immediately imperiled American access to important natural resources such as tungsten, manganese, and nickel. Likewise, a Europe dominated by the militaristic National Socialism of Hitler gravely threatened American economic interests. Fearing trade would drag America into another world war, isolationists mobilized. Trade with belligerent nations became the most bitterly debated controversy of the late 1930s. In Congress, isolationists passed a series of neutrality acts, curtailing trade with nations at war. Eager to aid Britain and China, Roosevelt desperately sought flexibility, often clashing angrily with isolationists.

In Asia, the president supported trade restrictions against Japan as a particularly stinging weapon. Japan had limited resources of its own and depended on America for 44 percent of its imports in the late 1930s. Roosevelt aimed, an adviser explained, to "slip the noose around Japan's head and give it a jerk now and then."[23] But the Japanese recoiled, especially at Roosevelt's oil embargo, declared in the summer of 1941 after Japanese troops moved into Indochina. Determined to break the U.S. stranglehold, on December 7, 1941, Japanese planes attacked Pearl Harbor.

Even before Pearl Harbor, American sales of war materiel under the Lend-Lease Act (discussed in chapter 7) effectively ended the depression.

Unemployment that had stood just below 15 percent in 1940 virtually disappeared by 1941. After the December 7 attack, American industry moved into overdrive. As the war opened, Roosevelt set out what seemed terribly ambitious goals of doubling the U.S. combat fleet and fabricating some 7,800 aircraft. Quickly U.S. industry surpassed FDR's markers. The automobile sector hastily converted the majority of its 1,000 U.S. plants to wartime production. By 1943, unemployment had fallen to 1.2 percent.

During the war, the U.S. government also lavishly funded research and development (R&D) projects. Military research expenditures rose from $29.6 million in 1940 to $423.6 million in 1945. Breakthroughs in electronics and radar directly emanated from these investments. The Manhattan Project, which developed the first nuclear bomb, towered over all R&D initiatives. At a cost of almost $2 billion, the project eventually employed over 100,000 workers at some 37 installations in the United States and Canada. The undertaking truly proved an international affair—bringing together scientists from around the western world. Hungarian Edward Teller, Italian Enrico Fermi, Swiss-born Felix Bloch, and Dane Niels Bohr all contributed their expertise. German-born Albert Einstein provided some of the impetus for the project in letters he wrote President Roosevelt, warning of German efforts to develop nuclear weaponry.

While scientists worked to develop nuclear technology, a more pressing concern emerged. "We're Running Out of Oil!" warned Secretary of the Interior Harold Ickes in a January 1944 article in *American Magazine*. The war had dramatically taxed U.S. oil resources. A shortage would be a potentially fatal handicap. "In all surveys of the situation," explained State Department economic adviser Herbert Feis, "the pencil came to an awed pause at one point and place—the Middle East."[24] Increasingly, Americans pushed into the Middle East, especially Saudi Arabia, promising postwar loans in return for vital concessions. Oil, it was growing clear, would be the most important world commodity in the second half of the twentieth century.

World War II sent Americans to all corners of the earth, spreading American culture, commerce—and Coca-Cola along the way. Before World War II, Coca-Cola had a strong presence in only a few countries, but the war transformed Coke into a global commodity. "We'll see that every man in uniform gets a bottle of coca cola wherever he is and whatever it costs this company," announced Coke's CEO just after Pearl Harbor. Exempted from wartime sugar rationing and awarded a monopoly on U.S. bases in exchange for providing GIs free Cokes, Coca-Cola kept its pledge—a promise that quickly proved a marketer's dream. "Wherever a U.S. battleship may be—so naturally Coca-Cola is there too," waxed one advertisement.[25] People from South Pacific islanders to Russian soldiers (who drank Coke with caramel coloring removed and a red star on the bottle) developed a taste for the American beverage. Increasingly Coca-Cola became synonymous with American culture.

—⟨∘⟩ ⟨∘⟩—

As the war wound down, America increasingly embraced its role as world economic leader. In July 1944, representatives from 44 nations gathered in the serene mountains of New Hampshire at the Bretton Woods resort. Guided by their American hosts, they mapped a plan for future global economic cooperation. Delegates created the International Monetary Fund to stabilize international currencies and the World Bank to provide loans for "reconstruction and development." Undergirding the new system was an American commitment to buy and sell gold at a rate of $35 an ounce. Countries around the world now cast their lot with the United States, shelving fears that local cultures and practices would be subsumed by capitalist "Americanism." In the decades to come, American commercial power would grow to new heights—its commercial empire expanding well beyond its own hemisphere. But as it grew, so too did international opposition and the challenge of maintaining so far-reaching an informal empire.

CHAPTER NINE

Reforming a Chaotic World

JANE ADDAMS AND THE SOCIAL QUESTION

Twenty-three-year-old Jane Addams arrived in Europe in 1883 at a pivotal point in her young life. She had recently dropped out of a women's medical school and suffered what appeared to be a nervous breakdown. Lacking real direction in life, she set out on a "grand tour"—an extended sojourn to soak up European culture. But stark poverty rather than uplifting culture proved the most memorable aspect of the "old world" for Jane. In London, a missionary took her "to witness the Saturday night sale of decaying vegetables and fruit" to the city's poorest residents. As Jane gaped in shock, an auctioneer "flung" food at bidders who stretched out their hands "empty, pathetic nerveless and workworn—clutching forward for food which was already unfit to eat." The impressionable mid-westerner could not shake the appalling images. She "went about London almost furtively, afraid to look down narrow streets and alleys lest they disclose again the hideous human need and suffering."

As she continued her tour, attending operas and museums, Addams increasingly felt a calling. Instead of foreboding, she felt herself "irresistibly drawn to the poorer quarters of each city." By the time she was ready to return home, Addams had conceived the plan that would become her life's work: "to rent a house in a part of the city where many primitive and actual needs are found, in which young women who had been given over too exclusively to study, might—learn of life from life itself."[1] In 1889, Addams founded Hull House in a poor neighborhood of Chicago. Modeled on Toynbee Hall, a British "settlement house," Hull House became a vital social welfare center staffed by middle-class men and women devoted to addressing the "social question"—the most pressing issue of the time. Addams proved remarkable in pursuing such an ambitious plan. But she was also typical of a generation of Americans who, dissatisfied with aspects of their native society, looked beyond U.S. borders for solutions to its problems. The late nineteenth and early twentieth centuries witnessed an extraordinary acceleration and expansion of the industrial revolution (as discussed in chapter 8). By the time Jane Addams toured Europe, the social ramifications of industrialization had emerged as the most discussed matter of the day. Indeed some version of the "social question"—the quest to reconcile a competitive, industrial economy with the needs of the poor and workers—became the central intellectual challenge wherever industrialization and modernity reared their heads. In the United States, a host of groups and individuals, running the gambit from anarchists to conservative factory owners, offered prescriptions to this social conundrum. As Jane Addams's experience suggests, this American quest for remedies cannot be understood outside its international context.

SOCIAL CRISIS AND RADICAL RESPONSES

As the nineteenth century wound down, the United States enjoyed the fastest-growing economy in the world. Fueled by abundant natural resources, a facilitating government, and swarms of immigrant laborers from Europe and Asia, industrial America grew at an unprecedented rate. But the dizzying pace of change brought social upheaval and crisis, as was the case worldwide. Industrialization spurred urbanization around the world; the populations of Berlin, Tokyo, and several cities in South America all neared or surpassed 1 million by 1900. Meanwhile, New York City's population soared to 3.4 million, eclipsing all other cities in growth. Worldwide rural-to-urban migration upended both city and countryside. Squalid housing, primitive sanitation, poor air quality, and constant earsplitting noise greeted migrants. "Noise, noise, nothing but noise," recorded English Fabian socialist Beatrice Webb on her first visit to New York City in 1898. "In the city your senses are disturbed, your ears are defamed, your eyes are wearied by constant rush." Chicago, home to some 1.7 million in 1900, instilled even greater disdain in Webb. It was "an unspeakable city, viler than the tongue can allow, and as hopeless as the Inferno," she wrote her friend George Bernard Shaw.[2] Americans, in turn, proved no less impressed by British cities. Writing on Britain's urban crisis in 1907, Frederic Howe ruminated "here poverty seems worse than any place in the civilized world. The problem of the city and the condition of the city dweller has become a question of national existence."[3]

Conditions in factories mirrored the general chaotic state of industrial cities. Workers toiled for long hours; factory owners strove to keep pay low; and safety and health conditions were abysmal. Increasingly, improved technology did away with the need for technical skills, depriving workers of leverage to improve conditions. Frequent economic downturns, resulting in long durations of unemployment, rendered life ever more precarious for laborers and their families. Difficult circumstances often mandated that work be a family affair. Both women and children frequently took their places on factory lines as the only way to sustain a hand-to-mouth living.

Facing penury, workers organized and rebelled—often resulting in violence. When industrialization spread to Russia, encouraged by a group of activist modernizers (including Czar Nicholas II), the result proved lethal. "We have become beggars, we have become oppressed, we are burdened by toils beyond our powers—we are not recognized as human beings," petitioned laborers in 1905.[4] Workers hoped to present their petition personally to the czar at his Winter Palace in Saint Petersburg. Yet, rather than the czar, armed troops met the protesters. The troops opened fire, killing at least 100 workers in the horrific "bloody Sunday" massacre. Similar violent clashes between workers and authorities occurred in America and throughout the industrial world, leading many to doubt the direction of progress.

As workers in the western world struggled with the full implications of industrialization, the wealthy—who were the primary beneficiaries of soaring industrial growth—often appeared oblivious to the crisis, focusing instead on "conspicuous consumption" of their riches. George Washington Vanderbilt, heir to a fortune in railroad holdings, completed construction in 1895 of a mammoth "summer home" known as Biltmore in the Blue Ridge Mountains of North Carolina. Directly modeled on the aristocratic homes of the French renaissance period, the 250-room mansion sat on a property of 146,000 acres.

Rather than the dawning of a brighter future, industrialization and urbanization seemed to be casting much of the western world into chaos and confrontation. In response, reformers, policy makers, writers, union leaders, intellectuals, and workers themselves searched in desperation for adequate responses to the burning "social question." With many parts of the world all facing the same crisis, information, ideas, and potential solutions surfaced and inevitably traversed borders and oceans, resulting in a remarkable global cross-fertilization. Ultimately, most societies, America included, embraced a moderate reform agenda. More radical approaches, however, also gained currency.

For some, socialism—especially the ideas associated with Karl Marx—offered the crucial insights and remedies necessary to address the complex social chaos. By the late nineteenth century, socialism in a variety of forms had crossed the ocean from Europe to America. While differing dramatically in emphasis, all socialists rejected the laissez-faire economics and politics of the time in favor of more democratic governance and some level of shared ownership of the forces of production. Most were rooted in Marxist theories of class conflict and the transforming, inexorable process of industrialization. As factories and cities grew, Marxists argued, workers would become alienated, eventually making common cause against the exploitative capitalist bourgeoisie. Citing Marx's famous phrase, "Workers of the World Unite," they envisioned a worldwide worker revolution.

Marxism had a natural constituency among some workers and labor leaders. By the turn of the century, immigrants, many well schooled in Marxism, anarchism (a philosophy that called for the abolition, sometimes violently, of all government and authority), and other forms of radicalism had swelled the ranks of America's workers. Prominent among them was Samuel Gompers, the British-born Jewish son of parents originally from the Netherlands. Arriving in New York City in his early teens, Gompers became a cigar maker, joining Cigarmakers' International Union in 1864. To help pass the often tedious workday, an apprentice or a fellow worker would read aloud to the cigarmakers at their workbenches. Marxist and other socialist tracts ranked high on the reading lists and made a deep impression on young Gompers. Moved by his on-the-job education, he became convinced only a strong labor movement could protect workers from the ravages of capitalism. Gompers rose quickly within the cigarmakers' union and sought new means for consolidating and strengthening organized labor. He also remained a student of Marx, keeping up a running correspondence with prominent European Marxists, including Marx's daughter and his collaborator, Friedrich Engels, whom Gompers once assured of his "respect for your judgment, having been a student of your writing and those of Marx."[5]

Ironically, as historian Michael Kazin noted, Gompers became a "Marxist who forged an anti-Marxist labor movement."[6] Unlike many socialists, Gompers rejected any role for the state and focused on organizing skilled workers (eschewing the unskilled) as the best route to achieving his goals. In 1886, Gompers formed the American Federation of Labor (AFL) as an antidote to what he saw as the unrealistic, utopian goals of other labor organizers, in particular radical socialists. Increasingly he denounced radicals in bitter terms. "Economically you are wrong; socially you are unsound, and industrially you are an impossibility," Gompers blasted in 1905.[7]

The Industrial Workers of the World (IWW), better known as the Wobblies, ranked high among the organizations Gompers dismissed as "impossibilities."

Certainly the most aggressive and controversial American manifestation of socialism during the early twentieth century, the IWW exemplified direct action and confrontation. "IWW beliefs," explained historian Melvin Dubofsky, offered a "particular amalgam of Marxism and Darwin, anarchism and syndicalism—all overlaid with a singularly American patina."[8] In particular, the Wobblies traded on the European notion of syndicalism—the goal of banding together all workers into one large union. Wobblie leaders such as the charismatic "Big" Bill Haywood openly espoused revolution. "Those of us who are in jail," wrote the frequently imprisoned Haywood, "those of us who have been in jail—all of us who are willing to go to jail—We are the Revolution." Far more than their meager numbers would suggest (at its peak there were perhaps 150,000 Wobblies), the IWW had the capacity to inspire both admiration and disdain, even beyond U.S. borders. In 1910, Haywood toured Europe attending socialist conventions and meeting the leading lights of European socialism, including German activist Rosa Luxemburg and possibly even Vladimir Lenin, leader of the Russian Revolution. Watching the Wobblie chieftain stir a crowd in England, future British prime minister J. Ramsay MacDonald marveled that his "crude appeals moved his listeners to wild applause—their hearts bounded to be up and doing."[9]

Wobblies envisioned the IWW, as its name suggests, as an international movement. They established branches in Europe and even Australia. They also embraced the Mexican Revolution that began in 1910, supporting radicals and recruiting Mexican-Americans into their ranks. "[W]e are here as one brotherhood and one sisterhood, as one humanity, with a responsibility to the down-trodden and the oppressed of all humanity," exhorted prominent anarchist Lucy Parsons, at the IWW's founding convention. "[I]t matters not under what flag or in what country they happened to be born. Let us have that idea of Thomas Paine, that 'The world is my country, and mankind are my countrymen.'"[10]

Originating in Europe, anarchism, a political philosophy that viewed all forms of political and economic organization as essentially corrupt, appealed to many Wobblies and others eager to challenge injustice. Prominent among anarchists was Emma Goldman, who immigrated to the United States from Russia as a teenager. Almost immediately, she devoted herself to radical causes with an unmatched energy and zeal. In 1892 she and her lover, Alexander Berkman, conspired to assassinate Henry Clay Frick, part owner of the Homestead Steel Works, then in the throes of a violent confrontation with his workforce. This act, Goldman believed, would "bring the teachings of Anarchism before the world."[11] The assassination attempt failed, but Goldman remained committed to agitation and anarchism.

REFORMING A CHAOTIC WORLD   179

The IWW and radicals such as Goldman unnerved many Americans, who saw such developments as the noxious influence of dangerous European radicalism. As a young man, Eugene Debs, a politician and trade union leader from Terre Haute, Indiana, shared that outlook. He complained of those "saturated with ideas born of European methods," who saw "nothing, or little in American institutions worthy of favorable consideration."[12] The calamitous Pullman Strike in 1894, however, did much to change Debs's perspective. Leading the American Railroad Union's strike against the Pullman Corporation, which had drastically cut worker wages during a severe depression, Debs suddenly found himself jailed for violating a court injunction. Behind bars, Debs began reading the work of Karl Marx, leading him to believe that no reconciliation could be reached between labor and capital. Embracing socialism, he became leader of the Socialist Party of America, eventually running for president six times. Still, Debs represented a tamer brand of socialism. He aimed to "Americanize" socialism—seeking, for instance, to link Abraham Lincoln to the battle to improve the lot of workers. Debs also rejected calls for violent revolution. Although an early supporter of the IWW, he later broke ranks as the Wobblies grew more radical.[13]

World War I and the Bolshevik Revolution in Russia posed grave challenges to socialists of all kinds. With the outbreak of war in Europe in the summer of 1914, American socialists, like their worldwide counterparts, divided on the issue. Debs's Socialist Party denounced the war and urged members to remain dedicated to the "imperishable principles of international socialism."[14] Debs himself proclaimed, "I am against all war except one—the worldwide war for socialist revolution."[15] But other socialists, fearing German militarism supported the allies.

Meanwhile, events in Russia inspired many radicals. The first Marxist-inspired revolution spurred aspirations and fears across the world. In America, radicals embraced Lenin and the Bolsheviks—viewing them as kindred spirits in a common cause. "Bolshevism was but the Russian name for IWW," enthused one Wobblie. "From the crown of my head to the soles of my feet," proclaimed Debs. "I am a Bolshevik and proud of it."[16]

If the Bolshevik revolution, however, stirred hopes for some, it bred dread in others. Encouraged by President Wilson, who sought to stamp out all opposition to his war to end all wars, a wave of anti-radicalism swept the country. In one of the darkest hours of American constitutional history, Congress passed the Wilson-supported Espionage Act (1917) and an amendment, commonly called the Sedition Act (1918), both sharply curbing antiwar speech. Government officials wielded the Espionage Act against Debs and Haywood, both of whom landed in prison. Authorities deported Goldman to Russia in 1919. Elsewhere angry mobs, often sailors and soldiers, attacked IWW members. In Oklahoma, "patriotic" rioters tarred and feathered Wobblies. The organization, once in the vanguard of American radicalism, struggled to survive under the government-inspired barrage. More broadly, German-Americans came under attack. Lynchings occurred, and even teaching the German language became controversial; both Nebraska and Iowa banned German instruction in public schools.

The atmosphere of wartime intolerance also spilled over to peacetime. A. Mitchell Palmer, the U.S. attorney general, led a campaign against what he believed were communists or "reds" organizing across the country. Disillusion and repression jointly ushered in a new era in which intellectuals increasingly looked inward, while wearing their disenchantment on their sleeves.

THE INTERNATIONAL REFORM MOVEMENT

While Marxist-influenced radicals and intellectuals drew attention—and often scorn—they had limited influence shaping pitted battles over the "social question." Progressive middle-class reformers, rather, proved most proficient at implementing their agenda. Rejecting the wholesale revolution demanded by most radicals, progressives sought pragmatic reforms aimed at easing the social crisis gripping the industrial world. Like the radicals, however, American progressives often drew inspiration from Europe. Saddled with similar crises in cities and industries, middle-class reformers in Europe, Australia, and New Zealand began searching for answers, driven by the belief that city and state planning offered the promise of addressing the social question without revolutionary upheaval. Reformers around the world remained in close contact. The late nineteenth century through to World War I, according to historian Daniel Rodgers, offered "a moment when American politics was peculiarly open to foreign models and imported ideas—when the North Atlantic economy formed, for many strategically placed Americans, a world mart of useful and intensely interesting experiments."[17]

Jane Addams was one such "strategically placed American." Her upper-middle class family's resources financed her "grand tour" of Europe where she encountered the settlement house movement. Influenced by socialist currents flowing through Europe and a profound sense of the crisis posed by industrialization, English university students had begun the settlement movement as a means of better understanding and addressing the urban crisis. In 1884, students opened Toynbee Hall, the first settlement house, in a poor section of London. Within several years, activists opened hundreds of settlement houses across Europe and North America. Profoundly moved by what they saw at Toynbee Hall, Addams and Ellen Gates Starr launched Hull House in Chicago in 1889. Addams's "salon in the slums" quickly became the most prominent of many such American settlement houses. Addams and her housemates dove into the issues of the day, such as playground reform, suffrage, immigration policy, sweatshop reform, and child labor. By 1907 Hull House had grown into a complex of 13 buildings. It offered classes, inexpensive meals for workers, art exhibits, and the first public playground in the city of Chicago. But residents understood that grave social problems remained unaddressed. Increasingly Hull House reformers looked to government to spur the sort of fundamental changes already afoot in Europe.

Socialism inevitably provoked intense discussion among residents of and visitors to Hull House. Addams herself, however, remained typical of the middle-class reformers. She held no concrete ideology save an impulse to improve urban/industrial life through organization and reform. She recalled longing "for the comfort of a definite social creed, which would afford—an explanation of the social chaos and the logical steps toward its better ordering."[18] Yet none of the radical prescriptions of the time seemed a good fit. Instead Addams continued to seek out pragmatic solutions to the evils of the day, staying closely appraised of international developments. Hull House hosted a constant stream of visitors from abroad seeking exposure to the American scene while sharing their experiments back home. Likewise, Hull House residents and veterans frequently joined fact-finding tours of Europe offered to American reformers.

Throughout the early twentieth century more and more progressive Americans toured Europe in search of inspiration. During this era, Americans often suffered a profound sense of lagging behind Europe, where experiments in public housing, social insurance, public utilities, and workmen's compensation were well under way. Packaged tours of the continent, designed to introduce Americans to European innovations, proliferated. In 1914, American groups sponsored by organizations such as the National Housing Association, the Chicago Railway Terminal Commission, the National Civic Federation, and the Institute of Education Travel, blanketed Western Europe, blissfully unaware of the looming maelstrom. (Some 200,000 Americans, in fact, found themselves stranded with the outbreak of World War I.) "Tourists" returned with a host of new ideas and approaches to addressing the ever-pressing social question.

The social gospel movement, which often overlapped with the settlement movement, also drew inspiration from Europe. Moved by the poverty and turmoil of the times, social gospel advocates believed Christian ethics might profitably be applied directly to the social question. In 1891, Walter Rauschenbusch, a Protestant minister from New York, traveled to Europe. In England, after expressing shock at the poverty of Liverpool, he marveled at the orderly, progressive industrial city of Birmingham, which had introduced a series of dramatic reforms under Mayor Joseph Chamberlain. America, Rauschenbusch wrote, "should do by foresight what Birmingham has done by hindsight." Later on the trip, while in Germany, he experienced something of an epiphany, leading him to conclude that the mission of the church should be "to penetrate and transform the world."[19]

Even New Zealand, the remote Pacific island settled by Europeans in the early nineteenth century, became an alluring model for American reformers. Despite its picturesque setting, New Zealand initially seemed prone to the same violence and social upheaval so prevalent in the rest of the industrial world. In 1890, authorities brutally suppressed a series of violent strikes that had swept across both Australia and New Zealand. A decade later, however, American progressive journalist Henry Demarest Lloyd toured New Zealand and discovered a "renaissance of reform." The island had adopted a host of social reform initiatives, including old age pensions, anti-monopoly legislation, a state-owned railroad, and government life insurance. New Zealand's compulsory arbitration laws particularly impressed Lloyd as a potential antidote to the labor turmoil and conflict raging through the industrial world. He had found, Lloyd raved in his book detailing his trip, "a country without strikes." Typical of progressive reformers, Lloyd delighted in finding little evidence of "sectarian socialism." Rather he noted with pleasure, "New Zealand's policy is a deliberate exploitation of both capitalists and proletariat by the middle class."[20]

While the urban crisis demanded the majority of progressive attention, the struggles of rural America were not forgotten—and again the search for solutions went international. In the 1860s Friedrich Wilhelm Raiffeisen began the rural credit cooperative movement in his native Rhineland. The idea of pooling agricultural resources rapidly caught on in Europe. Horace Plunkett, an energetic Irish reformer and politician, immediately grasped the applicability of Raiffeisen cooperatatives to Ireland. Plunkett soon became the leading international apostle of agricultural cooperatives. He urged his friend President

Theodore Roosevelt to adopt similar programs for struggling American farmers. On hearing Plunkett's slogan, "Better Farming, Better Business, Better Living," Roosevelt was supposed to have burst out, "I'll megaphone it to the world!"[21] Eventually Plunkett inspired the president to appoint the influential Country Life Commission in 1908.

Charged currents running between Europe and America increasingly inspired American political leaders, who often cited continental reforms as models to be followed. "It is humiliating," lamented Theodore Roosevelt in his push for workmen's insurance, "that at European international conferences on accidents the US should be singled out as the most belated among the nationals in respect of employers' liability legislation." Running for president in 1912, Woodrow Wilson told a Massachusetts crowd that the Scottish city of Glasgow, known for its generous municipal services, was "one of the best governed cities in the world—They are way ahead of us."[22] As president, Wilson modeled his reform initiatives after Prime Minister David Lloyd George's Liberal Party's program. (Ironically, in the 1930s, Lloyd George would announce a British version of the New Deal, modeled on American reforms.) The international progressive agenda had risen to the highest levels of American government.

THE INTERNATIONAL WOMEN'S MOVEMENT

Nowhere, however, was internationalism more prevalent than among the leadership of the resurgent women's movement in the early twentieth century. Women and women's organizations long had been on the front lines of the international reform movement (see chapter 4). By the twentieth century, a younger generation of activists had reignited the suffrage movement, which began in America with the 1848 Seneca Falls Convention. Similar developments took place in Europe, and activists maintained close contacts across the Atlantic Ocean. In 1901, Carrie Chapman Catt, president of the National Woman Suffrage Association (NWSA), distributed a questionnaire to feminists around the world. She received encouraging responses from 32 countries, inspiring her to launch the International Woman Suffrage Alliance (IWSA) a year later. The IWSA, over which Catt presided as president and British suffragette Millicent Fawcett as vice president, held meetings around the world with delegates gathering from almost every imaginable corner of the globe. Between 1911 and 1913, Catt toured the world to promote her cause. In South Africa she met Gandhi, and in China she joined sympathetic locals in making a banner reading "Helping Each Other, All of One Mind." "Our audiences," Catt reflected at the end of her tour, "have included the followers of every major religion—and representatives of all the human races—we have left the seeds of revolution behind."[23]

Catt and her British counterpart, Dame Millicent Fawcett, represented the moderate branch of the suffrage movement. Even as Catt toured Europe, other transatlantic networks of women pursued more militant tactics. Tired of slow progress, Emmeline Pankhurst, a British suffragette, and a group of sympathizers announced in 1910 a dramatic campaign of arson, violence, and civil disobedience aimed at challenging the status quo. Most famously, Emily Wilding Davison flung herself in protest onto a race track where a horse owned by King George V tramped her to death.

Alice Paul, an American studying at the London School of Economics, quickly found herself immersed in the radical suffragette movement after hearing Pankhurst speak. Originally attracted to the settlement movement, Paul redirected her considerable energies to the suffrage cause. Working alongside Pankhurst, Paul earned an education in militant feminism. Arrested several times in England, Paul joined British suffragettes on a hunger strike while in jail. She then returned to the United States eager to apply British militancy to the suffrage stalemate in her native land. Eventually she formed the National Women's Party in 1916 to press for a constitutional amendment to allow women the vote. In January 1917, Paul organized a protest outside the gates of the White House to push a reluctant Woodrow Wilson to action (Meanwhile Catt's NWSA supported Wilson's war). Arrested for "obstructing traffic," Paul served a seven-month sentence, partly in solitary confinement. Like her British "sisters," Paul went on a hunger strike, and authorities responded by force feeding her through a tube pushed down her throat.

More than any other factor, World War I, the great conflagration enveloping Europe and then the United States, brought results for the suffragists. A year after Paul's audacious picketing of the White House, Wilson endorsed women's suffrage as "a war measure." The president pleaded that the service of women as nurses on the battlefield and their work in wartime factories warranted expanding the franchise. Congress finally guaranteed women the vote when it ratified the Nineteenth Amendment a year later (winning support of the requisite number of states in 1920). The war also hastened the arrival of women's suffrage in Britain and Germany in 1918 for many of the same reasons. In 1919 French women came close to receiving the vote, but the French Senate defeated the bill, delaying suffrage reform until after World War II.

THE PEACE MOVEMENT

The women's movement overlapped with another important international movement brewing among reformers—the peace movement. Inspired by the same impulse to bring order to a chaotic world that drove efforts to address the social question, peace advocates formed influential networks and organizations around the world, and often these groups were led by women. While unable to stop the violence that so marked the first half of the twentieth century, these groups did fundamentally shape events.

As imperialists pressed for U.S. annexation of the Philippines and other territories (discussed in chapter 7), opponents organized under the banner of the Anti-Imperialist League. Figures as diverse as labor leader Samuel Gompers, who feared the "open competition of millions of semi-barbaric laborers," Jane Addams, and humorist Mark Twain joined the movement.[24] "It should, it seems to me, to be our pleasure and duty," explained Twain, "to make those people free, and let them deal with their own domestic questions in their own way."[25] As frustrations with the costs of the guerrilla war in the Philippines mounted, support grew for the anti-imperialist position.

Anti-imperialists actively sought ties with like-minded individuals and groups around the world. Belgian excesses in the Congo drew the particular ire of anti-imperialists. Educator Booker T. Washington became vice president of the American branch of the Congo Reform Association, and Mark Twain penned his caustic "King Leopold's Soliloquy" in support of the cause.

Meanwhile, peace activists worked to create permanent structures and organizations to discourage war. American activists attended in 1899 the First Hague Conference dedicated to arms reduction and the promotion of peace. The conference, enthused Robert Treat Paine, president of the American Peace Society, "transcends any human event—It is the first Parliament of Man; it is the first step toward the federation of the world."[26] Steel magnate-turned-philanthropist and peace activist Andrew Carnegie donated millions to promote international peace, including money to construct the lavish Peace Palace (Vredespaleis) in the Hague.

Jane Addams in particular became an outspoken advocate for peace as the world veered into a cataclysmic war in 1914. For Addams the chaos of conflict directly threatened the struggles to address the social question. She became convinced that "if war prevailed all social efforts would be cast into an earlier and coarser mold."[27] In May 1915, as war engulfed Europe, Addams and 42 other American women undertook a perilous journey across the Atlantic to attend the Hague Congress of Women where they pushed for a mediated settlement to the conflict. Six months later, Hungarian peace activist Rosika Schwimmer, then touring the United States, persuaded automaker Henry Ford to lead a delegation of U.S. peace advocates to Europe, where the group hoped to spark negotiations between warring parties. In grand fashion Ford charted an ocean liner, quickly dubbed "The Peace Ship," to transport his group. Addams had planned to join the group, but she backed out at the last minute due to illness. As a band played "I Didn't Raise my Boy to be a Soldier," Ford's ship pulled out of Hoboken harbor. The hastily organized mission quickly fell apart when it arrived in Europe, but one American newspaper gave Ford credit despite the debacle: "No matter that he failed, he at least tried."[28]

After the war, the peace movement grew in influence as Americans recoiled at the brutality and losses from the war. Antiwar organizations formed during the war, such as the Women's International League for Peace and Freedom, co-founded by Jane Addams in 1915 and headquartered in Geneva, Switzerland, continued to draw support. Meanwhile new organizations proliferated in the 1920s, such as the American Committee for the Outlawry of War, the National Council for the Prevention of War, and the Women's Peace Union for the Western Hemisphere. The Women's Peace Union, founded in 1921 quickly established branches in Mexico, Latin America, and Canada. In 1927, the organization drafted a constitutional amendment banning war. Sympathetic legislators introduced the amendment in every session of congress between 1927 and 1940. During those years, the international peace movement maintained pressure on leaders both in America and worldwide, contributing significantly to a public mood that endorsed isolationism and appeasement as World War II approached.

THE NEW NEGRO AND THE FATE OF MARCUS GARVEY

While class issues dominated discussions of the social question, race also concerned radicals and reformers. African Americans, particularly conscious of the grave racial injustices characteristic of the era, strove to develop their own agenda for reform, often conceiving their search in international terms. "[T]he Negro problem in America is but a local phase of a world problem," wrote W. E. B. Du Bois in a 1903 essay attacking segregation entitled "The Color Line Belts the World."[29]

Few white reformers, however, shared Du Bois's urgent belief that "the problem of the twentieth century is the problem of the color line." Rather, many progressives sought to contain the race problem through segregation—keeping the races apart to limit violence and tension. One of the few willing to challenge segregation, Jane Addams, later admitted, "[W]e are no longer stirred as the Abolitionists—to lead the humblest to the banquet of civilization."[30]

Seeing few opportunities at their disposal and a rising tide of intolerance and violence at home, some African Americans began to look back to Africa. Reflecting on the state of blacks in America, Bishop Henry M. Turner of the Black Methodist Church felt a bitter sense of disdain. "To the negro in the country," he proclaimed, "the American flag is a dirty and contemptible rag."[31] Despairing of America, Turner urged blacks to migrate to Africa—visiting the continent himself four times. Ida B. Wells, an African American suffragist, similarly counseled American blacks to take up the "grand opportunity" of going "back to Africa."[32] Both Wells and Turner believed American blacks had much to share with Africans. Turner believed they could Christianize the continent, while Wells held they could bring development and knowledge to Africa.

Two of the most forceful spokespersons for African Americans during the early twentieth century, W. E. B. Du Bois and Marcus Garvey, could not have been more different in terms of their approaches or their class background. Both, however, believed African Americans needed to think internationally and embrace Africa. Du Bois, a Harvard-educated historian and sociologist, had studied in Berlin (as did many American academics at this time, seeking exposure to the sophistication and rigor of the German university). Returning to the United States, he helped found the NAACP and became editor of its dynamic journal, the *Crisis*. While attracted to socialism, Du Bois believed (at least early in his career) in pluralism—that African Americans through activism could ultimately find a respected place in American society. Nevertheless, Pan-Africanism, a movement to unify Africans everywhere in an international community, deeply appealed to Du Bois. In 1919, he helped organize the first conference of the Pan-African Congress, which met in Paris to coincide with the Versailles treaty negotiations. Some 57 delegates from 15 countries attended. Soon, Du Bois was describing himself as an "ambassador of Pan-Africanism." In 1924 Du Bois embarked on his first trip to Africa. "The Spell of Africa is upon me," he waxed. "This is not a country, it is a world, a universe of itself."[33] Eventually, Du Bois would make Africa his home; he died in Ghana in 1963.

Du Bois had little patience for Marcus Garvey, the other great advocate of Pan-Africanism. Editorializing in the *Crisis*, Du Bois described Garvey as "the most dangerous enemy of the Negro Race in America or the world" and "either a lunatic or a traitor."[34] Hundreds of thousands in America, the Caribbean, and Africa disagreed. They heralded the Jamaican-born Garvey as a visionary.

Garvey had come to the United States in 1916, lured by the possibility of meeting one of his inspirations, Booker T. Washington, an educator who advocated accommodation with segregation and a vigorous program of black self-determination. Garvey also hoped to find fertile soil for his Universal Negro Improvement Association (UNIA), a self-improvement organization he had begun in 1914. Garvey's Pan-African vision of uniting and uplifting all peoples of African descent rapidly found a following in the Harlem neighborhood of New York City. "Up you mighty race," the charismatic Garvey would exhort from the podium. "You can accomplish what you will!"[35]

Unlike Du Bois, Garvey fully embraced capitalism. He mapped out an ambitious plan whereby a steamship company, the Black Star Line, would link together enterprising Africans on both sides of the Atlantic. From his headquarters on 135th Street in Harlem, Garvey sold stock in the Black Star to supporters around the world. By 1920, Garvey had incorporated and raised several hundred thousand dollars for the Black Star Line, which had launched several ships. Garvey also launched a newspaper, the *Negro World*, which reached a large audience and became an important promoter of black culture.

Garvey, however, almost immediately encountered serious roadblocks. In promoting Pan-Africanism, he became an outspoken critic of European colonialism in Africa. In response, colonial governments in Africa and the Caribbean banned the *Negro World*. The Black Star Line also struggled with corruption and inefficiency. More ominously, the Bureau of Investigation (precursor to the FBI) began investigating Garvey and the UNIA. In 1923 a court sentenced Garvey to jail on mail fraud charges. His empire, already shaky, quickly crumbled. Authorities deported Garvey in 1927.

During his brief rise and fall, Garvey managed to inspire many around the world with his vision of a united African people. The general message of black pride also resounded widely with African Americans, especially those moving north in what became known as the Great Migration (part, in fact, of a larger worldwide migration from rural to urban areas). During World War I, the stream of African Americans leaving the South for jobs in the North became a flood. Also, some 370,000 blacks were inducted into the military. The experience opened these soldiers' eyes. After witnessing the hypocrisy of a segregated army fighting to "make the world safe for democracy," many black soldiers found themselves integrated into the French army, where they seemed more appreciated than in their own military. Likewise, France offered a glimpse of a world without segregation. Not one African American soldier received the Congressional Medal of Honor during the Great War, while France honored hundreds of blacks with its Legion of Honor award. White elites worried about the impact of such experiences on American blacks. "American Negro[es] returning from abroad," fretted President Wilson, might "be our greatest medium in conveying bolshevism to America."[36]

Returning to America after risking their lives for their country, many black veterans were unwilling to accept the segregationist status quo. "We return from fighting. We return fighting," editorialized the *Crisis* in May 1919.[37] Much fighting in fact resulted. Wartime racial tensions spilled over and poisoned the peace. A race riot erupted in Chicago during the hot summer of 1919; nearly 40 were killed, and several hundred injured. Other riots flared up across the country. The violence, combined with the migration and recent war experience of many blacks fostered a new racial consciousness. African Americans began speaking of a new defiant stance—the "new negro," an attitude certainly fed by Pan-Africanism and support for Garvey and Du Bois, whose visions caused the first stirrings of black nationalism.

MODERNISM

Many progressives in America and around the world also participated in modernism, a broad artistic and intellectual movement that rejected the staid conventions of nineteenth-century Victorian culture. Scientific advances, rapid urbanization, and industrialization seemed to throw into question the earlier certainties of a steady, secure world under a benevolent deity. In response, modernists embraced uncertainty, skepticism, freedom, and experimentation. Impressionist artists and symbolist poets began the artistic movement in Paris in the 1870s. It quickly spread. Soon modernism was shaping architecture, literature, religion, and all manner of culture throughout Europe and then the United States. Post–World War I disillusionment over the possibility of solving the social question also fed modernism.

Among the Americans deeply moved by the modernist movement was Gertrude Stein. Daughter of wealthy Jewish parents, she grew up partly in Oakland, California (about which she famously quipped, "there is no there there"). Moving to Paris in 1903, Gertrude and her brother Leo became major collectors and patrons of modern art, befriending Pablo Picasso, Henri Matisse, and a host of other artists. From her home on 27 Rue des Fleures, Stein established a vibrant "salon" for all wanting to discuss modern art and culture.

At home, those drawn to modernism and the avant-garde organized the Armory Show, a provocative and controversial art exhibition in 1913, featuring

1,200 works by European and American artists, including Picasso, Edvard Munch, Vincent Van Gogh, and Claude Monet. The French modernist Marcel Duchamp's *Nude Descending a Staircase, No.2*, among other works, attracted intense discussion at the show. Despite, or perhaps because of, the controversy, the show drew large crowds. Even President Theodore Roosevelt attended and described the art as the product of "forces that cannot be ignored."[38]

After the Great War, the ranks of American modernists grew—as did their discontent with their homeland. Embracing cosmopolitanism, American moderns loudly denounced the suffocating influence of Puritanism and provincialism in America. Many of the writers and artists associated with the "Lost Generation"—a term coined by Gertrude Stein—left America for the supposed freedom of Europe, in particular Paris. Some, including Ernest Hemingway and Malcolm Cowley had experienced personally the horror and disillusion of World War I. In Paris, the expatriate community bonded tightly, hosting a "moveable feast" of lively parties, travel, and animated discussions at cafes. In 1926, Hemingway published his first novel, *The Sun Also Rises*, chronicling the often drunken meanderings of a group of Americans in Europe.

An active black expatriate community also gathered in Paris. In 1923 poet Langston Hughes arrived after traveling in Africa and elsewhere in Europe. In 1925, *La Revu Nègre* opened in Paris. The musical review's star, nineteen-year-old Saint Louis native Josephine Baker, quickly became a sensation. To American expatriates, Baker's bare-breasted "Danse Sauvage" seemed a thrilling antidote to the prudishness and racism of their homeland. Baker herself became an outspoken critic of Jim Crow and an enthusiast for all things French. In 1937, she became a French citizen and later contributed to the French resistance during World War II.

As Baker's activism suggests, modernist authors, artists and thinkers had not entirely written off the social question. A pressing cause could still mobilize activism. Such was the case when Massachusetts authorities arrested Nicola Sacco and Bartolomeo Vanzetti in 1920 on charges of robbery and murder. Italian immigrants with anarchist sympathies, Sacco and Vanzetti faced a hostile court and a climate of mounting nativism. The presiding judge urged jurors to be guided by the "spirit of supreme American loyalty."[39] The subsequent conviction and execution of Sacco and Vanzetti ignited an international firestorm of protest. Demonstrators marched from New York to Paris to Australia. Some turned to art to express their outrage. Ben Shahn, a Lithuanian-born New York City–based artist produced posters protesting the case. After the executions, Shahn painted "The Passion of Sacco and Vanzetti"—memorializing the martyrs and indicting authorities for their deaths. Even in the supposedly nonpolitical 1920s, international networks committed to social progress persevered.

ECONOMIC CRISIS AND NEW DEAL

If the "social question" receded somewhat from public discourse during the "roaring twenties," it roared back with a vengeance during the Great Depression. Beginning in the United States with the October 1929 stock market crash, financial crisis, business failings, and unemployment eddied across the world. As misery mounted, the social question took on new urgency. Yet, unlike an earlier generation that had turned outward in quest of novel experiments and creative remedies in other countries, the severity of the depression led Americans and others concerned with the social question to look inward. The carnage of World War I had convinced many in the United States to erect barriers against the rest of the world. The depression only fed those sentiments.

Even in the world of art, this nationalistic tendency was unmistakable. Popular fascination with modern abstract art with its strong European overtones faded. Social realism and regionalism exploring nationalistic American themes increasingly flourished. Artists such as Thomas Hart Benton, Reginald Marsh, and photographer Margaret Bourke-White all devoted themselves to exploring American subjects. In 1931, the Whitney Museum of American Art, exclusively dedicated to American artists, opened its doors in New York City. In 1935 Iowan Grant Wood, whose painting "American Gothic" ranks among the most recognized works of American art, vehemently attacked the overbearing influence of European modernism in an essay entitled "Revolt against the City." The depression had an upside, argued Wood: American artists could no longer afford their obligatory pilgrimages to Europe and hence would be forced to create their own art. Yet, in reality, even regionalism and social realism, seeking to expose economic injustice and poverty, had roots in European art.

Likewise, while the steady cross-fertilization among international reformers seen earlier in the century slowed considerably, many New Dealers had spent their youths and early adulthood awash in transnational progressivism. Earlier international contacts had produced a wealth of knowledge and a battery of programs and experimentation on which New Dealers could draw. As a rising politician and reformer, Franklin Delano Roosevelt had significant exposure to international progressive trends. As a boy he spent time in France and Germany (so much so that he offered military officials first-hand advice on potential bombing targets during World War II). As governor of New York in

1931, Roosevelt sent Frances Perkins, his industrial commissioner (and later secretary of labor), on a mission to England to collect information on unemployment insurance. As president five years later, President Roosevelt dispatched adviser Harry Hopkins to the continent to study public housing and social insurance programs. When he returned, however, Hopkins echoed the nationalistic sentiments of the time. "It is clear we have to do this in an American way—Instead of copying foreign schemes," he concluded.[40]

Hopkins's reluctance to embrace foreign models may have been more a matter of politics than a matter of ideology. At the time, critics were painting the New Deal as communistic or socialistic. When the Roosevelt administration opened Greenbelt, a "model town" in Maryland, whose design borrowed heavily from European modernism, a Chicago newspaper branded it "the first communist town in America."[41] Thus New Dealers were politically astute to portray their programs and ideas as native-born.

As recovery proved illusory, however, some Americans began looking for alternatives to the capitalist system that seemed so obvious a failure. Journalist Marquis Childs argued a better model—"a well defined middle course"—could be found in Sweden. "The Swedes," Childs argued, "seem to have interrupted the process of self-destruction which marked the economic life of other industrial countries."[42] Sweden's "planned economy" and cooperative enterprises, providing such amenities as low-cost housing and consumer cooperatives, became a model for New Deal planners convinced the U.S. economy needed a greater dose of government regulation and direction.

Roosevelt read Childs's writing with interest and decided to investigate. In 1936, the president dispatched a delegation to Europe. "[C]o-ops in Europe are supposed to be good for relief of destitution," Roosevelt instructed the group. "Let's find out what they do in Europe."[43] The group spent the summer of 1936 visiting such organizations as the Brinagh Cooperative Creamery in Ireland, the Konsum Consumer Cooperative in Stockholm, and Glasgow's United Cooperative Baking Society. These endeavors, concluded one member of the delegation, "might be described as capitalism upside down. Consumers, not the capital which serves them, are on top."[44]

While Roosevelt's team explicitly sought a middle ground between harsh capitalism and controlling socialism, the continuing crisis drove some Americans in more radical directions. The Soviet Union, which in contrast to much of the west seemed to be making economic gains through stringent economic planning, appeared to some an attractive alternative. In 1932 African American poet Langston Hughes traveled to the Soviet Union to make a movie. "I yearned to stand taller than I ever had stood—Soviet Russia seemed the answer."[45] Although the Soviet government, desiring better relations with the Americans, eventually backed out of Hughes's planned cinematic expose of American racism, other African Americans, including actor and singer Paul Robeson also turned to the USSR as they watched their country remain mired in racism and descending into poverty.

Walter and Victor Reuther of Wheeling, West Virginia, sons of a German immigrant socialist, also gravitated toward the Soviet Union. In 1933, the brothers left their factory jobs at Ford Motor Company, determined to join fellow autoworker expatriates in Russia. Walter and Victor first traveled to Europe, where they personally witnessed the smoldering remains of the Reichstag and the frightening rise of Nazism. They then traveled to Gorky in the Soviet Union to take jobs at a massive new manufacturing plant modeled on Ford's expansive River Rouge factory near Detroit. (While rejecting U.S.-style capitalism, the Soviets were taken by the productive potential of American industry.) Compared to demoralized America and violent Germany, the USSR seemed to the Reuthers an oasis of cooperation and planned progress. In Gorky the brothers joined roughly 100 of their compatriots living in an "American village" apartment complex. They worked long but satisfying hours on the assembly line despite seeing some evidence of Stalinistic terror. Recounting the progress he witnessed, Victor waxed in a letter home, "Who would not be inspired by such events?"[46] Later, as leaders of the United Auto Workers, the brothers turned sharply against the Soviet Union, becoming outspoken anticommunists. But their youthful embrace of Russia reflects the hopes of many in the face of the apparent collapse of capitalism.

The American Communist Party made little headway in the 1930s, despite the enthusiasm of some like the Reuthers and Langston Hughes. Nor did authoritarian fascism, then sweeping through Germany and already a fixture of Italian life under Benito Mussolini, gain many converts. The German-American Bund under Fritz Kuhn and similar organizations did agitate in the United States but found few followers. Likewise, a few New Dealers expressed some interest in fascism, a hypernationalistic political philosophy emphasizing authoritarian, single-party rule. Rexford Tugwell, FDR's undersecretary of agriculture, toured fascist Italy in 1934 and declared himself "envious" of the "most effectively operating piece of social machinery I've ever seen."[47] Later, National Recovery Administration chief Hugh Johnson, apparently similarly enamored by the organized corporatism of fascist Italy, praised the "shining name of Mussolini."[48] Still, most New Dealers viewed Il Duce as little more than a colorful thug.

The crisis of capitalism and appeal of radicalism—either fascism or communism—worried many in America and Europe. It particularly concerned British economist John Maynard Keynes. In his economic formulations Keynes sought means to stabilize and soften capitalism through regulation and intervention. Government spending—even deficit spending—was necessary to stimulate stagnant or collapsing economies, argued Keynes, most famously in his 1936 book *The General Theory of Employment, Interest, and Money.* Many American economists, including many New Dealers, already had become intuitive Keynesians, believing public-sector spending to be the only way out of the depression. While some New Dealers advocated extensive economic planning along the lines of Sweden, these proto-Keynesians encouraged general government spending, hoping the resulting consumer spending would stimulate growth without greater government control. Keynes's ideas were to have their greatest impact in the postwar years, but already in the 1930s they were reshaping American economics.

The New Deal exerted influence beyond American borders, just as international developments shaped the New Deal. Around the world, Roosevelt's programs generated intense interest. "You have made yourself the trustee," wrote Keynes to Roosevelt, "for those in every country who seek to mend the evils of our condition."[49] In Britain, former prime minister David Lloyd George announced his own "New Deal" plan, hopping to piggy-back on popular interest in the American version. In France, the Popular Front government, elected in 1936 under Leon Blum, also explicitly sought to link itself to Roosevelt's program. As in the United States, a wave of strikes followed labor reforms—although in France the strikes paralyzed the government, resulting in its collapse in 1937.

Of all New Deal initiatives, the Tennessee Valley Authority (TVA)—a massive electrification, flood control, and economic development program along the Tennessee River—attracted the most international attention. A public corporation, the TVA aimed to address long-standing environmental, social, and economic problems in the American South. The TVA, its planners believed, epitomized "grass-roots" democracy, harnessing the forces of nature for the good of the many. The apparent success of the project, bringing prosperity and "modernization" to a previously stagnant region, brought visitors from around the world to witness it in operation. In the 1930s, for instance, the Chinese International Famine Relief Commission arranged for Chinese agriculturalists and engineers to visit and study the TVA as a potential model for "rural reconstruction" in China. "Our foreign visitors see with particular clarity," wrote TVA administrator David Lilienthal, "that the TVA speaks in a tongue that is universal, a language of things close to the people: soil fertility, forests, electricity, phosphates, factories, minerals, and rivers."[50] By World War II, Lilienthal and others such as the Rockefeller Foundation began actively proselytizing and promoting the TVA as a model for world development and modernization.

—⟶ ⟵—

Lilienthal's sweeping vision of large-scale, environmentally altering electrification projects, democratizing societies, and modernizing the world seems a far cry from Jane Addams's simple idea of working among the poor. Beginning early in the century with a sense they had much to learn from the world, by the 1940s key Americans believed they had much to teach the world. Their quest to develop and modernize lands well beyond America's borders would greatly shape the rest of the century. Meanwhile, at home and abroad, festering questions about race and gender—questions often sidelined by early reformers—soon would resurface dramatically and demand attention. Those issues, with their global implications, would shape the next half of the twentieth century.

Part IV
1945–2010

A shattered world emerged from the maelstrom of world war in 1945. Poverty and desperation ruled large swaths of the globe. Squarely facing the chaos, Americans determined to take a new leadership role in the world to prevent such a cataclysm from occurring ever again. They set out to reorder the world in their own image—with mixed results. By the end of the century, the United States became a "hyper power" with a thriving high-tech economy that attracted immigrants and investment from around the world. Globalization, in many ways, appeared to be occurring on American terms. This drive to power, however, proved anything but uncomplicated. Indeed, opposition sprang forth at almost every turn, from without and within, and that resistance also shaped globalization.

_____

The pace of globalization, especially by the final decade of the twentieth century, seemed to be moving at breakneck speed. Major advances in transportation and communication sped the process. In the immediate years after World War II, ocean liners continued to dominate transoceanic travel. Although record numbers of Americans traveled overseas on such ships (over one million in 1957), the journey from New York to Europe still took three to four days. The advent of jet airplane travel in the late 1950s, however, rang the death knell for the ocean liners. Suddenly, the Atlantic could be crossed in 8–9 hours. By 1976, the Concord jet slashed transatlantic flight crossings to a mere three and a half hours. Correspondingly, tourism, business travel, and immigration grew dramatically.

In particular, millions moved from less-developed regions, seeking brighter futures in industrialized areas. Between 1931 and 1965 a mere 5 million immigrants entered the United States, but with the passage of immigration reform in 1965, the United States saw a stunning influx of immigrants rivaling the great wave of the early twentieth century. This time, however, newcomers from Latin America, Asia, and Africa dominated. In the 1990s, some 9 million immigrants arrived, and by 2010, nearly 38 million immigrants made their homes in the United States—over 10 percent of the total population. Likewise, in 1945, much worldwide communication was still done by telegraph. By the 1960s, however, satellite technology transformed communication. The development of the Internet inaugurated yet another leap, instantly connecting people around the world.

None of this is to suggest that globalization—especially the American vision of open markets, democratic governments, and free enterprise—came without resistance. The Cold War presented the most profound challenge. Confronted by an equally determined opponent espousing a system that seemed the antithesis of the U.S. vision, Americans launched a prolonged struggle against international communism. Cold War conflict in less developed regions of the world proved particularly harrowing—costing 36,516 American lives in the Korean War and 58,159 in Vietnam, (alongside millions of Vietnamese and Koreans killed in each war). Hopes that the end of the Cold War would bring a respite from conflict quickly proved fanciful. The War on Terror, which began in response to the 9–11 terror attacks on New York City and Washington, D.C., has inaugurated a new era of international insecurity.

Nor was the flood of American products and cultural influence abroad greeted with universal enthusiasm. Throughout this period, organized opposition to the American invasion remained a challenge for U.S. business interests. American movies, recordings, sports heroes, and products like Coca-Cola and McDonald's proved wildly popular but also the object of scorn and sometimes violence. By the 1970s, even as U.S. culture and commerce remained under fire, Americans grew increasingly concerned by international competition—especially from Japan and later China. U.S. economic dominance, Americans fretted, seemed to be fading—a concern that continued despite a surging economy in the late 1990s. The specter of decline, as much as a sense of triumph, hung over Americans during this period.

—☙ ❧—

Concerns about the direction, and even morality, of U.S. foreign policy also drove many Americans to take an active role opposing their government's expansive agenda. By the 1960s, such sentiments boiled over into a large-scale revolt by American youth that circulated throughout the rest of the world. Even after the immediate upheaval died down, protests reminiscent of both the best and worst of the 1960s could flare, such as the antiapartheid movement of the 1980s or the challenge to globalization that resulted in violence at the 1999 meeting of the World Trade Organization (WTO) in Seattle.

Debates about the course of globalization have continued into the twenty-first century. While recognizing challenges, some view American-style globalization (or Americanization) as a welcome force, promising a rising tide of prosperity and democracy lifting all boats. Others see a darker picture: environmental threats, labor exploitation, and a crushing uniformity that endangers traditional cultures. Americans' attitudes about globalization, despite the lead their nation has taken in the process, remain profoundly ambivalent.

_○ ○_

Although many around the world immediately associate military might with American power, it was in the realm of commerce that America wielded the greatest worldwide influence in the late twentieth century. The American ideology of open markets, expanding trade, and consumer-driven mass production proved extremely popular and controversial. From the economic plans laid at Bretton Woods in 1944 through to the North American Free Trade Agreement (NAFTA) and the creation of the WTO in 1995, Americans pursued open trade with dogged determination, despite domestic and international opposition. Americans marketed to the world a seductive modern vision of the future, promoting individualism, convenience, and freedom of choice. Rapidly proliferating American commerce and the concomitant spread of American consumerism and popular culture, however, proved as controversial as it was potent. Proponents praise globalization for lifting literally hundreds of millions out of poverty in the last quarter of the twentieth century. Its critics continue to decry globalization as veiled American imperialism, destroying local cultures and enriching a select few.

Unprecedented military power backed American determination to reorder the world. America's leaders and large segments of its population viewed overseas commitments and conflict as part of a necessary mission to bring stability and progress to a world vulnerable to threats of poverty, ignorance, and totalitarianism. To counter the communist threat, policymakers embarked on a breathtaking buildup of America's conventional and unconventional forces. By the 1960s, however, with the United States bogged down in the Vietnam War, many

Americans became convinced their country suffered from a blinding arrogance of power. Efforts to scale back U.S. commitments followed the Vietnam War, but by the 1980s, President Ronald Reagan convinced Americans to recommit to the anticommunist agenda. The end of the Cold War led some to seek out a new American mission, again with an emphasis on promoting order and democratic governance. That mission morphed into the War on Terror as the new century began. All along the way, American power had no shortage of critics.

One group of domestic critics stood out in particular—instigating an ideological challenge that would have far-reaching cultural repercussions. By the late 1940s, a dedicated corps of African American activists emerged determined to take on Jim Crow at home and push for the end of odious colonialism abroad. The movement picked up steam in the 1950s and 1960s, generating intense national and international interest, especially for young people. By the 1960s, it inspired a widespread and diverse global revolt among the young. By the end of the decade, governments from Washington to Moscow to Paris to Beijing felt besieged by mounting demands of protesters. Even after the immediate tumult calmed, the movement among African Americans to globalize their worldview continued to inspire cultural and political change in America and the world.

CHAPTER TEN

Globalization and Americanization

THE KITCHEN DEBATE

Vice President Richard Nixon, tense by nature, suffered a sleepless night—with good reason. He had just arrived in the Soviet Union to open the first U.S. exhibition ever in that country. Nixon hoped to run for president the next year, and much was riding on his ability to appear statesmanlike but firm before the notoriously tough Nikita Khrushchev, the fiercely demanding Soviet leader.

That morning, July 24, 1959, Nixon and Khrushchev traveled the short distance from the Kremlin to Sokolniki Park to tour the exhibit before its official opening later that evening. The golden pavilion housing the show shimmered in the bright sun, but swarms of reporters and cameramen eclipsed all light as the two leaders emerged from their car. Aware their every move would be transmitted around the world, Nixon and Khrushchev immediately began sparring—each determined to get the upper hand. In a television studio, Khrushchev, already annoyed at the intense interest Muscovites were showing in the U.S. exhibit, assured the vice president that his country would soon outpace America and "wave bye-bye." The premier offered a slow, exaggerated wave to make his point. Smiling tightly, Nixon looked for an opening to strike back.

Leaving the studio, the rivals found themselves touring a model American ranch house and standing over a reproduction of the typical American "miracle kitchen," complete with stove, oven, and full-size refrigerator—items unavailable to the average Russian. Nixon quickly seized the scene of domestic prosperity and commercialism to make a greater point. "To us, diversity is the right to choose, the fact that we have a thousand different builders that is the spice of life," insisted the vice president. Khrushchev mocked his counterpart's claims, but Nixon pushed on, jabbing his finger at the Soviet leader as cameras clicked. "Isn't it better to be talking about the relative merits of our washing machines than of the relative strengths of our rockets?" he asked. Beyond mere materialism,

Nixon also contended that progress, commercial or otherwise, required "a free exchange of ideas." The Soviet leader seemed to have no response, other than to insist against all evidence that such freedom existed in the USSR.

Although dismissed by one historian as "bluff, bluster, and near buffoonery," the so-called Kitchen Debate became an iconic moment in the Cold War.[1] Nixon clearly linked open markets, the free flow of ideas, and the aura of "the American way of life" to U.S. global ambitions. Such a vision had its critics—from the scoffing Khrushchev, to others worldwide who feared an American cultural invasion, to protectionists at home. The American agenda also faced challenges: the economic burden of maintaining world leadership, powerful emergent economies in Asia and Europe, and the struggles to keep up with ever-evolving technology. Despite serious ups and downs, Nixon's vision of American commercialism as a transforming force proved prophetic. By the early twenty-first century, the consumer capitalism exemplified by the model ranch house that Nixon and Khrushchev visited on that hot, tense Moscow day had become a hallmark of globalism.

RESHAPING THE WORLD ECONOMY

Americans greeted the end of World War II with great relief but also anxiety. Would the stagnant, painful economy of the 1930s return as the wartime mandates faded? During the depression, unemployment had averaged 17 percent, and an estimated 45 percent of whites and 95 percent of blacks lived in poverty. As economists scrambled to plan for the postwar period, many emphasized foreign trade and an internationally integrated economic system as key to preventing a slide back into stagnation. "While we shall not take advantage of any country," wrote President Franklin Roosevelt in 1944, "we will see that American industry has its fair share in the world markets." International trade, U.S. officials believed, was not only necessary for American prosperity; it offered the promise of a friendlier, peaceful world. Americans blamed the protectionism of the 1930s for the economic dislocation that allowed fascists to rise to power. "A world in economic crisis would be forever a breeding ground for trouble and war," warned Secretary of State Cordell Hull in 1944.[2]

U.S. planners hoped that the Bretton Woods agreement, negotiated in 1944 under American auspices at a sprawling New Hampshire resort, would provide the basis for a new stable system of international trade and convertible currency exchange—anchored by an American promise to exchange dollars for gold at $35 an ounce. This arrangement, Americans believed, would allow countries to exchange their currencies freely so they could purchase goods worldwide. The International Monetary Fund (IMF), conceived at Bretton Woods, brought together 182 countries, each of whom contributed money to a fund designed to stabilize weak currencies. The IMF could impose deflationary policies, including devaluation, on errant members with trade imbalances and vulnerable currencies.

Bretton Woods also launched the World Bank, capitalized at $10 billion, aimed at making long-term loans to encourage development. Additionally, planners hoped to forge the International Trade Organization to closely supervise world trade. Domestic opposition in the United States—fears that the new organization would be too restrictive—however, brought about its defeat in Congress. In its place, in 1947, Congress did approve the General Agreement on Tariffs and Trade (GATT). The agreement between 22 nations responsible for 80 percent of world trade aimed at lowering tariffs and governing international commerce.

Compared to the economic isolationism that had prevailed a mere decade before, the transformation was dazzling. As the strongest industrial economy in the world, America assumed center stage, providing stability and direction to the western world. To the relief of Americans, depression conditions did not return. Instead, pent-up saving from the war years sparked an economic boom in America that would soon double its middle class.

As the only industrial economy left intact after the war, America also dominated international trade, accounting for one-third of the world's exports and providing 41 percent of its goods and services. "She sits bestride the world like a Colossus," waxed a British historian after visiting the United States in 1948. "Half the wealth of the world, more than half of the productivity, nearly two-thirds of the world's machines—the rest of the world lies in the shadow of American industry."[3] But the after-effects of the war dried up potential markets for American goods. A wide dollar gap opened, in which countries, particularly European nations, simply did not have the currency to buy U.S. goods. In contrast to America, Europe stumbled and struggled to recover. Making matters worse, a vicious arctic winter descended on Europe in late 1946, causing shortages, damaging crops, and wreaking untold human misery. As the Cold War began, Americans worried struggling Europeans would turn to communism. "[W]orld communism is like a malignant parasite that feeds on diseased tissue," U.S. diplomat George Kennan warned his superiors. Convinced that something had to be done to address the dollar gap and save Western Europe from communism, in 1947 Truman proposed the Marshall Plan, a massive foreign aid program for Europe. "We shall help," announced the president, "because we know that we ourselves cannot enjoy prosperity in a world of economic stagnation."[4]

Under the Marshall Plan, billions of U.S. taxpayers' dollars—mostly in grants rather than loans—pumped up Western Europe's economy (the Soviet Union and eastern bloc countries refused to participate). The transfusion of U.S. dollars allowed Europeans access to American goods and services. A program guaranteeing investments encouraged U.S. companies like General Motors, Ford, Goodyear, and Standard Oil to expand operations in Western Europe. "The Marshall Plan," wrote economic historian Diane Kunz, "offers a case study in how a nation does well by doing good."[5] But American motives went beyond creating new markets for U.S. goods. As historian Michael Hogan has suggested, the plan's designers aimed "to refashion Europe in the image of the United States."[6] U.S. advisers poured into Europe introducing American technology, management, and labor-relations techniques. Seeking to knit together Europe in a fashion akin to the United States, planners promoted, with some resistance, economic and political integration.

Defense spending in America, evolving from Cold War imperatives, continued to swell in the late 1940s and early 1950s. In late 1949, the National Security Council issued a report known as NSC-68 calling for massive increases in defense-related outlays. The subsequent Korean War created a crisis that guaranteed just such an arms buildup. Heavy military spending—$85 billion, representing 12 percent of the GNP—further drove the U.S. economy and pushed technology to new and often dangerous heights. When the Soviets exploded their own atomic bomb, the American government committed itself to developing a hydrogen bomb capable of even greater destruction. A strong federal government, viewing investment and economic growth as one of its primary raisons d'être, backed these developments. Virtually everywhere in the western world, the principles of Keynesian economics and supposed virtues of a mixed economy, in which government and business jointly formulated economic decisions, reigned supreme.

While trade networks grew among so-called First World nations, little commerce occurred across the iron curtain. When Chinese communists wrested control of the country from U.S.-allied forces, they seized American property, including the ITT-owned Shanghai telephone system and bottling plants owned by Coca-Cola. Meanwhile, in the developing world, Americans moved assertively to control important natural resources. U.S. businesses invested aggressively in mining in Latin America and elsewhere. But nowhere were

U.S. businessmen more assertive than in competing for control of Middle Eastern oil resources. In the late 1940s, ARAMCO, an enterprise owned jointly by several major U.S. oil companies, massively expanded its operations in Saudi Arabia, where it had purchased a concession larger than the state of Texas. As thousands of American ARAMCO employees poured into that country, U.S.-style homes, grocery stores, and schools sprang from the desert in the company's headquarters in Dhahran. Well aware that the 100,000 barrels shipped to America each day depended on goodwill and good relations with Saudi authorities, ARAMCO strove "to avoid the odium of old-style colonialism" in dealing with native workers. "The master manner is taboo, respect for local customs is required," explained *Life* magazine in a 1949 profile. ARAMCO also avoided employing Jews for fear of offending the Saudi government, which was at odds with the new nation of Israel.[7] By 1953 oil exports soared to 1 million barrels a day, accounting for 13 percent of U.S. consumption.

"LOVE THAT 'AMERICAN WAY OF LIFE'"

By the early 1940s, the Marshall Plan and other U.S. aid initiatives had helped spur economic recovery around the world. American business leaders took notice and ramped up international trade and investment. Exports to Western Europe, the United States' top trading partner, grew from $3.3 billion in 1950 to $7.4 billion in 1958—representing one-third of all U.S. exports. American direct investment in Western Europe ballooned from $12 billion to $27 billion during the same years. Recovery spread to Japan as well, where Korean War spending brought an investment boom and a resurgence of Japanese industry. In total, U.S. direct investment worldwide neared $50 billion by the end of the 1950s—up from $19 billion in 1950. Trade fed prosperity at home, and the world took notice. Visitors to the United States marveled at the cornucopia of consumer goods in stores—in marked contrast to persistent shortages around the world. The "proud abundance of everything, at the shop windows, the well dressed people—the queues of shinning cars on the road," mesmerized an Italian visitor. To British writer Malcolm Bradbury, America in the 1950s was "a paradise of consumer splendor."[8]

As in the early twentieth century, the automobile made the greatest international impact: 85 percent of cars sold worldwide in the postwar period were American. General Motors' Opel division in Europe maintained a large share of the European market, while Ford's Taunus model, sold in Europe beginning in 1952, could be seen throughout Western Europe. Even Chrysler, the perennial third among the "Big Three" U.S. automakers, made inroads in Europe. In 1958, Chrysler purchased 25 percent of Simca, France's largest privately owned automobile maker (it gained a controlling interest five years later). Chrysler also established foreign subsidiaries in Venezuela (1959), South Africa (1959), Turkey (1962), and the Philippines (1963).

Coca-Cola—the thirst-quencher William Allen White deemed the "sublimation of all that America stands for"—also made stunning worldwide strides during the 1950s. Beginning with a series of elaborate receptions for delegates at the United Nations organization conference in San Francisco in 1945, Coca-Cola mapped out an ambitious strategy to globalize its bubbly beverage. The Atlanta-based company licensed bottling plants around the world. In Egypt, for instance, the four Pathy brothers purchased rights to build six bottling plants. By the 1950s, they produced 350 million bottles of Coke annually, most hawked by street vendors out of sleek, bright red coolers. "We have become consciously and willingly intoxicated by Cola-Cola," explained one of the Pathy brothers. *Time* magazine honored the company's global reach with a May 15, 1950, cover cartoon portraying a thirsty globe gratefully imbibing a Coke. The caption read: "World and Friend: Love that piaster, that lira, that tickey, and that American Way of Life."[9]

Hollywood, another icon of American culture, also went increasingly global after World War II. Since few American films could be shown in Europe and Asia during the war, Hollywood had a huge backlog of movies ready to share with the world. It wasted little time moving into new markets. By 1958, international receipts amounted to more than half of Hollywood's total profits. Aware of their global audience and increasingly cosmopolitan viewers at home, studios began filming more movies outside U.S. borders. Italy provided backdrops for *Roman Holiday* (1953) and *Ben Hur* (1959). Director Alfred Hitchcock shot *To Catch a Thief* (1955) in the south of France, and *The African Queen* (1951) and *The Snows of Kilimanjaro* (1952) were filmed in Africa. Meanwhile, Hollywood continued to rely on a steady stream of international actors, directors, and producers in the 1950s, including Hitchcock, Ingrid Bergman, and Otto Preminger.

Cecil B. DeMille's epic *The Ten Commandments* (1956) stands out for its international flavor—and global box office appeal. Seeking authenticity, DeMille decided to film portions of his biblical epic in Egypt. A fan of DeMille's earlier films, General Gamal Nasser, Egypt's iron-fisted chief of state, welcomed the production to his country. An ardent cold warrior, DeMille hoped his retelling of an ancient story would speak directly to the current crisis by depicting an absolutist ruler (portrayed by Russian-born Yul Brynner) challenged by Moses, heroically guided by religious conviction (and played by handsome U.S. movie star Charlton Heston). Fortunately for all involved, on-location shooting ended well before the explosive Suez crisis in the fall of 1956.

Modestly marketing DeMille's film as "The Greatest Event in Motion Picture History!," Paramount Pictures labored to appeal to an international audience. DeMille toured Europe to publicize the movie. Studio promoters provided Latin American and European clerics with advanced screenings in return for testimonials used to advertise the film. Even the prime minister of Pakistan provided his endorsement aimed at Islamic audiences. The public relations work paid off. *The Ten Commandments* broke box office records around the world, placing it squarely among the top grossing movies of all time.

REACTION AGAINST AMERICANIZATION

To many around the world, American culture and commercialism suggested a near-fantasy world of luxury, modernity, and excitement. Yet not all welcomed this mounting force. As an obvious symbol of U.S. culture and pervasive capitalism, Coca-Cola became a target for those objecting to pernicious "Americanization." *Le Monde,* the most influential French newspaper, denounced the "dangers that Coca-Cola represents for the health and civilization of France."[10] Activists attacked trucks loaded with Coke and painted skull-and-crossbones over Coke signs on cafes. French communists introduced legislation into the National Assembly to ban the sale of Coca-Cola. "General Lafayette would think this decision [the attempt to ban Coca-Cola] was small reward for General Marshall's Plan," lamented James A. Farley, chairman of the Coca-Cola Export Corporation.[11]

Anti-Americanism also swelled in Latin America. Unlike Western Europe, U.S. officials directed no major Marshall Plan–type initiative to the region. It remained dominated by powerful American commercial interests and undemocratic, often military, leaders. When a left-leaning government in Guatemala threatened to expropriate hundreds of thousands of acres of land owned by United Fruit Company, the Eisenhower administration swung into action. In 1954, a CIA operation overthrew the Guatemalan government, replacing it with leaders more amenable to U.S. interests.

As American investment proliferated in the region, growth in Latin America stagnated and poverty seemed endemic. Increasingly frustrated, many Latin Americans embraced "dependency theory," a school of thought that emerged in the late 1940s, blaming chronic underdevelopment in peripheral countries on their exploitation by larger "core" economic powers. Vice President Richard Nixon's visit to South America in 1958 furnished him a firsthand taste of brewing anti-American sentiment. Protestors spit on the vice president and his wife and violently attacked his car. The Eisenhower administration blamed communists for the violence, but longstanding tensions, the result of often ruthless American financial interests in the region, clearly contributed. The next year, a revolution in Cuba placed Fidel Castro in power. Castro, renouncing a legacy of economic exploitation, soon nationalized American holdings in his country and forged an alliance with the Soviet Union.

Ironically, as resentment of U.S. cultural and economic power swelled, American officials began worrying that their hegemony was slipping away. By the late 1950s, European and Asian economies had recovered from the devastation of war. West Germany and Japan, America's wartime adversaries, led the way, rapidly developing their industrial capacity and becoming increasingly competitive. America's share of manufacturing worldwide fell from 70 percent in 1950 to 50 percent in 1960. As the decade ended, 10 percent of automobiles—representing some 600,000 cars annually (100,000 of which were Volkswagen Beetles)—sold in America were foreign made. "On a teacher's salary, there is no better car for the pocket book than a foreign one. With the gas and oil eaters the American companies are producing, a teacher couldn't hope to own one," explained a New York educator.[12]

While the United States maintained a trade surplus (exporting more than it imported), its overall "balance of payments" (measuring total credits and debts) fell into deficits in all but one year during the 1950s. Generous aid programs and military commitments overseas (as well as heavy direct investment abroad) contributed to the balance-of-payment woes. As European currencies recovered, maintaining the goal of convertibility set out by Bretton Woods—America's pledge to exchange dollars for gold at a rate of $35 an ounce—became an increasing burden. U.S. gold reserves dropped from $22 billion to $17 billion over the course of the 1950s. Meanwhile gold and U.S. dollars piled up in European and Japanese bank accounts.

Fearing the balance-of-payments deficit would snowball into a larger crisis, President Dwight Eisenhower dispatched his Treasury secretary to ask the West German government to foot a larger share of the bill for maintaining U.S. troops in their borders. The West Germans refused. Eisenhower also pleaded with American businessmen to limit overseas investments and ordered U.S.

military dependents overseas home in an effort to stem the outflow of U.S. dollars. Within a decade and a half of its founding, the Bretton Woods system, which relied on the United States as its anchor, appeared an increasing liability to Americans.

GUNS AND BUTTER

John F. Kennedy began his presidency in 1961 fully cognizant of the threats to Bretton Woods and the U.S. dollar, and he was determined to protect both. An adviser recalled that "above all [Kennedy] felt impaled on our balance of payments deficit—It humiliated him."[13] To combat that imbalance, Kennedy worked hard to promote U.S. exports. He pushed Congress to pass the Trade Expansion Act in 1962, granting him authority to lower tariffs significantly. The next year, Kennedy hosted 300 top businessmen for a two-day White House conference dedicated to expanding U.S. exports. "[F]or almost any American business," the president implored the gathering, "life can begin anew at the ocean's edge."[14] Kennedy's State Department also increased the "buy American" provision attached to foreign aid appropriations. To ease the balance-of-payments burden, the U.S. government had required countries receiving U.S. aid dollars to spend two-thirds of them purchasing American products; Kennedy increased the mandate to four-fifths of total aid.

Yet JFK simultaneously unveiled an expansive agenda for U.S. foreign policy—plans that included expensive modernization initiatives coupled with a military buildup. This expensive guns-and-butter approach ran counter to his efforts to redress the balance-of-payments problem. A series of international crises in Berlin, Cuba, Vietnam, and elsewhere precluded any cutback in America's military commitments around the world. Kennedy's Keynesian spending policies, aimed at generating domestic growth, also undermined his work to promote exports and limit imports. Americans, enjoying the bounty of growing paychecks due to Kennedy's policies, were able to purchase more imports, while rising U.S wages made American exports more expensive.

Lyndon Johnson only accelerated American commitments overseas when he took the presidency following Kennedy's assassination. Above all, the Vietnam War, beginning in 1965, dashed hopes of reversing America's international financial crisis. Billions of U.S. dollars flowed into South Vietnam to remake the Third World country so that hundreds of thousands of Americans could fight a modern war. Across South Vietnam, Americans constructed huge bases, deep water ports, and a stunning array of support features—including beer distribution systems, creameries for ice cream, movie theaters, and night clubs. Surrounding countries prospered from the American war. The U.S. military, for instance, purchased $200 million of Japanese products for the war in Vietnam in 1967. The economies of South Korea, Taiwan, Thailand, and the Philippines likewise thrived.

At home, foreign competition continued to make dents in fields traditionally dominated by Americans. By the early 1960s, the U.S. textile industry was in full retreat as foreign competitors, especially Japan, aided by cheap labor and hefty import restrictions implemented by its own government, undercut American manufacturers. From 1948 to 1961 some 800 textile mills closed in the United States, costing some quarter million American jobs. "Frankly, Rome is burning," conceded the president of a major textile firm in an address to the 1963 annual convention of the American Textile Manufacturers' Institute.[15]

By the mid-1960s, Japan also conquered the U.S. market for sewing machines, watches, cameras, transistor chips, and binoculars. Japanese motorcycle maker Honda increasingly dominated U.S. sales with its low-cost, high-quality motorbikes (in 1972 Honda entered the U.S automobile market with its Civic, a two-door coupe). The 1967 James Bond film *You Only Live Twice* featured the Toyota GT as the dashing "Bond car." The priceless publicity helped propel Toyota sales worldwide. The next year Toyota introduced its Corolla, destined one day to be the bestselling car in the United States. Even more stunning were Japanese inroads into the U.S. steel market. After World War II, American occupational authorities deemed Japanese steel an essential industry—providing it important protections and subsidies. By 1951, Japan produced six million tons annually. During the 1960s, the international share of the U.S. steel market more than doubled to 12 percent—much of the imports coming from Japan.

Americans still provided many of the world's products and dominated many sectors, especially entertainment. By the 1960s, television programming became a new source of American exports. *Bonanza*, a television western following the exploits of the Cartwright family, could be seen in 59 countries. In Italy Perry Mason's name became synonymous with "lawyer." *Doctor Kildare* topped ratings in Rhodesia and Poland. Meanwhile *The Flintstones*, an animated cartoon, sat at number one in Sweden.

Still, after leading the world in the aftermath of World War II, Americans could not escape a panicky sense of losing ground. In early 1968, a series of crises—war in Vietnam, political assassinations, urban violence, inflation, a trade imbalance, and worsening balance of payments—resulted in a frightening monetary crisis. The emergency began in November 1967 with Britain's decision to devalue its pound by over 14 percent. The Tet Offensive in Vietnam and political turmoil in America prompted fears the dollar would collapse. Nervous investors scrambled to cash in dollars for gold. U.S. gold reserves, already low, sank to new depths. Fear enveloped the Johnson administration. "Everyone was just petrified," recalled a Treasury Department official.[16] To a generation of leaders haunted by firsthand memories of the Great Depression, the possibility of a worldwide financial collapse rang alarm bells.

Desperate to restore order and determined to protect the dollar's vaulted status, Johnson moved to limit direct investment overseas and U.S. tourism. He persuaded the British to shut down the London gold markets, and the president slapped a 10-percent tax surcharge on individual and corporate incomes in hopes of addressing a growing budget deficit that was feeding inflation. When his military advisers asked for some additional 200,000 troops for the war in Vietnam (in addition to the already half million fighting there), Johnson felt compelled to decline—fearing the economic and political costs of such a commitment. Additional troops in Southeast Asia, Senator Michael Mansfield explained to the president, would mean "more inflation, more balance of payments complications, and possible financial panic and collapse."[17]

By midyear the crises eased. Student riots in Paris and the Soviet invasion of Czechoslovakia, in the spring and summer of 1968 (discussed in chapter 11), suddenly reversed the flow of gold into the United States, which now appeared a comparatively safe haven. Johnson could breathe a sigh of relief, but even with serious adjustments, such as erecting separations between the dollar and the private gold market, the U.S. dollar seemed overvalued and the international system overburdened.

By 1971, the ground again began to give way under the U.S. dollar and the Bretton Woods system. Foreigners held three times as many dollars as the U.S. government could redeem for gold at the $35 mark. U.S. gold reserves continued to slip—by 1971 to the lowest levels since the Great Depression. Meanwhile, America experienced its first trade deficit since 1883. "The simple fact is that in many areas, others are outproducing us, outthinking us, outworking us, and outtrading us," lamented Treasury secretary John Connally.[18] Some sectors, such as trade unions and industries hard hit by increasing imports, began calling for protective tariffs. Japan, which exported 50 times more textiles than it imported, became a favorite target of trade critics. Desperate for help, President Nixon waived limits on foreign arms sales, hoping to generate more exports in at least one sector.

By the summer of 1971, the president felt compelled to act. In mid-August he ordered his economic team to the presidential retreat at Camp David. Secluded in the mountains of western Maryland, Nixon and Connally orchestrated a redesign of American and world economics. Nixon's advisers determined America could no longer afford its pledge to convert dollars to gold—the costly promise at the heart of Bretton Woods. The unilateral decision to terminate convertibility, announced when Nixon came down from Camp David, effectively devalued the dollar (an actual devaluation of 8.6 percent occurred later in the year), rendering U.S. exports more competitive. Nixon also slapped a 10-percent surcharge on imports. Never consulted by Nixon, stunned leaders worldwide cut short their August vacations to deal with a troubling new economic world. With gold shunted aside (although still a valuable commodity), the dollar eventually "floated" with all world currencies, the international market determining its value.

Secretary Connally, a Texan, enjoyed betting big. "What's the sense of losing small?" he liked to ask.[19] Nixon's gamble on ending convertibility did revitalize the struggling U.S. export sector, especially in technology and agriculture. The Camp David shake-up, which included temporary price and wage controls, improved the U.S. economy in time for Nixon's 1972 reelection. Yet other nations also devalued their currencies to keep their imports marketable, prompting a new worldwide bout of inflation.

OIL SHOCK AND STAGFLATION

The brief economic upswing of 1972, however, proved the calm before the storm. Already by the early 1970s, mounting concerns about America's energy supply reverberated among policy planners. Still, most Americans gave little thought to the cheap, presumably limitless supply of oil that fueled the American way of life. For several decades U.S.-based oil companies had profited handsomely from deals with Middle Eastern countries. By the late 1960s, however, Arab countries began to push back—insisting on renegotiating agreements and cutting production to drive up prices. Although the Middle East supplied less than 10 percent of the oil consumed in the United States, production cuts combined with restrictive controls and regulation imposed by the U.S. government caused supplies to tighten in the early 1970s.

Then foreign policy came into play. On October 6, 1973, Egypt and Syria launched a coordinated attack on Israel. Supporting the attack, Arab oil-producing nations slashed production to warn the Americans against support of Israel. After some hesitation, Nixon defied the Arabs and initiated a massive resupply of Israel, which quickly overcame the attacks. Spurned and stung by defeat, Arab states slapped a total embargo on their oil sales to America. Oil prices immediately shot up in the United States and across the world. The New York Stock Exchange lost $100 billion in value in the first six weeks of the embargo. Spot shortages occurred across the country. Other oil-producing countries took advantage of the crisis and drove prices up 400 percent. Western economies reeled. Industrial production fell in America, causing layoffs and plant closings. Meanwhile, prices on other products soared due to the high cost of oil needed to manufacture and transport them. For five painful months, the embargo dragged on, while the Nixon administration desperately sought a diplomatic solution. Finally, in mid-March 1974, the Arab nations called off their protest. The damage, however, had been done. The price of oil had quadrupled, with devastating repercussions. By the summer of 1974, the Organization for Economic Cooperation and Development (OECD) announced that its member states had suffered an economic reversal of record proportions.

Shocked by their vulnerability, Americans briefly altered their habits. President Nixon announced Project Independence, designed to cut America's reliance on foreign oil in ten years. Many Americans shifted to smaller, fuel-efficient (often Japanese or European) cars, and automakers strove to improve fuel efficiency. A second energy crisis in 1979, the result of a revolution in Iran, again drove up oil prices, spurring further interest in alternative sources of energy. Nevertheless, U.S. reliance on outside sources for oil continued to rise, especially when oil prices began to fall in 1983 as surpluses grew.

The energy crisis combined with other factors, such as poor harvests, resulted in what became known as "stagflation"—rising unemployment coupled with inflation. Everywhere talk persisted that America had outstripped its resources and was entering a period of decline. In a nationally televised speech in 1979, President Jimmy Carter openly fretted that a malaise had overcome Americans, stripping the country of its enterprising, positive spirit. The problem, Carter concluded, was "deeper than gasoline lines or energy shortages, deeper even than inflation or recession—It is a crisis of confidence." Less than a year later, a group of scholars, politicians, and businessmen gathered at Harvard University to assess the economic crisis. The backdrop remained bleak—mounting trade deficits, soaring inflation, a deepening energy crisis, unemployment, and a weak dollar. "The 1980s will be a decisive decade," opined one economist. "[I]f we fail to come to grips with our problems, the United States will be taking a back seat to more disciplined countries such as West Germany and Japan."[20]

Indeed, America's problems seemed nearly insurmountable at the dawn of the 1980s. "Things just do not work now as they used to," lamented Arthur Burns, chairman of the Federal Reserve.[21] Japanese competition became an ever-growing concern to Americans as U.S. trade deficits mounted. By the 1970s, Japanese imports represented one half of the deficit. As Americans turned to smaller foreign cars in the wake of soaring gas prices, U.S. auto manufacturers cut back operations. By 1980, 215,000 of the United Auto Workers' 1.1 million members were laid off. The once omnipotent American steel industry also continued to wane in the face of foreign competition. U.S. steelmakers operated at 30 percent capacity in the early 1980s. Defenders of American steelmakers accused the Japanese and others of "dumping"—selling products below cost to gain market share. Others argued U.S. facilities had become outdated and American labor costs were stiflingly high. Concurrently, Japan threatened to dominate the market for electronics, such as radios and televisions, and began encroaching on the emerging semiconductor industry.

As Americans struggled with mounting challenges, Japan emerged as a model for some. Inspired by Japan's powerful Ministry of International Trade and Industry, a group of concerned Americans called for industrial planning along the lines practiced by West Germany and Japan. Senator Ted Kennedy called for an "American Reindustrial Corporation" to guide investment, development, trading policies, and planning. Others, however, insisted market forces and competition offered the best route to regaining lost market shares.

In fact, despite cries from organized labor and some industries, a distinct trend away from protectionism and toward open markets was unmistakable by the late 1970s. Free market economist Milton Friedman won the Nobel Prize in economics in 1976. Margaret Thatcher's election as Britain's prime minister in 1979 based on her calls to trim the welfare state and privatize government-owned industries also signaled change. In 1980, Ronald Reagan ran for president, vowing to reverse America's fortunes through a combination of tax cuts, deregulation, and free trade. Reaganites claimed their overwhelming victory in 1980 would inaugurate a new day. But the U.S. economy sank to new lows in 1981 and 1982 as high interest rates designed to curb inflation drove America into recession. U.S. goods became harder to sell overseas, and tighter monetary policy provoked a debt crisis in Latin America, where long-term indebtedness quadrupled between 1975 and 1982.

As unemployment topped 10 percent in 1982 and American industry appeared anemic, pressure built on Reagan to intervene. Pointing to severe barriers erected by countries such as Japan, protectionists assailed free trade, calling instead for "fair trade." At some political cost, Reagan resisted the pressure. "[I]f one partner in the boat shoots a hole in the boat, it doesn't make much sense for the other partner to shoot another hole in the boat," he explained to the Japanese Diet in 1983. "Some call that getting tough. I call it getting wet." Yet Reagan did push Japan to open its markets, and, with the cooperation of the Japanese, arranged voluntary restraints on automobile imports. The Reagan administration also placed temporary quotas on Japanese motorbikes and semiconductors, hoping to buy Americans time to improve productivity and competitiveness.

RADIATING "UNLIMITED FREEDOM"

After a shaky two years, Reagan's policies began to gain traction in 1983. An international oil glut drove prices down. A strong U.S. dollar drew low-cost imports into the United States, also helping to tame the inflation that ravaged the nation in the previous decade. Encouraged, the Federal Reserve dropped interest rates, spurring recovery. Soon unemployment was dropping at its fastest rate in 30 years. U.S. companies such as Harley-Davidson (maker of motorcycles), Xerox (makers of copiers), and Intel (semiconductors) turned back stiff international competition.

It was not, however, traditional sectors such as automobiles and steel, that led the way to recovery. Rather new "high-tech" industries—particularly computers and information technology—drove the resurgence. From the postwar UNIVAC, which took up an entire room, the computer had evolved rapidly. The IBM (International Business Machines) corporation initially set the pace, followed by seven smaller companies, dubbed the "seven dwarfs." Their dominance was challenged in 1976 when two college dropouts from California developed the first Apple Computer aimed at personal use. IBM soon countered with its own PC. Ever improving technology quickly allowed businesses and individuals easy access to inexpensive computers. *Time* magazine bestowed its coveted "man of the year" designation on the computer in 1982. Between 1981 and 1983 computer sales doubled. Innovative high-tech companies proliferated, springing up in areas such as Silicon Valley in northern California and along Route 128, connecting Boston to its suburbs. People began talking of a "Massachusetts Miracle," as unemployment in the Bay State remained below the national average despite the decline of its traditional industries.

As his policies began to bear fruit, Reagan pushed aggressively for open trade. Pressured by the president and aware of the threat from a protectionist-leaning

Congress, Japan made conciliatory gestures such as opening assembly plants in the United States. Meanwhile, in 1986, Reagan helped initiate a new series of GATT negotiations. Known as the Uruguay Round, the talks aimed at lowering tariffs and spurring trade worldwide. Closer to home, Reagan brokered the Free Trade Agreement with Canada and began similar discussions with Mexico. Embracing the liberalized atmosphere, American business flocked to the formerly closed People's Republic of China. Under Deng Xiaoping, the PRC opened itself to foreign investment and trade. "It doesn't matter whether the cat is white or black as long as it catches mice," Deng offered in explanation of why a communist country would dive headfirst into the global capitalist economy.

While trade deficits continued to grow, a spirit of optimism swept up U.S. businesses. American culture remained an ever-expanding and bankable global force. *Dallas,* a nighttime soap opera chronicling the triumphs and travails of a fabulously wealthy family of Texas oil tycoons, became the most popular show in the world, seen in 57 countries by 300 million viewers. While Jack Lang, France's minister of culture, dismissed *Dallas* as "the symbol of American cultural imperialism," his countrymen faithfully tuned in to follow the latest episode. Soon the French developed their own knock-off version of *Dallas,* entitled *Chateauvallon.*[22] Meanwhile McDonald's "fast food" restaurants spread worldwide. Soon hungry customers could order Big Macs in thousands of Golden Arches internationally. Disney, with its theme song "It's a Small World after All," opened an amusement park in Tokyo in 1983 (and Euro Disney in France in 1992). U.S. cigarette manufacturers also expanded their global operations. By the 1980s, Philip Morris and R. J. Reynolds generated half their profits from international markets, especially Asia. The "Marlboro Man" image of a cowboy relishing the rugged life became a worldwide icon, linking freedom with American commercialism. Even behind the iron curtain, American music and culture was celebrated. So prized were Levi's jeans in the Soviet Union that they often substituted for currency. "The image of America," commented a Japanese critic, "radiates unlimited freedom."[23] Richard Nixon's insight at the U.S. exhibit in Moscow about the global appeal of American culture and its byproducts seemed prescient.

For all these advances, many Americans remained skeptical of expanded international trade—as evidenced by the strong protectionist mood often on display in the U.S. Congress. Japan, with its aggressive export sector and resistance to imports, remained the focus of resentment. A 1986 Ron Howard movie entitled *Gung Ho* played American anxieties for laughs. In the film, a Japanese company buys an automobile manufacturing plant in Pennsylvania. Japanese bosses immediately clash with their informal and individualistic American workforce. *Gung Ho* ends on a hopeful note as employees team up with a Japanese executive to save the plant from a planned closing. Still the movie, which appeared in theaters the year after America became a net debtor country, betrayed lingering apprehensions as the economies of Japan and other Asian countries appeared on the march.

Off the silver screen hope for accommodation between the two economic competitors seemed less and less likely. The purchase of American landmarks such as Rockefeller Center by a Japanese real estate firm and Sony's acquisition of Columbia Records, both in the late 1980s, stirred resentment. Meanwhile a new challenge from the Asian Tigers—Singapore, South Korea, Taiwan, and Hong Kong—appeared on the horizon. Reagan and his successor George H. W. Bush resolutely avoided a trade war, but many Americans began openly expressing frustration. "Japan bashing" came in many forms—"buy American" campaigns, celebrations when the commissioner of baseball rejected a bid by Nintendo to buy the Seattle Mariners, even violence against Japanese cars.

Tensions peaked in early 1992 when President Bush, on a trade mission to Tokyo, grew violently ill during a state dinner. The image of an American president overcome by nausea beamed around the world and appeared a metaphor to some. "When the Japanese prime minister said he felt sympathy for the U.S., it made me sick," declared Governor Bill Clinton, then a candidate for Bush's job. "If I'd been with him, I'd have thrown up too!"[24] As Bush recovered and strove to keep his job, protectionism seemed the wave of the future. One Democratic candidate for president appeared in hockey goalie dress before a goal, vowing to protect U.S. industries and jobs. Within his own party, Bush faced a stiff challenge from conservative commentator Patrick Buchanan, who celebrated economic nationalism and assailed free trade. "The Cold War is over," went a popular joke, "and Japan won!"

Ironically, as Bush's trade record came under fire, evidence abounded that America's relationship with Japan had changed. Between 1985 and 1992 U.S. exports to Japan doubled, rising to $50 billion—more than American trade with Germany, Italy, and France combined. Likewise, as economist Robert Reich argued in 1991, the global economy was becoming so integrated that older notions of balance of trade and nation-against-nation competition were outdated. A "sports car is financed in Japan, designed in Italy, and assembled in Indiana, Mexico, and France. Does it matter?" asked Reich.[25] Meanwhile the Japanese economy entered a sharp recession, slowing growth for the next decade.

NEOLIBERAL GLOBALIZATION

Reich's close friend, Governor Clinton, became the Democratic Party's nominee for president in 1992. Clinton largely sided with Reich, believing America must embrace a more global approach to trade and economics, and he looked to continue the international trade agenda of Reagan and Bush when he became president in 1993. By the early 1990s the end of the Cold War accelerated movement toward open, liberalized economies. Where once mixed, heavily regulated systems seemed the wave of the future, a "neoliberal" movement, espousing free-market, free-trade policies, now appeared inexorable. The accelerating high-tech, information revolution drove neoliberal globalization. The emergence of the Internet in particular seemed to herald a new age of almost overwhelming communication potential—a "third industrial revolution of communications and technology," some proclaimed, had arrived.[26] The Internet quickly transformed and cheapened traditional communications with the introduction of e-mail, e-commerce, and a host of other new services and resources. By the late 1990s, hundreds of millions worldwide were "surfing the net" (by 2010, that figure had ballooned to several billion). Recognizing the potential of revolutionary emerging technology, Clinton resisted any efforts to regulate the Internet, insisting it should remain accessible and democratic.

The president faced dogged opposition from congressional Republicans on a host of issues, but on world trade, he often found the GOP more amenable than his own protectionist-leaning Democratic Party. Clinton enthusiastically embraced work begun by his predecessors to link Canada, the United States, and Mexico into a free trade bloc. Despite ardent support from three former presidents—Ford, Carter, and Bush—Clinton encountered strong resistance to passing the treaty. Ross Perot, a popular businessman and presidential candidate, warned of the giant "sucking sound" of jobs leaving the United States for cheaper labor markets. In the end Clinton relied heavily on House Republicans to pass the NAFTA measure. When Mexico's economy floundered in 1994, Clinton called on Congress to bail out his new trading partner. After Democrats blocked his efforts, the president turned to monies already appropriated to the Treasury Department. Clinton also wrapped up the sweeping Uruguay Round of GATT negotiations in 1994, reducing tariffs by an average of 40 percent, protecting intellectual property rights (particularly important to preserve U.S. dominance of the entertainment sector), and creating the World Trade Organization (WTO), an international body to enforce global trade agreements. After heated debate, Congress passed the broad trade revisions. A grateful Clinton credited Republicans with saving the agreement.

This groundwork further spurred an international trade boom already under way. By the mid-1990s, "globalization" became the popular buzzword to describe the transforming world economy. National borders no longer defined trade. Even regional alliances such as NAFTA and the European Union, while of increasing importance, seemed part of a larger, unrelenting trend toward the global integration of markets. The Internet and high-tech resources sped communications and finance, connecting commerce around the world. Seeing the potential of free markets, more states adopted the non-interventionist model. The IMF and World Bank, increasingly powerful in the shaping economies worldwide, also pushed neoliberal reforms, especially on states mired in debt.

World commerce flourished in this atmosphere. Global trade expanded 85 percent in the 1990s (compared to 11 percent between 1980 and 1985). The United States, with its large markets and innovative environment, sat at the center of many of these developments. A roaring stock market in the second half of the 1990s financed a "dot-com" boom, thrusting small, inventive information-technology firms to the forefront of the U.S. economy. Liberal immigration laws in America drew technically savvy individuals from around the world—leading less-developed countries to complain of "brain drains." By the 1990s, one-third of the high-tech innovators in Silicon Valley were foreign born.

Among the cultural products marketed so effectively to the world was American sports. In 1986, the National Football League inaugurated annual "American Bowl" preseason games played internationally in cities that included Berlin, Tokyo, Mexico City, and Sydney. By the twenty-first century, the NFL was actively considering launching international franchises. Meanwhile, no single figure more exemplified the globalization of U.S. sports than Michael Jordan. Satellite television beamed Jordan's gravity-defying feats around the globe. Along the way Jordan marketed a dizzying array of products to the world—especially Nike athletic shoes, manufactured by low-wage labor in developing countries then sold at considerable profit to consumers eager to "be like Mike," as advertisers promised. Driven in part by the commanding image of Jordan, basketball went increasingly global (although the International Basketball Federation began in Geneva in 1932, and in 1936 basketball became an Olympic sport). Meanwhile, the NBA itself became increasingly international as standouts such as China's Yao Ming (2002's top NBA pick) filled its ranks.

Yao Ming's unlikely ascension to NBA fame and fortune mirrored his country's rise. For sheer pace of growth and rapid integration into the global economy China outpaced the rest of the world. Deng Xiaoping's invitation to foreign investors rekindled old dreams of a "China Market" among Americans. Congress granted China most favored nation (MFN) status in 1980, and U.S. dollars flowed into China. The Tiananmen Square massacre in 1989, in which Chinese troops mercilessly crushed a reform movement, stalled the emerging Sino-U.S. trading relationship. However, both Presidents Bush and Clinton worked to maintain good relations. Despite opposition, Congress reaffirmed MFN status for China. Clinton also strove to resolve disputes over intellectual property rights without initiating a trade war with China.

As a result, China's economy soared, growing at a pace of near 10 percent during the 1990s, and over 10 percent in the new century. Chinese products—from clothing to computers to electronics—filled American stores. Chinese corporations such as Haier, maker of large appliances, came seemingly out of nowhere to seize a large share of the American market. So lopsided was trade that the Chinese began manufacturing their own disposable shipping containers—since there was no need to ship empty containers back to China (millions of empty containers, in fact, had been clogging West Coast ports). As they had with Japan, Americans complained of barriers to trade, which drove up U.S. trade deficits with China from $100 billion in 1994 to $251 billion by 2007. Yet despite tension, the U.S. trade relationship with China only deepened. In 2000, Congress granted China "permanent normal trade relations," and the next year China entered the WTO as its 143rd member.

Supporters of globalization crowed that mushrooming global commerce and stunning technological developments promised a bright future of growth and spreading democracy. *New York Times* columnist Thomas Friedman, a leading globalization cheerleader, advanced his McDonald's theory of conflict resolution: No two countries both hosting the ubiquitous fast food franchise had ever gone to war (nor presumably would they ever). Peace, apparently, was a by-product of the new integrated world. "There's now a universal sense that democracy is humankind's chosen form of political organization and that the free market is its chosen form of economic organization," waxed Vice President Albert Gore.[27]

Not all, however, shared this ebullience. The steady resistance Clinton encountered from within his own party only mounted. Although never able to halt the momentum of globalization, opponents were able to slow it. When President Clinton, in his second term, asked for "fast track" authority to negotiate trade treaties that Congress could only vote up or down (without amendments), Republicans and Democrats joined forces to defeat the proposal—twice. Exasperated, Clinton urged his opponents to recognize the new global realities. "[N]othing we can do can change the fact that factories or information can flash across the world, that people can move money around the world in the blink of an eye," he pleaded.[28]

As trade took off, so, too, did worldwide resistance to globalization. In France, California-raised activist Jose Bove became a folk hero for attacking and defacing a McDonald's near Montpellier. Bove and many Europeans particularly objected to the introduction of genetically altered foods forced on them, they believed, by trade agreements with America. Violence also resulted after the IMF imposed strict reforms on Asian countries in the wake of the "Asian Flu" economic downturn that afflicted key economies in Asia in the late 1990s. IMF-imposed austerity measures on Indonesia contributed to rioting that brought down the government in 1998. In Latin America, resentment built against what became known as the "Washington Consensus," a series of free-market reforms many felt the IMF and U.S. Treasury Department imposed on countries in the region.

Many such critics also warned that globalization, a process supposedly weaving together the world, amounted to American economic imperialism, the triumph of U.S. culture and commerce. "Globalization," lamented a Jordanian professor in the *Jordan Times*, "is nothing but Americanization."[29] Even Michael Jordan came under fire as an ambassador of an exploitative capitalism that benefited only his country. "Imperialism, that's what Michael Jordan stands for. Economic and cultural imperialism," blasted economist Michael Veseth.[30] By this time, of course, such fears were nearly a century old. Likewise, some observers noted that far from collapsing in the wake of "Americanization," local cultures often co-opted globalization. Still, critics sprang fresh from every corner of the globe, especially as U.S. military might rendered it the sole superpower (see chapter 11).

Anger reached its apex at the Seattle meeting of the WTO in 1999. Protestors, many calling themselves anarchists, converged on the gathering. Violent clashes, property damage, and arrests shocked WTO members, including President Clinton. "[W]hat all those people in the street tell us is that they would also like to be heard. I think we need to do a better job of making the basic case," concluded the president. Despite Clinton's pledge to open communications, the WTO arranged to have future meetings in locations guaranteeing greater security and privacy for members. In 2001, antiglobalization protestors again moved to disrupt an international conference, this time a Quebec City meeting of Western Hemisphere democracies. The meeting aimed to pave ground for a Free Trade Area of the Americas (an arrangement still under negotiation in 2011) to promote free trade among the 800 million inhabitants representing some $11 trillion in commerce from Cape Horn to Canada. Police, relying on tear gas, struggled to control some 20,000 protestors who tore down fences, set bonfires, and vandalized property.

As the Seattle and Quebec City protests suggest, by the end of the century, a broad cross-section of activists was coalescing against globalization. Deep concerns about labor, human rights, and the environment led many to seek alternatives to the emerging global regime geared around the logic of the market. "Fair trade" coffee, a movement to provide western consumers with coffee and other products produced by justly compensated workers and favorable environmental conditions, has proved popular. Likewise, environmental concerns have led to a worldwide "sustainability" movement aimed at promoting environment-friendly lifestyles. The horrific terrorist acts of September 11, 2001, also contributed to the sobering realization that technology (al-Qaeda uses the Internet for recruiting and organization) can promote anarchy as easily as democracy.

Even some among the original proponents of globalization have joined the dissenters. Joseph Stiglitz, a Nobel Prize–winning economist and key adviser to President Clinton, increasingly has emerged a leading critic of the American role in promoting globalization. "While we talked about democracy, we did everything we could to maintain our control of the global economic system," Stiglitz confessed in 2003.[31]

Likewise a global recession beginning in 2008 made painfully clear that an integrated world economy, with countries and industries deeply intertwined, could as easily spiral downward as soar upward. The bursting of the U.S. housing bubble and related banking crisis triggered shock waves that reverberated around the world. The collapse of Lehman Brothers, a major global investment firm, led banks worldwide to curtail their lending. Soon, economies were reeling. Nations around the world feared they would soon follow the path of little Iceland, which saw its entire banking system fold like a house of cards in the fall of 2008.

Convinced the lesson of the 1930s depression mandated strong international cooperation, world leaders sought joint action to preserve the global economy. At a meeting of the G-20 (a forum for finance ministers and central bank leaders from 20 nations and the European Union, begun in 1999 in response to the Asian financial crisis), delegates disavowed protectionism and pledged $1 trillion to stimulating the ailing global economy. U.S. president

Barack Obama praised the agreement as "a turning point in our pursuit of global economic recovery."

Still the world economy struggled. Unemployment among youth (ages 15–24) in OEDC countries soared to 19 percent, while overall unemployment in the United States hit double digits. Nicknaming themselves the "Ant Tribe," three million unemployed Chinese college graduates faced uncertain futures. When the G-20 met in Pittsburgh in September 2009, the mood was decidedly darker. Protestors angry over high-profile bank bailouts while joblessness soared converged on the city, resulting in violent clashes with police and arrests.

By 2011 some signs of recovery showed through the global recession. Still, a debt crisis in Greece (abetted by U.S.-based global investment and banking firm Goldman Sachs, which helped mask Greek debts) threatened to derail gains. Meanwhile, some countries began insisting that bailout funds be concentrated domestically, potentially imperiling global recovery in favor of national recovery.

Despite its severity, however, the global recession does not appear as yet to have altered American commitment to free trade and globalization. U.S. trade representatives continue to push for open markets, and key American officials continue to argue that free trade will raise global standards of living and foster peaceful democracies—solving, along the way, many of the persistent problems so alarming to globalization critics. In 2009 at a "town hall" meeting with Chinese students in Shanghai, President Barack Obama attempted to make just that case. The president extolled the gains made through globalization and closer U.S.-Sino relations: lifting "hundreds of millions of people out of poverty—an accomplishment unparalleled in human history." He vowed to pursue even closer trade relations and pushed ever so gently issues related to human rights. He was clearer when it came to access to the Internet. "The more freely information flows the stronger the society becomes," he preached, his words echoing Nixon's Kitchen Debate contentions. The students seemed to appreciate the message. Chinese authorities, however, refused to broadcast the meeting to the rest of the country.

—◌ ◌—

At its best, U.S. commerce, culture, and technology has indeed enriched the world. The "freedom to choose," as Nixon put it, remains an alluring model for the world. In many ways globalization cannot be separated from Americanization. Yet skeptics abound, perhaps more numerous and organized than ever. Consensus about a rapidly integrating world—so much an American project since the end of World War II—remains elusive.

CHAPTER ELEVEN

Becoming the "Indispensable Nation"

UPROAR AT OHIO STATE

It was supposed to have been a civil exchange of views—in the grand tradition of American "town hall meetings." President Bill Clinton dispatched three of his top foreign policy advisers—secretary of state, defense secretary, and national security adviser—to Ohio State University to make the case publicly for military action against Iraq. Saddam Hussein, Iraq's dangerous and erratic leader, recently had denied United Nations inspectors access to sites suspected of concealing stockpiles of chemical, biological, and even nuclear weaponry. Furious, the Clinton administration prepared to retaliate.

The trio of policy makers hoped the Ohio State forum, to be broadcast internationally by the cable news network CNN, would increase pressure on Saddam and build support for their hard line. But the February 17, 1998, town hall hardly resembled the New England town hall ideal of thoughtful discussion. Chants of "One, two, three, four, we don't want your racist war" greeted the Clinton administration officials as they entered the cavernous basketball arena that served as the setting for the forum. Audience members openly booed the panelists—interrupting answers with cries of "Bullshit! Bullshit!" Police forcibly removed some protestors as others chanted "The whole world is watching." At one point nervous White House staffers debated pulling the plug before things got worse.

While the secretary of defense and national security adviser shrank from confrontation, Madeleine Albright, the secretary of state, took on the crowd. "As a former university professor," Albright shot back at a hostile questioner, "I suggest, sir, that you study carefully what American foreign policy is. I would be happy to spend 50 minutes with you after the forum to explain it." As tension grew, Albright refused to back down. "I am really surprised people feel it necessary to defend the rights of Saddam Hussein," she scolded, earning a smattering of applause from some among the 5,000 in attendance.[1]

Born in Czechoslovakia just before World War II, Albright twice fled her homeland with her family—first to escape the Nazis, then to flee the communists—before coming to the United States. "My mindset is Munich, not Vietnam," she liked to say, setting herself apart from a generation often squeamish about American power.[2] Albright believed deeply that her nation had a mission to spread democracy and fight tyranny—a point she tried to make one last time before the hostile Ohio State crowd. "[W]hat we are doing," she insisted over catcalls and boos, "is being the indispensable nation, willing to make the world safe for our children and grandchildren and for nations who follow the rules."[3]

The immediate crisis with Iraq passed—although President Clinton did unleash a series of air attacks later that year and the United States launched a costly invasion in 2003. Still, the raucous Ohio State forum and Albright's bold assertion of America as "the indispensable nation" reflect clashing currents that shaped America's interaction with the world. After World War II, American leaders, already imbued with notions of American exceptionalism, undertook what they saw as a mission to reorder and revive a world torn to pieces by war. Even after the Cold War, America's leaders continued to frame its military and foreign policy in terms of a mission to preserve order and spread democracy. Meanwhile, as Albright found in Ohio, not all Americans shared the crusading spirit; indeed, opposition both domestic and international, often shaped the conflicts and missions undertaken by Americans.

COLD WAR: "A SOLEMN RESPONSIBILITY"

The view from 1945 was harrowing. Most of Europe and large portions of Asia lay in rubble. Millions around the world had died in the brutal world war. Homelessness, disease, desperation, and fear of more violence portended a frightening future. In response, postwar American leaders cast off all lingering isolationism and set about to reorder a world veering toward chaos. Like Woodrow Wilson before them, they believed only the United States could usher in a new era of peace and stability. "History has bestowed upon us a solemn responsibility. We failed before to give a genuine peace—we dare not fail again," explained Harry S. Truman as the United States once again faced the daunting challenge of reordering the world after a cataclysmic war.[4]

Yet with the end of the war, pressure built to demobilize rapidly. Most Americans, while hardly isolationists, hoped to retreat from the horrors of war—and the 12 million Americans on active duty in the armed forces in the summer of 1945 wanted nothing more than to board the boats that would take them home. Policy makers responded to popular slogans like "no boats, no votes." Within a year of Japan's surrender, only three million remained in service, and by 1947 that figure was halved again. Despite its popularity with the public, President Truman worried "the program we were following was no longer demobilization—it was disintegration of our armed forces."[5]

To Truman, ominous threats to world order remained, especially in the form of the Soviet Union, America's wartime ally. Washington officials worried about the future of Eastern Europe occupied by Soviet troops at war's end. The Soviet system seemed the antithesis of the democratic ideals American leaders had espoused and hoped to spread to the world. As White House aide Harry Hopkins explained, "We should not be timid about blazoning to the world our desire for the rights of all people to have a genuine civil liberty. We believe our dynamic democracy is the best in the world."[6]

A clash between wartime allies seemed inevitable. Wartime losses that easily topped 20 million (compared to 400,000 Americans killed) left the USSR reeling and determined to better secure its borders. Meanwhile the United States resented the continuing presence of Soviet troops in Eastern Europe. At an April 22, 1945 meeting, Truman lashed out at Soviet foreign minister V. M. Molotov, assailing the Soviets for sabotaging planned elections in Poland. "I have never been talked to like that in my life," protested Molotov. "Carry out your agreements and you won't get talked to like that," the president shot back.[7] Despite the exchange, Truman continued to seek accommodation with the Soviets in the first several months after the war. Likewise, Stalin appeared willing to compromise on some issues. Still, tensions in Eastern Europe combined with clashes over Iran, postwar loans, German reparations, and other issues inexorably pushed the two superpowers toward discord. By May 1946 a *Life* magazine headline blared, "Why Kid Around? There is no 'Misunderstanding' between Russia and the West. There is Conflict."[8] That same year Winston Churchill toured the United States ominously warning of a Soviet "iron curtain" descending over Eastern Europe.

Set on challenging communism, Truman moved to make his case to the American public. Taking Senator Arthur Vandenberg's advice, the president decided to "scare the hell out of the country"—believing he had to jolt Americans to take responsibility for the brewing crisis.[9] Before a joint session of Congress on March 12, 1947, Truman portrayed a clash between the American vision "based on representative government, free elections, guarantees of individual liberty, freedom of speech and religion, and freedom from political oppression" and a rival system "based upon terror and oppression, a controlled press and radio; fixed elections, and the suppression of personal freedoms." Truman petitioned Congress for $400 million for Greece and Turkey, both facing threats from communist insurgencies. He also asked the country to dedicate itself and its resources to a new conflict—a Cold War against the Soviet Union. Exaggerating only a bit, the *Los Angeles Times* editorialized, "Americans have never been called on to make a decision which would commit them so far and so heavily as that proposed by Mr. Truman."[10] Truman spared little drama in generating public support for his initiatives. Indeed, most historians now believe the president overestimated the threat from the Soviets. Truman's worldview, however, sprang directly from the horrors of the recent world war, a conflict he and many believed could have been avoided had the United States taken an earlier, more effective leadership role resisting Hitler.

Gearing up, Truman moved to reorganize the federal government. The National Security Act of 1947 took a dramatic step toward creating a national security state—a powerful centralized government organized around a strong military and security sector. The act created a permanent Central Intelligence Agency, a separate Department of Defense, and a National Security Council operating inside the White House. Truman also initiated an unprecedented federal program of economic aid to Europe, a continent in severe distress—in the words of Winston Churchill, "a rubble heap, a charnel house, a breeding-ground of pestilence and hate." Besides spurring economic growth in Europe (as discussed in chapter 10), the Marshall Plan also aimed to cement Western Europe's allegiance to the capitalist West. Initially the U.S. government also offered Marshall Plan aid to the Soviet Union and countries increasingly in its orbit. Soviet leaders, however, concluded too many strings came attached to the program.

Challenges to the American Cold War mission grew when the Soviets detonated their own atomic bomb in 1949, ending American monopoly on the dangerous weapon. In China, communist insurgents led by Mao Zedong overthrew the U.S.–supported government of Jiang Jieshi. For America and the West, it was a devastating loss. U.S. containment policy appeared to be losing ground.

228 PART IV. 1945-2010

Determined to regain the upper hand, the United States joined Canada, Iceland, and nine Western European countries in forging the North American Treaty Organization (NATO), an alliance aimed at protecting Western Europe. Concurrently, the National Security Council drafted an extensive proposal entitled NSC-68, advocating greater defense spending and an uncompromising response to communism worldwide. This new mindset led directly to U.S. intervention on behalf of South Korea following its invasion by communist North Korea on June 24, 1950. Fighting as part of a U.N.-sanctioned coalition, U.S. forces struggled under difficult conditions. Challenges grew astronomically when over 200,000 Chinese troops intervened to support North Korea in November 1950. The war continued for over two years at a cost of several million lives (including 36,516 Americans).

NATO and America's increased worldwide military presence worried many critics in Europe and at home. From a paltry 14 bases outside American borders in 1938, U.S. military installations expanded to over 2,000 worldwide by 1948. U.S. bases, big and small, became home to some one million American military personnel and their families by the late 1950s. They became outposts of U.S. culture and commercialism in the midst of distant lands—"little Americas" replete with schools, stores, eateries, and recreational facilities. The pronounced U.S. military presence garnered mixed reactions overseas—some welcoming, some less so. Signs reading "Ami Go Home" met Americans in France. Seeking to cast itself in a positive light, the U.S. military organized events such as "German-American Friendship Week," featuring lectures, exhibits, and "open-house" tours of U.S. bases. In Libya, a nation that celebrated horses, Americans sponsored rodeos. Such public relations bore some fruit in the early years of the Cold War, but by the Vietnam years, relations with local communities grew tense.

Concerns about militarism also preoccupied many Americans. Both Truman and his successor, Dwight Eisenhower, feared the massive military buildup might result in a "garrison state," undermining U.S. liberties in the very same battle to preserve them. In his farewell address in 1960, Eisenhower warned that the effects of the emerging "military industrial complex" were "felt in every city, every Statehouse, every office of the Federal government . . . we must not fail to comprehend its grave implications." Guided by such concerns, U.S. policy makers strove to contain the growing influence of defense spending; proposals such as universal military training, for instance, gained little traction despite the imperatives of the Cold War.

AMERICA AND THE DEVELOPING WORLD

By the mid-1950s, the "clarity" of a bipolar world, grounded in competition between the Soviets and Americans, was rapidly giving way to the complexities of a multipolar world. While Cold War competition continued to define international relations, new players increasingly took the stage—creating a new mandate for American cold warriors. "We want the uncommitted peoples of the Middle East, Asia and Africa to remain free from the ever-reaching tentacles of Soviet influence and responsive to the leadership of the United States," proclaimed Senator John F. Kennedy to a Missouri crowd in 1956. "[T]his issue confronts us in Algeria, Cyprus, West New Guinea and elsewhere. Tomorrow it may be in Portuguese Goa or Singapore—and the next day it may be in Togoland or Tanganyika."[11]

No single event more confirmed the rise of the developing world than the Bandung conference in 1955. Organizers of the conference, held in the mountain city of Bandung in Indonesia, aimed to forge a coalition of nonaligned countries to challenge both colonialism and exploitation of countries emerging from colonialism. American officials fretted the new organization would become a tool for communist designs on the "Third World" (the designation for developing countries). People's Republic of China premier Zhou Enlai's pronouncement at the conference opening that "[t]he population of Asia will not forget that the first atomic bomb exploded on Asian soil" validated U.S. fears that communist nations would use the conference for their own ends. Representative Adam Clayton Powell, an African American congressman from Harlem representing the United States at Bandung, shot back, labeling Zhou a fraud, concerned only with sowing "the seeds of distrust" between America and the Third World.[12]

Still, as Cold War competition shifted to the Third World, Americans felt themselves at a distinct disadvantage. The Chinese and Soviets, with long histories of opposing colonialism, seemed better positioned to make inroads. A 1958 best-seller entitled *The Ugly American* reflected these anxieties. The authors, William Lederer and Eugene Burdick, depicted American diplomats in a fictional Southeast Asian country as arrogantly content to remain isolated and alienated from the local community. Ignorant of the local language and customs, Americans in the novel present little competition to the dedicated communists undermining Southeast Asia. An antidote to these "ugly Americans" comes in the form of Colonel Edwin Hillandale, modeled on real-life Colonel

Edward Lansdale and his work in the Philippines and Vietnam. In marked contrast to U.S. diplomats, Hillandale is accessible, speaks the local language, and mingles with the native population—even serenading locals with native songs on his harmonica. Americans, Lederer and Burdick admonished, needed to emulate Hillandale before it was too late.

Liberals quickly echoed the "ugly American" thesis. "Men who do not even know how to pronounce the name of the head of the country to which they are accredited," complained Senator Kennedy to a California audience, "have been sent to important countries, essential countries, in the struggle between East and West."[13] Alongside an improved diplomatic corps and enhanced foreign aid, Kennedy and others urged that the military adopt "counterinsurgency" strategies, guerilla-style techniques to battle insurgencies at the grassroots level. Counterinsurgency proponents liked to quote Mao Zedong's edict that "guerillas must move among the people as fish swim in the ocean."[14]

Social scientists also eagerly took up the mission of advancing the U.S. cause in the Third World. An influential group of economists and political scientists began advocating a series of ideas dubbed "modernization." According to modernizers, all societies move along a "common linear path."[15] As the apotheosis of modernity, the United States, through investment and support in Third World countries, could rapidly move societies from poverty (and susceptibility to communism) toward modernity, where the benefits of free enterprise and democratic institutions could readily be realized. Proponents frequently cited the success of the Tennessee Valley Authority, the New Deal program that brought electricity, jobs and relief from economic stagnation in the American South, as a model for what could be done overseas (see chapter 9).

Decrying the Eisenhower administration's pusillanimity in foreign aid, modernizers insisted that investment in large-scale river projects, green revolutions in agriculture, technical education, and other such programs would pay great dividends for the U.S. cause in the Third World. By the late 1950s, faith in technology and the virtues of modernization had grown exponentially and become key components of the U.S. Cold War mission. In his 1961 inaugural, newly elected President John F. Kennedy addressed "those peoples in the huts and villages across the globe struggling to break the bonds of mass misery," adding "we pledge our best efforts to help them help themselves." Endorsing the United Nation's call for a "decade of development," Kennedy brought key advocates of modernization into his administration. Among them was Walt Rostow, an economist whose influential book, *The Stages of Economic Growth: A Non-Communist Manifesto*, provided a blueprint for modernizers. Among other initiatives, Rostow recommended putting "television sets in the thatch hutches of the world" as one means of propelling "traditional" societies toward modernization.[16]

Kennedy lost no time in launching the modernization mission by reorganizing and revitalizing foreign aid under the umbrella of the Agency for International Development and initiating an ambitious program to encourage economic development in Latin America. To great fanfare, the president also launched the Peace Corps, a high-profile undertaking that sent young American volunteers to underdeveloped countries around the world. By 1963, over 7,000 Peace Corps volunteers—"carriers of America's best values and ideals"—operated in 44 countries around the world.[17]

VIETNAM: THE AMERICAN MISSION IN CRISIS

Confidence that Americans could effectively modernize less-developed countries, bettering lives and battling communism in the process, drove the Kennedy and Johnson administrations to invest further in the Third World. The Alliance for Progress program in Latin America, which ultimately yielded mixed results, aimed to foster development and counter the influence of Fidel Castro, the communist head of Cuba who deeply vexed U.S. leaders. In Southeast Asia as well, Kennedy pushed foreign aid programs aimed at immunizing local populations from infectious communism. By 1963, South Vietnam emerged as a problematic yet important test of Kennedy's sweeping mission to "bear any burden, meet any hardship, support any friend, oppose any foe" to stem the tide of communism.

An international conference at Geneva in 1954 had divided Vietnam in half. With the northern portion of the country turned over to a coalition allied with the Soviets and Chinese, the Americans hoped to cultivate an anticommunist bulwark in the south that might halt further communist penetration in Southeast Asia. Eager to build a viable nation, Americans turned to Ngo Dinh Diem, a reclusive nationalist who had fought both French and Vietnamese communists and had lived for a time in the United States. Thanks in part to the good counsel of Colonel Edward Lansdale (the real-life Colonel Hillandale), Diem managed to stabilize South Vietnam, although poverty and violent opposition continued to plague the new country. Determined they could build a nation, American modernizers moved in. The U.S. government contracted with Michigan State University to provide training for South Vietnamese public officials and police. Dr. Wesley Fishel, a political science professor who headed the Michigan State initiative, became Diem's close adviser and confidant.

Diem, however, failed to live up to American aspirations. He proved embarrassingly autocratic and mercurial. Worse, well aware that his political enemies painted him as a puppet of the Americans, Diem often defied U.S. counsel, seeking to portray himself to his people as an independent leader. In 1960, Diem's opponents banded together, with encouragement from the North Vietnamese, now fully in the Soviet-Chinese orbit, to create the National Liberation Front (NLF), dedicated to ousting Diem and the Americans from South Vietnam. Kennedy, increasingly convinced Diem was contributing mightily to his own problems, tacitly supported the coup that resulted in Diem's assassination in 1963. Weeks later, Kennedy himself was killed.

Having watched the New Deal transform his native Hill Country in East Texas, Kennedy's successor, Lyndon Baines Johnson, needed little convincing of the virtues of modernization. As the NLF picked up support, Johnson fully understood that U.S. troops would be necessary to save South Vietnam but that committing such forces would be costly, painful, and no guarantee of success. His faith in modernization, however, led him to move ahead. In a speech at Johns Hopkins University in early 1965, the president spoke boldly of the transforming power of development: "The vast Mekong River can provide food and water and power on a scale to dwarf even our own TVA. The wonders of modern medicine can be spread through villages. Schools can be established to train people in the skills that are needed to manage the process of development." Within two years, a half million Americans were in Southeast Asia fighting the NLF and North Vietnamese. Although fighting the war became his priority, Johnson continued to press modernizing projects, including a "miracle rice" initiative, the Mekong River project, job training programs, and even a plan to introduce public television to Southeast Asia. Whatever progress or goodwill such initiatives generated, however, was undercut by the war in Vietnam. Bombings, population relocations, high casualty rates, and growing South Vietnamese resentment of their overbearing patron soon created a quagmire for Johnson's nation-building mission in South Vietnam.

Originally, Johnson hoped to cloak his intervention in the garb of international support. Promising to cover all costs, he desperately searched for nations willing to commit even a token force to fight alongside the United States. Despite financial inducements, few countries took up his offer. Johnson aggressively sought British support but found little forthcoming. At one point British prime minister Harold Wilson telephoned Johnson at 3:00 a.m. Washington, D.C., time to urge restraint in Vietnam. An irate LBJ let "fly an outburst of Texas temper," telling the prime minister, "[D]on't tell us how to run Vietnam. If you want to help us in Vietnam send us some men." [18]

Meanwhile public pressure both in the United States and internationally built against the American presence in Vietnam. Worldwide, protests grew in size and intensity (see chapter 12). In January 1968 the NLF launched a daring series of attacks on South Vietnamese cities using the cover of the Vietnamese Tet (New Year's) holiday. While the eventual outcome was a resounding defeat for the NLF, the brutality of the attacks and counterattacks turned growing numbers around the world against the war. Johnson, feeling increasingly isolated, began to suspect an international communist conspiracy when the North Koreans captured and held the crew of the USS Pueblo almost concurrently with the Tet attacks. Adding to his woes were mounting problems in the Middle East, where the United States had supported Israel in the 1967 Six-Day War against its Arab neighbors, and in Latin America where Johnson faced anti-American riots in Panama and what he believed were Castro's continuing efforts to undermine the region. Everywhere, U.S. power, once hegemonic, appeared threatened.

Under pressure financially and militarily at home and throughout the world, Johnson announced in March 1968 that he would seek negotiations in Vietnam—something he essentially resisted in the past. In addition, tired and disillusioned by the host of problems at his doorstep, Johnson chose not to seek reelection in 1968.

AMERICA IN DECLINE?

As he took office in 1969, President Richard Nixon fully understood the transformed world he faced—a world vastly different than that confronting Johnson just four years earlier. American resources were stretched to the breaking point and anti-American sentiment was growing at home and overseas. Large-scale modernization projects, once the toast of the world, were now in disrepute—seen as ineffective and environmentally unsound.

Nixon fretted about the dangers of a "new isolationism." Long acknowledged as a virulent anticommunist, the new president believed America must remain an active force in the world. In 1970, announcing the U.S. invasion of Cambodia, where NLF and North Vietnamese guerillas had established sanctuaries, he famously warned: "If, when the chips are down, the world's most powerful nation, the United States of America, acts like a pitiful, helpless giant, the forces of totalitarianism and anarchy will threaten free nations and free institutions throughout the world."

Still Nixon recognized America's far-reaching commitments contributed to its global woes. He vowed to chart a foreign policy that "steers a course between the past danger of over-involvement and the new temptation of under-involvement."[19] A major part of Nixon's strategy involved disengagement to preserve dwindling American power. In Vietnam, alongside the Cambodian incursion, this meant a tortuous pursuit of negotiations leading to an American exit "with honor." Elsewhere Nixon sought to deputize regional allies to shore up American and Western interests. Under the so-called Nixon Doctrine, America armed and backed problematic surrogates such as Iran, South Africa, and Pakistan rather than become embroiled in difficulties in those regions itself. To many observers, Nixon's actions and the sorry state of world affairs suggested an America in decline. Books with titles such as *The Retreat of American Power* and *Retreat from Empire* proliferated in the early 1970s.

Charting his "grand design," or redesign, of American foreign policy, Nixon relied heavily on Dr. Henry Kissinger, his national security adviser. A German-born Jew, Kissinger and his family had barely escaped the Holocaust. Having watched Europe descend into the horrors of Nazism, Kissinger became a devotee of realpolitik, the European school of thought that emphasized the virtues of "realism" and "balance of power" rather than the American predilection for idealism and mission in international relations. Kissinger greatly admired nineteenth-century European diplomat Klemens Wenzel von Metternich and sought to emulate him in formulating international stability to halt the hemorrhaging of American power. Despite their frequent bickering, in Nixon, Kissinger found a philosophical soul mate.

Together the pair dusted off one of the oldest rules of diplomacy: the enemy of my enemy is my friend. Already, European leaders such as De Gaulle in France and Willy Brandt in West Germany had been seeking opportunities to ease Cold War tensions—a movement known as détente. American officials had long understood there to be tension between China and its former Soviet ally. As Nixon took office in 1969, that tension briefly broke out into a bloody border dispute. Seeking to counterbalance the threat from their north, Chinese moderates, especially Zhou Enlai, sent faint signals to the Americans of an interest in improving relations, frozen since the Chinese revolution in 1949. Nixon and Kissinger seized the moment; the president stunned the world by journeying to China in February 1972 (not coincidentally an election year). The president masterfully executed the mission. He cultivated a potential new ally and divided the communist bloc. "[T]his was the week that changed the world," Nixon proclaimed as he departed Beijing.[20] In May, Nixon traveled to Moscow for a summit with Soviet leader Leonid Brezhnev—who had watched apprehensively the specter of his two enemies warming to each other. The meeting in

Moscow led to the Strategic Arms Limitation Treaty (SALT), the first comprehensive effort to limit arms proliferation. Détente seemed to be blossoming, and Nixon and Kissinger appeared skilled gardeners. The president's landslide reelection in 1972 and the Paris Accords of 1973 allowing for the removal of U.S. troops from Vietnam seemed to confirm his new status as global statesman.

Nixon, however, had little time to enjoy his success. Within a few months, he was embroiled in the Watergate scandal that would force his resignation. Meanwhile the Middle East descended into chaos that quickly proved toxic to the rest of the world. In September 1973, coordinated attacks by Egypt and Syria threatened the very existence of Israel, which the U.S. had strongly supported after the Six-Day War of 1967. Initially, Kissinger and Nixon sought to avoid offending Arab states by overtly aiding Israel. But as the conflict expanded into its second week, the White House (largely Kissinger, with Nixon tied up in the Watergate scandal) made its move. The United States airlifted 11,000 tons of military equipment and ammunition to Israel, which soon repelled the invaders and grabbed significant land in both Syria and Egypt. Infuriated, the vanquished Arab states moved to embargo oil to the United States. Gasoline prices soared, and the American economy sputtered (see chapter 10).

Meanwhile despite the promise of détente and the budding Sino-U.S. amity, American fortunes continued to decline. In 1974, a mob in Cyprus, angry over U.S. support for Turkey in the disputed territory, attacked the U.S. embassy and killed the American ambassador. Then in April 1975, the North Vietnamese overran Saigon, the capital city of South Vietnam. Helicopters frantically ferried Americans and loyal South Vietnamese from the U.S. embassy in Saigon's final hours. To many it appeared a shameful conclusion to a sorrowful affair. By this time, Nixon had resigned and been replaced by Gerald Ford. Kissinger remained as secretary of state, but he seemed an ever-more burdened man. A cover of *Newsweek* magazine in 1975 depicted Kissinger as a confused Gulliver, tied down by Lilliputians around the world.

Like Nixon, Jimmy Carter, elected president in 1976, saw the need for a major reorientation of American international relations—albeit in a very different direction. Rather than the relentless pursuit of American self-interest and balance of power, Carter preached that morality and human rights should guide U.S. international relations. Impressed by the international movement for human rights (see chapter 12), Carter, a born-again Christian, believed "the expansion of human rights might be the wave of the future throughout the world," and he "wanted the United States to be on the crest of this movement."[21] Carter doggedly pursued peace in the Middle East, successfully bringing

Egypt and Israel to the negotiating table. Attempting to redress a sordid past in Latin America, he arranged the transfer of the Panama Canal to Panama—a move that mirrored Nixon's efforts to scale back global commitments but also aimed to recast America's foreign policy on a moral plain.

Yet Carter's human rights crusade proved problematic, as the president himself later acknowledged. "In spite of my own study of the past and planning for the future," he confessed, "I did not fully grasp the ramifications of our new policy."[22] Seeking to distance himself from General Anastasio Somoza, the dictator and U.S. ally who ruled Nicaragua with an iron fist, Carter fruitlessly sought some middle ground between an authoritarian government and leftist Sandinista rebels. When the Sandinistas triumphed, Carter initially extended aid to the new government but withdrew it later, responding to critics who believed Nicaragua was aligning itself with communist Cuba.

The most serious challenge to Carter's human rights policies came in Iran. Strongman Shah Mohammad Reza Pahlavi, like Somoza, long had been a trusted American ally. But the shah's brutal repression of his own people fed widespread internal disaffection. His embrace of large-scale modernization schemes, which he called his "White Revolution," brought only hardship and further alienation to working-class Iranians. Carter fully understood the value and rarity of the shah as an oil-producing ally in a troubled region. Yet the shah's human rights record disturbed the president—as did mounting opposition to the monarch in Iran. Carter hoped to use the shah's state visit to Washington in November 1977 to quietly persuade the monarch to clean up his act. The visit, however, proved a disaster. The shah's supporters fought with anti-regime demonstrators just outside the White House. Tear gas used by police to separate the demonstrators blew into the White House grounds—ruining an outdoor ceremony for the shah. Afterward, Carter took the shah aside and recited by memory a carefully worded plea. "Is there anything that can be done" to address human rights concerns "by easing off on some of the strict police policies," Carter asked the shah. "No, there is nothing I can do," the shah replied sadly.[23]

A little over a year later, angry mobs fed by the anti-American, anti-Western Shi'ite leader Ayatollah Khomeini drove the shah from power. When Carter reluctantly admitted the exiled shah to the United States for cancer treatment, a group of radical students seized the U.S. embassy in Tehran, holding 52 Americans hostage. Day and night, demonstrators chanted slogans denouncing the United States as the "Great Satan." They burnt Carter in effigy and trampled on American flags. The international scene grew even gloomier for Carter in

December 1979 when the Soviet Union invaded Afghanistan. Fearing it the first step to expanding Soviet influence in the Middle East, Carter organized a boycott of the 1980 Summer Olympics in Moscow, eventually persuading some 64 other nations to join the boycott.

America appeared to have hit rock bottom in April 1980 with the depressing failure of a rescue mission to free the hostages. The collision of helicopters and transport aircraft at a staging ground in the Iranian desert left eight Americans dead. Talk earlier in the decade of an America in decline, now seemed confirmed. "We Europeans, along with the rest of the world," asserted the editor of *L'Express*, a French newspaper, "hear the bell of U.S. military supremacy toll in Iran."[24]

REVIVAL OF AMERICAN POWER

Carter faced not only a grave crisis in Iran in 1980, but he also faced a tough re-election campaign. Magnifying his problems, the crisis abroad increasingly undermined the U.S. economy (as discussed in chapter 10). Carter faced a spirited challenger in Republican Ronald Reagan. Like Carter, Reagan believed morality an essential ingredient of foreign policy. The former Hollywood star turned politician, however, explicitly rejected any retrenchment of American power. "I will not stand by and watch this great country destroy itself. We need a rebirth of the American tradition of leadership," Reagan proclaimed.[25] Reagan made it his mission to revive and reassert U.S. influence, especially in relation to the Cold War. With Carter weakened by the Iran hostage crisis, the collapsing economy, and renewed evidence of Soviet aggression in Afghanistan, Reagan strode to victory in 1980. (Iran finally released the hostages literally during Reagan's inaugural ceremonies.)

Reagan, a friend explained, "was obsessed by the Soviet threat. Everything else was second tier."[26] He immediately lay to rest any thoughts he might moderate his views at his first news conference. "[T]he only morality [the Soviets] recognize is what will further their cause, meaning they reserve unto themselves the right to commit any crime, to lie, to cheat," pronounced the new president in response to a question. By contrast, as Reagan frequently insisted, America was a "shining city on a hill."

Believing the communist foundation of the Soviet economy to be fatally weak, Reagan embarked on an aggressive arms buildup aimed at breaking the Russians. In 1983 he proposed an initiative to construct a system of satellites and lasers in outer space to shield the United States from nuclear attack. The plan, dubbed "Star Wars," proved controversial. Even some among Reagan's advisers, believing "mutually assured destruction" between the United States and USSR to be the best avenue to preventing war, expressed doubts.

Latin America soon emerged as the testing ground for the Reagan mission to arrest Soviet expansion in the Third World. The new president pumped money and arms into the hands of an often-brutal government in El Salvador, which faced a violent insurgency alleged by Reagan to be tied to Cuban and Soviet aggression. He also authorized and funded a private, CIA-trained militia to overthrow the Sandinista government in Nicaragua, which the president saw as linked to Soviet ambitions in the region. Congressional Democrats loudly objected, setting off a series of confrontations that eventually severely limited funding for Reagan's Latin American operations.

International outrage, not seen since the Vietnam era, swelled swiftly in opposition to Reagan's policies. In 1981, 15,000 German students protesting U.S. aid to the El Salvadoran government rampaged through downtown Frankfurt—defacing American cars and other symbols of the United States. Across Europe hundreds of thousands took to the streets to show disgust with Reagan's policies. Four hundred thousand demonstrators loudly protested Reagan's speech before the Bundestag (German Parliament) in 1982. In Great Britain, a group of Welsh women chained themselves to a fence encircling a U.S. military base. Calling themselves the Greenham Common Women's Peace Camp, the women occupied the site for ten years until the United States removed its missiles. Likewise, many Americans joined the antinuclear movement. On June 12, 1982, throngs—estimates ranged as high as a million—gathered in New York City for demonstrations and a concert dedicated to the antinuclear cause. "We're thinking of our babies. There are no communist babies; there are no capitalist babies," preached an Australian pediatrician to the record crowd.[27] Protest spilled over into popular music. In 1984 "99 Luftballons" charged up the charts in several countries including the United States. The song by West German singer Nena depicted an overzealous military responding violently to the innocent release of balloons.

Unbeknownst to the protestors, Reagan shared their revulsion for nuclear weaponry. Such weapons, he believed, were a dangerous, unsatisfactory means of keeping the peace. Driven by deep idealism, he hoped for a day when nuclear arms would be superfluous. Such talk dismayed the president's hardcore advisers. "Reagan," recalled his aide Kenneth Adelman, "had a totally naïve view against nuclear weapons."[28] Before the Bundestag in 1982 Reagan tried to reach his noisy critics protesting just outside. "To those who march for peace, my heart is with you. I would be at the head of your parade if I believed marching alone could bring about a more secure world." His words moved few among the demonstrators.

In his second term, however, Reagan got just the chance he craved to move toward abolition of nuclear weapons. The Soviet Union, as Reagan well understood, was in the throes of an economic meltdown. In 1985, after the deaths in rapid succession of three older Soviet heads of state, Mikhail Gorbachev, a 54-year-old pragmatist emerged as the new general secretary. Gorbachev had few illusions about the challenges facing his country. He feared, as he told his Politburo, being "drawn into an arms race that we cannot handle." Despite initial distrust, Gorbachev and Reagan quickly warmed to each other, finding they shared an interest in diminishing their mutual nuclear arsenals. The two almost managed a major breakthrough at a summit in Reykjavik, Iceland, but Reagan refused to sacrifice his Star Wars defense system plan. Nevertheless, the tide had clearly turned. "Ronnie, you just won the Cold War. They admitted they can't compete," marveled an old Reagan friend to the dejected president after the summit.[29]

The two leaders continued to meet and make progress. Soon Gorbachev was pulling Soviet troops out of Afghanistan. For Reagan it still was not enough. On June 12, 1987, Reagan addressed a cheering crowd in front of West Berlin's Brandenburg Gate. "[I]f you seek peace, if you seek prosperity for the Soviet Union and Eastern Europe," he fatefully pronounced with his voice rising, "Mr. Gorbachev, tear down this wall!"

As Reagan played the role of peacemaker, however, his overzealousness in Latin America came back to haunt him. When Congress cut support for his "Contra" counterrevolutionaries in Central America, Reagan aides found funding in the unlikeliest of places—Iran. Hoping Iran had some influence over Hezbollah terrorists holding American hostages in Lebanon, Reagan authorized the sales of military parts to the religious radicals in control of Tehran. Overcharging the Iranians, the Reagan staffers then diverted the profits to the CIA's militia charged with harassing the Sandinistas. When revelations of the diversion became public, made so by Reagan himself, the resulting controversy nearly derailed his presidency.

Completing Reagan's Cold War mission fell to his successor George H. W. Bush. As with Reagan, Bush's initial coolness turned to a close relationship with Gorbachev. When the cracking Soviet bloc began to crumble in 1989, Bush worked hard to manage the situation. One after another, Eastern European countries shook loose their communist governments as it became clear

Gorbachev would not stand in the way. The culmination came on November 9, 1989, with the fall of the Berlin Wall. While managing change in Europe, Bush still faced retrenchment in China, where Chinese authorities violently broke a pro-democracy movement. Again, Bush followed his inclinations toward "prudence," maintaining the Sino-American alliance without condoning the violence. He applied the same traits of caution and personal diplomacy when facing the collapse of the Soviet Union in 1991, following an aborted coup by Kremlin hardliners. "We could have overreacted and moved in troops," recorded Bush in his diary. "We could have underreacted by saying well, we'll deal with whoever is there. I think we found the proper balance."[30] Thus, finesse rather than force brought the end of the Cold War—completing, on American terms, Reagan's mission to eliminate the conflict that so plagued the world.

"A NEW WORLD ORDER"

Absent the Cold War, Bush seemed to step into a mission vacuum, particularly ill-suited for a man lacking, by his own admission, "the vision thing."[31] On one hand, the dramatic thawing of the Cold War seemed to spur democratization and opportunity for America around the world. At the ballot box, Nicaraguans ousted the Sandinistas in favor of a reform candidate. Apartheid collapsed in South Africa. Likewise, when Iraqi leader Saddam Hussein invaded the small neighboring country of Kuwait in August 1990, Bush knit together an alliance to reverse the action. The Soviets, to the surprise of many, joined the U.S. in condemning Saddam. Backed by his coalition, Bush easily dislodged the Iraqis from Kuwait.

On the other hand, Americans, Bush included, seemed perplexed and intimidated by what the president amorphously called the "new world order." What new mission might a mission-oriented country undertake in this new world? Academics scrambled to define the post–Cold War world. Harvard professor Samuel Huntington wrote of a "clash of civilizations" that would next dominate the world, with religious and cultural conflict replacing rivalries between nations. Political scientist Francis Fukuyama argued that the denouement of the ideological struggle driving the Cold War represented "the end of history." Henceforth a consensus surrounding free markets and democratization would define global developments. Concurrently debate sparked about America's place in the new order. A group of neoconservatives in Bush's Defense Department under Secretary Richard Cheney urged that America must remain strong as the sole force capable of maintaining order and stability in the world. America must assume the role of "globocop," they seemed to argue. By contrast, newspaper columnist and presidential candidate Patrick Buchanan advocated a new isolationism, "a new nationalism, a new patriotism, a new foreign policy that puts America first."[32]

Into the vacuum stepped Arkansas governor Bill Clinton. Believing most "Americans are basically isolationists," Clinton's campaign road map for the presidency stressed domestic rather than international affairs.[33] When he did focus on the larger world, Clinton attacked Bush's lack of vision. His victory in the 1992 election seemed to suggest that international relations, in an age of American dominance, would take a back seat to pressing internal problems.

The world, however, proved hard to ignore and even harder to control. A peacekeeping mission undertaken by Americans in the war-torn African country of Somalia turned violent in 1993, resulting in the deaths of 18 U.S. soldiers. Days later, the *USS Harlan County* steaming toward Haiti on a humanitarian mission, turned around when angry mobs shouting "Somalia, Somalia" took over the Port-au-Prince docks. Meanwhile, genocidal horrors overtook Yugoslavia in southern Europe and Rwanda in Africa.

Despite the apparent chaos, Clinton persevered. He managed to drive through Congress the North American Free Trade Act (NAFTA) and push Israel and the Palestine Liberation Organization toward a peace agreement. Clinton also facilitated a settlement in Yugoslavia between warring Serbians and Bosnians. An improving economy—partly the result of Clinton's globalization initiatives—brought the president re-election in 1996. Increasingly Clinton found his voice and his mission. He began talking of America as "an indispensable nation" charged with spreading democracy and the benefits of free trade. The president also appeared more comfortable using force to impose his vision. In 1998, he unleashed Operation Desert Fox, involving 650 sorties and 400 cruise missiles in retaliation for Saddam's interference with the work of UN weapons inspectors. That same year, Clinton signed into law the Iraq Liberation Act, calling for regime change in the country that had so vexed the United States since 1990.

America's mastery of air power and growing willingness to wield force, however, discomforted many both at home and abroad. In France, officials grumbled that the United States had become a "hyperpower," and others in Europe complained American leaders were lacking in sensitivity. Opposition to America's increasing power also grew at home—as evidenced by the uproar at Ohio State depicted in the introduction to this chapter. Even as the United

States entered what was arguably the apogee of its power, Americans and the world remained deeply conflicted about its ever-growing role.

THE WAR ON TERROR

All sense that America lacked mission disappeared suddenly on September 11, 2001. "Our war on terror will not end until every terrorist group of global reach has been found, stopped and defeated," announced President George W. Bush only days after the horrific attacks on New York City's World Trade Center and the Pentagon in Washington, D.C., killed nearly 3,000. In the wake of the 9–11 horrors, members of Congress—both Democrats and Republicans— stood shoulder-to-shoulder on the steps of the U.S. capital and spontaneously sang "God Bless America." The brief bipartisan moment allowed President George W. Bush, in office a scant nine months, to reorganize the federal government in a manner not seen since the early days of the Cold War. He consolidated the country's intelligence organizations and created a new cabinet-level Department of Homeland Security. He also waged war against the Taliban leaders of Afghanistan who had been harboring al-Qaeda members responsible for the 9–11 attacks.

The Bush administration then faced the issue of where to go next with its War on Terror. Iraq and Saddam Hussein remained a persistent worry. "Neoconservatives" among Bush's advisers urged him to take action to prevent use of what U.S. intelligence agencies insisted were caches of "weapons of mass destruction" held by the Iraqi leader in violation of UN strictures. Bush administration officials also attempted to link al-Qaeda to Saddam—although no direct connections proved credible. In October 2002, in a contentious vote, Congress authorized Bush to act against Iraq. The United Nations proved less amenable, rejecting a resolution to use force. Undeterred, Bush, with much help from British prime minister Tony Blair, cobbled together a "coalition of the willing"—including Australia, Denmark, Poland, and Spain—to move against Saddam. Meanwhile, traditional U.S. allies, in particular France, rejected the rationale for war.

On March 20, 2003, the invasion of Iraq began with an overwhelming show of air power the U.S. military code-named "Shock and Awe." By April 9, Baghdad had fallen. Despite early successes, the occupation of Iraq proved a lengthy, troubled affair. Inspectors could find no weapons of mass destruction, one of the principle justifications for the invasion. Likewise resistance from al-Qaeda and former Saddam loyalists hampered efforts to remake the country. Improvised explosive devices (IEDs) victimized Iraqi civilians and coalition soldiers alike.

Worldwide, protests exploded in response to Bush and Blair's war. Coordinated demonstrations across Europe on April 14, 2003, took special aim at America's growing power. Hundreds of thousands carried signs reading, "Fight the New Colonialism" and led chants of "Bush, Blair, CIA—How many kids have you killed today?"[34] The insurgency and continued conflict in Iraq also led to growing opposition at home. While U.S. voters reelected Bush in 2004, the U.S. mission in Iraq remained problematic. Casualty and death rates remained high. In 2007, overcoming significant resistance from political opponents, Bush chose to send additional troops to Iraq—the "surge" as it became known. This action, combined with counterinsurgency strategies aimed at converting former enemies, brought a dramatic decline in violence within a year. By 2009, under a new Democratic regime led by President Barack Obama, trouble shifted back to Afghanistan, where the U.S. military faced a resurgent Taliban determined to use the same combination of guerrilla tactics, including IEDs, ambushes, and kidnappings, to tax and exhaust the U.S. presence. Attempting to distance himself from Bush, Obama renounced the term "war on terror," but fighting terror remained a major preoccupation—indeed mission—of his administration, even as debates remained about what such a fight should entail.

Americans after World War II approached the world with a sense of mission—a crusading drive to bring order, peace, and democracy to the world—that was an outgrowth of a powerful sense of national exceptionalism. Combating communism, modernizing the Third World, spreading democracy and free markets, and fighting global terrorism inspired sacrifice and ever-greater involvement in global affairs. Americans in large numbers remain committed to maintaining a leadership role in the world. But debates remain about what such leadership should entail. Meanwhile, a steady minority, both at home and abroad, continue to question American motives and aims. These dynamics seem destined to persist well into the new century.

CHAPTER TWELVE

Civil Rights and World Culture

ALI'S "RUMBLE IN THE JUNGLE"

"Ali! Boma ye! Ali! Boma ye!" The thunderous chant—translated "Kill him! Kill him, Ali!"—followed 32-year-old Muhammad Ali everywhere that autumn of 1974. Ali had traveled to Africa to reclaim his boxing title from reigning champion, George Foreman. Few gave him much of a chance, but the people of Zaire, the war-torn former Belgian Congo, believed in Ali. His outspoken bravado, charisma, and commitment to black rights in America and around the world made him a hero in Zaire.

Controversy had dogged Ali since his debut, when he won a gold medal at the Rome Olympics in 1960. In 1964, he defeated Sonny Liston for the heavyweight championship of the world, but his conversion that same year to the Nation of Islam, which promoted black pride and separateness, set off anxieties among white Americans. Embracing a new Muslim identity, he also dropped his given name of Cassius Clay in favor of Muhammad Ali. Then at the height of the Vietnam War in 1967, Ali refused induction into the army. "I ain't got no quarrel with them Viet Cong; they never called me a nigger," he blustered. For his audacity, officials stripped him of his title and sentenced him to five years in prison. Ali immediately appealed, but it would not be until 1970 that the Supreme Court reversed his conviction, allowing him to box again.

Ali jumped at the opportunity not only to fight Foreman but to fight him in Africa. "Africa is the home of the black man; I'm going back home to fight for my brothers," he proclaimed. President Mobutu Sese Seku of Zaire put up the money for the fight, and promoter Don King arranged an all-star soul concert, featuring James Brown, the Spinners, and B. B. King to accompany the heavyweight bout. It was to be a fusion of African and African American cultures drawing on the worldwide interest in American music and sports.

Although the underdog, Ali remained the center of attention. The specter of the bold, confident Ali, defiant of the white power structure, riveted the local population. Crowds, especially children, could not get enough of Ali. The contender in turn played off the throngs who greeted him. Foreman, while heavily favored and an African American himself, was cast as the villain—the stand-in for the oppressive power structure. Zairians had faced a long line of struggles, dating back to extreme exploitation at the hands of Belgian colonizers. In 1960, the Congo gained its independence, but it quickly dissolved into civil war, culminating with the torture and murder of Patrice Lumumba, a former prime minister. Strongman Mobutu had stabilized the country but only through coercive and often corrupt means.

By October 30, 1974, the day of the fight, Ali had become a national hero in Zaire. True to form, in the ring the contender brilliantly outmaneuvered the younger, stronger Foreman. Executing a "rope-a-dope" strategy designed to exhaust his opponent by absorbing blows, Ali drained the champion. Then in the eighth round, Ali struck, knocking Foreman to the mat. The crowd exploded in celebration—"the most joyous scene in the history of boxing," according to announcer David Frost.[1] Ali, once scorned, had reemerged champion. Two months later, as if to complete the journey to redemption, President Gerald Ford hosted the new champion at the White House.

The vibrant, outspoken Ali comes as close as anyone to encapsulating the spirit of the age: defiant, young, dismissive of barriers, and unapologetically political. The issue of race in particular drove social, cultural, and political change in the second half of the twentieth century. African Americans, often casting their struggle as part of a worldwide battle, aggressively challenged the status quo in America. This challenge in turn inspired a cultural revolution that went far beyond the boundaries of America to spark youthful rebellion around the world. The ideas put forth so aggressively by the American civil rights movement changed the world. By the last decades of the twentieth century, the pace of change slowed, yet the American model of race relations continued to influence the world.

"A NONVIOLENT REBIRTH"

The horrors of World War II led many American reformers to shift priorities away from grand quests to address the "social problem." The horrifying bigotry of militaristic Japan and Nazi Germany forced many to reexamine the racism so prevalent in American life. While the New Deal of the 1930s barely addressed the issue of racism, postwar liberals began to recognize the issue as America's Achilles' heel. Increasingly for liberals, race superseded the older, early-twentieth-century emphasis on reordering capitalism. Unnerved by mass movements that led to communism and fascism, liberals focused instead on protecting minorities from the prejudices of the majority. Spurred by African Americans, who saw their battle as part of an international war against colonialism and racism, and by fears that Jim Crow put America at a distinct disadvantage in the Cold War, the issue of civil rights rose to the forefront of the reform agenda.

An outsider in fact proved pivotal in crystallizing the issue for Americans. In 1938, Swedish economist Gunnar Myrdal began an exhaustive study of the place of blacks in American society. Six years later he published his conclusions in *An American Dilemma: The Negro Problem and Modern Democracy*. Myrdal found a fundamental tension between America's ideals and practices when it came to its black citizens. This American "dilemma" was a "moral" blight that undercut the nation's claim to world leadership. "America for its international prestige, power and future," explained Myrdal, "needs to demonstrate to the world that American Negroes can be satisfactorily integrated into democracy."[2]

The realization that America tolerated elements of the same odious racism against which it fought a world war moved liberals to rededicate themselves to the principles of liberal universalism—the notion, rooted in Enlightenment thought, that all peoples, no matter their surface differences, share an essential likeness and equality. These sentiments saw their strongest statement in the United Nation's Universal Declaration of Human Rights in 1948. Drafted under the supervision of Eleanor Roosevelt among others, the declaration called for the recognition of "the inherent dignity and the equality and inalienable right of all members of the human family."

Yet it was black activists rather than white liberals who provided the primary push for addressing the global agenda for civil rights. Some one million black veterans returned from World War II (where they fought in a segregated army) eager to challenge the status quo in the Jim Crow South. But the racist system refused to budge. Instead, a torrent of violence swept through the South. As was the case after World War I, black veterans often became victims of mob violence. Infuriated, key black leaders mobilized for action. With the foundations of colonialism shaken by World War II, African Americans rallied to push for decolonization abroad and civil rights at home. Increasingly, American blacks began to think of themselves as members of a worldwide African diaspora. The Council on African Affairs (CAA), founded in 1942, spearheaded the movement, mobilizing blacks to support a host of causes, including the 1946 general strike by South African miners. The 15,000 in attendance at a June 6, 1946, CAA rally at Madison Square Garden heard speakers assail the Truman administration for "striking a blow against the American people themselves" by failing to oppose colonialism. "[C]olonialism—that bankrupt, plundering and wasteful system of the past—must be done away with," inveighed one speaker.[3]

Understanding the United States' new role as global leader, African Americans sought to expose Jim Crow practices internationally. Several times, black groups introduced petitions to the UN calling on the international body to address racism in the United States. In 1947, W. E. B. Du Bois, representing the National Association for the Advancement of Colored People (NAACP), presented the UN with "An Appeal to the World," an extensively documented study of discrimination and oppression against black Americans. "It is not Russia so much that threatens the United States," concluded Du Bois, in reference to the emerging Cold War, "as Mississippi."[4] While the UN never took action, the NAACP initiatives did embarrass American officials. "I was humiliated . . . to realize that in our America there could be the slightest foundation for such a petition," lamented U.S. attorney general Thomas Clark.[5]

The emerging Cold War presented both challenges and obstacles to blacks seeking to contest colonialism and spur civil rights at home. Groups such as the CAA, which had ties to communists, found themselves under increasing suspicion for airing their country's racist dirty laundry. The State Department moved to revoke the passports of black activists who criticized America overseas, including Du Bois and Paul Robeson. The Soviet Union wasted no time drawing attention to America's racial hypocrisy. *Pravda,* the official Soviet state newspaper, devoted heavy coverage to lynchings and racial violence in the South. "The Constitution of the United States guarantees to all citizens equal rights," reported *Pravda,* "however, [r]acial discrimination continues to exist in all forms and in all branches of the economy and culture of the country." The Russian media, warned the U.S. embassy in Moscow in 1949, "hammers away on such things as 'lynch laws,' segregation, racial discrimination, deprivation of political rights etc. . . . seeking to build up a picture of an America in which Negroes are brutally downtrodden."[6] Not only did the Soviet Union use Jim Crow to embarrass America, but it also found U.S. racism convenient for deflecting criticism of Soviet actions. When James Byrnes, the U.S. secretary of state, complained of Soviet resistance to allowing free elections in satellite countries, a Soviet spokesperson reminded him that "the Negroes of Mr. Byrnes' own state of South Carolina" were "denied the same right."[7]

Worse still, U.S. racism also drew negative press in nonaligned countries, which the United States hoped to draw to its cause in the Cold War. As far away as the Fiji islands, Jim Crow earned unwanted notice. "The United States has within its own borders, one of the most oppressed and persecuted minorities in the world today," railed the *Fiji Times and Herald* in 1946, under the headline "Persecution of Negroes Still Strong in America." The U.S. embassy in Ceylon warned Washington of "Asian preoccupation with racial discrimination in the United States."[8] Even America's allies reported on the issue. The *Manchester Guardian* for instance ran reports on Ku Klux Klan activities in the South.

U.S. officials fully understood that Jim Crow was no longer just an internal issue; rather, it threatened America's global agenda. Secretary of State George C. Marshall cautioned that the "moral influence of the United States is weakened" by reports of American racism. "The eyes of the world," warned the State Department's legal adviser, "will be upon the United States." Partly to address international concerns, partly to preserve the black vote for his Democratic Party, President Harry S. Truman appointed a Presidential Committee on Civil Rights, which laid the groundwork for his executive orders in 1948 desegregating the armed forces and prohibiting racial discrimination in hiring federal employees. As the first U.S. president to address the NAACP in 1947, Truman framed his comments in international terms: "[O]ur case for democracy should rest on practical evidence that we have been able to put our own house in order."[9]

Seeking to counteract the wave of bad publicity, the U.S. government acknowledged racial problems but insisted the country was making good progress toward rectifying injustice. "The Negro in American Life," a booklet produced by the U.S. Information Agency and translated into several different languages, featured glossy photographs of integrated schools and workplaces. The State Department urged African Americans traveling abroad to make the case for racial progress in the United States. The most popular State Department initiative, however, was sending African American jazz musicians on international tours. "When I played Berlin," recalled Louis Armstrong, "a lot of them Russian cats jumped the Iron Fence to hear Satchmo, which goes to prove that music is stronger than nations." Understanding the growing global appeal of sports, the State Department also dispatched the Harlem Globetrotters on multiple tours. Between 1951 and 1955, the Globetrotters dazzled audiences in Berlin, Indonesia, Burma, South Africa, and other locations worldwide. "With their special brand of diplomacy," waxed *Bantu World*, the antiapartheid South African newspaper, the Globetrotters have "become one of the United States' most effective weapons in the Cold War against communism."[10]

The U.S. government's project to improve America's image, however, faced challenges—not the least of which was continuing brutality in the American South, as the civil rights movement began in earnest. Angered by violence against black schoolchildren trying to integrate a Little Rock, Arkansas, high school, Louis Armstrong canceled a planned 1957 tour of the USSR. "[T]he way they are treating my people in the South, the government can go to hell," blasted Armstrong.[11] Conversely, many Americans objected to any acknowledgment of past failings. When the State Department organized an exhibit entitled "Unfinished Business" for the 1958 Brussels world's fair, planners sought to "face squarely" persistent racial problems while pointing to improvements. "Democracy is our method," concluded the exhibit's literature. "Slowly but surely, it works." But these frank admissions proved too much for southern congressmen, who denounced the show. Finally, pressed by President Dwight Eisenhower, who worried that America was not putting its "best foot forward," organizers closed the exhibit for "renovations."[12] Still, whether Ike liked it or not, the race issue and emerging civil rights movement had become an international issue, and a troublesome one for the United States. On a tour of Africa in 1960, one American reported, "Little Rock seemed to be the best known town in America."[13]

Key leaders of the burgeoning civil rights movement drew inspiration from the thoughts and actions of Indian leader Mohandas Gandhi and his nonviolent movement against British colonial rule. In a remarkable example of transnational exchange, Gandhi borrowed some of his approach and vision from nineteenth-century American author Henry David Thoreau's booklet "On the Duty of Civil Disobedience." Thoreau's ideas as interpreted by Gandhi then bounced back to inspire the twentieth-century U.S. civil rights movement. Bayard Rustin, a brilliant and controversial black activist, for instance, became particularly taken with Gandhi and traveled to India in 1948 (arriving just after Gandhi's assassination) to study Gandhian principles firsthand. By the late 1950s, Rustin became a key adviser to Martin Luther King, who was already deeply interested in the philosophy of nonviolence.

Although not a Pan-Africanist, King did look to Africa for inspiration. In 1957 he journeyed to West Africa for ceremonies marking Ghanaian independence from Britain. Deeply moved, King described the experience as "a nonviolent rebirth." He remained passionate about Africa the rest of his life. "[W]e share a mutual struggle for freedom and brotherhood," he wrote to Rhodesian activists.[14] King worked to bring African students to the United States and developed strong relations with African activists. He frequently called for a

Marshall Plan to address the extreme poverty of Africa and loudly protested apartheid in South Africa.

The American civil rights movement in turn inspired Africans. As early as 1946, Nigerian activist Nnamdi Azkiwe rallied support for a general strike against British rule with references to "If We Must Die," a fiery call-to-action by Jamaican-born Harlem Renaissance poet Claude McKay. African newspapers devoted heavy coverage to the U.S. civil rights movement, and anticolonial leaders developed networks in the United States. In 1959, for instance, King's Southern Christian Leadership Conference hosted Kenyan labor leader Tom Mboya in Atlanta. I "read your book [*Stride toward Freedom*]," Mboya told King, "and want you to know that I have never found myself so completely captured by a book and ideas."[15]

Meanwhile, American blacks, like King, passionately supported the struggles of Africans emerging from colonialism. "Black Africa today is sending rejuvenating currents of liberty over all the earth reaching even as far as Little Rock, Birmingham, and Jackson Mississippi," waxed poet Langston Hughes.[16] The crisis in the Congo (the future Zaire) particularly galvanized the attention of young African Americans. The 1961 murder of Congolese prime minister Patrice Lumumba, ostensibly under UN protection at the time, outraged many American blacks, who suspected the United States or Belgian governments of involvement in the killing. On February 15, 1961, 60 African American protesters, including future American poet laureate Maya Angelou, stormed the gallery of the UN Security Council, interrupting a speech by U.S. ambassador Adlai Stevenson. Guards forcibly removed the protesters, but others gathered outside UN headquarters, throwing rocks and snowballs. Eventually, mounted police charged the group and broke the demonstration.

By the early 1960s interest in Africa among African Americans was growing. Civil rights leaders such as Fannie Lou Hamer and Robert Moses toured the continent in 1964. That same year, black Muslim leader Malcolm X formed the Organization for Afro-American Unity. While not envisioning a return-to-Africa movement, Malcolm X urged his followers to move "spiritually, culturally, and philosophically" toward Africa.[17] Many blacks followed Malcolm X's advice, exploring African culture and forging a new identity that would soon lead to the emergence of the black power movement. Meanwhile, by the early 1960s, the example of the civil rights movement began inspiring a broader movement for social, political, and cultural change.

YOUTH IN REVOLT

The African American rights struggle provided young people everywhere with a language and model with which to challenge the status quo. Civil rights activists viewed their struggle as part and parcel of a larger war against oppression everywhere, one that mandated young people "to put their bodies on the line" to evoke change. Moved by this message, youth of all colors increasingly envisioned themselves part of a larger battle against injustice and intolerance—even as the vanguard of a worldwide revolution.

Americans coming of age after World War II—by sheer numbers the largest generation to that date—grew up in a cosmopolitan world in which the leadership of the United States was never in question. Postwar prosperity, radio, television, and all manner of mass media shrank the world as never before. The growth of higher education meant that more young Americans (and Europeans) than ever went to college where they learned of influential ideas such as Marx's socialism and Albert Camus's existentialism.

The specter of young African Americans bravely challenging corrupt authority forced many young whites to reexamine their country and themselves. The shared commitment to a common humanity moved many to join the civil rights movement, the Peace Corps, or other cause-oriented groups flourishing during the early 1960s. "If there hadn't been a civil rights movement, there wouldn't have been an SDS," recalled a member of the Students for a Democratic Society, the leading radical student group of the time. Overseas the U.S. civil rights movement had a similar impact. Daniel Cohn-Bendit, a key leader of the Paris uprising of 1968, recalled being deeply moved by a memorial service he attended in New York City in 1964 for slain civil rights workers. "I was very impressed with the atmosphere. These two white Jewish guys who went to Mississippi. How dangerous. That was something different than what I was prepared to do," remembered Cohn-Bendit.[18]

Beyond politics, culture played perhaps an even greater role in linking and mobilizing young people. Music—especially the rebellious, edgy beat of rock and roll—spread like wildfire around the world. The roots of the music revolution, like the origins of the political and cultural revolution, again lay in the African American experience. Rhythm and blues, an infectious beat-driven amalgam of several forms of music emerged in the South among African Americans during the mid-twentieth century. Sensing potential for a broader market, in the mid-1950s, ambitious music producers recruited white artists such as Elvis Presley to record rhythm-and-blues standards aimed at a larger white audience. The impact was immediate and overwhelming. Elvis, Bill Haley, Buddy Holly, the Everly Brothers, and others became instant youth icons.

In a shrinking world, rock and roll could hardly be contained within U.S. borders. American military personnel and armed forces radio were among the transmitters of the new music genre. At age 18, future Rolling Stone Bill Wyman found himself drafted into Britain's Royal Air Force and sent to Germany—also temporary home to thousands of American military personnel, including many African Americans. In Germany, Wyman heard country music over U.S. Armed Forces Radio and listened to records by Fats Domino, Elvis, and Little Richard before those artists ever penetrated Britain. The bustling port city of Liverpool, home of four young lads later to become the Beatles, saw the constant coming and going of travelers, including American soldiers eager to share their music. American music and culture became an obsession for many European youth. "The first books I ever bought were about America. The first records were American. I was just devoted to the American way of life without ever having been there," recalled British-born Eric Clapton, who later emerged as a rock guitar legend. By the late 1950s, U.S. rockers such as Gene Vincent and Eddie Cochran (who tragically died in an automobile accident in London in 1960) were touring Britain and France to sold-out audiences. In turn, European youth, especially the British, quickly developed their own unique take on rock and roll and sold it back to America. The "British invasion," beginning in 1964 and led by the Beatles and Rolling Stones, nearly drove American artists off their own record charts. Soon Carnaby Street in London became the fashion center of the young world, and the irreverence and wit of the Beatles proved infectious. American rock and folk singer David Crosby remembered "coming out of the theater" after seeing the Beatles' movie *A Hard Day's Night*, "so jazzed that I was swinging around sign poles at arm's length."[19]

The idealism and activism of American youth, particularly the example of civil rights workers, also generated waves worldwide. Beginning with a dedicated few at the onset of the 1960s, activism and radical politics proliferated rapidly. Decrying the "imperialist" example of the United States and its rival the USSR, young people, especially college students, explicitly rejected materialism and militarism, embracing countercultural values and politics. Early leaders of "the movement," as it became known, were cosmopolitan, and transnational exchange flourished. Martin Vester, a member of the Socialist German Students' League, for instance, participated directly in drafting SDS's June 1962 declaration of principles entitled the Port Huron Statement. Young activists around the world shared similar intellectual influences as well, including the radical political philosophies of Herbert Marcuse, Frantz Fanon, Jean Paul Sartre, and others. Early anti-establishment demonstrations in Europe adopted strategies developed by Americans. Radical students worldwide also idolized Third World revolutionaries such as Mao Zedong, Fidel Castro, and Che Guevara. SDS, violating American law, began sending members to Cuba for closer exposure to "real" revolutionaries. "You North Americans are lucky," Che told a visiting delegation. "You live in the middle of the beast. You are engaged in the most important fight of all."[20]

Music and a shared culture continued to inspire and bond students throughout the 1960s. Drugs, hippie-style clothes, long hair, and music bridged youth movements. An Italian student newspaper summed up the global nature of the counterculture with the headline: "Proletarian Youth of Europe, Jimi Hendrix Unites Us."[21] In a phenomenon dubbed "hippie tourism," youthful Americans and young people everywhere began traveling abroad in record numbers— some 800,000 young Americans visiting Europe in the late 1960s. With its low fares and no minimum stay requirements, Icelandic Airlines quickly became known as the "Hippie Carrier." Exotic locations, such as the Moroccan city of Marrakesh—known for its hashish—also drew hippies from across the globe. Increasingly, a common countercultural identity emerged among youth, based not on nationality but rather on shared culture, values, and politics.

American intervention in Vietnam in 1965 dramatically radicalized youth around the world. Vietnam, recalled leading activist Tom Hayden, "became the dominant feature of our lives in the second half of the sixties." Increasing numbers of young people interpreted the war as an unacceptable act of aggressive imperialism. Protests began almost immediately in the United States and quickly spilled over into Europe and Asia. Picking up an American tactic, activists organized anti-Vietnam teach-ins at universities across Europe. In February 1966 German demonstrators, in an act they dubbed the "Custard Assassination"— egged American House (one of several cultural centers set up by the U.S. government in West Germany) in West Berlin. Others took a darker approach, such as when protesters scrawled "Vietnam, the Auschwitz of America" on the wall at the former Nazi death camp at Dachau.[22] Increasingly, youthful activists across the world aligned themselves with South Vietnam's National Liberation Front (NLF) in its struggle against America. "The common bond between the New Left and the NLF is . . . not a common experience but a common enemy: the U.S. government," explained the *New Republic* magazine.[23] Seeking to strengthen the alliance, in 1967 representatives of the North Vietnamese and NLF met with 40 young American activists in Czechoslovakia.

"YEAR OF THE BARRICADES": 1968

Mounting frustration over the Vietnam War and fury at stagnant social and education systems exploded beyond control in 1968—a year of earthshaking international turmoil. Across the world, militant young people, especially college students, drove the violence and chaos. For young rebels, America served both a model and an object of scorn. The methods and causes extolled by the American protest movement, with its roots in the nonviolent civil rights movement remained an inspiration even as violence increasingly competed for the allegiance of the young. Likewise, American culture, with its embrace of youth and freedom, remained an international force. Yet even as the American counterculture inspired, America writ large increasingly represented imperialism, racism, and grotesque materialism to many young people around the world. Anti-Americanism often provided the fuel that drove angry protests, particularly in reaction to the Vietnam War. "Tell the Americans the day and hours will come when we will drive you out unless you yourselves throw out imperialism," exhorted German student leader Rudi Dutschke, as he fired up West Berlin protestors in 1968.[24]

Violence and protest seemed ubiquitous in 1968, and college campuses were the epicenter of the tumult. That year demonstrators literally shut down hundreds of colleges and universities around the world. Students took over Hornsey College of Art and Design in London, holding it for several weeks. In Uruguay, nearly all students and teachers at both the college and secondary level went on strike in June 1968. Meanwhile, Columbia University in New York City became the scene of a lengthy siege when student radicals, offended by a planned university expansion into a surrounding ghetto community, seized several campus buildings. Mark Rudd, leader of the Columbia students (who had visited Cuba earlier that year), set the tone for the revolt by quoting poet LeRoi Jones to the university's president: "Up against the wall, motherfucker, this is a stick-up."[25] While Rudd's movement at Columbia ended in violence, the student movement in Mexico ended in massacre. On October 2, 1968, government troops fired into a student rally in Mexico City. Hundreds were killed and thousands jailed. The most far-reaching student protests came in Paris, where the student population rose up in force to challenge the French government, paralyzing the country in the process. Violence similarly flared in Japan, where huge student protests greeted the visit of the aircraft carrier USS Enterprise in early 1968. In Japan, as elsewhere, police met student violence with vicious brutality.

As he watched chaos envelop his country and much of the world, French president Charles de Gaulle, in another twist on anti-Americanism, bitterly blamed the CIA for a coordinated plot against France. "It is not possible that all of these movements could be unleashed at the same time, in so many different countries without orchestration," lamented the aging leader.[26] Some communist officials in Czechoslovakia similarly blamed American hippies and "foreign" elements for stirring up dissent during what became known as Prague Spring (a brief political and cultural awakening soon crushed by Soviet tanks).[27] Meanwhile an embittered President Lyndon Johnson futilely ordered his CIA to find evidence the Soviet Union and communist world had incited the disruption in his country's streets.

In fact, a general spirit rather than any direct orchestration united the youth movements. The aforementioned youth culture, seeded by the African American struggle for freedom, provided adhesion. A common global craving for political and cultural freedom to match rising material gains also united protesters. Certainly the worldwide media spread word of the movements from nation to nation. "In 1968 Mexican students read with fascination about Paris, Czechoslovakia, Berkeley, Columbia and other U.S. universities," recalled a Mexican journalist.[28] Students also traveled around the world, allowing movements and ideas to cross-fertilize. Militants in far-flung locations such as Israel, India, and Bermuda formed groups modeled after the Black Panthers, a radical self-defense organization begun in Oakland, California, in 1966.

Activists organized international meetings, such as the German SDS's International Vietnam Conference in February 1968 and an international meeting at the London School of Economics later that year. Yet no international student leadership ever emerged to direct or even link the various movements. Nor did outsiders—despite the suspicions of Johnson and De Gaulle—gain substantial control over any sector of the youth movement. Vietnam and anti-Americanism provided touchstones, but local frustrations, particular to a country and culture, more often lent the crucial motivations for students in revolt. Even in attacking the United States, protestors often were using America as a convenient stand-in for their own authorities. Reflecting years later on the complex, often personal, motives driving the protests, a Mexican activist mused, "If they ask me what the student movement of 1968 was all about, I could tell them that it was the history of how a son rebelled against his government because he could not confront his father, while a president who felt impotent against his own son's rocker lifestyle, took revenge against hundreds of students."[29]

After 1968, the scale of the demonstrations and violence died down. World leaders on both sides of the iron curtain, shaken by the tumult, embraced détente, partly as a means of subverting the chaos in their midst. In response, some protesters embraced a dangerous anarchism. In America, the Weather Underground attempted to harness and redirect the collapsing student movement toward violence. Ultimately, members usually did more harm to themselves than others, as in 1970, when three Weather Underground members blew themselves up while preparing bombs in a Greenwich Village townhouse. Elsewhere similar movements emerged, for instance the Red Brigades (Brigate Rosse) in Italy and the Shining Path (Sendero Luminoso) in Peru.

Despite the waning of the international student movement by the early 1970s, the counterculture persisted, often morphing into the mainstream culture. Across the world, jeans, long hair, rock music, sexual openness, and a defiant embrace of freedom became the marker of style. A 1971 photograph of future terrorist Osama Bin Laden, on vacation with his large Saudi Arabian family, reinforces the point. Smiling confidently, sporting bell-bottom jeans amidst his brothers and sisters, similarly clad in the latest youth fashion—long hair, denim suits, sunglasses, and turtle necks—young Bin Laden seemed the stereotypical western youth. His subsequent violent rejection of western culture stands in marked contrast.

FROM THE ERA OF CIVIL RIGHTS
TO THE ERA OF HUMAN RIGHTS

Hopes of an international movement to protect minorities and encourage political and social freedom, however, did not fully fade. Out of the chaos and violence of 1968 emerged a revived women's movement. Again the U.S. civil rights movement provided the seedbed. While exhilarated by the experience of challenging Jim Crow, women activists in the South often found themselves subject to the sexism of male movement leaders who expected them to act as secretaries at meetings and cooks and housekeepers in common living quarters. By the mid-1960s, women began to strike back, demanding equity and an end to the ubiquitous sexism surrounding them. Fighting to liberate the oppressed, women had discovered their own oppression.

Women in student-based movements around the world felt similar grievances. "The compañeros wanted to send us to the kitchen," recalled a Mexican activist, "but we wanted to dedicate ourselves to learning to propagandize and to do what they were doing."[30] When male members of the German SDS appeared contemptuous of women-related issues raised at a September 1968 conference, a female delegate pelted them with tomatoes. Publicity generated by such early activity, in particular the demonstrations organized at the September 1968 Miss America Contest in Atlantic City, New Jersey (where protesters famously crowned a sheep in a mock beauty contest), helped spread word of the emerging American movement, which in turn inspired offshoot movements throughout the world.

Made up of largely middle-class, college-educated women, the women's movement had a cosmopolitan air from the beginning. Works such as Simone de Beauvoir's influential *The Second Sex* (1949), for instance were required reading for emerging female activists. Likewise, as members of a self-defined movement promoting world transformation, women traveled frequently, facilitating the early cross-fertilization of the movement.

Of all the causes born in the 1960s, the women's movement enjoyed the most success. Between 1970 and 1975 the percentage of women college students in the United States grew by 45 percent. During the 1970s, the portion of female lawyers tripled and the number of female doctors doubled. Around the world, women made similar gains. In France, for instance, where laws prohibited women from opening bank accounts without their husband's permission until the mid-1960s, the portion of women doctors grew at a rate outpacing that of the United States—to one-third of all physicians in the 1970s.

The "human rights" movement of the 1970s shared similar roots. During the heyday of the civil rights movement, American blacks had sought to harness the term "human rights" in their battle against Jim Crow. In 1960, twenty-year-old activist Julian Bond, a student at Morehouse University, published "An Appeal for Human Rights" in several Atlanta newspapers. He aimed to broaden support for the local battle for civil rights by casting it in universal terms. Later, as Martin Luther King likewise strove to broaden and internationalize his movement in 1967, he told his supporters that "we have moved from the era of civil rights to the era of human rights."[31] By the mid-1970s, activists who cut their teeth working in the South were deeply ensconced in the human rights movement. Attorney Gay McDougall, who began her career working in the South with King, moved to New York City where she worked with the United Nations on human rights issues, especially in Africa.

By the 1970s, the human rights movement had broadened to attract people and organizations from all parts of the political spectrum. International organizations such as Amnesty International and Human Rights Watch, both begun in Europe but quickly spread to America, gained increasing political power and public support in their struggle to address human rights abuses such as torture, female circumcision, and genocide. Anticommunists embraced human rights as a means of exposing Soviet abuses. Liberals, in turn, argued that reorienting U.S. foreign policy toward human rights would restore America's lost moral authority after Vietnam. In 1976, Jimmy Carter, a man with deep ties to the civil rights movement in his home state of Georgia, won the presidency. Throughout his campaign, Carter made clear his "absolute" commitment to human rights. As if to reinforce the linkage between human rights and civil rights, he appointed Congressman Andrew Young, an ordained minister and close confidant of Martin Luther King, as his ambassador to the United Nations. Young attacked his job with vigor, focusing on improving relations with emerging African countries. Having first met members of the African National Congress and other African anti-colonialists in the late 1950s, Young's internationalism and human rights orientation descended directly from that of W. E. B. Du Bois and early black activists who sought to use the United Nations to attack colonialism and racism. In Africa, in particular, Young's presence at the UN had immediate resonance. "For President Carter to appoint not just a black man, but a black man who believes in human rights, is more than a symbol," declared Tanzanian president Julius Nyerere.[32]

To the surprise of many, human rights (for a few short years at least) became a dominant theme both in America and around the world. "Human rights is suddenly chic," reported one supporter. Nongovernmental organizations such as Amnesty International and Human Rights Watch managed to wield power though publicity and information campaigns, harnessing the strength of the international media. Innovative programs like "adoption" letter-writing campaigns on behalf of political prisoners, helped spur public support. At times the U.S. government found such initiatives embarrassing, such as when human rights groups targeted capital punishment in the United States. Ambassador Young himself complained at one point that there were hundreds of political prisoners in the United States, generating sharp criticism and a political headache for the Carter administration. Still, the international human rights movement, born of the civil rights movement, significantly shaped international relations in the 1970s and 1980s.

Challenging South Africa's rigid, racist apartheid system stood among Young's priorities at the UN. In 1977, he traveled to South Africa to meet with black activists. Young counseled nonviolence and cited the successes of the American civil rights movement as a model. While appreciating the support, black South Africans saw little congruity between the U.S. experience, where the civil rights movement enjoyed the support of large segments of the federal government, and their situation in South Africa, where blacks faced a state dedicated to their violent subjugation. South African militant Steve Biko actually refused to meet with Young, viewing him as naïve. Still, American activists grew increasingly committed to challenging apartheid. Biko's killing in September 1977 while in police custody alarmed many around the world. The United Nations organized a special memorial service for Biko as protests raged outside on the streets of New York City. Determined to push for U.S. sanctions and international condemnation, veterans of the civil rights movement, led by Randall Robinson, organized TransAfrica to push their cause.

The labors of Young, Robinson, and Jesse Jackson (another former member of King's inner circle, who was a frequent visitor to South Africa by the late 1970s and vehement critic of apartheid), sparked a broader movement demanding change in South Africa. TransAfrica led the way, beginning with a dramatic sit-in at the South African embassy in Washington, D.C., on November 21, 1984 (the first sit-in at the South African embassy had, in fact, occurred in 1965 at the height of the civil rights movement, as did the first calls for economic sanctions). The nonviolent protest, which ended with the arrests of several prominent members of TransAfrica, harked back to the heyday of the civil rights revolution and generated a greater following for the burgeoning movement.

As in the 1960s, college students quickly seized the cause as their own. In the spring of 1985, beginning at Cornell University and spreading to 40 other campuses, students erected shantytowns on campus property to push university administrators to withdraw investments (divest) from South Africa. While encountering some resistance, (police leveled the shantytown built by Berkeley students), the student movement enjoyed real success. Within a year, hundreds of colleges, universities, cities, churches, and other organizations had divested—costing South Africa some $220 billion.

Also reminiscent of the 1960s, popular culture, particularly music, played a role in the movement. Concern about famine in Africa led British musicians to produce a star-studded recording entitled "Do They Know It's Christmas?" in 1984. American artists released their own fund-raising song entitled "We Are the World" several months later. Live Aid, a massive musical festival simultaneously held in England and the United States in the summer of 1985, further raised awareness of African issues in the United States. Following the success of Live Aid, Steven Van Zandt, guitarist for Bruce Springsteen's E Street Band, organized Artists Against Apartheid to raise money and support for the antiapartheid movement. The presence of Coretta Scott King, widow of Martin

Luther King, on the board of Artists Against Apartheid helped reinforce its connection to the civil rights movement of the 1960s.

Perhaps even more important than its success pushing for divestment, the antiapartheid movement managed to push Congress to take stronger action against South Africa. In 1986 Congress passed, over President Ronald Reagan's veto, the Comprehensive Anti-Apartheid Act, slapping far-reaching sanctions on a country that was increasingly an international pariah. "This has now become a Civil Rights issue," explained Senate Republican majority leader Robert Dole.

Reeling from international pressure, and well aware that with the end of the Cold War its value to the West as a bulwark against communism had diminished, South Africa moved to end apartheid. In early 1990, South African officials released ANC leader Nelson Mandela after nearly three decades in prison. Later that year, Mandela toured the United States to enthusiastic crowds. Before a rally at Yankee Stadium, Mandela noted the inspiring examples of Marcus Garvey, W. E. B. Du Bois, and Martin Luther King, adding that "an unbreakable umbilical cord connected black South Africans and black Americans."[33]

MULTICULTURALISM—A NEW AMERICAN IDENTITY?

Multiculturalism, another outgrowth of the civil rights movement, became the center of intense debate by the 1990s. Ethnic and racial diversity was nothing new in America. Immigration and race long had generated deep controversies. Campaigns to promote cooperation and tolerance among diverse groups also were hardly novel. In the early twentieth century, for instance, German-born social philosopher Horace Kallen talked of the virtues of cultural pluralism as an alternative to a one-size-fits-all melting pot. Still, by the late 1980s, educators, public planners and others embraced multiculturalism as a new approach to managing the nation's challenging diversity. The American experience both shaped and was shaped by other societies experiencing similar demographic challenges. And in America as elsewhere, multiculturalism generated controversy and intense debate.

Late in the 1960s a discernible challenge to the ideals of universalism that drove the early civil rights movement set up the emergence of multiculturalism. Most prominently, the black power movement renounced the supposed benefits of integration in favor of a separate celebration of the virtues of African American culture and tradition. Following this lead, other groups demanded recognition based on race, ethnicity, sexual orientation, or gender. A surge in immigration from non-Western regions (initiated by the Immigration and Nationality Act of 1965) added to a sense among some that the nation must redefine its identity. Educational institutions, universities in particular, were first to respond to the sea change by introducing new programs in black studies, Latino studies, women's studies, and queer studies.

By the early 1990s, the term *multiculturalism* began to be applied to policies aimed at encouraging diversity and tolerance between cultures. The term actually came from Canada, like the United States a diverse country struggling to maintain a balance amidst expanding immigration and demands for group recognition. Canada's 1985 Multiculturalism Act essentially made multiculturalism the law of the land. While no such federal mandate ever passed in the United States, multiculturalism became an unmistakable force in the country by the 1990s—from hiring practices to refashioning educational curricula to redefining acceptable behavior in the workplace. A bustling industry of diversity consultants even emerged to "facilitate" and encourage multiculturalism.

Many of the most far-reaching multicultural initiatives came in the field of education. Colleges and universities, pressured by student and faculty activists, did away with traditional western civilization courses, replacing them with broader world history offerings that brought Asian, Latin American, and African history and literature into the educational canon. The federal government also undertook an initiative to identify key historical issues that should be taught in schools. The resulting National Standards for History aimed to broaden traditional approaches to American history with more attention to the experiences of women and minorities. Surveying these developments in 1997, one prominent former critic announced, "We are all multiculturalists now." Generously funded by patrons such as the Ford Foundation, multiculturalism seemed to be thriving. The global success of African American athletes, artists, and celebrities—none more impressive nor ubiquitous than Michael Jordan—also helped to broadcast to the world the potential of multiculturalism (see chapter 9).

Yet, as in other countries, critics soon emerged. By the mid-1990s, they complained that multiculturalism was fostering a rigid "political correctness"— a knee-jerk obeisance to the politics of diversity at the expense of free speech and, frequently, common sense. Initiatives to impose campus speech codes led critics to warn of threats to free expression. Soon a backlash of sorts was brewing. The U.S. Senate rejected by a vote of 99–1 the multiculturalist National History Standards as excessively revisionist to the point of unfairly abrogating key elements of the national historical narrative.

Fallout from multicultural initiatives caused similar controversy in other countries. In Canada, critics of multiculturalism flocked to the new Reform Party which explicitly called for immigration restriction and a curtailment of multiculturalism. Both Britain and Germany, which embraced multiculturalism in response to waves of immigrants, began to back away—reacting in particular to challenges of large-scale Muslim immigration. In 2007, Australian prime minister John Howard, a longtime critic of multiculturalism, introduced a controversial "Citizen Test"—a series of questions about Australian values and traditions required of those applying for citizenship. Three years later, German chancellor Angela Merkel blasted *multikulti* (the German version of multiculturalism) as having "utterly failed."[34] In early 2011, British prime minister David Cameron echoed Merkel, urging Europeans to abandon the "passive tolerance of recent years" and embrace a "much more active, muscular liberalism."[35]

Still, multiculturalism as a broad approach to organizing society seems to have survived the onslaught in the United States. Among his first official acts after the 9–11 terrorist attacks in 2001, President George W. Bush and his wife visited an Islamic mosque. "Muslims need to be treated with respect," he told reporters during the visit.[36] Likewise, American multiculturalism and some of its successes addressing racial, ethnic, social, and gender schisms have become something of a model for the world. James A. Banks, born in the Jim Crow South to an African American farming family, has become a leading proponent of multicultural education both in the United States and abroad. Known as "the father of multicultural education," Banks has traveled the world, serving as a consultant to schools and universities in diverse locales such as China, Ireland, Japan, Portugal, and Israel.

—⁂—

In many ways the election of President Barack Obama in 2008—with his roots in Africa and America—could be seen as the final triumph of the civil rights movement and multiculturalism. The union in 1962 of a white American college student named Anne Dunham and Barack Obama Sr., a Kenyan studying in the United States was one product of the cultural sea change prompted by the youth movement of the 1960s and the civil rights movement. Even as those movements lost intensity by the early 1970s, elements persisted, most obviously in the antiapartheid battles of the 1980s and the culture wars over multiculturalism in the 1990s. By the 1980s, the once controversial Muhammad Ali was serving as a goodwill ambassador for the United States (even going to

Africa at the behest of President Carter in 1980 to explain the U.S. boycott of the Olympics). Such developments not only helped make Obama's academic and legal career successful but, no doubt, helped prepare ordinary Americans to elect him president in 2008.

Conclusion

Most Americans tend to view globalization as a linear process: a steady progression toward economic, political, and cultural integration. This process is frequently depicted as a recent phenomenon—often associated with the post–World War II era, sometimes dated to the end of the Cold War in 1989. The proceeding pages, however, make essentially the opposite argument: globalization has long, deep, complex roots. It is hardly a recent phenomenon, and it has operated in anything but a linear fashion. As historians, our intent in this book has been both to problematize and to clarify. Globalization has been a long-term, multifaceted process, making great advances in some eras and receding in others. To depict this process clearly, this study organized issues related to America and globalization under three broad rubrics: commerce, culture, and conflict. In no way are these to be perceived as mutually exclusive categories. To the contrary, they are mutually reinforcing and overlapping groupings. Indeed, the story of America and the world cannot be told exclusively in terms of either cultural interaction, commerce, warfare, or "foreign" policy.

Commerce, the force perhaps most frequently associated with globalization, had international dimensions from the time of Columbus. From the earliest encounters between Europeans and Native Americans, America quickly became integrated into an evolving global economic system. The reality of Europeans enslaving Africans in America to grow commodities to be shipped worldwide underscores the remarkably integrated nature of trade even in this early period. The mercantile system to some extent constrained commercial activity, but by the late eighteenth century Americans had seized on the potential of free trade. Easy access to natural resources and strong internal markets similarly retarded overseas trade in the nineteenth century, yet immigration and foreign investment proved key to American industrial development.

By the turn of the century, America had moved from the economic periphery to the center. Still, setbacks occurred, such as the Great Depression of the 1930s and the "oil shocks" of the 1970s. Many around the world resented growing American commercial influence, while some at home demanded that bulwarks be erected to protect jobs and fragile sectors of the U.S. economy. Toward the end of the twentieth century, even as many prepared to sound the death knell for American commerce, new information-based technologies and an international easing of trade barriers led to great gains for both the American economy and globalization in general. Again complaints about growing "Americanization" sounded around the globe. While the war on terrorism and a global economic downturn that began in 2008 threaten what some were celebrating as a new age of globalization and democracy, the growth and reaction cycle of world economic globalization will most likely continue.

Without question, warfare and diplomacy also served as vehicles for globalization, although hardly in a neat, linear manner. From the first encounters between Europeans and natives, America became an important, albeit often peripheral, theater in the expansive world wars of the eighteenth and early nineteenth centuries. After the War of 1812, Americans focused on expansion—often engendered by warfare—within their own hemisphere. As announced by the Monroe Doctrine and Roosevelt Corollary, Americans increasingly viewed Latin America and the Caribbean as part of an informal empire.

Full engagement in the affairs of the wider world proved difficult to avoid by the early twentieth century. America initially recoiled from "the Great War" that began in Europe in 1914. Faith that it might bring order to a chaotic world, however, brought the United States into the war in 1917—marking its first military engagement on European soil. The foray proved costly and disillusioning for many Americans. Following the war, many sought refuge and comfort in a renewed isolationism—a fanciful hope America could fashion a destiny separate from a chaotic world. Such sentiments grew during the 1930s, only to be eviscerated by American engagement in the second World War. The shedding of American blood in Europe and Asia fed an emerging consciousness (first conceptualized by Woodrow Wilson) that America must pilot the world toward a new democratic, capitalist synthesis. This consciousness guided America through much of the rest of the century.

American leadership, however, has not been without opposition and controversy. Both at home and worldwide, persistent voices have protested growing American power, sometimes forcing retrenchment such as during and after the Vietnam War. Such debates continued into the twenty-first century as prolonged engagements in Iraq and Afghanistan tested the endurance of America's international commitments.

From English clergy sparking the Great Awakening in America, to European reforms aimed at addressing the pressing "social question," to Africans boldly challenging colonialism and racism on their continent, a steady stream of global culture and ideology has shaped the United States. In turn, American culture and ideology has greatly influenced world development, from the political culture of the American Revolution to the ideology of Progressive reformers at the turn of the twentieth century, to the counterculture of the 1960s and modern-day American popular culture.

From the United States' inception, American political culture—in particular the espousal of individual rights and self-government—proffered a potent model for the world. At times the model has also occasioned bitter controversy among both Americans and peoples worldwide. To some, the vaulted ideals celebrated by Americans amount to little more than veiled justifications for a brazen quest for global hegemony while others continue to see America as an exceptional "shining city on a hill."

Americans have inherited a long and complex history of interaction with the world—a history that resists easy characterization. Furthermore, Americans have frequently reacted to the outside world in wildly divergent ways. The combination of exaltation and anxiety with which Americans approach the world today is very much manifest in our past. Indeed, at no time has America's global interaction been without severe critics both at home and abroad. As students of history and informed citizens, we proceed best if we try to comprehend modern globalization by understanding its historical context, a history replete with triumphs, horrors, contractions, twists, and turns.

Notes

CHAPTER 1: COMMERCE AND CONQUEST

1. William Bradford, *Of Plymouth Plantation 1620–1647* (Modern Library, 1967), 288.

2. Quoted in Felipe Fernandez-Armesto, *Pathfinders: A Global History of Exploration* (W. W. Norton, 2007), 172.

3. Christopher Columbus, *The Journal of Christopher Columbus*, ed. Clements R. Markham (Hakluyt Society, 1893), 37.

4. Alan Taylor, *American Colonies: The Settling of North America* (Penguin, 2002), 38.

5. Alfred Crosby, *The Columbian Exchange* (Greenwood, 1973) 48.

6. Ibid., 80.

7. Ibid., 97.

8. Daniel Richter, *Facing East from Indian Country* (Harvard University Press, 2003), 59.

9. Charles C. Mann, *1491: New Revelations of the Americas before Columbus* (Vintage, 2006), 218.

10. Taylor, *American Colonies*, 46.

11. Marcy Norton, *Sacred Gifts, Profane Pleasures* (Cornell University Press, 2010), 102–3.

12. James Axtell, *Natives and Newcomers* (Oxford University Press, 2000), 108.

13. Richter, *Facing East*, 50.

14. James Merrell, *The Indians' New World* (W. W. Norton, 1991), 52.

15. John J. McCusker and R. R. Menard, *The Economy of British America, 1607–1785* (University of North Carolina Press, 1985), 150.

16. Taylor, *American Colonies*, 134.

17. Edmund S. Morgan, *American Slavery, American Freedom* (W. W. Norton, 1975), 109.

18. McCusker and Menard, *Economy of British America*, 119.

19. S. Max Edelson, *Plantation Enterprise in Colonial South Carolina* (Harvard University Press, 2006), 76.

20. Robin Law, *The Slave Coast of West Africa 1550–1750* (Clarendon, 1991), 161.

21. Lawrence A. Peskin, *Manufacturing Revolution* (Johns Hopkins University Press, 2003), 18.

22. *Four Dissertations on the Reciprocal Advantage of a Perpetual Union between Great-Britain and Her American Colonies* (Philadelphia, 1766), 28.

CHAPTER 2: THE MANY WARS FOR AMERICA

1. John P. Demos, *The Unredeemed Captive* (Vintage, 1995), 18.
2. Ian K. Steele, *Warpaths* (Oxford University Press, 1994), 16.
3. Kris E. Lane, *Pillaging the Empire* (M. E. Sharpe, 1998), 24.
4. Kenneth R. Andrews, *Trade, Plunder, and Settlement* (Cambridge University Press, 1984), 144.
5. Ibid., 289.
6. Michael A. Bellesisles, *Arming America* (Knopf, 2000), 120.
7. Steele, *Warpaths*, 171.
8. Luke Tyerman, *The Life of the Rev. George Whitefield* (Anson D. Randolph & Co., 1877), 151.
9. Fred Anderson, *Crucible of War* (Vintage, 2001), 55.
10. T. R. Clayton, "The Duke of Newcastle, the Earl of Halifax, and the American Origins of the Seven Years' War," *The Historical Journal* 24 (1981): 590.

CHAPTER 3: DE-INDIANIZING AMERICAN CULTURE

1. *The Journal of Christopher Columbus,* ed. Clements R. Markham (Hakluyt Society, 1893) 37.
2. Luca Codiginola, "The Holy See and the Conversion of the Indians in French and British North America," in *America in European Consciousness,* ed. Karen O. Kupperman (Institute of Early American History and Culture / University of North Carolina Press, 1995), 195.
3. J. H. Eliot, *Empires of the Atlantic World* (Yale University Press, 2006), 202.
4. David J. Weber, *The Spanish Frontier in North America* (Yale University Press, 1992), 98.
5. Eliot, *Empires of the Atlantic World,* 72.
6. Alison Games, *Migration and the Origins of the English Atlantic World* (Harvard University Press, 2001), 134.
7. Jonathan Butler, *Awash in a Sea of Faith* (Harvard University Press, 1991), 53, 64.
8. Michel de Montaigne, *The Complete Essays* (Stanford University Press, 1955), 155.
9. Susan O'Brien, "A Transatlantic Community of Saints: The Great Awakening and the First Evangelical Network, 1735–1755," *American Historical Review* 91 (1986): 817.
10. Jon Butler, *Becoming America* (Harvard University Press, 2000), 703.
11. Winthrop D. Jordan, *White over Black* (Penguin, 1969), 230.
12. I. Bernard Cohen, *Science and the Founding Fathers* (W.W. Norton, 1995), 180, 182.
13. John Locke, *Two Treatises of Government* (Cambridge University Press, 1960), 343 (2.5.49).
14. Barbara Arneil, *John Locke and America* (Oxford University Press, 1996), 49.
15. David S. Lovejoy, *The Glorious Revolution in America* (Harper & Rowe, 1972), 267, 291.
16. Locke, *Two Treatises,* 332 (2.5.32).
17. Adam Smith, *The Wealth of Nations* (Cook & Hale, 1818), 2:105.

CHAPTER 4: THE IDEA OF FREEDOM IN AN AGE OF SLAVERY

1. Susan Dunn, *Sister Revolutions* (Faber & Faber, 2000), 4.
2. Gary Nash and Graham R. G. Hodges, *Friends of Liberty* (Basic Books, 2008).
3. Laurent Dubois, *Avengers of the New World* (Belknap, 2005).
4. Richard W. Slatta and Jane Lucas De Grummond, *Simon Bolivar's Quest for Glory* (Texas A&M University Press, 2003), 6.
5. Alexis de Tocqueville, *Democracy in America* (Harper Perennial, 2007), 14.
6. Francis Trollope, *Domestic Manners of the Americans* (Whittaker, Treacher, & Co., 1832), 55.
7. Tocqueville, *Democracy in America*, 38.
8. Margaret Bayard Smith, *The First Forty Years of Washington Society* (Gaillard Hunt, 1906), 296.
9. Margaret H. McFadden, *Golden Cables of Sympathy* (University Press of Kentucky, 1999), 144.
10. Ibid.
11. *The Works of Lord Byron*, 5 vols. (Bernhard Tauchnitz, 1866) 1:477.
12. Robert Dale Owen, *Discourses on a New System of Society*, 11, cited in Alice Felt Tyler, *Freedom's Ferment* (1944; reprint, Harper & Rowe, 1962).
13. Cited in Tyler, *Freedom's Ferment*, 206.
14. *Niles Historical Register*, Aug. 16, 1848, p. 99.
15. Thomas Bender, *A Nation among Nations* (Hill & Wang, 2006), 127–28.
16. Harriet Martineau, *Society in America* (Saunders & Otley, 1837), 2:368.
17. McFadden, *Golden Cables of Sympathy*, 109.
18. Eric Foner, *Nothing but Freedom* (Louisiana State University Press, 2007), 8.
19. George Fitzhugh, *Sociology for the South* (A. Morris, 1854), 83.
20. Cited in Howard Jones, *Crucible of Power* (Rowman & Littlefield, 2009), 149.

CHAPTER 5: DEVELOPING A CONTINENTAL MARKET

1. Stanley Elkins and Eric McKitrick, *The Age of Federalism* (Oxford University Press, 1995), 72.
2. Jefferson to John Jay, 1785, in Merrill D. Peterson, ed., *The Portable Thomas Jefferson* (Penguin, 1975), 382.
3. William L. Neumann, "Religion, Morality, and Freedom: The Ideological Background of the Perry Expedition," *Pacific Historical Review* 23 (August 1954): 247; Walter LaFeber, *The Clash* (W. W. Norton, 1998).
4. Robert Vincent Remini, *Daniel Webster: The Man and His Time* (W.W. Norton, 1997), 712.
5. Quoted in LaFeber, *Clash*, 24.
6. Lawrence A. Peskin, *Manufacturing Revolution* (Johns Hopkins University Press, 2003), 48.
7. Jefferson to Benjamin Austin, 1816, in Peterson, *The Portable Jefferson*, 549.
8. Doron Ben Atar, *Trade Secrets* (Yale University Press, 2004), 79.

9. Peskin, *Manufacturing Revolution*, 221.

10. Cited in Richard Hofstadter, *The Age of Reform* (Vintage, 1955), 175, 278–79.

11. Cited in Richard D. Heffner, *A Documentary History of the United States* (New American Library, 2002), 245.

CHAPTER 6: FROM COLONIES TO THE THRESHOLD OF EMPIRE

1. Lawrence A. Peskin, *Captives and Countrymen* (Johns Hopkins University Press, 2009), 202.

2. Frank Lambert, *The Barbary Wars* (Hill & Wang, 2007), 196; Robert J. Allison, *Stephen Decatur* (University of Massachusetts Press, 2005) 167.

3. Lawrence Kaplan, *Colonies into Nation* (Macmillan, 1972), 91.

4. Ibid., 105.

5. R. Ernest Dupuy, Gay Hammerman, and Grace P. Hayes, *The American Revolution: A Global War* (David McKay, 1960), 49.

6. Colin G. Calloway, *American Revolution in Indian Country* (Cambridge University Press, 1995), 281.

7. U.S. State Papers, Military Affairs (1798), 120.

8. Jon Latimer, *1812: War with America* (Belknap, 2007) 400; emphasis in original.

9. Thomas Jefferson to Robert R. Livingston, April 18, 1802, Thomas Jefferson Papers, Library of Congress.

10. Ramon E. Ruiz, *Triumphs and Tragedy* (W. W. Norton, 1993), 209.

11. Ibid., 213–14.

12. Allan Peskin, *Volunteers* (Kent State University Press, 1991), 181.

13. Dean B. Mahin, *One War at a Time: The International Dimensions of the American Civil War* (Brassey's, 1999), 24.

14. Peter H. Smith, *Talons of the Eagle* (Oxford University Press, 2007), 25.

CHAPTER 7: RELUCTANT GLOBAL WARRIORS

1. Edward K. Eckert, ed., *In War and Peace: An American Military History Anthology* (Wadsworth, 1990), 226–37.

2. Thomas Paterson, "United States Intervention in Cuba, 1898: Interpretations of the Spanish-American-Cuban-Filipino War," *The History Teacher* 29 (May 1996): 345–46.

3. Trevor McCrisken, "Exceptionalism," in *Encyclopedia of American Foreign Policy*, ed. Alexander DeConde et al. (Scribner, 2001), 63.

4. Theodore Roosevelt, *The Rough Riders* (Charles Scribner's Sons, 1899), 1.

5. Eric Love, *Race Over Empire: Racism and U.S. Imperialism, 1865–1900* (University of North Carolina Press, 2004), 162.

6. Robert David Johnson, *Peace Progressives and American Foreign Policy* (Harvard University Press, 1995), 24.

7. Ibid., 27.

8. Paul Kramer, *The Blood of Government: Race, Empire, the United States, and the Philippines* (University of North Carolina Press, 2006), 108.

9. William Jennings Bryan, "Imperialism (1900)," in *Speeches of William Jennings Bryan,* ed. William Jennings Bryan and Mary Baird Bryan (Funk & Wagnalls, 1913), 2:41.

10. McCrisken, "Exceptionalism," 70.

11. Mathew Jacobson, *Barbarian Virtues: The United States Encounters Foreign Peoples at Home and Abroad,* (Hill & Wang, 2001), 45.

12. Theodore Roosevelt, *The Autobiography of Theodore Roosevelt* (Macmillan, 1913), 566.

13. George Herring, *From Colony to Superpower: U.S. Foreign Relations Since 1776* (Oxford University Press, 2008), 391.

14. "Wilson's Address at the Salesmanship Congress Detroit," July 10, 1916, in *President Wilson's State Papers and Addresses* (George H. Horan Co., 1918), 282.

15. Woodrow Wilson, "The Meaning of Liberty," Address at Independence Hall, July 4, 1914, in *President Wilson's Foreign Policy: Messages, Addresses, Papers,* ed. James Brown Scott (Oxford University Press), 65.

16. McCrisken, "Exceptionalism," 71.

17. J. W. Schulte Nordholt, *Woodrow Wilson: A Life for World Peace,* trans. Herbert Rowen (University of California Press, 1991), 131.

18. Ibid., 146.

19. Theodore Roosevelt, *America and the World War* (Charles Scribner's Sons, 1915), 276, xv, 277, xi.

20. Nordholt, *Woodrow Wilson,* 275.

21. Joan Hoff, *A Faustian Bargain, Foreign Policy from Woodrow Wilson to George W. Bush: Dreams of Perfectibility* (Cambridge University Press, 2008), 46.

22. Thomas Fleming, *The Illusion of Victory: America in World War I* (Basic Books, 2004), 47.

23. Tim Madigan, *The Burning: Massacre, Destruction, and the Tulsa Riot of 1921* (Macmillian, 2001), 35.

24. Charles A. Lindbergh, *Why Your Country Is at War and What Happens to You after the War and Related Subjects* (National Capital Press, 1917), 8.

25. Eliot A. Cohen, *Supreme Command: Soldiers, Statesmen and Leadership in Wartime* (Simon & Schuster, 2002), 69.

26. David Kennedy, *Over Here: The First World War and American Society* (Oxford University Press, 1980), 144.

27. Erez Manela, *The Wilsonian Moment: Self-Determination and the International Origins of Anticolonial Nationalism* (Oxford University Press, 2007), 93, 99.

28. Ruth Henig, *Versailles and After, 1919–1933* (Routledge, 1995), 28.

29. Woodrow Wilson, Address at Hotel Alexandria, Los Angeles, 20 September 1919, in *Addresses of President Wilson: Addresses Delivered by President Wilson on His Western Tour* (U.S. Government Printing Office, 1919), 286.

30. Nathan Miller, *New World Coming: The 1920s and the Making of Modern America* (Scribner, 2003), 88.

31. Jean Edward Smith, *FDR* (Random House, 2007), 420.

32. Justus Donecke, ed., *In Danger Undaunted: The Anti-Interventionist Movement of 1940–1941 as Revealed in the Papers of the America First Movement* (Hoover Institution Press, 1990), 36.

33. Ibid., 18.

34. "Did You Know the Implications behind the Roosevelt-Churchill 18 Points?" 23 August 1941, in ibid., 315.

35. Franklin D. Roosevelt, "The Arsenal of Democracy," 29 December 1940, in *FDR's Fireside Chats*, ed. Russell Buhite and David Levy (University of Oklahoma Press, 1992), 166.

36. Smith, *FDR*, 477.

37. Chester Bowles to R. Douglas Stuart, 15 July 1941, in Donecke, *In Danger Undaunted*, 279.

38. "Text of the Addresses by Lindbergh and Wheeler before 22,000 at Garden," *New York Times*, 24 May 1941.

39. Franklin D. Roosevelt, "Inaugural Address," 20 January 1941, in *Rendezvous with Destiny: Addresses and Opinions of Franklin D. Roosevelt*, ed. Franklin D. Roosevelt and J.B.S. Hardman (Dryden Press, 1944), 59.

40. Franklin D. Roosevelt, "State of the Union," 6 January 1941, in *Rendezvous with Destiny*, 172.

41. John Lewis Gaddis, *The United States and the Origins of the Cold War, 1941–1947* (Columbia University Press, 1972), 27.

42. Henry Luce, "The American Century," *Life*, 6 January 1941.

CHAPTER 8: EMERGING ECONOMIC HEGEMON

1. John Kobler, "Sam the Banana Man," *Life Magazine*, 19 February 1951, p. 87.

2. Stephen Kinzer, *Overthrow: America's Century of Regime Change from Hawaii to Iraq* (Henry Holt, 2007), 100.

3. Kobler, 94.

4. William Thomas Stead, *Americanization of the World* (Horace Markley, 1901), 4.

5. Mathew Jacobson, *Barbarian Virtues: The United States Encounters Foreign Peoples at Home and Abroad, 1876–1917* (Farrar, Straus & Giroux, 2000), 22.

6. H. W. Brands, *T.R.: The Last Romantic* (Basic Books, 1997), 395.

7. Louis Perez, *Cuba and the United States: Ties of Singular Intimacy* (University of Georgia Press, 2003), 147.

8. Alan McPherson, *Yankee No!: Anti-Americanism in U.S.–Latin American Relations* (Harvard University Press, 2003), 40; Perez, *Cuba and the United States*, 146.

9. William Dickson Boyce, *Illustrated South America* (Rand-McNally, 1913), 50–51, 37.

10. McPherson, *Yankee No!*, 81.

11. Jason Colby, "Banana Growing and Negro Management: Race, Labor, and the Jim Crow Colonialism in Guatemala, 1884–1930," *Diplomatic History* 30 (September 2006): 617.

12. Emily Rosenberg, *Spreading the American Dream: American Cultural and Economic Expansion, 1890–1945* (Hill & Wang, 1982), 17.

13. William Appleman Williams, *The Tragedy of American Diplomacy* (W. W. Norton, 1972), 62.

14. David Mowery and Nathan Rosenberg, "Twentieth-Century Technological Change," in *The Cambridge Economic History of the United States*, vol. 3, ed. Stanley Engerman and Robert Gallman (Cambridge University Press, 2000), 834.

15. Michael Hunt, *The American Ascendancy: How the United States Gained and Wielded Global Dominance* (University of North Carolina Press, 2007), 87.

16. Geir Lundestad, "Empire by Invitation," in *Ambiguous Legacy: U.S. Foreign Relations in the American Century*, ed. Michael J. Hogan (Cambridge University Press, 1999), 58.

17. Hunt, *American Ascendancy*, 88.

18. Mary Beth Norton et al., *A People and a Nation: A History of the United States* (Houghton Mifflin, 1982), 753–54.

19. Mira Wilkins, *The Maturing of the Multinational Enterprise: American Business Abroad from 1914 to 1970* (Harvard University Press, 1974), 159.

20. Alonzo Hamby, *For the Survival of Democracy: Franklin Roosevelt and the World Crisis of the 1930s* (Free Press, 2004), 131–34.

21. Dana Frank, *Buy American: The Untold Story of Economic Nationalism* (Beacon, 2000), 59.

22. Peter Trubowitz, *Defining National Interest: Conflict and Change in American Foreign Policy* (University of Chicago Press, 1998), 128.

23. Jean Edward Smith, *FDR* (Random House, 2008), 515.

24. Daniel Yergin, *The Prize: The Epic Quest for Oil, Money and Power* (Simon & Schuster, 2008), 377, 378.

25. Mark Pendergrast, *For God, Country, and Coca-Cola: The Definitive History of the Great American Soft Drink and the Company That Makes It*, 2nd ed. (Basic Books, 2000), 195, 202.

CHAPTER 9: REFORMING A CHAOTIC WORLD

1. Jane Addams, *Twenty Years at Hull House with Autobiographical Notes* (Macmillan, 1951), 66–68.

2. Robert Frankel, *Observing America: The Commentary of British Visitors to the United States, 1890–1950* (University of Wisconsin Press, 2007), 48.

3. Frederic Howe, *The British City: The Beginnings of Democracy* (Charles Scribner's Sons, 1907), 5.

4. David Welch, *Modern European History, 1871–2000: A Documentary Reader* (Routledge, 1999), 48.

5. Sidney Lens, *Radicalism in America* (Thomas Y. Crowell, 1969), 183.

6. Michael Kazin, interview, "Heaven On Earth: The Rise and Fall of Socialism," New River Media, accessed February 25, 2011, www.pbs.org/heavenonearth/interviews_kazin .html.

7. Lens, *Radicalism in America*, 213.

8. Melvyn Dubofsky, *We Shall Be All: A History of the Industrial Workers of the World* (University of Illinois Press, 1988), 86–87.

9. John P. Diggins, *Rise and Fall of the American Left* (W. W. Norton, 1992), 88, 89.

10. "Minutes of IWW Founding Convention," accessed February 25, 2011, www.iww .org/culture/library/founding/.

11. Alice Wexler, *Emma Goldman: Intimate Life* (Pantheon, 1984) 63.

12. Nick Salvatore, *Eugene V. Debs: Citizen and Socialist* (University of Illinois Press, 2007), 70.

13. James Chace, *1912: Wilson, Roosevelt, Taft & Debs—The Election that Changed the Country* (Simon & Schuster, 2004), 81, 179.

14. Diggins, *Rise and Fall*, 101.

15. Lens, *Radicalism in America*, 247.

16. Diggins, *Rise and Fall*, 105, 108.

17. Daniel Rodgers, *Atlantic Crossings: Social Politics in a Progressive Age* (Harvard University Press, 1998), 4.

18. Addams, *Twenty Years*, 118.

19. Gary Dorrien, *The Making of American Liberal Theology: Idealism, Realism, and Modernity* (John Knox Press, 2003), 88, 89.

20. Henry Demarest Lloyd, *Newest England: Note of a Democratic Traveller in New Zealand with some Australian Comparisons* (Doubleday, Page, 1902), 234, 376.

21. Trevor West, *Horace Plunkett: Co-operation and Politics: An Irish Biography* (C. Smythe/Catholic University of America, 1986), 133.

22. Rodgers, *Atlantic Crossings*, 247, 144.

23. Patricia Ward D'Itri, *Cross Currents in the International Women's Movement, 1848–1948* (Bowling Green State University Press, 1999), 104.

24. Eric Love, *Race over Empire: Racism and U.S. Imperialism, 1865–1900* (University of North Carolina Press, 2004), 184.

25. Milton Meltzer, *Mark Twain Himself: A Pictorial Biography* (University of Missouri Press, 2002), 255.

26. Charles DeBenedetti, *The Peace Reform in American History* (Indiana University Press, 1980), 78.

27. Jane Addams, *Peace and Bread in a Time of War* (Macmillan, 1922), 4.

28. Ray Batchelor, *Henry Ford: Mass Production, Modernism, and Design* (University of Manchester Press, 1994), 26.

29. W. E. B. Du Bois, "The Color Line Belts the World," in *W. E. B. Du Bois: A Reader*, eds. William Edward Burghardt Du Bois and David L. Lewis (Macmillan, 1995), 42.

30. Michael McGerr, *A Fierce Discontent: The Rise and Fall of the Progressive Movement in America* (Oxford University Press, 2003), 196.

31. Ibid., 200–201.

32. Kristin Hoganson, "'As Badly Off as the Filipinos': U.S. Women's Suffragists and the Imperial Issue at the Turn of the Twentieth Century," *Journal of Women's History* 13, 2 (Summer 2001): 20.

33. David Levering Lewis, *W. E. B. Du Bois: The Fight for Equality and the American Century, 1919–1963* (Holt, 2000), 118, 119.

34. Ibid., 149.

35. Alan Dawley, *Struggles for Justice: American Progressives in War and Revolution* (Harvard University Press, 1991), 273.

36. Melvyn P. Leffler, *The Specter of Communism: The United States and the Origins of the Cold War, 1917–1953* (Hill & Wang, 1994), 14.

37. John Hope Franklin and Alfred Moss, *From Slavery to Freedom: A History of African Americans* (Knopf, 1988), 331.

38. McGerr, *Fierce Discontent*, 242.

39. Dawley, *Struggles for Justice*, 289.

40. Arthur Schlesinger Jr., *The Politics of Upheaval, 1935–1936, Vol. 3: The Age of Roosevelt* (Mariner, 2003), 191.

41. Rodgers, *Atlantic Crossings*, 469.

42. Marquis Childs, *Sweden: The Middle Way* (Yale University Press, 1936), 160.

43. Oral history interview with Jacob Baker, 25 September 1963, Archives of American Art, Smithsonian Institution, available at www.aaa.si.edu/collections/interviews/oral-history -interview-jacob-baker-11712.

44. Inquiry on Cooperative Enterprise, *Report of the Inquiry on Cooperative Enterprise in Europe, 1937* (U.S. Government Printing Office, 1937), 99.

45. Joy Gleason Carew, *Blacks, Reds, and Russians: Sojourners in Search of the Soviet Promise* (Rutgers University Press, 2008), 115.

46. Nelson Lichtenstein, *Walter Reuther: The Most Dangerous Man in Detroit* (University of Illinois Press, 1997), 40.

47. Rodgers, *Atlantic Crossings*, 420.

48. Peter Irons, *The New Deal Lawyers* (Princeton University Press, 1993), 27.

49. William Leuchtenburg, "The Great Depression," in *The Comparative Approach to American History*, ed. C. Vann Woodward (Basic Books, 1968), 307.

50. David Lilienthal, *TVA: Democracy on the March* (Harper, 1944), 204.

CHAPTER 10: GLOBALIZATION AND AMERICANIZATION

1. Stephen Ambrose, *Nixon: The Education of a Politician, 1913–1962* (Simon & Schuster, 1987), 525.

2. John Lewis Gaddis, *The United States and the Origins of the Cold War, 1941–1947* (Columbia University Press, 1972), 21, 18.

3. David Halberstam, *The Fifties* (Villard, 1993), 116.

4. Gaddis, *Origins*, 342.

5. Diane B. Kunz, *Butter and Guns: America's Cold War Diplomacy* (Free Press, 1997), 54.

6. Michael Hogan, *The Marshall Plan: America, Britain, and the Reconstruction of Europe, 1947–1952* (Cambridge University Press, 1987), 89.

7. "High Pay, Good Housing Win Arab Friendship," *Life*, 28 March 1949, 66.

8. Richard Pells, *Not Like Us: How Europeans Have Loved, Hated, and Transformed American Culture* (Basic Books, 1997), 164.

9. "The Sun Never Sets on Coca-Cola," *Time*, 15 May 1950.

10. Mark Pendergrast, *For God, Country, and Coca-Cola: The Definitive History of the Great American Soft Drink and the Company That Makes It*, 2nd ed. (Basic Books, 2000), 237.

11. *New York Times*, 5 March 1950.

12. "Should You Buy a Foreign Car?" *Popular Mechanics*, August 1959, 98.

13. William S. Borden, "Defending Hegemony: American Foreign Economic Policy," in Thomas J. Paterson ed. *Kennedy's Quest for Victory* (Oxford University Press, 1989), 63.

14. Edwin Dale, "President Exhorts Business to Strive for More Exports," *New York Times*, 18 September 1963.

15. "Industry: Textile Troubles," *Time*, 29 March 1963.

16. Robert Collins, "The Economic Crisis of 1968 and the Waning of the 'American Century,'" *American Historical Review* 101 (April 1996): 396.

17. Ibid., 415.

18. "The Economy: Struggle to Stay Competitive," *Time*, 31 May 1971.

19. Robert M. Collins, *More: The Politics of Economic Growth in Postwar America* (Oxford University Press, 2000), 105.

20. "Business: Why the U.S. Is Slipping," *Time*, 12 May 1980.

21. "To Set the Economy Right," *Time*, 27 August 1980.

22. John Tomlinson, *Cultural Imperialism: A Critical Introduction* (Continuum, 2001), 45.

23. Richard Barnet and John Cavanaugh, *Global Dreams and the New World Economy* (Touchstone, 1994), 36.

24. "Bashing Japan on the Campaign Trail," *Time*, 10 February 1992.

25. Robert Reich, *The Work of Nations: Preparing Ourselves for 21st Century Capitalism* (Vintage, 1992), 112-13.

26. James Patterson, *Restless Giant: The United States from Watergate to Bush v. Gore* (Oxford University Press, 2005), 361.

27. Derek Chollet and James Goldgeier, *America between Wars from 11/9 to 9/11: The Misunderstood Years between the Fall of the Berlin Wall and the Start of the War on Terror* (Public Affairs, 2008), 100.

28. Ibid, 159.

29. Andrew Kohut and Bruce Stokes, *America against the World: How We Are Different and Why We Are Disliked* (Henry Holt, 2007), 142.

30. Michael Veseth, *Globaloney: Unraveling the Myths of Globalization* (Rowman & Littlefield, 2005), 66.

31. Joseph Stiglitz, *The Roaring Nineties: A New History of the World's Most Prosperous Decade* (W. W. Norton, 2003), 204.

CHAPTER 11: BECOMING THE "INDISPENSABLE NATION"

1. Thomas Lippman, *Madeleine Albright and the New American Diplomacy* (Westview, 2004), 158.

2. Ibid., 89.

3. "U.S. Policy on Iraq Draws Fire," www.cnn.com/WORLD/9802/18/town.meeting.folo/.

4. Thomas Paterson, *On Every Front: The Making and Unmaking of the Cold War* (W. W. Norton, 1992), 102.

5. John Lewis Gaddis, *The United States and the Origins of the Cold War, 1941-1947* (Columbia University Press, 1972), 261.

6. Paterson, *On Every Front*, 100.

7. Gaddis, *Origins*, 204.

8. *Life*, 27 May 1946,

9. George Herring, *From Colony to Superpower: U.S. Foreign Relations since 1776* (Oxford University Press, 2008), 615.

10. "Extracts from American Editorial Comment on President Truman's Message," *New York Times*, 13 March 1947.

11. Remarks of Senator John F. Kennedy at the Fourth Annual Rockhurst Day Banquet of Rockhurst College in Kansas City, Missouri, Saturday June 2, 1956, accessed 31 October 2009, www.jfklibrary.org/Historical+Resources/Archives/Reference+Desk/Speeches/JFK/JFK+Pre-Pres/1956/002PREPRES12SPEECHES_56JUN02.htm.

12. *New York Times*, 18 April 1955.

13. Speech of Senator John F. Kennedy, Cow Palace, San Francisco, CA, 2 November 1960, accessed 31 October 2009, www.presidency.ucsb.edu/ws/index.php?pid<#213>25928.

14. Arthur Schlesinger Jr., *A Thousand Days: John F. Kennedy in the White House* (Houghton Mifflin, 2002), 341.

15. Michael Lanham, *Modernization as Ideology: American Social Sciences and "Nation Building" in the Kennedy Era* (University of North Carolina Press, 2000), 4.

16. Nick Cullather, "Miracles of Modernization: The Green Revolution and the Apotheosis of Technology" *Diplomatic History* 28 (April 2004): 231.

17. Bill Moyers, "The Peace Corps," *The Alcalde*, October 1961, 9.

18. Sylvia Ellis, *Britain, America, and the Vietnam War* (Praeger, 2002), 49.

19. Richard Melanson, *American Foreign Policy since the Vietnam War: From Richard Nixon to George Bush* (M. E. Sharpe, 2005), 73.

20. Margaret MacMillan, *Nixon and Kissinger: The Week that Changed the World* (Random House, 2008), xxi.

21. Jimmy Carter, *Keeping Faith: Memoirs of a President* (Bantam, 1982), 144.

22. Ibid.

23. Ibid., 436.

24. "Nation: The U.S. Is No Longer #1," *Time*, 30 June 1980.

25. David Farber, *Taken Hostage: The Iranian Hostage Crisis and America's First Encounter with Radical Islam* (Princeton University Press, 2005), 176.

26. James Mann, *The Rebellion of Ronald Reagan: A History of the End of the Cold War* (Viking, 2009), 18.

27. *New York Times*, 13 June 1982.

28. Mann, *Rebellion of Ronald Reagan*, 29.

29. Richard Reeves, *President Reagan: The Triumph of the Imagination* (Simon & Schuster, 2005), 340, 343.

30. George Bush and Brent Scowcroft, *A World Transformed* (Knopf, 1998), 532.

31. Herbert Parmet, *George Bush: The Life of a Lone Star Yankee* (Transaction, 2000), 341.

32. Derek Chollet and James Goldgeier, *America between Wars from 11/9 to 9/11: The Misunderstood Years between the Fall of the Berlin Wall and the Start of the War on Terror* (Public Affairs, 2008), 23.

33. Nigel Hamilton, *Bill Clinton: Mastering the Presidency* (Public Affairs, 2007), 197.

34. *New York Times*, 14 April 2003.

CHAPTER 12: CIVIL RIGHTS AND WORLD CULTURE

1. Mike Marqusee, *Redemption Song: Muhammad Ali and the Spirit of the Sixties* (Verso, 2005), 273–74.

2. Mary L. Dudziak, *Cold War Civil Rights: Race and the Image of American Democracy* (Princeton University Press, 2002), 8.

3. *New York Times*, 7 June 1946.

4. Thomas Borstelmann, *The Cold War and the Color Line* (Harvard University Press, 2003), 77.

5. Dudziak, *Cold War Civil Rights*, 45.

6. Paul Gordon Lauren, "Seen from the Outside: The International Perspective on the American Dilemma," in *Window on Freedom: Race, Civil Rights, and Foreign Affairs, 1945–1988*, ed. Brenda Gayle Plummer (University of North Carolina Press, 2003), 27; Dudziak, 38.

7. Borstelmann, *Cold War and the Color Line*, 75.

8. Lauren, "Seen from the Outside," 26; Dudziak, *Cold War Civil Rights*, 31.

9. Lauren, "Seen from the Outside," 28; Borstelmann, *Cold War and the Color Line*, 59.

10. Penny Von Eschen, *Satchmo Blows Up the World: Jazz Ambassadors and the Cold War* (Harvard University Press, 2004), 11, 177.

11. Dudziak, *Cold War Civil Rights*, 66.

12. Michael Krenn, "Unfinished Business: Segregation and U.S. Diplomacy at the 1958 World's Fair," *Diplomatic History* 20, 4 (Fall 1996): 595, 599, 607.

13. Elizabeth Cobbs Hoffman, *All You Need Is Love: The Peace Corps and the Spirit of the 1960s* (Harvard University Press, 1998) 28.

14. Stephen Oates, *Let the Trumpet Sound: The Life of Martin Luther King Jr.* (Harper-Collins, 1994), 118.

15. Lewis V. Baldwin, *To Make the Wounded Whole: The Cultural Legacy of Martin Luther King* (Augsburg Fortress, 1992), 174.

16. Andrew J. DeRoche, *Andrew Young: Civil Rights Ambassador* (Scholarly Resources, 2003), 18.

17. Kevin Gains, "The Civil Rights Movement in World Perspective," in *America on the World Stage: A Global Approach to U.S. History*, ed. Gary Reichard and Ted Dickson (University of Illinois Press), 201.

18. Mark Kurlansky, *1968: The Year That Rocked the World* (Random House, 2005), 219.

19. Alice Echols, *Shaky Ground: The Sixties and Its Aftershocks* (Columbia University Press, 2002), 24, 25.

20. Melvin Small, *AntiWarriors: The Vietnam War and the Battle for America's Hearts and Minds* (Scholarly Resources, 2002), 8.

21. Tony Judt, *Postwar: A History of Europe since 1945* (New York: Penguin Press, 2006), 407.

22. Tom Hayden, "The Future of 1969's Restless Youth" in *1968 in Europe: A History of Protest and Activism*, ed. Martin Klimke and Joachim Schrloth (Palgrave Macmillan, 2008), 326; Judt, 419.

23. Todd Gitlin, *The Sixties: Years of Hope, Days of Rage* (Bantam, 1993), 271.

24. Kurlansky, *1968*, 152.

25. Ibid., 197.

26. Ibid., 224.

27. Richard Ivan Jobs, "Youth Movements: Travel, Protest, and Europe in 1968," *American Historical Review* 114, 3 (April 2009): 391.

28. Kurlansky, *1968*, 333.

29. Sara Evans, "Sons, Daughters, and Patriarchy: Gender and the 1968 Generation," *American Historical Review* 114, 3 (April 2009): 338.

30. Ibid., 340.

31. Vanita Guputa, "Blazing a Path from Civil Rights to Human Rights: The Pioneering Career of Gay McDougall," in *Bringing Human Rights Home*, vol. 1, ed. Cynthia Soohoo et al. (Praeger, 2008), 143.

32. DeRoche, *Andrew Young*, 86.

33. Nelson Mandela, *Long Walk to Freedom: The Autobiography of Nelson Mandela* (Little, Brown, 1994), 508.

34. *New York Times*, 18 October 2010.

35. *New York Times*, 5 February 2011.

36. "Bush Visits Mosque, Warns against Violence," *Christian Century*, 26 September 2001.

Suggested Further Reading

CHAPTER 1: COMMERCE AND CONQUEST

For general overviews of the European encounter with the Americas, see Alan Taylor, *American Colonies: The Settling of North America* (Penguin, 2001); John McCusker and Russell Menard, *The Economy of British America, 1607–1789* (University of North Carolina Press, 1991); James Axtell, *Natives and Newcomers* (Oxford University Press, 2001); Lyle N. McAlister, *Spain and Portugal in the New World* (University of Minnesota Press, 1984); and J. H. Elliott, *Empires of the Atlantic World* (Yale University Press, 2006).

On the pre-Columbian era and the Columbian exchange, see Charles Mann, *1491: New Revelations of the Americas before Columbus* (Vintage, 2006); Fernand Braudel, *Civilization and Capitalism*, 3 vols. (Harper & Row, 1982–84); Colin Calloway, *New Worlds for All* (Johns Hopkins University Press, 1997); Felipe Fernandez-Armesto, *Pathfinders* (W. W. Norton, 2006); A. J. Russell-Wood, *The Portuguese Empire, 1415–1808* (Johns Hopkins University Press, 1998); Samuel Eliot Morison, *Admiral of the Ocean Sea: A Life of Christopher Columbus* (Little, Brown, 1970); Alfred W. Crosby, *The Columbian Exchange* (Greenwood, 1973); Peter Mancall, *Envisioning America* (Bedford St. Martin's, 1995); Daniel K. Richter, *Facing East from Indian Country* (Harvard University Press, 2001); Andrew F. Smith, *The Tomato in America* (University of South Carolina Press, 1994); Marcy Norton, *Sacred Gifts, Profane Pleasures: A History of Tobacco and Chocolate in the Atlantic World* (Cornell University Press, 2008); and David Hackett Fischer, *The Great Wave: Price Revolutions and the Rhythm of History* (Oxford University Press, 1996).

On the extractive economy, see Charles E. Clark, *The Eastern Frontier* (University Press of New England, 1983); William Cronon, *Changes in the Land* (Hill & Wang, 2003); James Merrell, *The Indians' New World* (University of North Carolina Press, 1989); Bernard Bailyn, *The New England Merchants in the Seventeenth Century* (Harvard University Press, 1955); and Allan Gallay, *The Indian Slave Trade* (Yale University Press, 2002).

On the "plantation complex," see Philip D. Curtin, *The Rise and Fall of the Plantation Complex* (Cambridge University Press, 1990); Sidney Mintz, *Sweetness and Power: The Place of Sugar in Modern History* (Penguin, 1986); Edmund Morgan, *American Slavery, American Freedom* (W. W. Norton, 1975); S. Max Edelson, *Plantation Enterprise in Colonial South Carolina* (Harvard University Press, 2006); Andrew M. Watson, *Agricultural Innovation in the Early Islamic World* (Cambridge University Press, 1983); Peter Coclanis, *The Shadow of a Dream: Economic Life and Death in the South Carolina Low Country, 1670–1920* (Oxford University

Press, 1989); Philip D. Curtin, *The Atlantic Slave Trade: A Census* (University of Wisconsin Press, 1969); William D. Phillips Jr., *Slavery from Roman Times to the Early Transatlantic Trade* (University of Minnesota Press, 1985); Ira Berlin, *Many Thousands Gone: The First Two Centuries of Slavery in North America* (Harvard University Press, 1998); Robin Law, *The Slave Coast of West Africa, 1550–1750* (Clarendon, 1991); and John Thornton, *Africa and Africans in the Making of the Atlantic World, 1400–1680* (Cambridge University Press, 1992).

CHAPTER 2: THE MANY WARS FOR AMERICA

For general overviews of the many wars for America, see Douglas E. Leach, *Arms for Empire* (Macmillan, 1973), and Frances Jennings, *The Invasion of America* (University of North Carolina Press, 1975).

On the Spanish conquest, see Hugh Thomas, *Conquest* (Simon & Schuster, 1993); Inga Clendinnen, *Aztecs: An Interpretation* (Cambridge University Press, 1995); David J. Weber, *The Spanish Frontier in North America* (Yale University Press, 1992); and David Hurst Thomas, ed., *Columbian Consequences: Archaeological and Historical Perspectives on the Spanish Borderlands East* (Smithsonian Institution Press, 1993).

On Atlantic pirates and privateers, see Kris E. Lane, *Pillaging the Empire* (M. E. Sharpe, 1998); Kenneth R. Andrews, *Trade, Plunder, and Settlement* (Cambridge University Press, 1984); Wim Klooster, *The Dutch in the Americas, 1600–1800* (John Carter Brown Library, 1997); Edwin G. Burrows and Mike Wallace, *Gotham* (Oxford University Press, 2000); Paul Seaward, *The Cavalier Parliament and the Reconstruction of the Old Regime, 1661–1667* (Cambridge University Press, 2003); Jonathan Israel, *The Dutch Republic* (Clarendon, 1995); and Robert C. Ritchie, *The Duke's Province* (University of North Carolina Press, 1977).

On warfare in British North America, see Karen Kupperman, *The Jamestown Project*, (Harvard University Press, 2009); William Saunders Webb, *1676: The End of American Independence* (Syracuse University Press, 1995); and Ian K. Steele, *Warpaths: Invasions of North America* (Oxford University Press, 1994).

On the Anglo-French conflict, see Richard White, *The Middle Ground* (Cambridge University Press, 1994); Fred Anderson, *Crucible of War* (Vintage, 2001); and P. J. Marshall, ed., *The Oxford History of the British Empire, Vol. 2: The Eighteenth Century* (Oxford University Press, 1998).

CHAPTER 3: DE-INDIANIZING AMERICAN CULTURE

For overviews of the "de-Indianizing" of American culture, see J. H. Elliott, *Empires of the Atlantic World* (Yale University Press, 2006); Karen O. Kupperman, ed., *America in European Consciousness 1493–1750* (University of North Carolina Press, 1995); and David Hurst Thomas, ed., *Columbian Consequences: Archaeological and Historical Perspectives on the Spanish Borderlands East* (Smithsonian Institution Press, 1993).

On global Christianity, see Robert Bireley, *The Refashioning of Catholicism, 1450–1700* (Catholic University of America Press, 1999); Jonathan Butler, *Awash in a Sea of Faith* (Harvard University Press, 1992); Alison Games, *Migration and the Origins of the English Atlantic World* (Harvard University Press, 1999); Ramon Guttierez, *When Jesus Came the Corn Mothers*

Went Away (Stanford University Press, 1991); R. Po-chia Hsia, *The World of Catholic Renewal, 1540–1700* (Cambridge University Press, 2004); Samuel Eliot Morrison, *Builders of the Bay Colony* (Houghton Mifflin, 1958); and David J. Weber, *The Spanish Frontier in North America* (Yale University Press, 1992).

On geography and anthropology, see Felipe Fernandez Armesto, *Pathfinders: A Global History of Exploration* (W. W. Norton, 2006); James Axtell, *Natives and Newcomers* (Oxford University Press, 2001); Colin G. Calloway, *New Worlds for All* (Johns Hopkins University Press, 1998); Joyce Chaplin, *Subject Matter: Technology, the Body, and Science on the Anglo-American Frontier, 1500–1676* (Harvard University Press, 2003); Fredi Chiappelli, ed., *First Images of America* (University of California Press, 1976); J. H. Elliott, *The Old World and the New* (Cambridge University Press, 1970); Samuel Eliot Morrison, *Admiral of the Ocean Sea* (Little, Brown, 1942).

On Enlightenment thought and the Glorious Revolution, see David Armitage, *The Ideological Origins of the British Empire* (Cambridge University Press, 2000); Barbara Arneil, *John Locke and America* (Oxford University Press, 1996); I. Bernard Cohen, *Science and the Founding Fathers* (W. W. Norton, 1997); David Lovejoy, *The Glorious Revolution in America* (Wesleyan University Press, 1987); Henry F. May, *The Enlightenment in America* (Oxford University Press, 1976).

CHAPTER 4: THE IDEA OF FREEDOM IN AN AGE OF SLAVERY

On Atlantic revolutions, see Laurent Dubois, *Avengers of the New World: The Story of the Haitian Revolution* (Harvard University Press, 2004); Susan Dunn, *Sister Revolutions: French Lightning, American Light* (Faber & Faber, 2000); Jack Fruchtman Jr., *Atlantic Cousins: Benjamin Franklin and His Visionary Friends* (Basic Books, 2007); David P. Geggus and Norman Fiering, eds., *The World of the Haitian Revolution* (Indiana University Press, 2008); Eric Hobsbawm, *The Age of Revolution, 1789–1848* (Vintage, 1996); Jay Kinsbruner, *Independence in Spanish America* (University of New Mexico Press, 1994); Lester D. Langley, *The Americas in the Age of Revolution, 1750–1850* (Yale University Press, 1996); Gary B. Nash and Graham Russell Gao Hodges, *Friends of Liberty: Thomas Jefferson, Tadeusz Kosciuszko, and Agrippa Hall* (Basic Books, 2008); R. R. Palmer, *The Age of Democratic Revolution*, 2 vols. (Princeton University Press, 1969); and Richard W. Slatta and Jane Lucas De Grummond, *Simon Bolivar's Quest for Glory* (Texas A & M University Press, 2003).

On utopian communities and reform, see Arthur Bestor, *Backwoods Utopias* (University of Pennsylvania Press, 1971); Daniel Walker Howe, *What Hath God Wrought: The Transformation of America, 1815–1848* (Oxford University Press, 2007); Margaret H. McFadden, *Golden Cables of Sympathy: The Transatlantic Sources of Nineteenth-Century Feminism* (University Press of Kentucky, 1999); David Rothman, *The Discovery of the Asylum* (Little, Brown, 1971); Alice Felt Tyler, *Freedom's Ferment* (Harper & Rowe, 1944); and Sean Wilentz, *Chants Democratic* (Oxford University Press, 1984).

On international dimensions of slavery and reconstruction, see Robin Blackburn, *The Overthrow of Colonial Slavery, 1776–1848* (Verson, 1988); David Brion Davis, *Inhuman Bondage: The Rise and Fall of Slavery in the New World* (Oxford University Press, 2006); Seymour Drescher, *Abolition: A History of Slavery and Antislavery* (Cambridge University Press, 2009);

Stanley Engerman, *Slavery, Emancipation, and Freedom: Comparative Perspectives* (Louisiana State University Press, 2007); Don E. Fehrenbacher, *The Slaveholding Republic: An Account of the United States Government's Relations to Slavery* (Oxford University Press, 2001); Eric Foner, *Nothing but Freedom: Emancipation and Its Legacy* (Louisiana State University Press, 1983); Peter Kolchin, *Unfree Labor: American Slavery and Russian Serfdom* (Harvard University Press, 1987); and Benjamin Quarles, *Black Abolitionists* (Da Capo, 1991).

CHAPTER 5: DEVELOPING A CONTINENTAL MARKET

On the antebellum search for new markets, see James Fichter, *So Great a Profit: How the East Indies Trade Transformed Anglo-American Capitalism* (Harvard University Press, 2010); Merrill Jensen, *The New Nation* (Random House, 1966); Walter LaFeber, *Clash: U.S.-Japanese Relations throughout History* (W. W. Norton, 1988); Curtis Nettles, *The Emergence of a National Economy: 1775–1815* (Holt, Rinehart, & Winston, 1962); Douglass North, *The Economic Growth of the United States, 1790–1860* (W. W. Norton, 1966); and Kenneth Pomeranz, *The Great Divergence: China, Europe, and the Making of the Modern World Economy* (Princeton University Press, 2000).

On antebellum westward expansion and manufacturing, see Doron Ben-Atar, *Trade Secrets* (Yale University Press, 2004); Thomas Dublin, *Women at Work* (Columbia University Press, 1981); Clyde Milner, Carol O'Connor, and Nancy Sandweiss, eds., *The Oxford Encyclopedia of the West* (Oxford University Press, 1996); Walter K. Nugent, *Habits of Empire: A History of American Expansion* (Knopf, 2008); Lawrence Peskin, *Manufacturing Revolution* (Johns Hopkins University Press, 2003); George R. Taylor, *The Transportation Revolution, 1815–1860* (M. E. Sharpe, 1977).

On turn-of-the century industrialism and anti-globalism, see Lawrence Goodwyn, *The Populist Moment* (Oxford University Press, 1978); Steven Hahn, *The Roots of Southern Populism* (Oxford University Press, 2006); Richard Hofstadter, *The Age of Reform* (Vintage, 1960); Walter Licht, *Industrializing America* (Johns Hopkins University Press, 1995); and Mira Wilkins, *The History of Foreign Investment in the United States to 1914* (Harvard University Press, 1989).

CHAPTER 6: FROM COLONIES TO THE THRESHOLD OF EMPIRE

For studies of diplomacy of the post-revolutionary era, see George Herring, *From Colony to Superpower: U.S. Foreign Relations since 1776* (Oxford University Press, 2008), and Robert Kagan, *Dangerous Nation: America's Foreign Policy from Its Earliest Days to the Dawn of the Twentieth Century* (Vintage, 2007).

On international aspects of the American Revolution, see Troy Bickham, *Making Headlines: The American Revolution as Seen through the British Press* (Northern Illinois University Press, 2008); Colin Callaway, *The American Revolution in Indian Country* (Cambridge University Press, 1995); Jonathan Dull, *A Diplomatic History of the American Revolution* (Yale University Press, 1987); R. Ernest Dupuy, Gay Hammerman, and Grace Hayes, *The American Revolution: A Global War* (D. McKay, 1977); Lawrence Kaplan, *Colonies into Nation: American Diplomacy, 1763–1801* (Macmillan, 1972); Robert Middlekauf, *The Glorious Cause: The Ameri-*

can Revolution, 1763–1789 (Oxford University Press, 2007); Cassandra Pybus, *Epic Journeys of Freedom: Runaway Slaves of the American Revolution and Their Global Quest for Liberty* (Beacon, 2007).

On manifest destiny and westward expansion, see Walter Nugent, *Habits of Empire: A History of American Expansion* (Knopf, 2008); David M. Pletcher, *The Diplomacy of Annexation: Texas, Oregon, and the Mexican War* (University of Missouri Press, 1973); and Peter H. Smith, *Talons of the Eagle: Latin America, the United States, and the World* (Oxford University Press, 2007).

On Civil War–era diplomacy, see Dean B. Mahin, *One War at a Time: The International Dimensions of the American Civil War* (Brassey's, 1999); Robert E. May, ed., *The Union, the Confederacy, and the Atlantic Rim* (Purdue University Press, 1995); and Brian Schoen, *The Fragile Fabric of Union: Cotton, Federal Politics, and the Global Origins of the Civil War* (Johns Hopkins University Press, 2009).

CHAPTER 7: RELUCTANT GLOBAL WARRIORS

The broad topic of American exceptionalism is covered by Deborah Madsen, *American Exceptionalism* (University Press of Mississippi, 1998), and Godfrey Hodgson, *The Myth of American Exceptionalism* (Yale University Press, 2009).

On the American experience with imperialism, see Thomas Paterson, "United States Intervention in Cuba, 1898: Interpretations of the Spanish-American-Cuban-Filipino War," *History Teacher* 29 (May 1996): 341–61; Kristin Hoganson, *Fighting for American Manhood: How Gender Politics Provoked the Spanish-American and Philippine-American Wars* (Yale University Press, 2000); and Walter Lafeber, *Inevitable Revolutions: The United States in Central America* (W. W. Norton, 1993).

On the debate over U.S. imperialism, see Robert David Johnson, *Peace Progressives and American Foreign Policy* (Harvard University Press, 1995); Robert Beisner, *Twelve against Empire: The Anti-Imperialists, 1898–1900* (McGraw-Hill, 1968); and Eric Love, *Race over Empire: Racism and U.S. Imperialism, 1865–1900* (University of North Carolina Press, 2004). Brian McAllister Linn, *The Philippine War, 1899–1902* (University of Kansas Press, 2000); Paul A. Kramer, *The Blood of Government: Race, Empire, the United States, and the Philippines* (University of North Carolina Press, 2006); and Stuart Creighton Miller, *Benevolent Assimilation: The American Conquest of the Philippines, 1899–1903* (Yale University Press, 1984), cover the painful Philippines-American War. On American intervention in Mexico, see John Eisenhower, *Intervention: The United States and the Mexican Revolution, 1913–1917* (W. W. Norton, 1995).

On World War I and Wilsonianism, see John Keegan, *The First World War* (Knopf, 1999); Thomas Knock, *To End All Wars: Woodrow Wilson and the Quest for a New World Order* (Princeton University Press, 1992); Erez Manela, *The Wilsonian Moment: Self-Determination and the International Origins of Anticolonial Nationalism* (Oxford University Press, 2009); and Margaret MacMillan, *Paris 1919: Six Months That Changed the World* (Random House, 2003).

On the battle between isolationists and interventionists, see Justus Doenecke, *Storm on the Horizon: The Challenge to American Intervention, 1939–1941* (Rowman & Littlefield, 2003).

For divergent views on Franklin Roosevelt's handling of the growing world crisis, see Robert Divine, *The Reluctant Belligerent: American Entry into World War II* (Wiley, 1965), and Robert Dallek, *Franklin D. Roosevelt and American Foreign Policy, 1932–1945* (Oxford University Press, 1979). Gaddis Smith, *American Diplomacy during the Second World War, 1941–1945* (Wiley, 1965), provides an excellent introduction to diplomatic and military issues during the war.

CHAPTER 8: EMERGING ECONOMIC HEGEMON

For excellent treatments of America and globalization in the first half of the twentieth century, see Emily Rosenberg, *Spreading the American Dream: American Economic and Cultural Expansion, 1890–1945* (Hill & Wang, 1982), and Alfred Eckes and Thomas Zeiler, *Globalization and the American Century* (Cambridge University Press, 2003). John Steele Gordon, *Empire of Wealth: The Epic History of American Economic Power* (Harper Collins, 2004), offers a lively overview of economic issues during the period.

On dollar diplomacy, see Emily Rosenberg, *Financial Missionaries to the World: The Politics and Culture of Dollar Diplomacy, 1900—1930* (Duke University Press, 2004), and Cryus Vesser, *A World Safe for Capitalism: Dollar Diplomacy and America's Rise to Globalism* (Columbia University Press, 2002).

Kristin Hoganson, *Consumers' Imperium: The Global Production of American Domesticity, 1865–1920* (University of North Carolina Press, 2007); Frank Costigliola, *Awkward Dominion: American Political, Economic, and Cultural Relations with Europe, 1919–1933* (Cornell University Press, 1984); and Ian Jarvie, *Hollywood's Overseas Campaign: The North Atlantic Movie Trade, 1920–1950* (Cambridge University Press, 1985), explore the cultural side of U.S. economic expansion.

The role of economics in U.S. relations with China is treated in Michael Hunt's *Making of a Special Relationship: The United States and China since 1914* (Columbia University Press, 1985). U.S.-Latin American ties are treated in Walter LaFeber, *Inevitable Revolutions: The United States in Central America* (W. W. Norton, 1993), and Peter Chapman, *Bananas: How United Fruit Company Shaped the World* (Canongate, 2007).

For an overview of U.S. companies operating aboard, see Mira Wilkins, *The Maturing of Multinational Enterprise: American Businesses Abroad from 1914–1970* (Harvard University Press, 1970). Fascinating case studies can be found in Greg Grandin, *Fordlandia: The Rise and Fall of Henry Ford's Forgotten Jungle City* (Henry Holt, 2009); Mark Pendergrast, *For God, Country, and Coca-Cola: The Definitive History of the Great American Soft Drink and the Company That Makes It* (Basic Books, 2000); and Daniel Yergin, *The Prize: The Epic Quest for Oil, Money and Power* (Simon & Schuster, 2008).

On domestic resistance to economic trade, see Dana Frank, *Buy American: The Untold Story of Economic Nationalism* (Beacon, 2000).

On the global depression of the 1930s, see Charles Kindleberger, *The World in Depression, 1929–1939* (University of California Press, 1986); John Garraty, *The Great Depression: An Inquiry into the Causes and Consequences of the Worldwide Depression of the 1930s* (Anchor, 1986); Robert Skidelsky, *John Maynard Keynes, 1883–1946: Economist, Philosopher, States-*

man (Penguin, 2005); and Barry Eichengreen, *Gold Fetters: The Gold Standard and the Great Depression, 1919–1935* (Oxford University Press, 1992).

CHAPTER 9: REFORMING A CHAOTIC WORLD

For a remarkable survey of America and international reform, see Daniel Rodgers, *Atlantic Crossings: Social Politics in a Progressive Age* (Harvard University Press, 1998). Also see James Kloppenberg, *Uncertain Victory: Socialism and Progressivism in European and American Thought* (Oxford University Press), and Alan Dawley, *Changing the World: American Progressives in War and Revolution* (Princeton University Press, 2003). John P. Diggins, The *Rise and Fall of the American Left* (W. W. Norton, 1992), offers a wonderfully clear and concise introduction to American intellectual history in the twentieth century. For lively surveys of the Progressive period through World War I, see Nell Painter, *Standing at Armageddon: The United States, 1877–1919* (W. W. Norton, 1989), and Michael McGerr, *A Fierce Discontent: The Rise and Fall of the Progressive Movement in America* (Oxford University Press, 2003).

On Marx and socialism in the United States, see David Shannon, *The Socialist Party of America: A History* (Quadrangle, 1967); Irving Howe, *Socialism and America* (Harcourt Brace Jovanovich, 1986); Melvyn Dubofsky, *We Shall Be All: A History of the Industrial Workers of the World* (University of Illinois Press, 1988); and Nick Salvatore, *Eugene Debs: Citizen and Socialist* (University of Illinois Press, 1984).

On modernism and Greenwich Village, see Christine Stansell, *American Moderns: Bohemian New York and the Creation of a New Century* (Henry Holt, 2001). Warren Beatty's 1981 film *Reds* depicts the odyssey of John Reed and the Greenwich Village circle.

On the international women's movement, see Leila Rupp, *World of Women: The Making of the International Women's Movement* (Princeton University Press, 1998); Patricia Ward D'Itri, *Cross Currents in the International Women's Movement, 1848–1948* (Bowling Green State University Press, 1999); and Katherine H. Adams and Michael L. Keene, *Alice Paul and the American Suffrage Campaign* (University of Illinois Press, 2008).

Excellent treatments of key figures from this period include Jean Bethke Elshtain, *Jane Addams and the Dream of American Democracy: A Life* (Basic Books, 2002); Judith Stein, *The World of Marcus Garvey: Race and Class in Modern Society* (Louisiana State University Press, 1986); Mark David Huddle, *Marcus Garvey: Black Nationalism and the New Negro Renaissance* (Ivan R. Dee, 2010); David Levering Lewis, *W. E. B. Du Bois: The Fight for Equality and the American Century, 1919–1963* (Henry Holt, 2000); and Bennetta Jules-Rosette, *Josephine Baker in Art and Life: The Icon and the Image* (University of Illinois Press, 2007).

On the international influence of the New Deal, see David Ekbladh, *The Great American Mission: Modernization and the Construction of an American World Order* (Princeton University Press, 2010).

CHAPTER 10: GLOBALIZATION AND AMERICANIZATION

Alfred Eckes and Thomas Zeiler, *Globalization and the American Century* (Cambridge University Press, 2003), and Diane B. Kunz, *Butter and Guns: America's Cold War Diplomacy* (Free

Press, 1997), offer excellent starting points for further investigation; also see Michael Hunt, *The American Ascendancy: How the United States Gained and Wielded Global Dominance* (University of North Carolina Press, 2007); D. Clayton Brown, *Globalization and America since 1945* (Scholarly Resources, 2007); and Peter Lindert, "U.S. Foreign Trade and Trade Policy in the Twentieth Century," in *The Cambridge Economic History of the United States: The Twentieth Century*, ed. Stanley L. Engerman and Robert E. Gallman (Cambridge University Press, 2000).

Treatments of the American economy in the postwar period include Robert M. Collins, *More: The Politics of Economic Growth in Postwar America* (Oxford University Press, 2000); and David Calleo, *The Imperious Economy* (Harvard University Press, 1982).

On the Bretton Woods system and the early Cold War economy, see Barry Eichengreen, *Globalizing Capital: A History of the International Monetary System* (Princeton University Press, 2008); Michael Hogan, *The Marshall Plan: America, Britain, and the Reconstruction of Europe, 1947–1952* (Cambridge University Press, 1987); and Christopher Endy, *Cold War Holidays: American Tourism in France* (University of North Carolina Press, 2004).

On U.S. commercial influence, see Victoria de Grazia, *Irresistible Empire: America's Advance through Twentieth-Century Europe* (Harvard University Press, 1995), and Richard Pells, *Not Like Us: How Europeans Have Loved, Hated, and Transformed American Culture since World War II* (Basic Books, 1997).

On the impact of the Vietnam War, see Anthony Campagna, *The Economic Consequences of the Vietnam War* (Praeger, 1991), and Irving Bernstein, *Guns or Butter: The Presidency of Lyndon Baines Johnson* (Oxford University Press, 1996). Nixon's reshaping of the American and world economies is covered in Allen Matusow, *Nixon's Economy: Booms, Busts, Dollars, and Votes* (University of Kansas Press, 1998). Daniel Yergin, *The Prize: The Epic Quest for Oil, Money, and Power* (Simon & Schuster, 2008), and Robert Samuelson, *The Great Inflation and Its Aftermath* (Random House, 2008), treat the economic turmoil of the 1970s.

On the shift to a global neoliberal economy see Daniel Yergin and Joseph Stanislaw, *The Commanding Heights: The Battle for the World Economy* (Simon & Schuster, 2002), and Derek Chollet and James Goldgeier, *America between Wars from 11/9 to 9/11: The Misunderstood Years between the Fall of the Berlin Wall and the Start of the War on Terror* (Public Affairs, 2008).

For differing views on the post–Cold War rise of globalization, see Thomas Friedman, *The Lexus and the Olive Tree* (Farrar, Straus & Giroux, 1999); Joseph Stiglitz, *Globalization and Its Discontents* (W. W. Norton, 2003); and Benjamin Barber, *Jihad vs. McWorld: How Globalism and Tribalism Are Reshaping the World* (Random House, 1995).

CHAPTER 11: BECOMING THE "INDISPENSABLE NATION"

For a general overview, see Stephen Ambrose and Douglas Brinkley, *Rise to Globalism: American Foreign Policy since 1938* (Penguin, 1998).

On the Cold War, see Thomas Paterson, *On Every Front: The Making and Unmaking of the Cold War* (W. W. Norton, 1992); Melvin Leffler, *For the Soul of Mankind: The United States, the Soviet Union, and the Cold War* (Hill & Wang, 2008); and John Lewis Gaddis, *Strategies of Containment* (Oxford University Press, 2008).

On modernization, see Michael Lanham, *Modernization as Ideology: American Social Sciences and Nation Building in the Kennedy Era* (University of North Carolina Press, 2000), and Nils Gilman, *Mandarins of the Future: Modernization Theory in Cold War America* (Johns Hopkins University Press, 2007).

Treatments of the Cold War in the Third World include Nick Cullather, *The Hungry World: America's Cold War Battle against Poverty in Asia* (Harvard University Press, 2010); Robert J. McMahon, *The Cold War on the Periphery: The United States, India, and Pakistan* (Columbia University Press, 1996); and Kyle Longley, *In the Eagle's Shadow: The United States, and Latin America* (Harlan Davidson, 2002).

On Sino-American relations, see Warren I. Cohen, *America's Response to China: A History of Sino-American Relations* (Columbia University Press, 2010).

George Herring, *America's Longest War* (McGraw-Hill, 1996), and Mark A. Lawrence, *The Vietnam War: A Concise International History* (Oxford University Press, 2008), provide excellent introductions to the Vietnam War. Jeremi Suri, *Power and Protest: Global Revolution and the Rise of Détente* (Harvard University Press, 2003), offers a provocative international interpretation of the tumult of the 1960s and 1970s.

On the Middle East, see Douglas Little, *American Orientalism: United States and the Middle East since 1945* (I. B. Tauris, 2003). On Iran, see Mark Bowden, *Guests of the Ayatollah* (Atlantic Monthly Press, 2006).

On the end of the Cold War, see James Mann, *The Rebellion of Ronald Reagan: A History of the End of the Cold War* (Viking, 2009); Michael Hogan, ed., *The End of the Cold War: Its Meaning and Implications* (Cambridge University Press, 1992); and John Lewis Gaddis, *Now We Know: Rethinking Cold War History* (Oxford University Press, 1997).

On international relations in the post–Cold War era see Derek Chollet and James Goldgeier, *America between Wars from 11/9 to 9/11: The Misunderstood Years between the Fall of the Berlin Wall and the Start of the War on Terror* (Public Affairs, 2008); Samuel Huntington, *Clash of Civilizations and the Remaking of the World Order* (Simon & Schuster, 1996); and Fareed Zakaria, *The Post-American World* (W. W. Norton, 2008).

CHAPTER 12: CIVIL RIGHTS AND WORLD CULTURE

On the civil rights movement and international politics, see Thomas Borstelman, *The Cold War and the Color Line* (Harvard University Press, 2003); Brenda Gayle Plummer, ed., *Window on Freedom: Race, Civil Rights, and Foreign Affairs, 1945–1988* (University of North Carolina Press, 2003); Mary L. Dudziak, *Cold War Civil Rights: Race and the Image of American Democracy* (Princeton University Press, 2002); Kevin Gains, "The Civil Rights Movement in World Perspective," in *America on the World Stage: A Global Approach to U.S. History*, ed. Gary Reichard and Ted Dickson (University of Illinois Press, 2008); Penny Von Eschen, *Satchmo Blows Up the World: Jazz Ambassadors Play the Cold War* (Harvard University Press, 2006); Penny Von Eschen, *Race against Empire: Black Americans and Anticolonialism, 1937–1957* (Cornell University Press, 1997); Michael Krenn, *The African American Voice in U.S. Foreign Policy since World War II* (Routledge, 1999).

For a sense of the spirit of the 1960s, see Elizabeth Cobbs Hoffman, *All You Need Is Love: The Peace Corps and the Spirit of the 1960s* (Harvard University Press, 1998); David Maraniss, *They Marched into Sunlight: War and Peace, Vietnam and America, October 1967* (Simon & Schuster, 2003); Todd Gitlin, *The Sixties: Years of Hope, Days of Rage* (Bantam, 1993); Kenneth

J. Heineman, *Put Your Bodies upon the Wheels: Student Revolt in the 1960s* (Ivan R. Dee, 2010); and Catherine Krull et al., eds., *New World Coming: The Sixties and the Shaping of Global Consciousness* (Between the Lines, 2009).

On the pivotal year of 1968, see Mark Kurlansky, *1968: The Year That Rocked the World* (Random House, 2005); Martin Klimke and Joachim Scharloth, eds., *1968 in Europe: A History of Protest and Activism* (Palgrave Macmillan, 2008); and Carole Fink, Philipp Gassert, and Detlef Junker, eds., *1968: The World Transformed* (Cambridge University Press, 1998).

On the international women's movement, see Sara Evans, "Sons, Daughters, and Patriarchy: Gender and the 1968 Generation," *American Historical Review* 114, 2 (April 2009): 331–47, and Bonnie Smith, ed., *Global Feminisms since 1945* (Routledge, 2000).

On the antiapartheid movement, see David Hostetter, *Movement Matters: American Anti-Apartheid Activism and the Rise of Multiculturalism* (Taylor & Francis, 2009), and Francis Nesbitt, *Race for Sanctions: African Americans Against Apartheid, 1946–1994* (Indiana University Press, 2004).

For scholarly reflections on multiculturalism, see Nathan Glazer, "Multiculturalism and a New America," in *Civil Rights and Social Wrongs: Black and White Relations since World War II*, ed. John Higham (Penn State University Press, 1994); David Hollinger, *Postethnic America: Beyond Multiculturalism* (Basic Books, 1995); and Arthur Schlesinger Jr., *The Disuniting of America* (W.W. Norton, 1998).

Index

Martineau, Harriet, 79, 82

Martinique, 75

Marx, Karl, 81–82, 176–178, 251

Maryland, 54, 62

Mascarene Islands, 94

"Massachusetts Miracle," 215

Mayan Indians, 30–31, 51

Mboya, Tom, 250

McCormick Reapers, 106

McDonald's restaurants, 216, 220, 221

McDougall, Gay, 257

McKay, Claude, 250

McKinley, William, 137–8

Mekong River Project, 232

Mercantilism, 26–27, 91–92, 100

Merkel, Angela, 262

Methodism, 78–79, 83

Mexican War, 122–124

Mexico, 11; Christianity in, 50–51; conquest of, 30–32; French, 123–125; mineral wealth, 16; revolution in, 141–2, 161, 178; and U.S. investment, 161–162, 218; and WWI, 145, 160–161, 218; and youth protests, 254

Michigan State University, 231

Middle East: and Carter administration, 235, 237; and oil resources, 172, 205, 212–213; and Six-Day War, 233, and Yom Kippur War, 235

Military spending, 209, 228

Ministry of International Trade and Industry (Japan), 214

Miranda, Francisco de, 75

Mobutu Sese Seku, 244

Moctezuma II, 31–32

Modernism, 189–191

Modernization theory, 230, 232

Molotov, V.M., 226

Monroe Doctrine, 119, 124, 128

Montaigne, Michel de, 56

More, Thomas, 56

Morgan, J. P., 144, 164–166

Mormonism, 79

Movies. *See* Cinema

Muhammad, Ali, 244–245, 262–263

Multiculturalism, 260–263; and German *multi-kulti*, 262

Multiculturalism Act (1985), 261–262

Mussolini, Benito, 193

Myrdal, Gunnar, 246

Narvaez, Panfilo, 33

Nassar, Gamal, 206

National Association for the Advancement of Colored People (NAACP), 187, 247

National Basketball Association (NBA), 219

National Football League (NFL), 219

National Recovery Association, 193

National Security Act (1947), 227

National Standards for History, 261

National Women's Party, 184

National Woman Suffrage Association (NWSA), 183–184

Native Americans: and American Revolution, 114–115; and Civil War, 125–126; in Europe, 56; and race, 55–57. *See also specific tribes*

Navigation Acts, 25–26

Neutrality Acts, 149

New Deal, 134, 191–192, 230

Newfoundland, 17

New Harmony, IN, 80

New Model Treaty, 92

"New Negro," 189

New York City, 175

New Zealand, 180, 182

Ngo Dinh Diem, 231–232

Nicaragua, 141, 236, 240; Sandinistas, 236, 239, 240

Nike, Inc., 219

Nineteenth Amendment, 184

Nixon, Richard: and Bretton Woods system, 211–212; and "Kitchen Debate," 201–202, 216, 223; and Latin America, 208; and Nixon Doctrine, 233–235

North American Free Trade Act (NAFTA), 199, 218, 219, 241

North Atlantic Treaty Organization (NATO), 228

Norton, Charles Eliot, 137

Nott, Josiah, 89

NSC-68, 204

Nye, Gerald, 149, 170

Nyerere, Julius, 258

Obama, Barack, 223, 243, 262

O'Connell, Daniel, 85